SGT FROG

CHARACTER RELATIONSHI

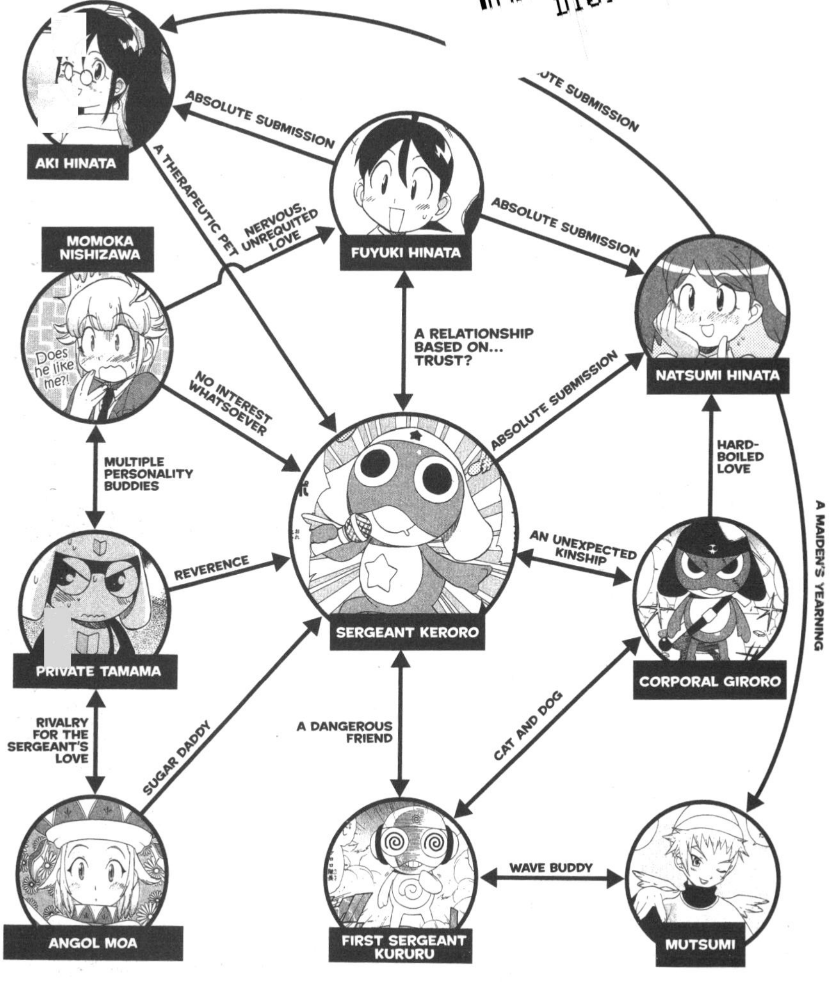
AKI HINATA
ABSOLUTE SUBMISSION
UTE SUBMISSION
FUYUKI HINATA
A THERAPEUTIC PET
NERVOUS, UNREQUITED LOVE
ABSOLUTE SUBMISSION
MOMOKA NISHIZAWA
Does he like me?!
A RELATIONSHIP BASED ON... TRUST?
NATSUMI HINATA
NO INTEREST WHATSOEVER
ABSOLUTE SUBMISSION
HARD-BOILED LOVE
MULTIPLE PERSONALITY BUDDIES
A MAIDEN'S YEARNING
AN UNEXPECTED KINSHIP
REVERENCE
SERGEANT KERORO
PRIVATE TAMAMA
CORPORAL GIRORO
RIVALRY FOR THE SERGEANT'S LOVE
SUGAR DADDY
A DANGEROUS FRIEND
CAT AND DOG
WAVE BUDDY
ANGOL MOA
FIRST SERGEANT KURURU
MUTSUMI

AS CAPTAIN OF THE SPACE INVASION FORCE'S SPECIAL ADVANCE TEAM OF THE 58TH PLANET OF THE GAMMA STORM CLOUD SYSTEM, SGT. KERORO ENTERED THE HINATA FAMILY OF POKOPEN WHEN HIS PREPARATION FOR THE INVASION OF EARTH RAN AFOUL VIA HIS CAPTURE BY HINATA CHILDREN, FUYUKI AND NATSUMI. THANKS TO FUYUKI'S KINDNESS, OR AT LEAST HIS CURIOSITY, SGT. KERORO QUICKLY BECOMES A BONA FIDE MEMBER OF THE HINATA FAMILY...IN OTHER WORDS, A TOTAL FREELOADER. SOON HIS LOYAL SUBORDINATE, PRIVATE TAMAMA, AND UNLIKELY RELATIVE ANGOL MOA (A.K.A. THE LORD OF TERROR FORETOLD BY NOSTRADAMUS) ARE FOISTING FURTHER CHAOS ONTO THE HINATA FAMILY UNIT. MEANWHILE, THE SERGEANT AND HIS GANG CONTINUE TO HATCH THEIR PLANS TO INVADE THE EARTH, RIGHT UNDER THE HINATAS' WELL-INTENTIONED NOSES...

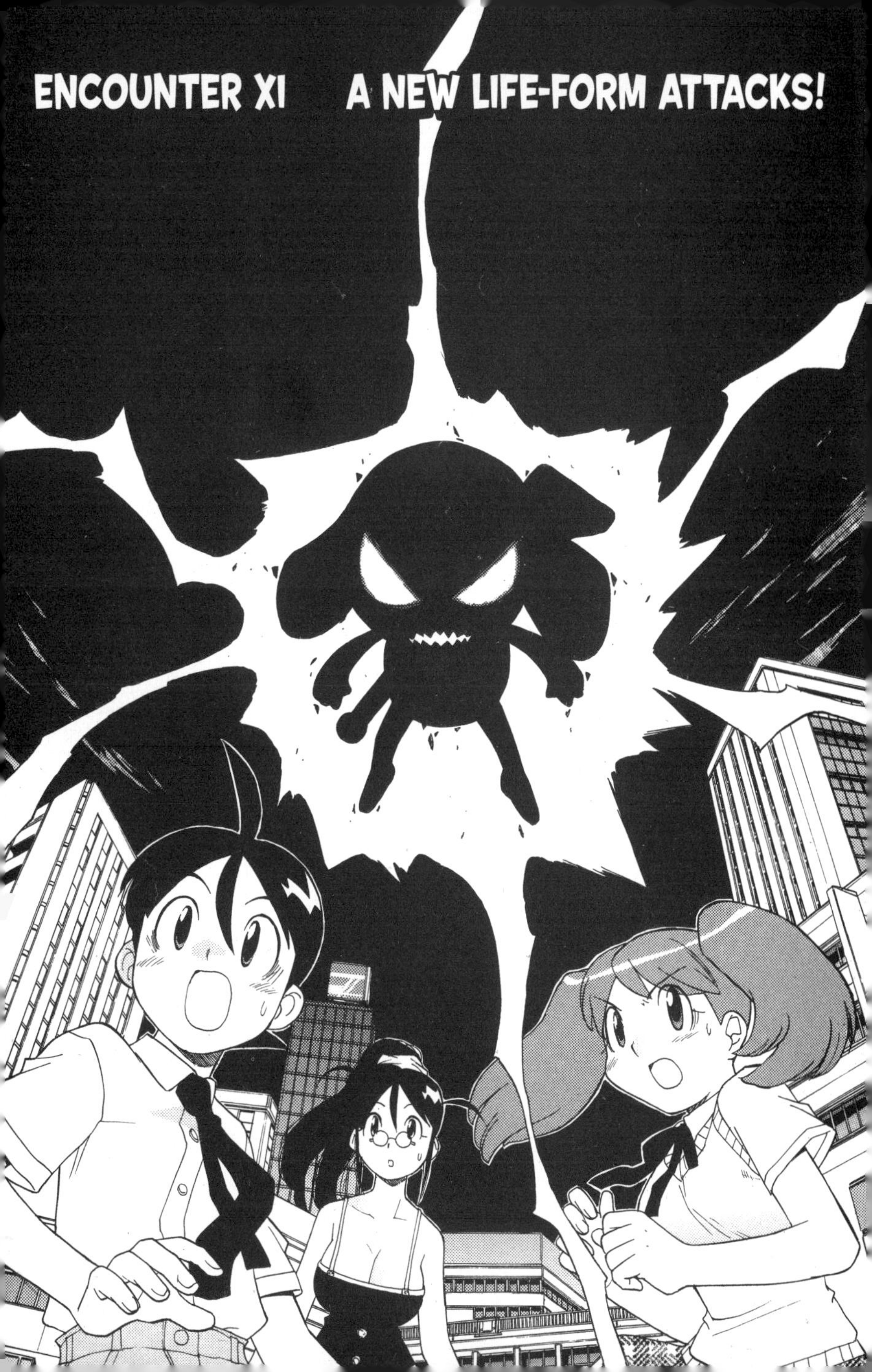
ENCOUNTER XI A NEW LIFE-FORM ATTACKS!

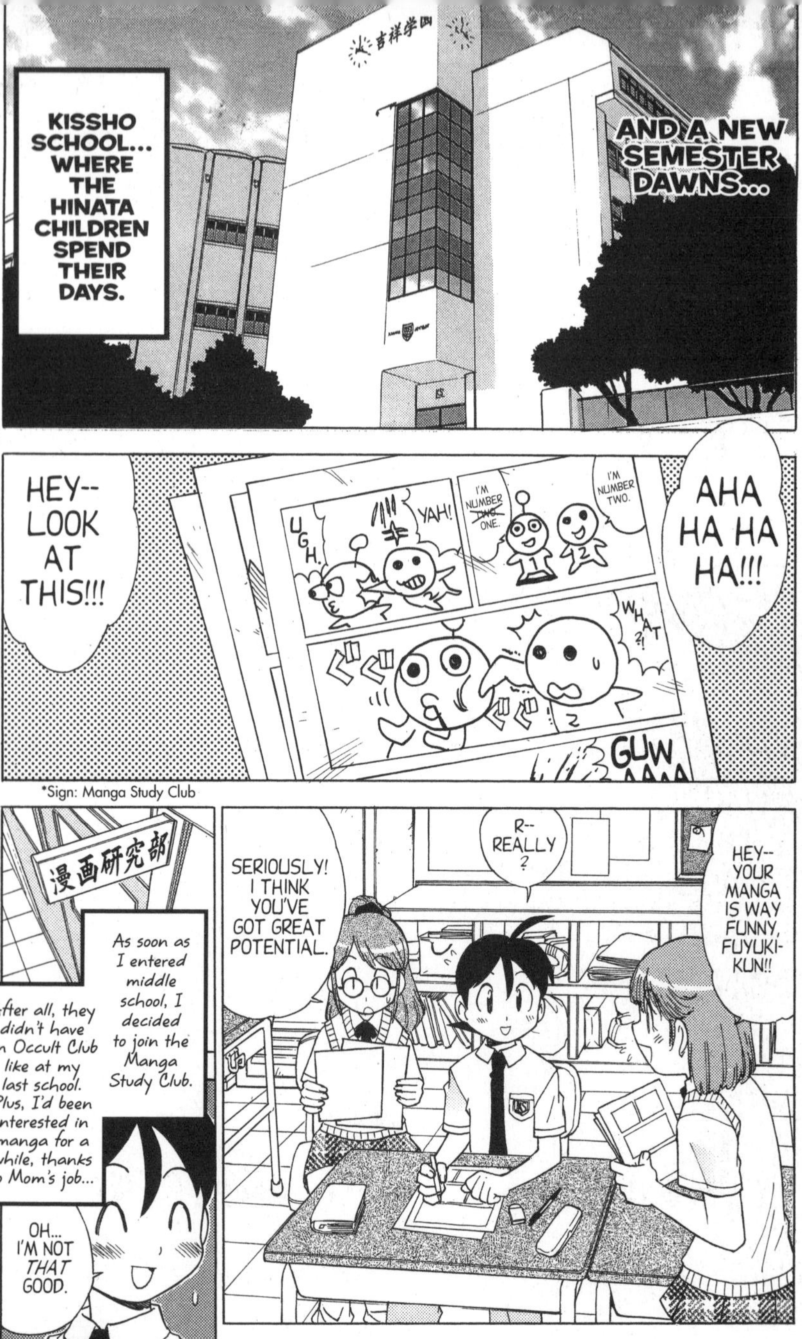
KISSHO SCHOOL... WHERE THE HINATA CHILDREN SPEND THEIR DAYS.
AND A NEW SEMESTER DAWNS...
AHA HA HA HA!!!
I'M NUMBER TWO.
I'M NUMBER ~~TWO~~ ONE.
YAH!
UGH.
WHAT ?!
GUW AAA
HEY-- LOOK AT THIS!!!
HEY-- YOUR MANGA IS WAY FUNNY, FUYUKI-KUN!!
R-- REALLY ?
SERIOUSLY! I THINK YOU'VE GOT GREAT POTENTIAL.
漫画研究部
As soon as I entered middle school, I decided to join the Manga Study Club.
After all, they didn't have an Occult Club like at my last school. Plus, I'd been interested in manga for a while, thanks to Mom's job...
OH... I'M NOT *THAT* GOOD.
*Sign: Manga Study Club

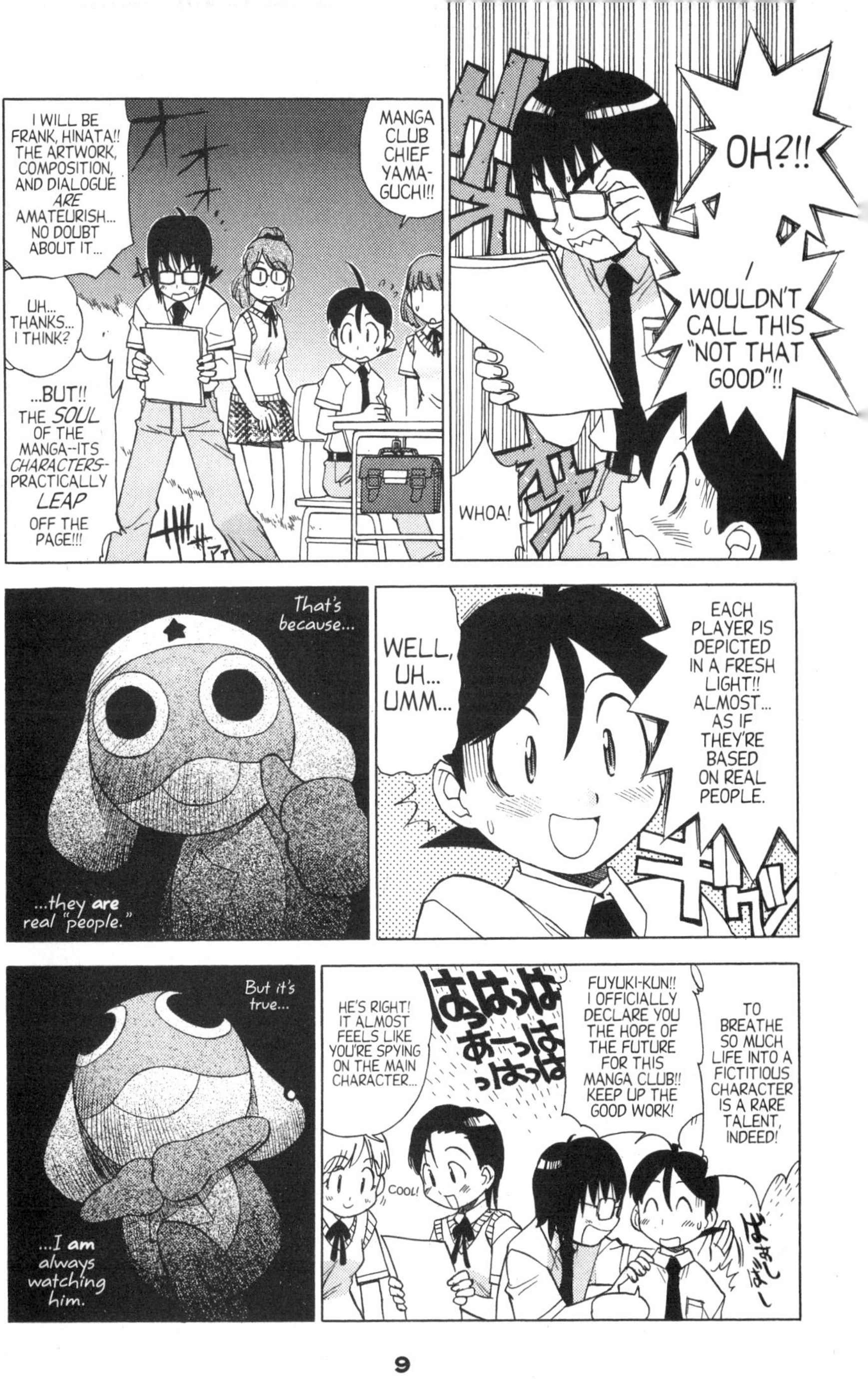
OH?!! I WOULDN'T CALL THIS "NOT THAT GOOD"!!
WHOA!
MANGA CLUB CHIEF YAMAGUCHI!!
I WILL BE FRANK, HINATA!! THE ARTWORK, COMPOSITION, AND DIALOGUE ARE AMATEURISH... NO DOUBT ABOUT IT...
UH... THANKS... I THINK?
...BUT!! THE SOUL OF THE MANGA--ITS CHARACTERS-PRACTICALLY LEAP OFF THE PAGE!!!
EACH PLAYER IS DEPICTED IN A FRESH LIGHT!! ALMOST... AS IF THEY'RE BASED ON REAL PEOPLE.
WELL, UH... UMM...
That's because...
...they are real "people."
TO BREATHE SO MUCH LIFE INTO A FICTITIOUS CHARACTER IS A RARE TALENT, INDEED!
FUYUKI-KUN!! I OFFICIALLY DECLARE YOU THE HOPE OF THE FUTURE FOR THIS MANGA CLUB!! KEEP UP THE GOOD WORK!
HE'S RIGHT! IT ALMOST FEELS LIKE YOU'RE SPYING ON THE MAIN CHARACTER...
COOL!
But it's true...
...I am always watching him.

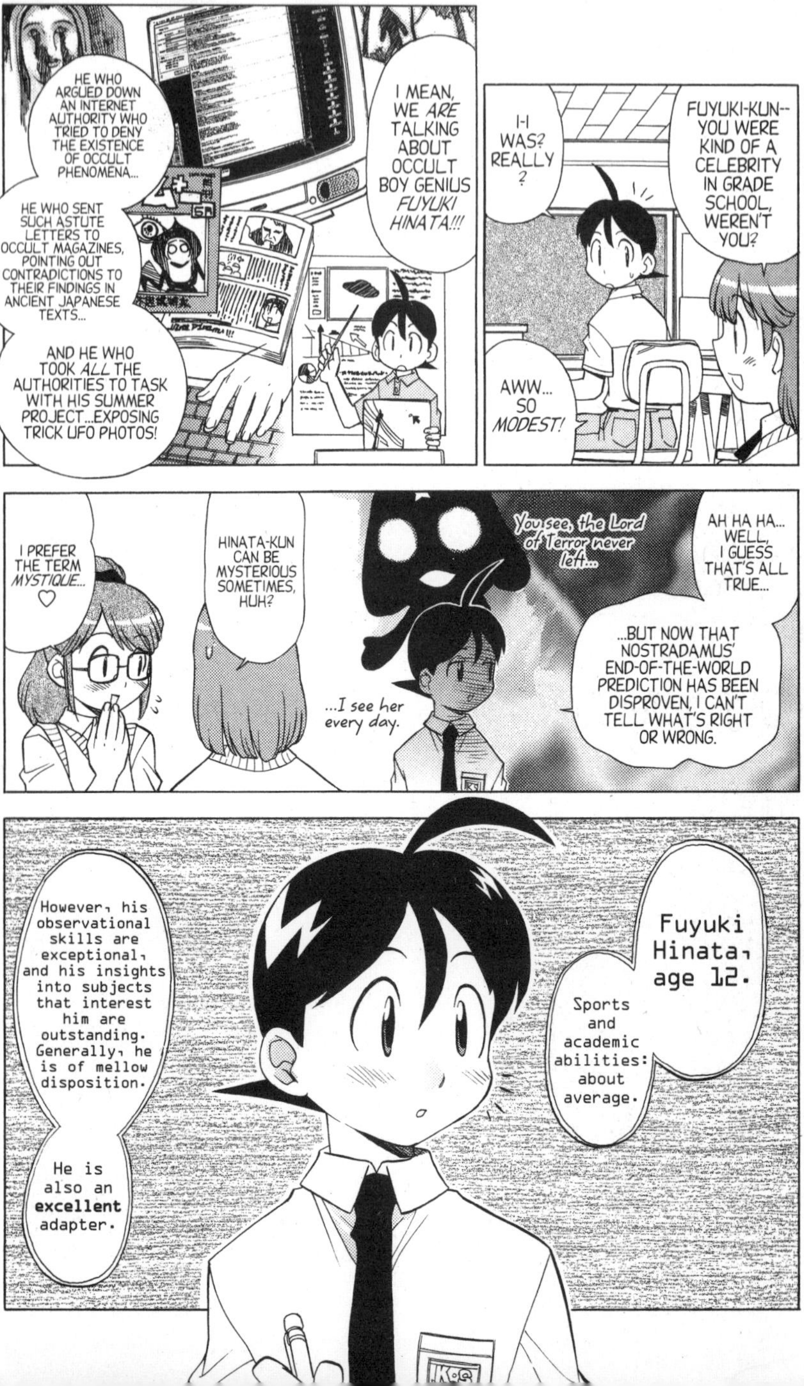
FUYUKI-KUN-- YOU WERE KIND OF A CELEBRITY IN GRADE SCHOOL, WEREN'T YOU?
I-I WAS? REALLY?
AWW... SO *MODEST!*
I MEAN, WE *ARE* TALKING ABOUT OCCULT BOY GENIUS *FUYUKI HINATA!!!*
HE WHO ARGUED DOWN AN INTERNET AUTHORITY WHO TRIED TO DENY THE EXISTENCE OF OCCULT PHENOMENA...
HE WHO SENT SUCH ASTUTE LETTERS TO OCCULT MAGAZINES, POINTING OUT CONTRADICTIONS TO THEIR FINDINGS IN ANCIENT JAPANESE TEXTS...
AND HE WHO TOOK *ALL* THE AUTHORITIES TO TASK WITH HIS SUMMER PROJECT...EXPOSING TRICK UFO PHOTOS!
AH HA HA... WELL, I GUESS THAT'S ALL TRUE...
...BUT NOW THAT NOSTRADAMUS' END-OF-THE-WORLD PREDICTION HAS BEEN DISPROVEN, I CAN'T TELL WHAT'S RIGHT OR WRONG.
You see, the Lord of Terror never left...
...I see her every day.
HINATA-KUN CAN BE MYSTERIOUS SOMETIMES, HUH?
I PREFER THE TERM *MYSTIQUE...* ♡
Fuyuki Hinata, age 12.
Sports and academic abilities: about average.
However, his observational skills are exceptional, and his insights into subjects that interest him are outstanding. Generally, he is of mellow disposition.
He is also an **excellent** adapter.

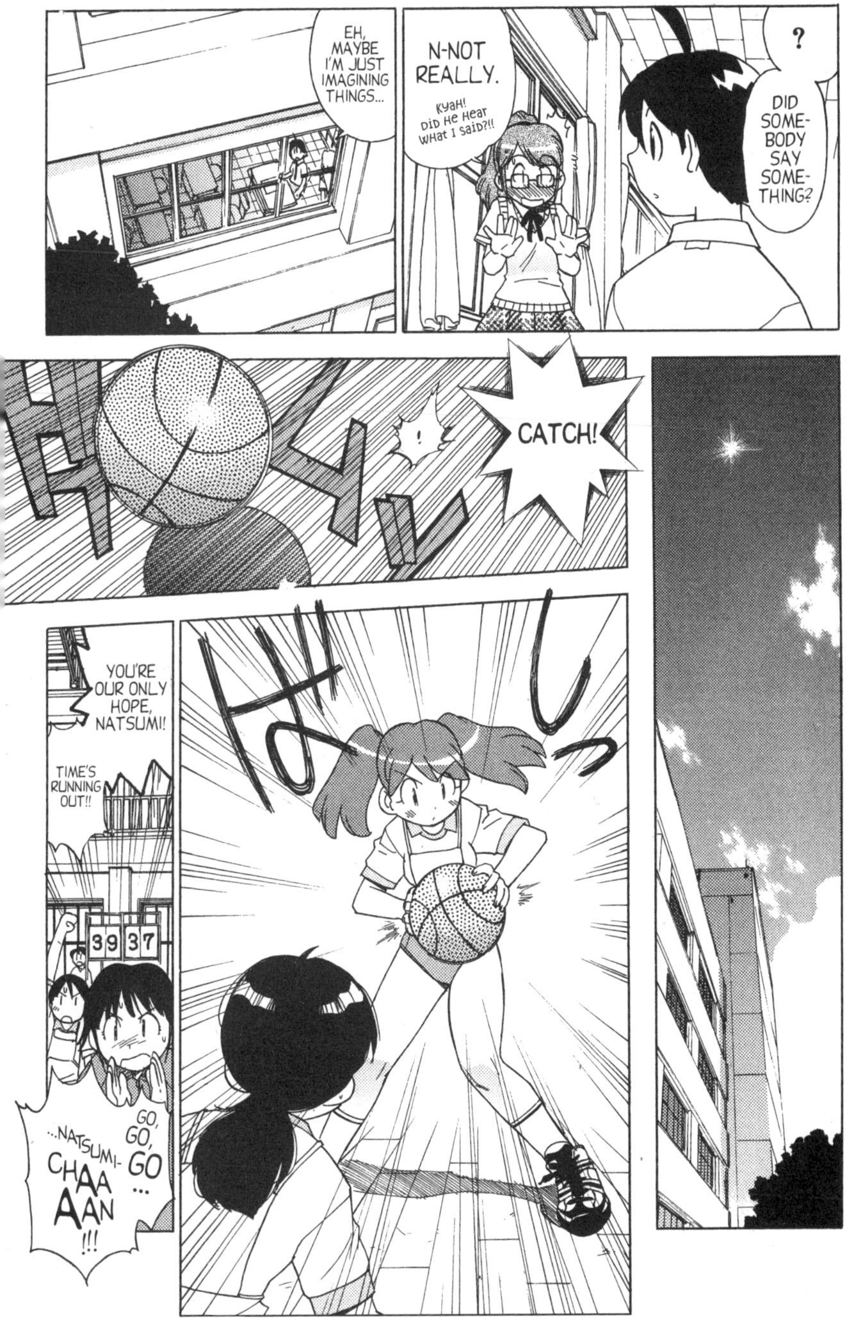
?
DID SOMEBODY SAY SOMETHING?
N-NOT REALLY.
Kyah! Did he hear what I said?!!
EH, MAYBE I'M JUST IMAGINING THINGS...
CATCH!
!
YOU'RE OUR ONLY HOPE, NATSUMI!
TIME'S RUNNING OUT!!
39 37
GO, GO, GO...
...NATSUMI-CHAAAAN!!!

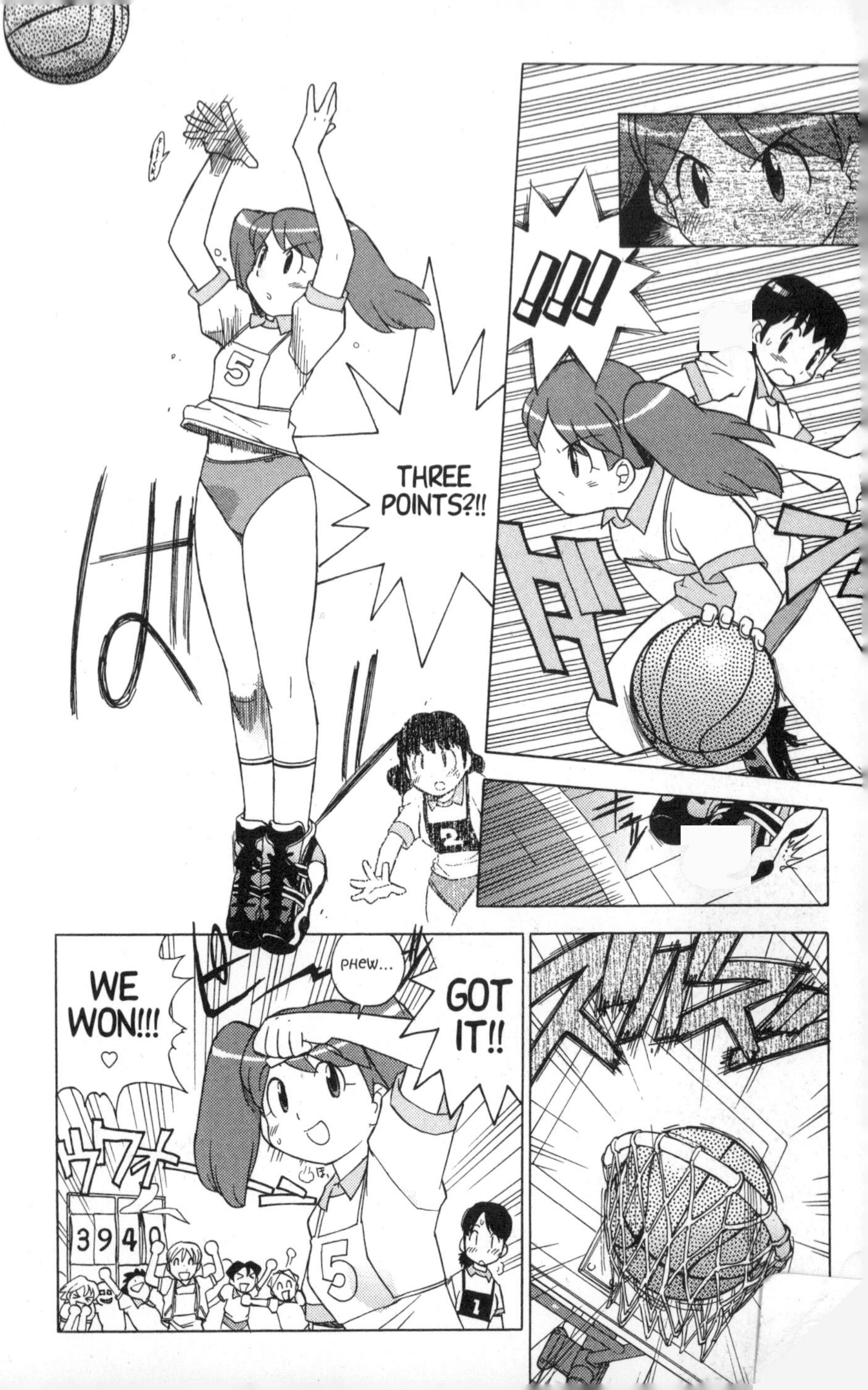
!!!
THREE POINTS?!!
GOT IT!!
PHEW...
WE WON!!! ♡
ウワオー
3940

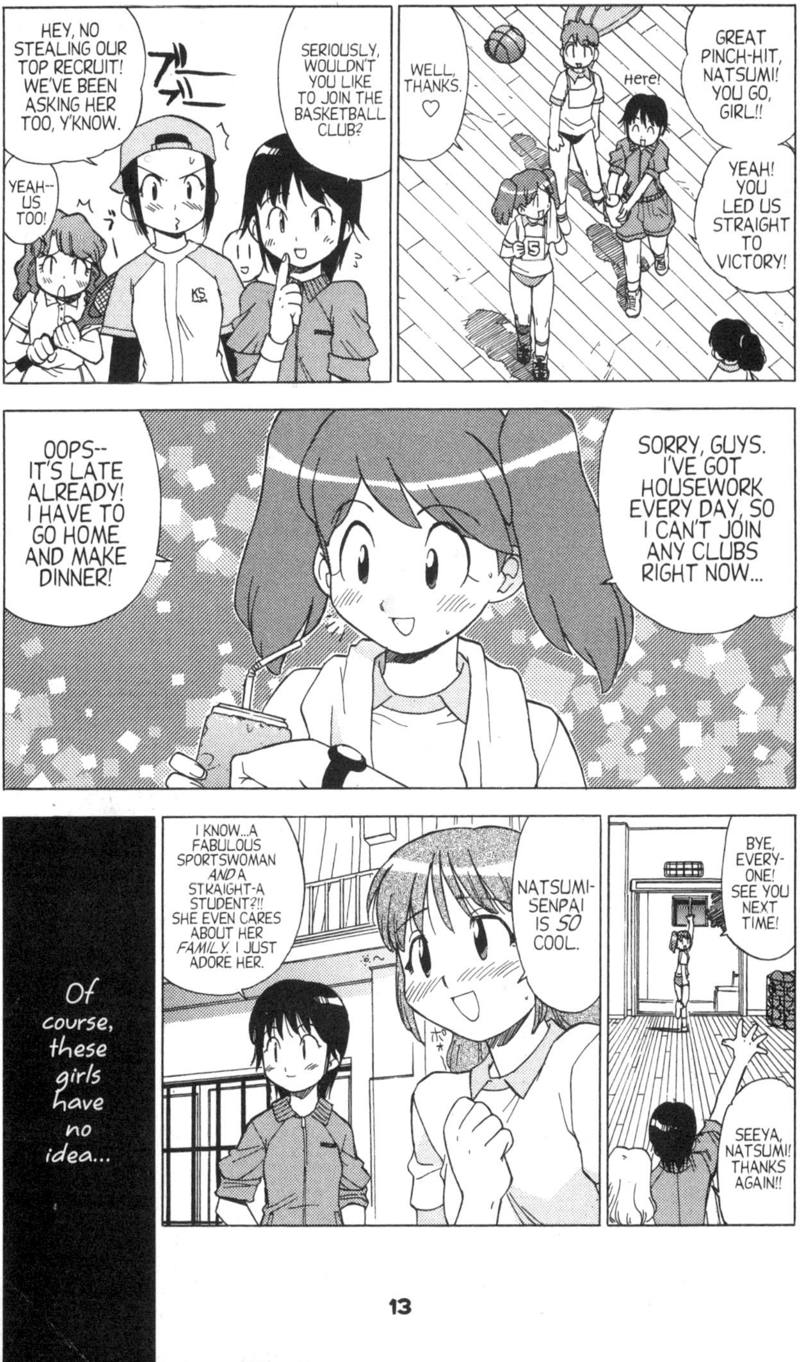
GREAT PINCH-HIT, NATSUMI! YOU GO, GIRL!!
YEAH! YOU LED US STRAIGHT TO VICTORY!
Here!
WELL, THANKS. ♡
SERIOUSLY, WOULDN'T YOU LIKE TO JOIN THE BASKETBALL CLUB?
HEY, NO STEALING OUR TOP RECRUIT! WE'VE BEEN ASKING HER TOO, Y'KNOW.
YEAH-- US TOO!
SORRY, GUYS. I'VE GOT HOUSEWORK EVERY DAY, SO I CAN'T JOIN ANY CLUBS RIGHT NOW...
OOPS-- IT'S LATE ALREADY! I HAVE TO GO HOME AND MAKE DINNER!
BYE, EVERY-ONE! SEE YOU NEXT TIME!
SEEYA, NATSUMI! THANKS AGAIN!!
NATSUMI-SENPAI IS *SO* COOL.
I KNOW...A FABULOUS SPORTSWOMAN *AND* A STRAIGHT-A STUDENT?!! SHE EVEN CARES ABOUT HER *FAMILY*. I JUST ADORE HER.
Of course, these girls have no idea...

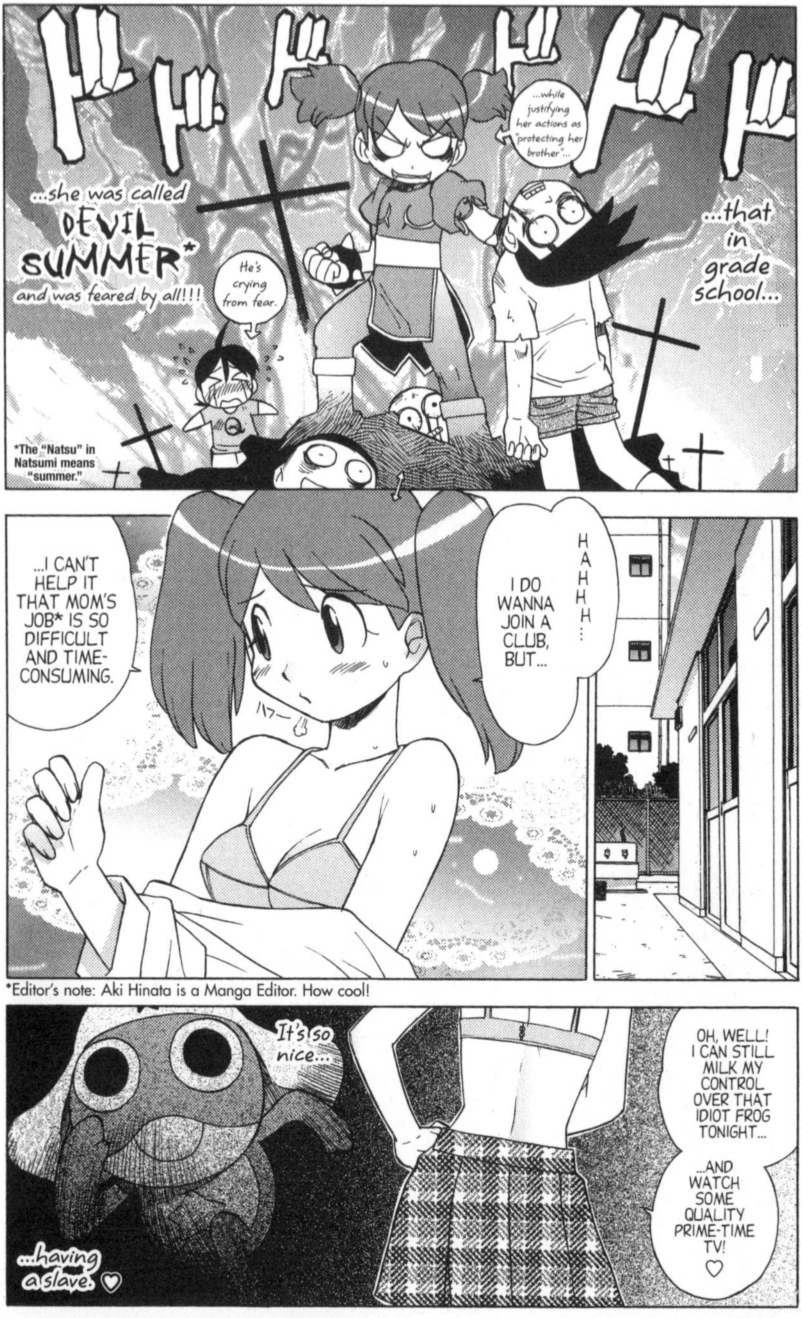

...that in grade school...
...while justifying her actions as "protecting her brother"...
...she was called DEVIL SUMMER* and was feared by all!!!
He's crying from fear.
*The "Natsu" in Natsumi means "summer."
HAHHH...
I DO WANNA JOIN A CLUB, BUT...
...I CAN'T HELP IT THAT MOM'S JOB* IS SO DIFFICULT AND TIME-CONSUMING.
ハァー
OH, WELL! I CAN STILL MILK MY CONTROL OVER THAT IDIOT FROG TONIGHT...
...AND WATCH SOME QUALITY PRIME-TIME TV! ♡
It's so nice...
...having a slave. ♡

*Editor's note: Aki Hinata is a Manga Editor. How cool!

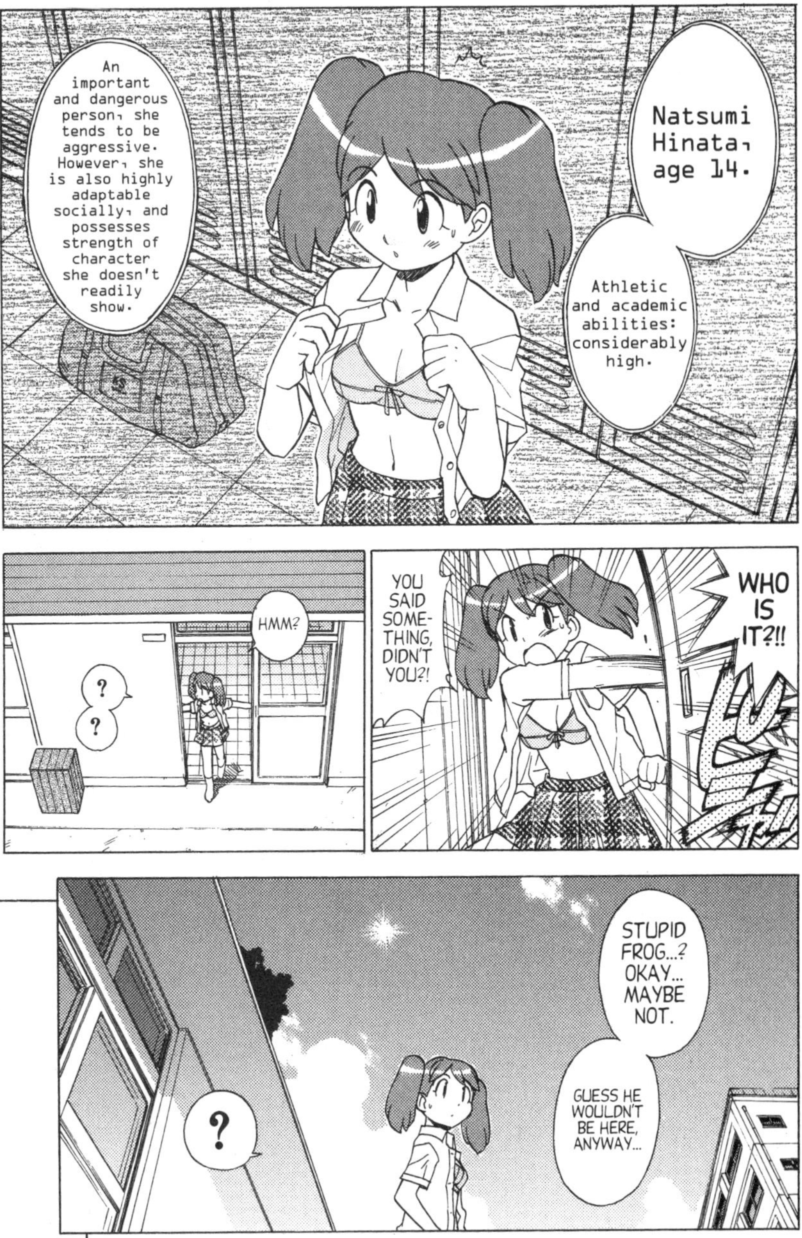
Natsumi Hinata, age 14.
Athletic and academic abilities: considerably high.
An important and dangerous person, she tends to be aggressive. However, she is also highly adaptable socially, and possesses strength of character she doesn't readily show.
WHO IS IT?!!
YOU SAID SOMETHING, DIDN'T YOU?!
HMM?
?
?
STUPID FROG...? OKAY... MAYBE NOT.
GUESS HE WOULDN'T BE HERE, ANYWAY...
?

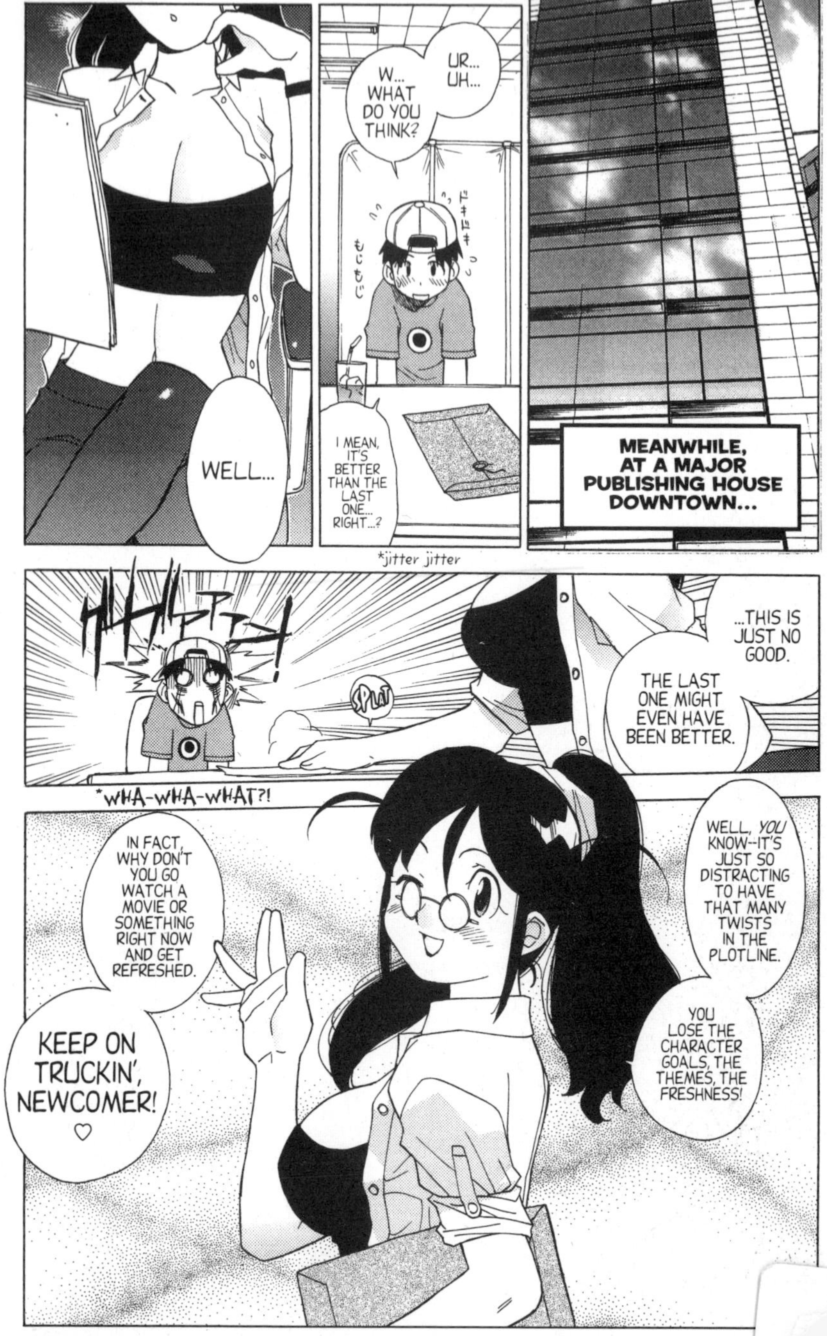
MEANWHILE, AT A MAJOR PUBLISHING HOUSE DOWNTOWN...
UR... UH...
W... WHAT DO YOU THINK?
I MEAN, IT'S BETTER THAN THE LAST ONE... RIGHT...?
*jitter jitter
WELL...
...THIS IS JUST NO GOOD.
THE LAST ONE MIGHT EVEN HAVE BEEN BETTER.
SPLAT
*WHA-WHA-WHAT?!
WELL, *YOU* KNOW--IT'S JUST SO DISTRACTING TO HAVE THAT MANY TWISTS IN THE PLOTLINE.
YOU LOSE THE CHARACTER GOALS, THE THEMES, THE FRESHNESS!
IN FACT, WHY DON'T YOU GO WATCH A MOVIE OR SOMETHING RIGHT NOW AND GET REFRESHED.
KEEP ON TRUCKIN', NEWCOMER! ♡

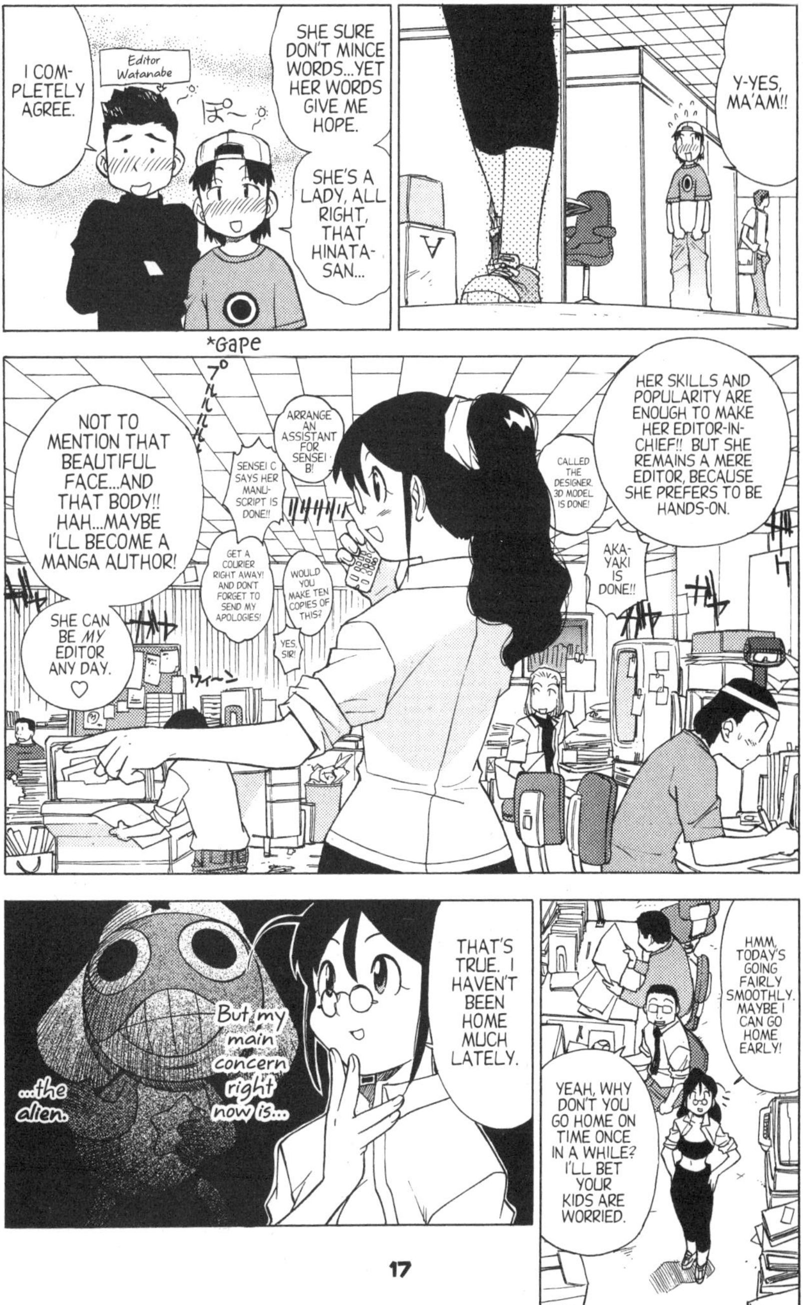

Y-YES, MA'AM!!
SHE SURE DON'T MINCE WORDS...YET HER WORDS GIVE ME HOPE.
SHE'S A LADY, ALL RIGHT, THAT HINATA-SAN...
ぽ〜
Editor Watanabe
I COMPLETELY AGREE.
*Gape
プルルル
HER SKILLS AND POPULARITY ARE ENOUGH TO MAKE HER EDITOR-IN-CHIEF!! BUT SHE REMAINS A MERE EDITOR, BECAUSE SHE PREFERS TO BE HANDS-ON.
CALLED THE DESIGNER. 3D MODEL IS DONE!
AKA-YAKI IS DONE!!
ARRANGE AN ASSISTANT FOR SENSEI B!
SENSEI C SAYS HER MANUSCRIPT IS DONE!!
NOT TO MENTION THAT BEAUTIFUL FACE...AND THAT BODY!! HAH...MAYBE I'LL BECOME A MANGA AUTHOR!
WOULD YOU MAKE TEN COPIES OF THIS?
YES, SIR!
GET A COURIER RIGHT AWAY! AND DON'T FORGET TO SEND MY APOLOGIES!
SHE CAN BE *MY* EDITOR ANY DAY. ♡
ウィ〜ン
HMM, TODAY'S GOING FAIRLY SMOOTHLY. MAYBE I CAN GO HOME EARLY!
YEAH, WHY DON'T YOU GO HOME ON TIME ONCE IN A WHILE? I'LL BET YOUR KIDS ARE WORRIED.
THAT'S TRUE. I HAVEN'T BEEN HOME MUCH LATELY.
But my main concern right now is...
...the alien.

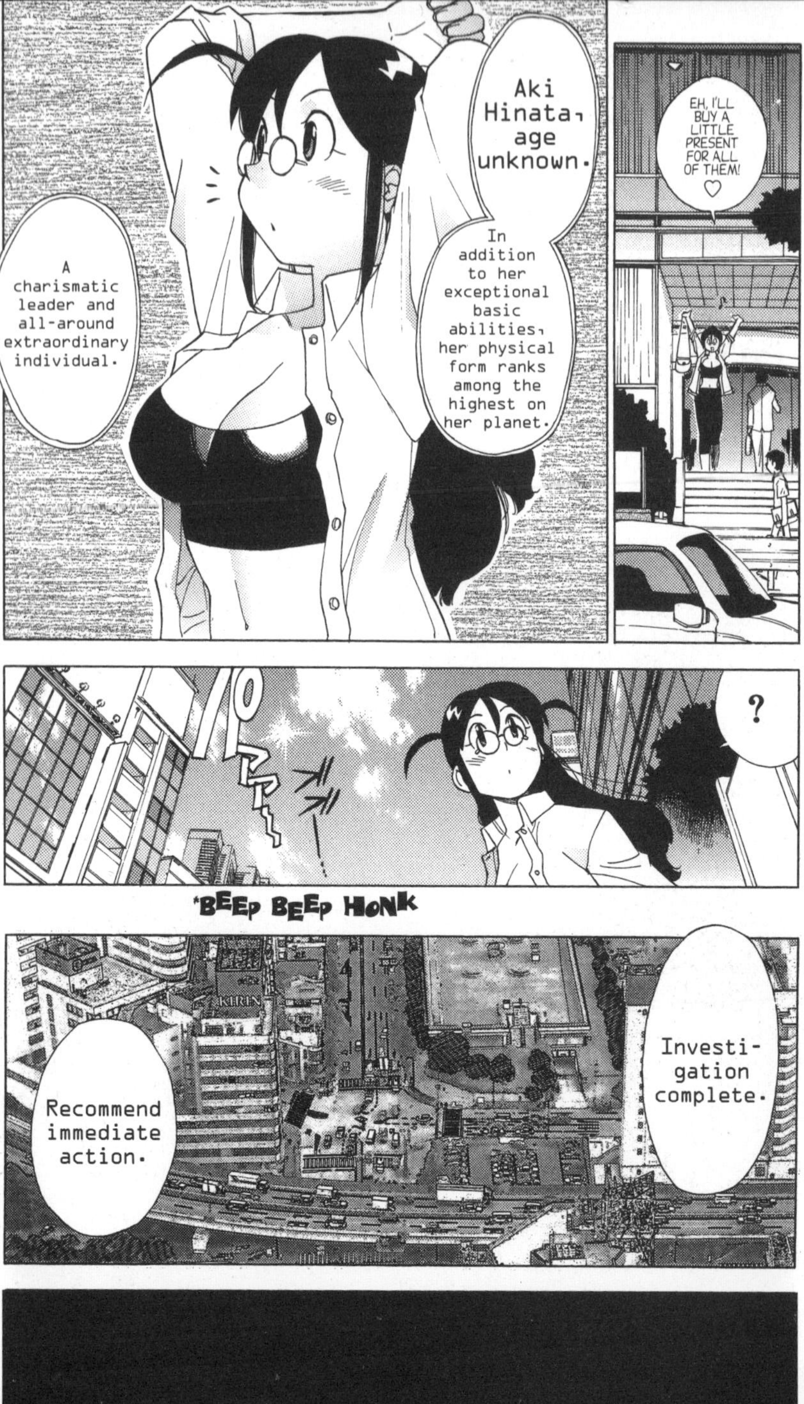
EH, I'LL BUY A LITTLE PRESENT FOR ALL OF THEM! ♡
Aki Hinata, age unknown.
In addition to her exceptional basic abilities, her physical form ranks among the highest on her planet.
A charismatic leader and all-around extraordinary individual.
?
*BEEP BEEP HONK
Investigation complete.
Recommend immediate action.
KIRIN

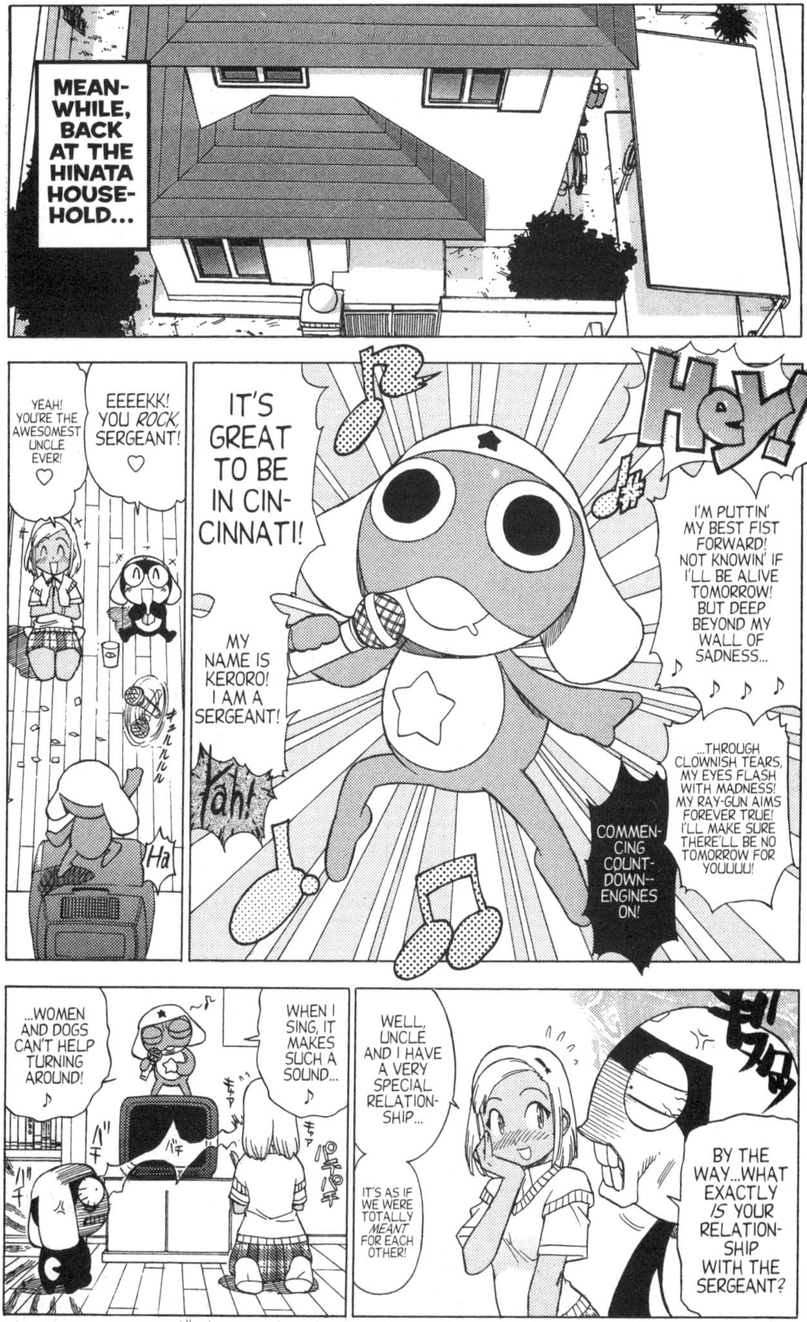
MEAN-WHILE, BACK AT THE HINATA HOUSE-HOLD...
Hey!
I'M PUTTIN' MY BEST FIST FORWARD! NOT KNOWIN' IF I'LL BE ALIVE TOMORROW! BUT DEEP BEYOND MY WALL OF SADNESS...
...THROUGH CLOWNISH TEARS, MY EYES FLASH WITH MADNESS! MY RAY-GUN AIMS FOREVER TRUE! I'LL MAKE SURE THERE'LL BE NO TOMORROW FOR YOUUUU!
COMMENCING COUNT-DOWN--ENGINES ON!
IT'S GREAT TO BE IN CINCINNATI!
MY NAME IS KERORO! I AM A SERGEANT!
Yah!
EEEEKK! YOU *ROCK*, SERGEANT! ♡
YEAH! YOU'RE THE AWESOMEST UNCLE EVER! ♡
Ha
BY THE WAY...WHAT EXACTLY *IS* YOUR RELATIONSHIP WITH THE SERGEANT?
WELL, UNCLE AND I HAVE A VERY SPECIAL RELATIONSHIP...
IT'S AS IF WE WERE TOTALLY *MEANT* FOR EACH OTHER!
WHEN I SING, IT MAKES SUCH A SOUND... ♪
...WOMEN AND DOGS CAN'T HELP TURNING AROUND! ♪

*ELECTRIC EYE-BEAM STARE

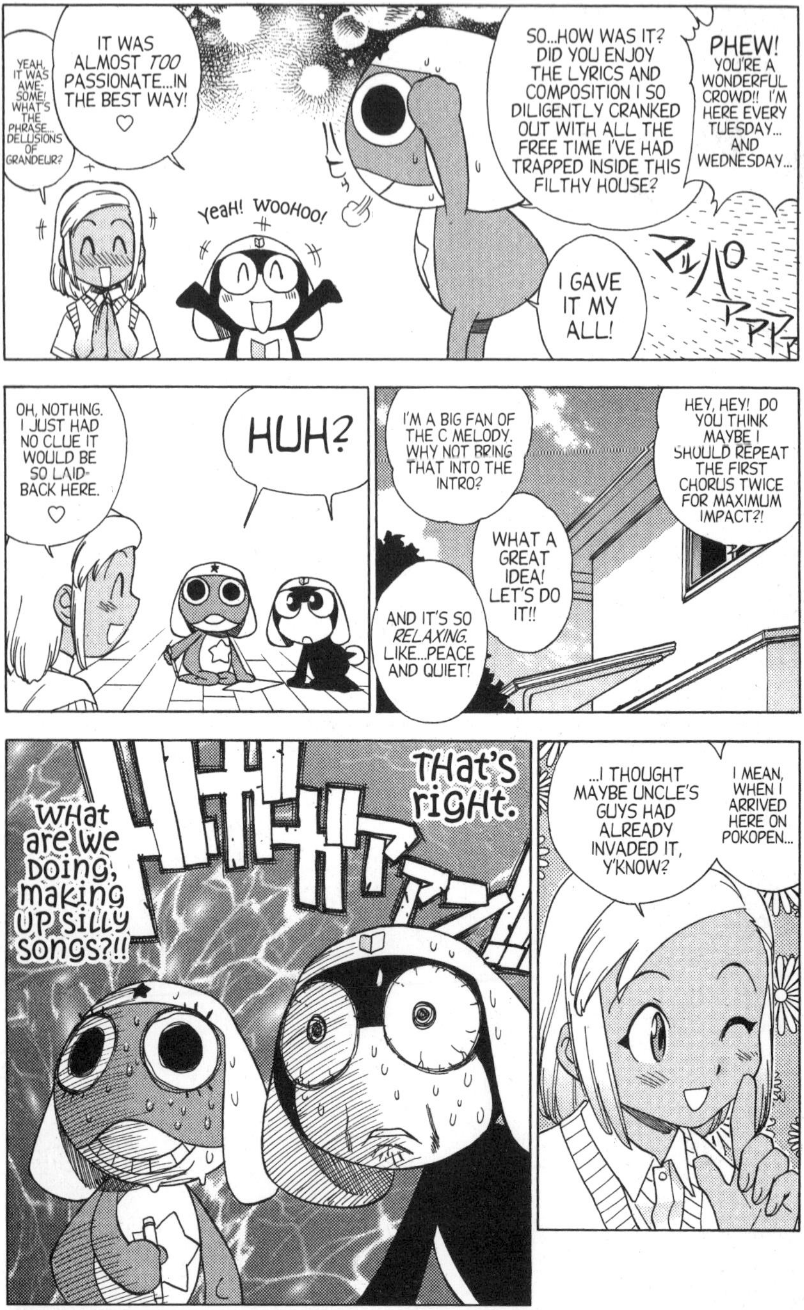
PHEW! YOU'RE A WONDERFUL CROWD!! I'M HERE EVERY TUESDAY... AND WEDNESDAY...
SO...HOW WAS IT? DID YOU ENJOY THE LYRICS AND COMPOSITION I SO DILIGENTLY CRANKED OUT WITH ALL THE FREE TIME I'VE HAD TRAPPED INSIDE THIS FILTHY HOUSE?
I GAVE IT MY ALL!
IT WAS ALMOST *TOO* PASSIONATE...IN THE BEST WAY! ♡
YEAH, IT WAS AWESOME! WHAT'S THE PHRASE... DELUSIONS OF GRANDEUR?
YeaH! WOOHOO!
HEY, HEY! DO YOU THINK MAYBE I SHOULD REPEAT THE FIRST CHORUS TWICE FOR MAXIMUM IMPACT?!
I'M A BIG FAN OF THE C MELODY. WHY NOT BRING THAT INTO THE INTRO?
WHAT A GREAT IDEA! LET'S DO IT!!
AND IT'S SO *RELAXING*. LIKE...PEACE AND QUIET!
HUH?
OH, NOTHING. I JUST HAD NO CLUE IT WOULD BE SO LAID-BACK HERE. ♡
I MEAN, WHEN I ARRIVED HERE ON POKOPEN...
...I THOUGHT MAYBE UNCLE'S GUYS HAD ALREADY INVADED IT, Y'KNOW?
THAT's right.
WHAT are we DOING, making UP Silly songs?!!

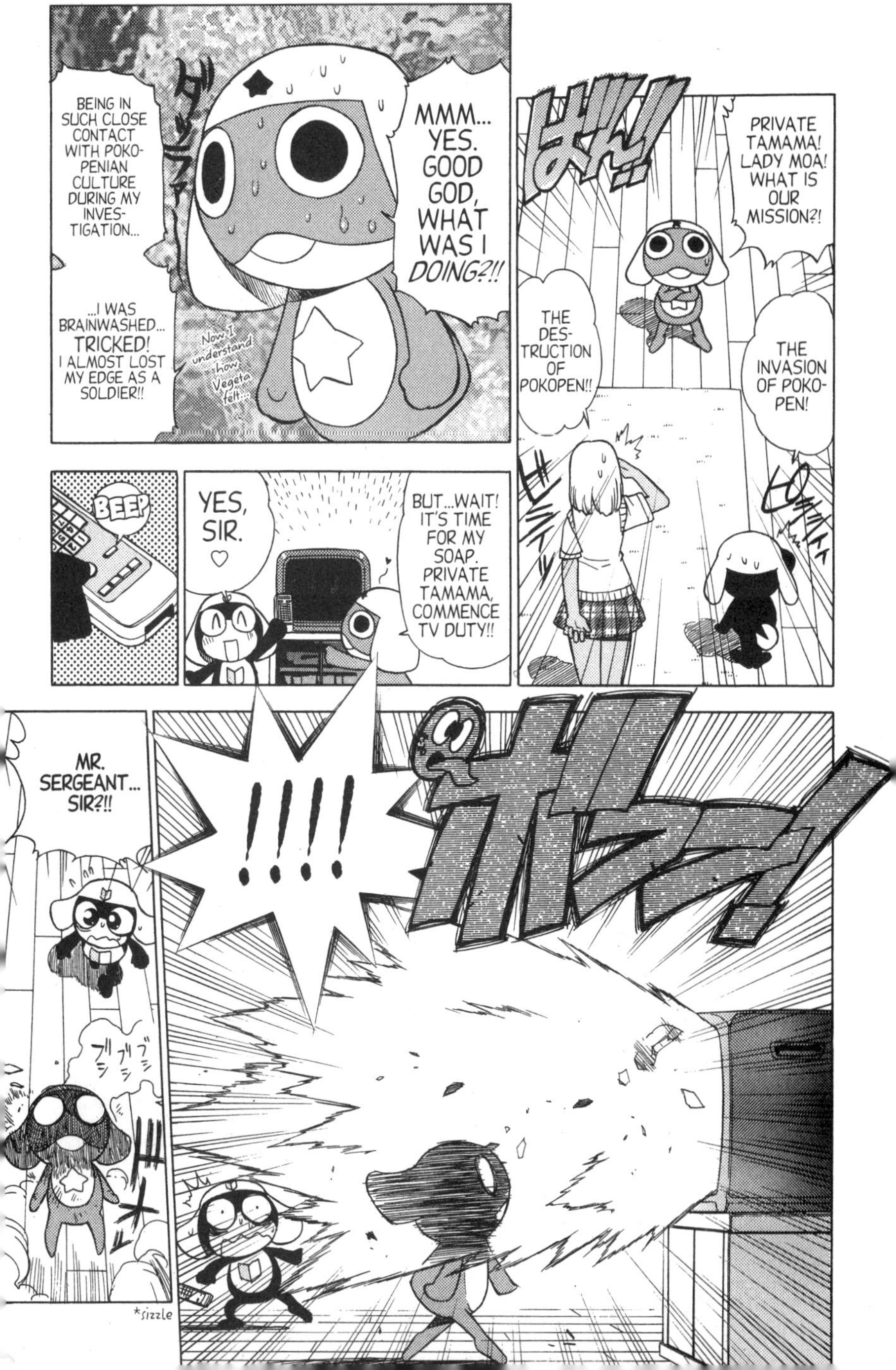
PRIVATE TAMAMA! LADY MOA! WHAT IS OUR MISSION?!
THE INVASION OF POKO-PEN!
THE DES-TRUCTION OF POKOPEN!!
MMM... YES. GOOD GOD, WHAT WAS I DOING?!!
BEING IN SUCH CLOSE CONTACT WITH POKO-PENIAN CULTURE DURING MY INVES-TIGATION...
...I WAS BRAINWASHED... TRICKED! I ALMOST LOST MY EDGE AS A SOLDIER!!
Now I understand how Vegeta felt...
BUT...WAIT! IT'S TIME FOR MY SOAP. PRIVATE TAMAMA, COMMENCE TV DUTY!!
YES, SIR. ♡
BEEP
!!!!!
MR. SERGEANT... SIR?!!
*sizzle

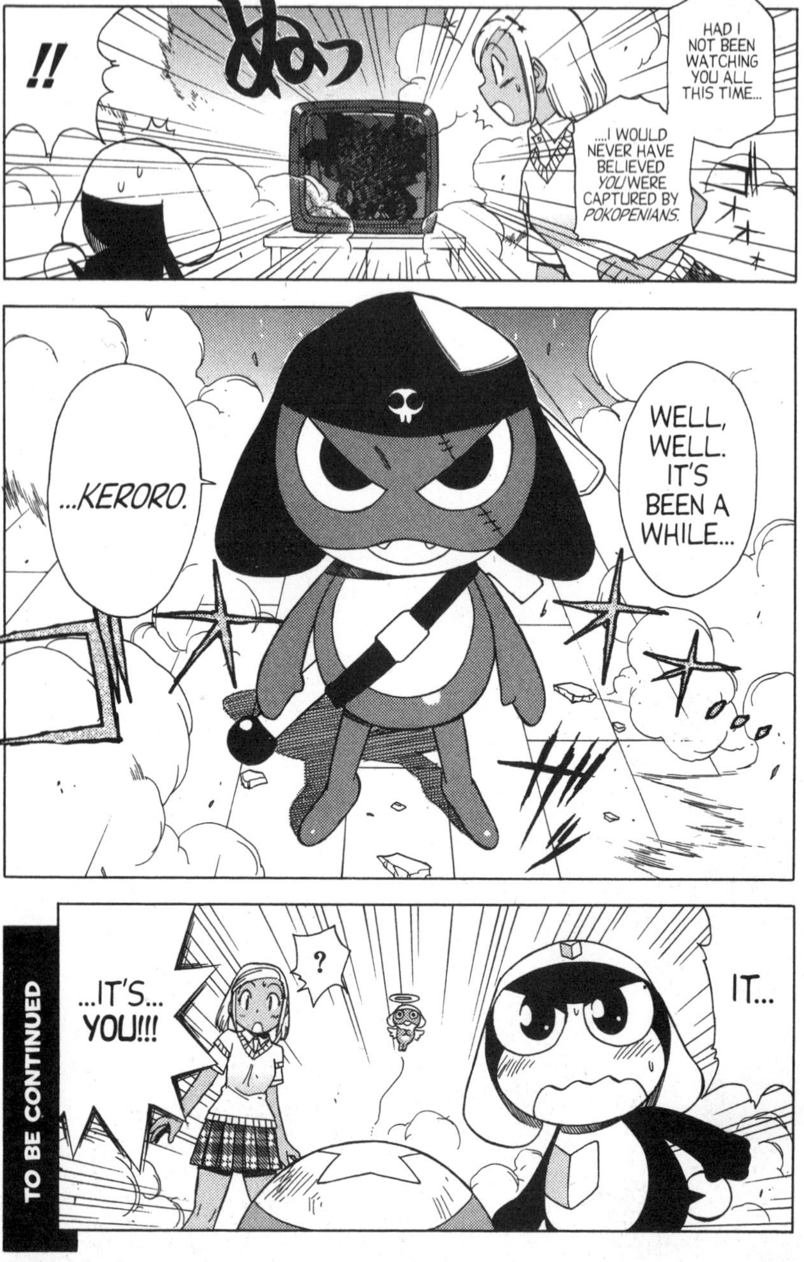
HAD I NOT BEEN WATCHING YOU ALL THIS TIME...
....I WOULD NEVER HAVE BELIEVED *YOU* WERE CAPTURED BY *POKOPENIANS.*
ぬっ
!!
WELL, WELL. IT'S BEEN A WHILE...
...KERORO.
IT...
?
...IT'S... YOU!!!
TO BE CONTINUED

ENCOUNTER XII

BATTLE ROYALE: KERORO VS. GIRORO

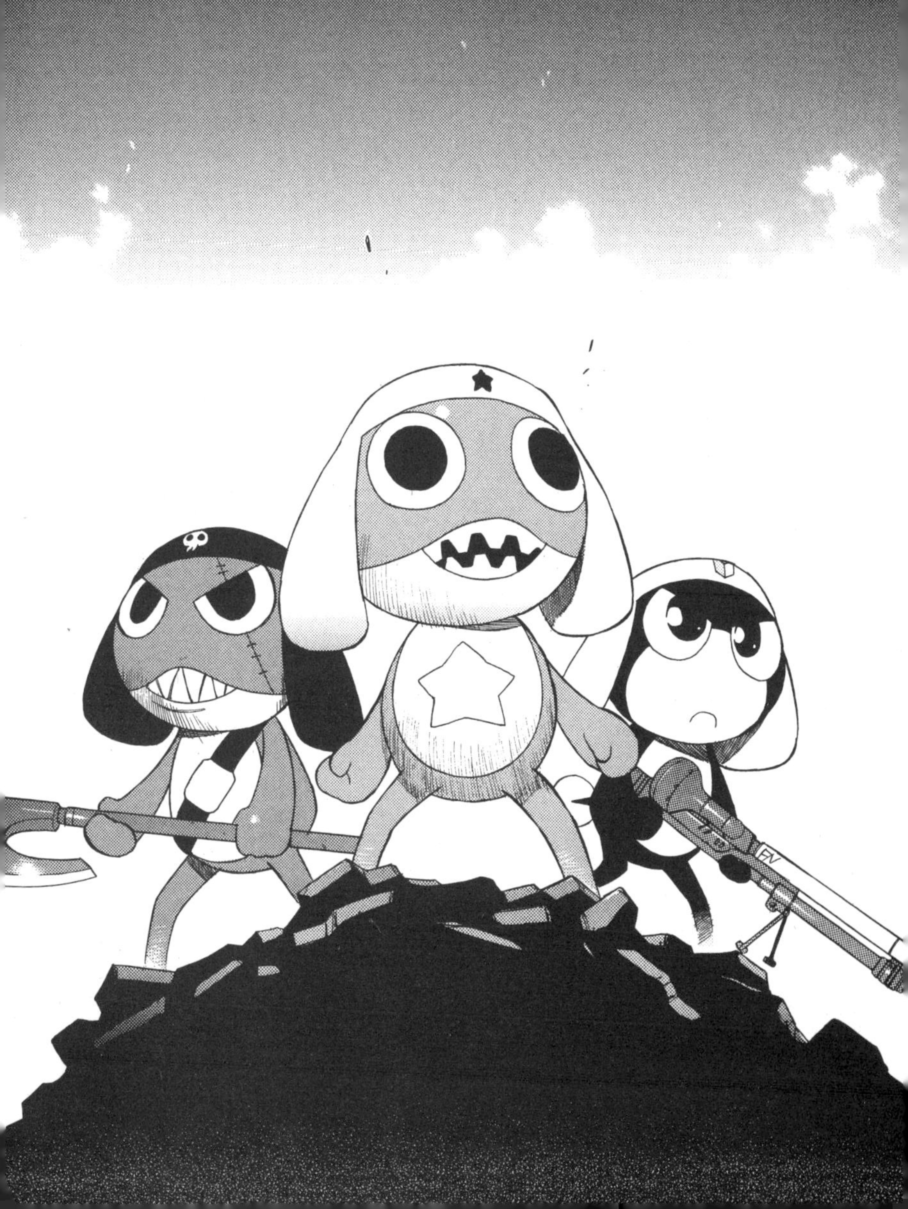

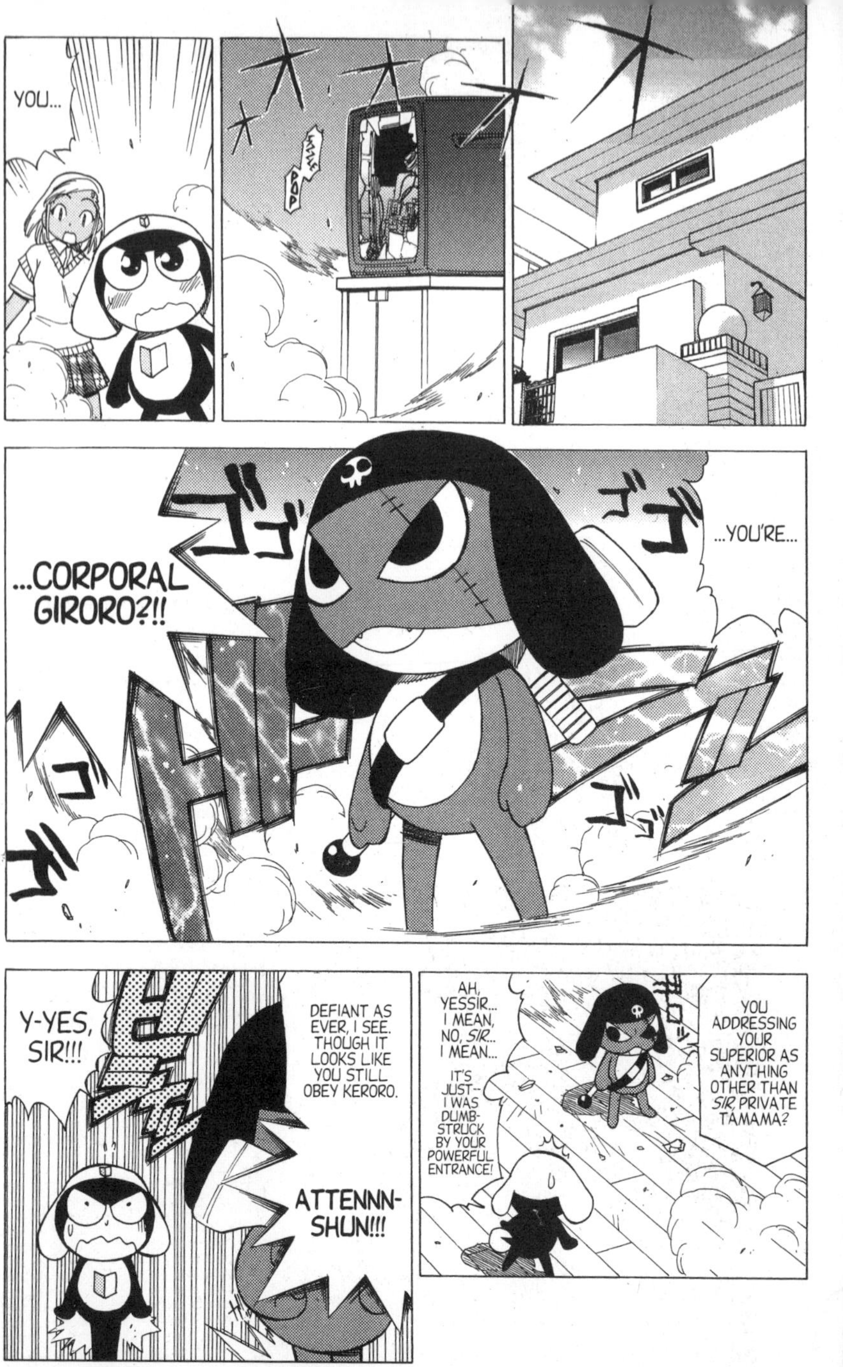
POP
YOU...
...YOU'RE...
...CORPORAL GIRORO?!!
YOU ADDRESSING YOUR SUPERIOR AS ANYTHING OTHER THAN *SIR*, PRIVATE TAMAMA?
AH, YESSIR... I MEAN, NO, *SIR*... I MEAN...
IT'S JUST-- I WAS DUMBSTRUCK BY YOUR POWERFUL ENTRANCE!
DEFIANT AS EVER, I SEE. THOUGH IT LOOKS LIKE YOU STILL OBEY KERORO.
Y-YES, SIR!!!
ATTENNN-SHUN!!!

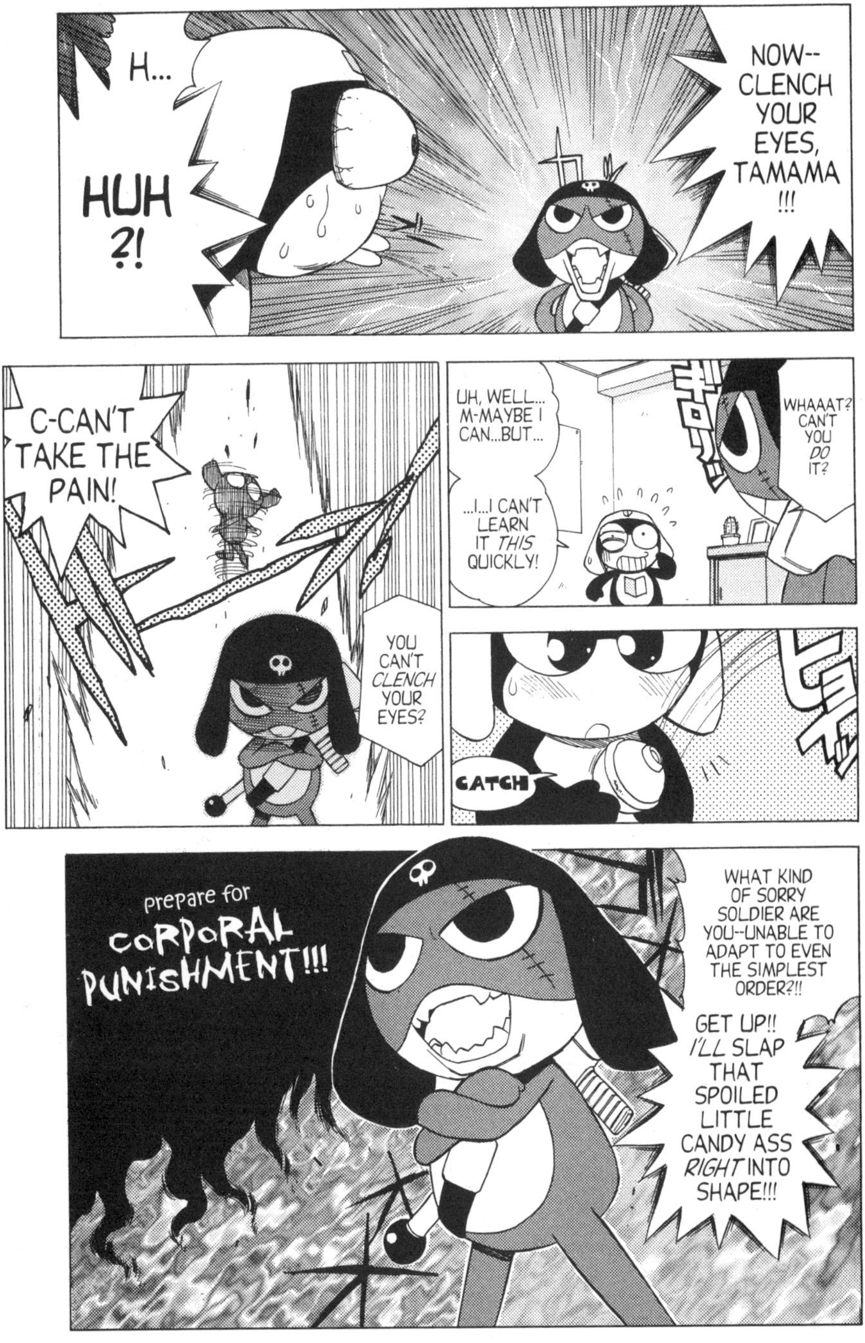
NOW-- CLENCH YOUR EYES, TAMAMA!!!
H...
HUH?!
WHAAAT? CAN'T YOU *DO* IT?
UH, WELL... M-MAYBE I CAN...BUT...
...I...I CAN'T LEARN IT *THIS* QUICKLY!
CATCH
YOU CAN'T *CLENCH* YOUR EYES?
C-CAN'T TAKE THE PAIN!
WHAT KIND OF SORRY SOLDIER ARE YOU--UNABLE TO ADAPT TO EVEN THE SIMPLEST ORDER?!!
GET UP!! *I'LL* SLAP THAT SPOILED LITTLE CANDY ASS *RIGHT* INTO SHAPE!!!
prepare for CORPORAL PUNISHMENT!!!

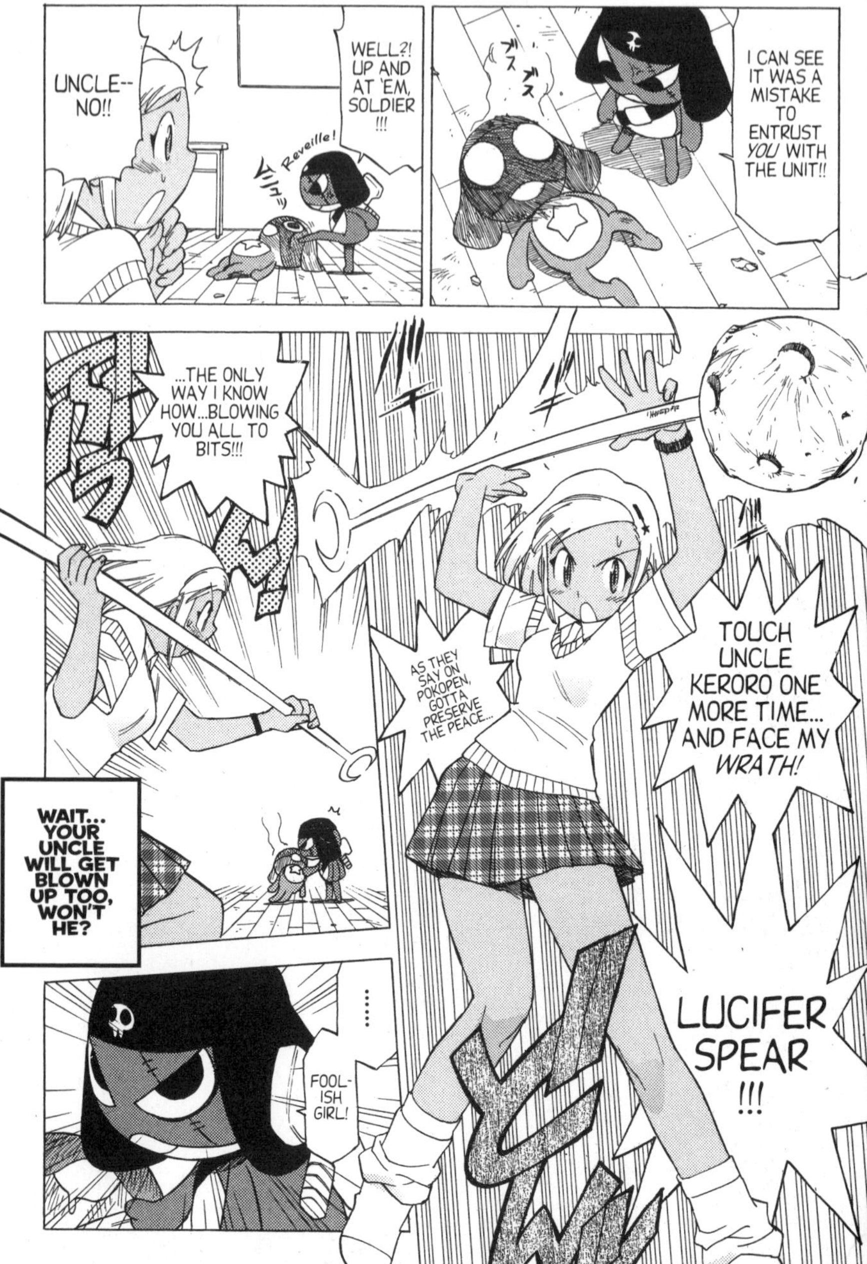
ブス ブス
I CAN SEE IT WAS A MISTAKE TO ENTRUST *YOU* WITH THE UNIT!!
WELL?! UP AND AT 'EM, SOLDIER!!!
Reveille!
UNCLE-- NO!!
TOUCH UNCLE KERORO ONE MORE TIME... AND FACE MY *WRATH!*
AS THEY SAY ON POKOPEN, GOTTA PRESERVE THE PEACE...
LUCIFER SPEAR!!!
...THE ONLY WAY I KNOW HOW...BLOWING YOU ALL TO BITS!!!
WAIT... YOUR UNCLE WILL GET BLOWN UP TOO, WON'T HE?
......
FOOL-ISH GIRL!

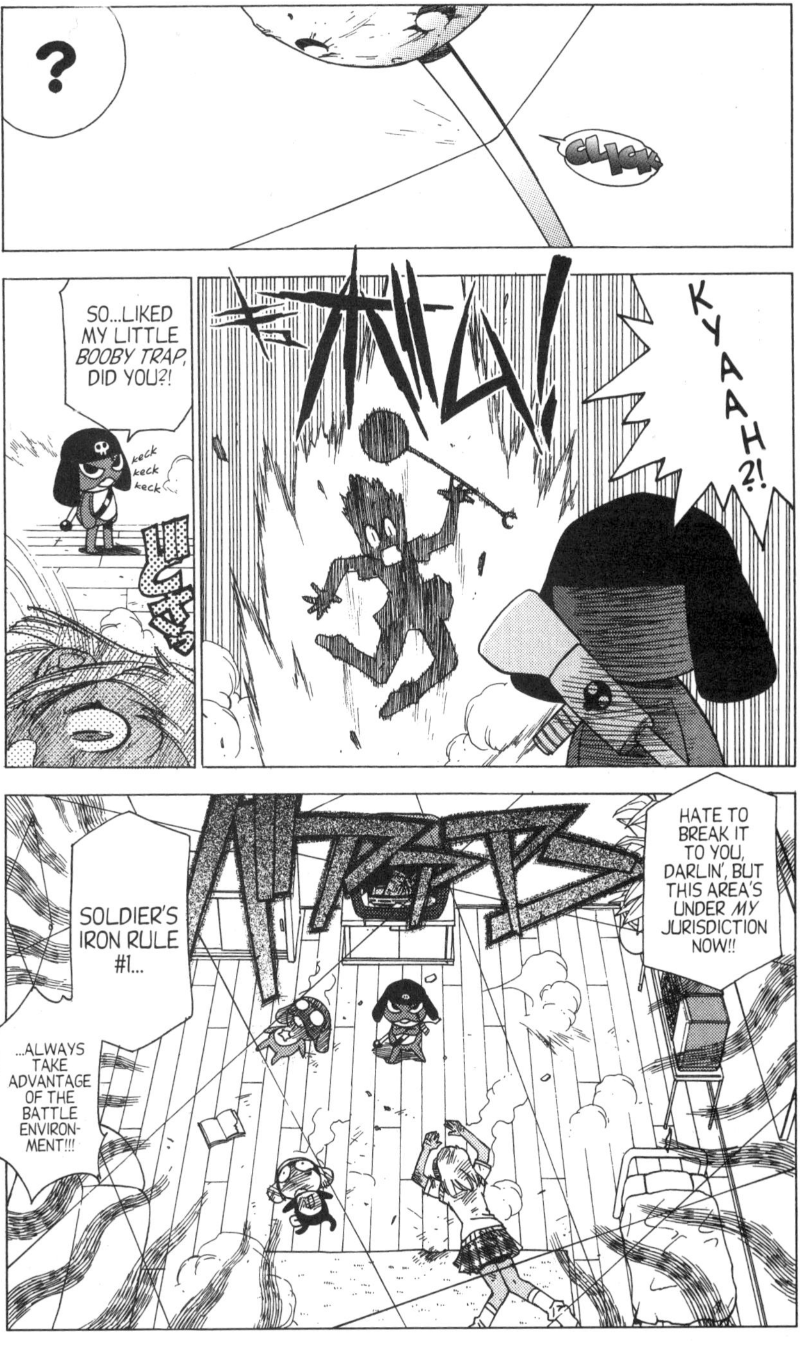
?
CLICK
KYAAH?!
SO...LIKED MY LITTLE *BOOBY TRAP*, DID YOU?!
keck keck keck
HATE TO BREAK IT TO YOU, DARLIN', BUT THIS AREA'S UNDER *MY* JURISDICTION NOW!!
SOLDIER'S IRON RULE #1...
...ALWAYS TAKE ADVANTAGE OF THE BATTLE ENVIRONMENT!!!

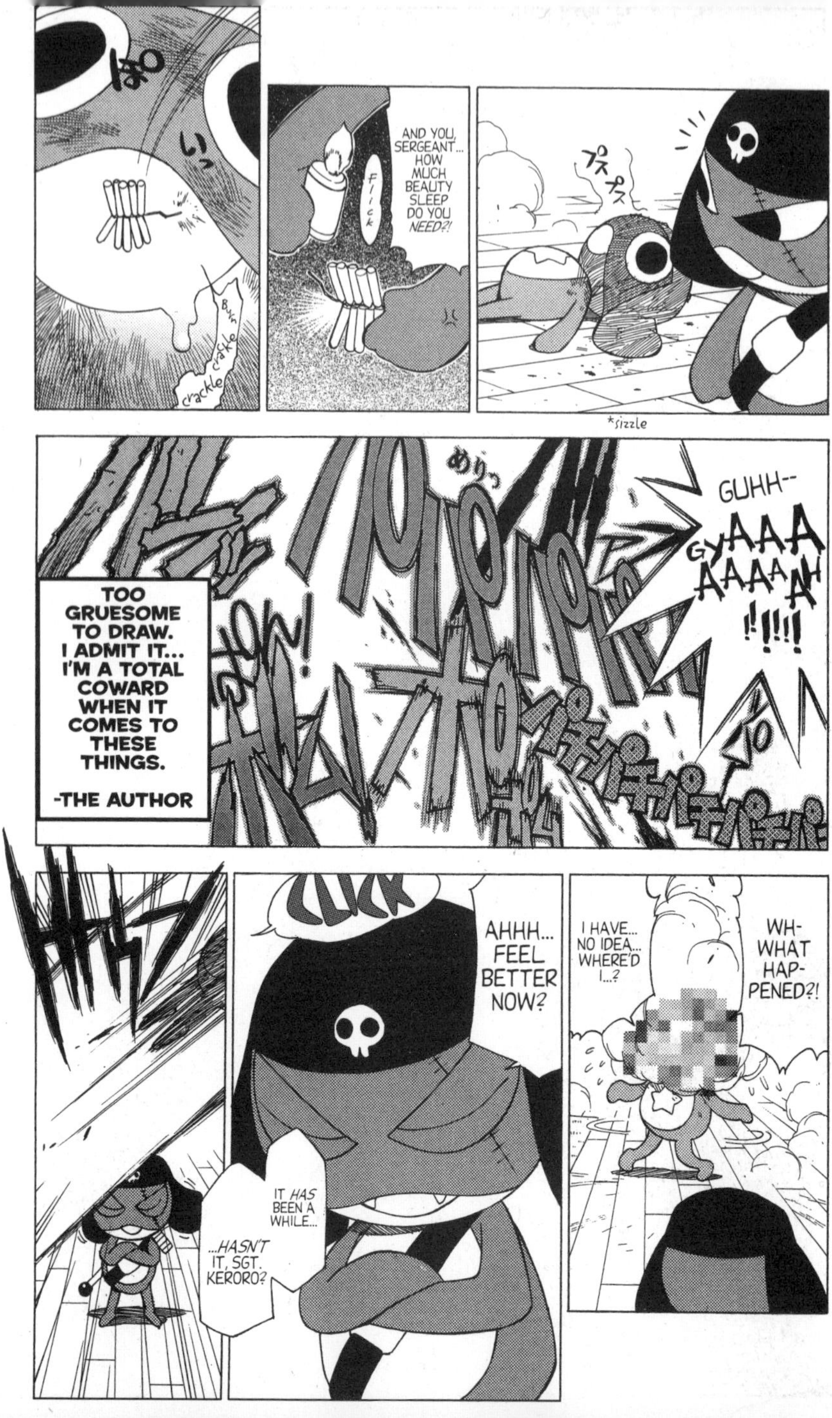
プスプス
*sizzle
AND YOU, SERGEANT... HOW MUCH BEAUTY SLEEP DO YOU *NEED?!*
Flick
Burn
crackle
crackle
crackle
GUHH-- GYAAAAAAAH!!!!!!
めりっ
TOO GRUESOME TO DRAW. I ADMIT IT... I'M A TOTAL COWARD WHEN IT COMES TO THESE THINGS.
-THE AUTHOR
WH- WHAT HAP- PENED?!
I HAVE... NO IDEA... WHERE'D I...?
AHHH... FEEL BETTER NOW?
IT *HAS* BEEN A WHILE...
...*HASN'T* IT, SGT. KERORO?

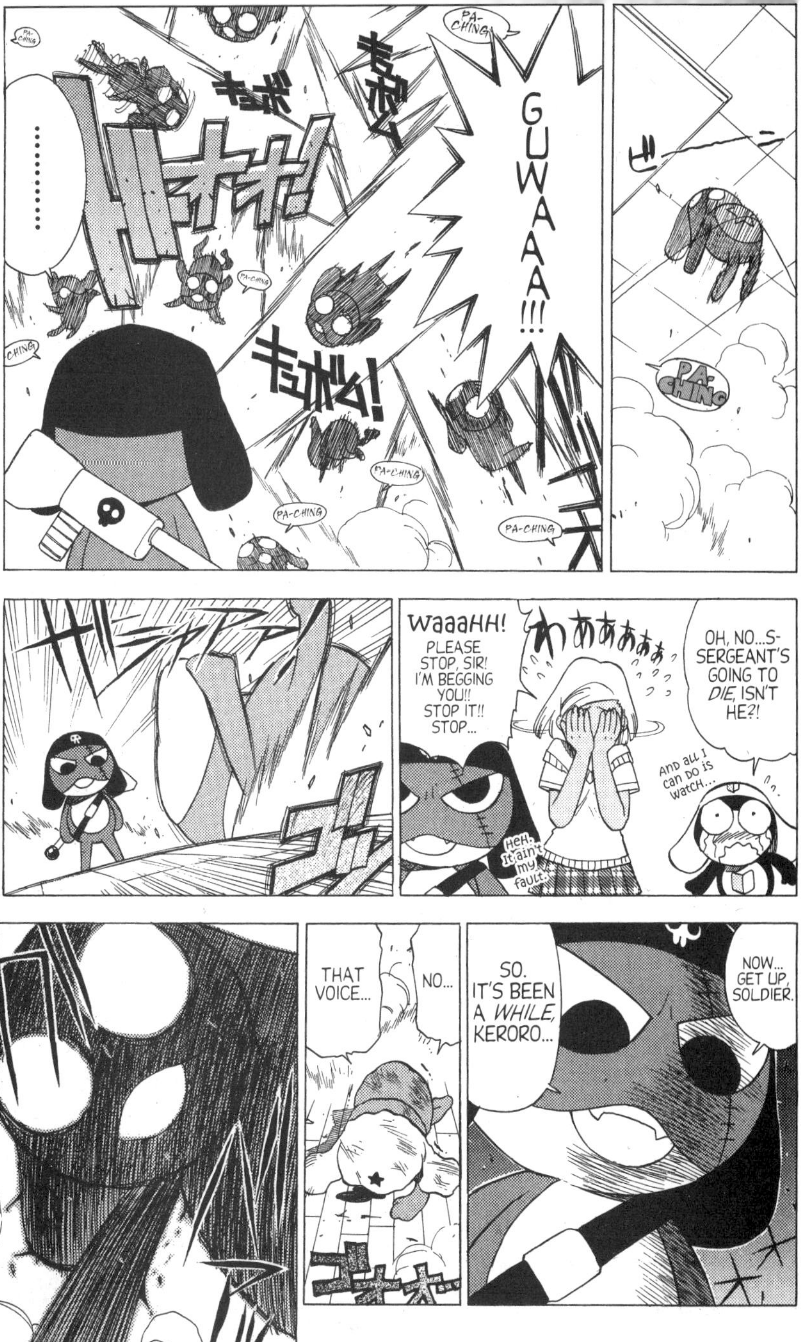
PA-CHING
PA-CHING
PA-CHING
....
GUWAAAA!!!
PA-CHING
CHING
PA-CHING
PA-CHING
PA-CHING
OH, NO...S-SERGEANT'S GOING TO *DIE*, ISN'T HE?!
And all I can do is watch...
WaaaHH! PLEASE STOP, SIR! I'M BEGGING YOU!! STOP IT!! STOP...
わあああああ
Heh. It ain't my fault.
NOW... GET UP, SOLDIER.
SO. IT'S BEEN A *WHILE*, KERORO...
NO...
THAT VOICE...

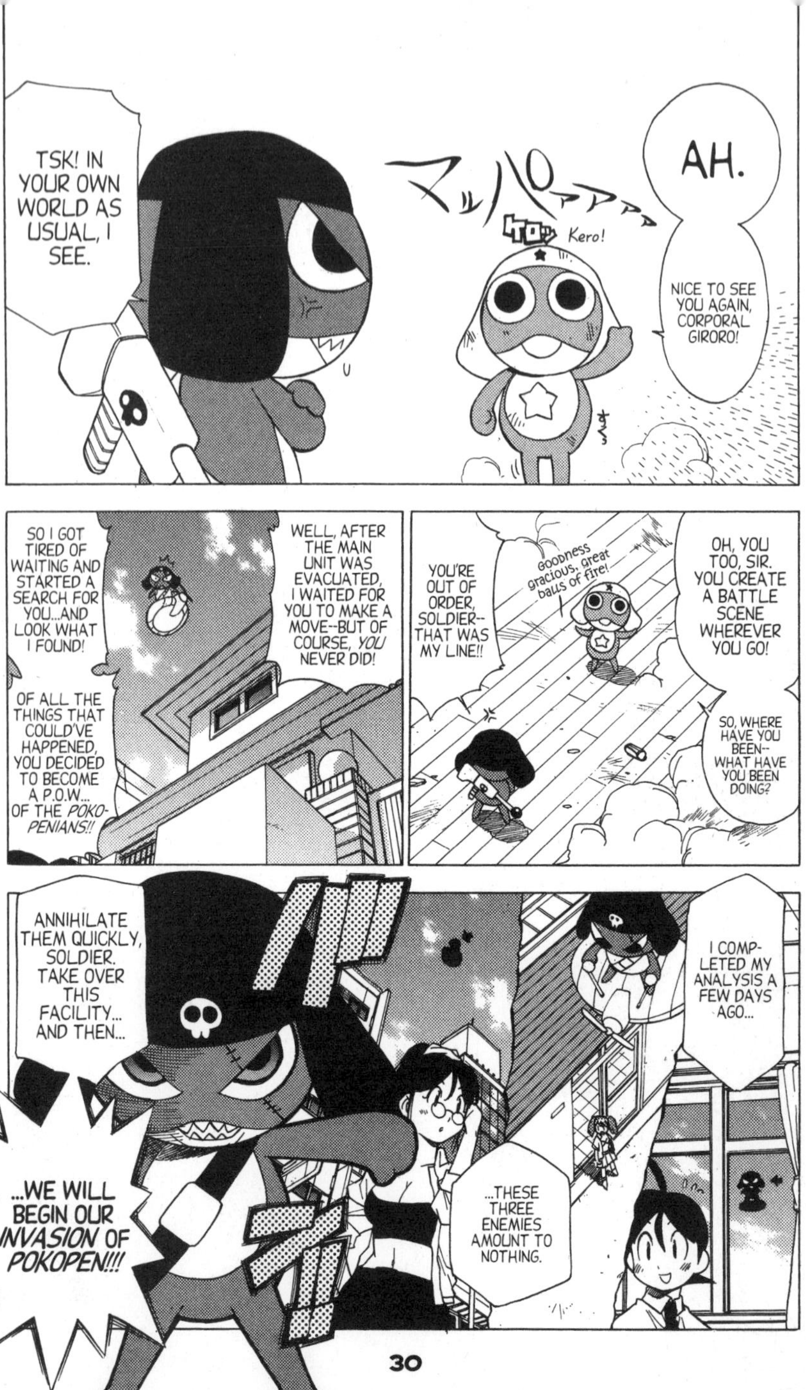
AH.
NICE TO SEE YOU AGAIN, CORPORAL GIRORO!
Kero!
TSK! IN YOUR OWN WORLD AS USUAL, I SEE.
OH, YOU TOO, SIR. YOU CREATE A BATTLE SCENE WHEREVER YOU GO!
Goodness gracious, great balls of fire!
YOU'RE OUT OF ORDER, SOLDIER--THAT WAS MY LINE!!
SO, WHERE HAVE YOU BEEN--WHAT HAVE YOU BEEN DOING?
WELL, AFTER THE MAIN UNIT WAS EVACUATED, I WAITED FOR YOU TO MAKE A MOVE--BUT OF COURSE, *YOU* NEVER DID!
SO I GOT TIRED OF WAITING AND STARTED A SEARCH FOR YOU...AND LOOK WHAT I FOUND!
OF ALL THE THINGS THAT COULD'VE HAPPENED, YOU DECIDED TO BECOME A P.O.W... OF THE *POKO-PENIANS!!*
I COMPLETED MY ANALYSIS A FEW DAYS AGO...
...THESE THREE ENEMIES AMOUNT TO NOTHING.
ANNIHILATE THEM QUICKLY, SOLDIER. TAKE OVER THIS FACILITY... AND THEN...
...WE WILL BEGIN OUR *INVASION* OF *POKOPEN!!!*

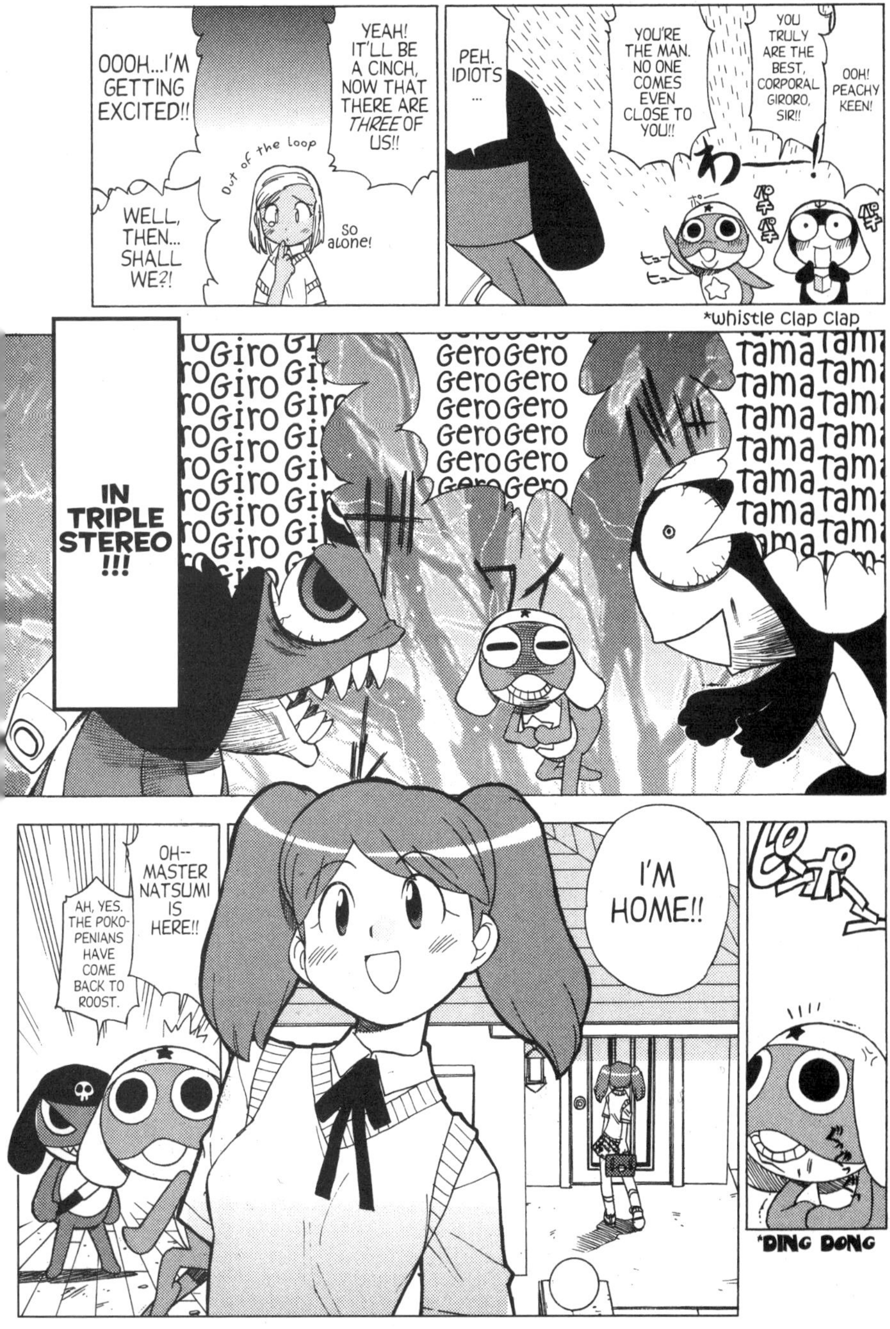
OOH! PEACHY KEEN!
YOU TRULY ARE THE BEST, CORPORAL GIRORO, SIR!!
YOU'RE THE MAN. NO ONE COMES EVEN CLOSE TO YOU!!
わーー!
PEH. IDIOTS ...
*whistle Clap Clap
YEAH! IT'LL BE A CINCH, NOW THAT THERE ARE *THREE* OF US!!
OOOH...I'M GETTING EXCITED!!
Out of the loop
WELL, THEN... SHALL WE?!
So alone!
Tama Tama Tama Tama Tama Tama Tama Tama
Gero Gero Gero Gero Gero Gero Gero Gero Gero Gero
Giro Giro Giro Giro Giro Giro Giro Giro
IN TRIPLE STEREO!!!
*DING DONG
I'M HOME!!
OH-- MASTER NATSUMI IS HERE!!
AH, YES. THE POKO-PENIANS HAVE COME BACK TO ROOST.

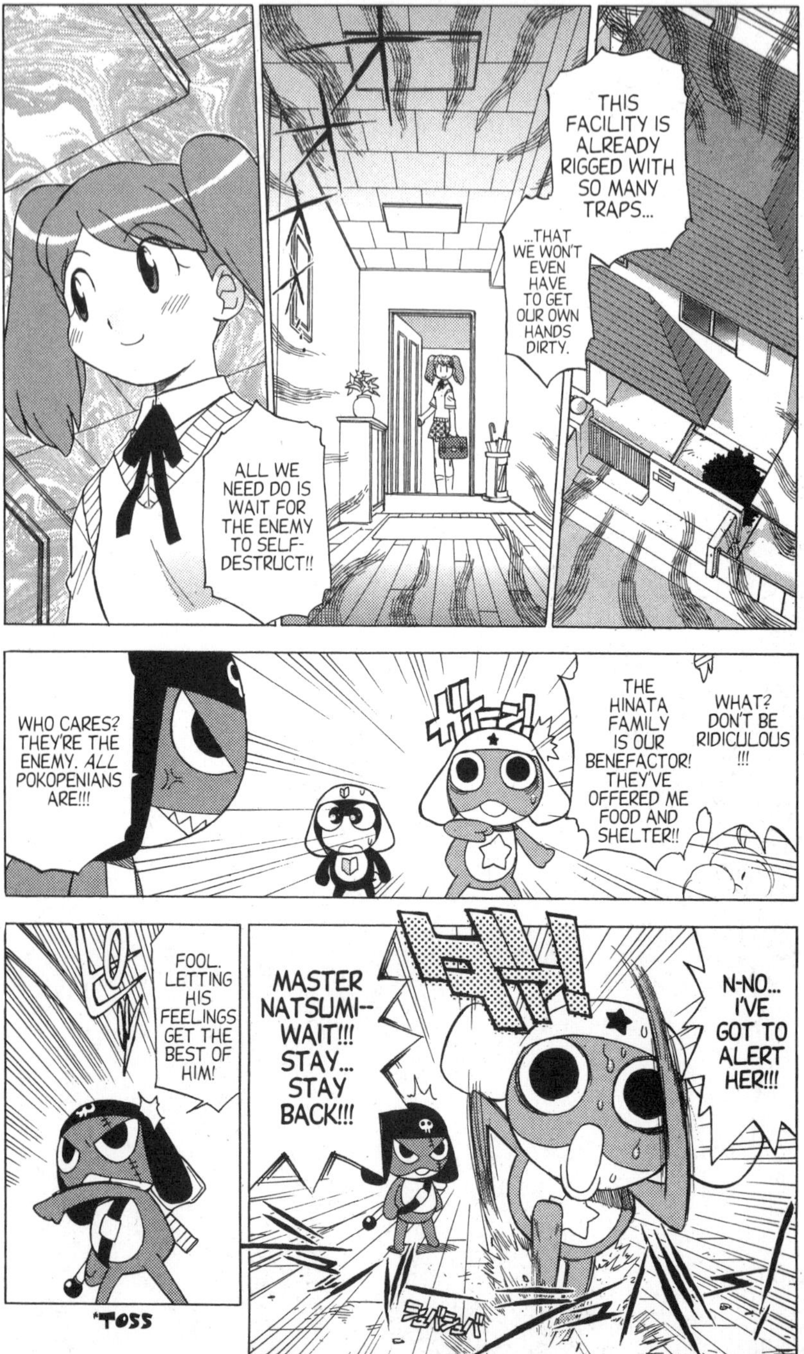
THIS FACILITY IS ALREADY RIGGED WITH SO MANY TRAPS...
...THAT WE WON'T EVEN HAVE TO GET OUR OWN HANDS DIRTY.
ALL WE NEED DO IS WAIT FOR THE ENEMY TO SELF-DESTRUCT!!
WHAT? DON'T BE RIDICULOUS!!!
THE HINATA FAMILY IS OUR BENEFACTOR! THEY'VE OFFERED ME FOOD AND SHELTER!!
WHO CARES? THEY'RE THE ENEMY. ALL POKOPENIANS ARE!!!
N-NO... I'VE GOT TO ALERT HER!!!
MASTER NATSUMI-- WAIT!!! STAY... STAY BACK!!!
FOOL. LETTING HIS FEELINGS GET THE BEST OF HIM!
*TOSS

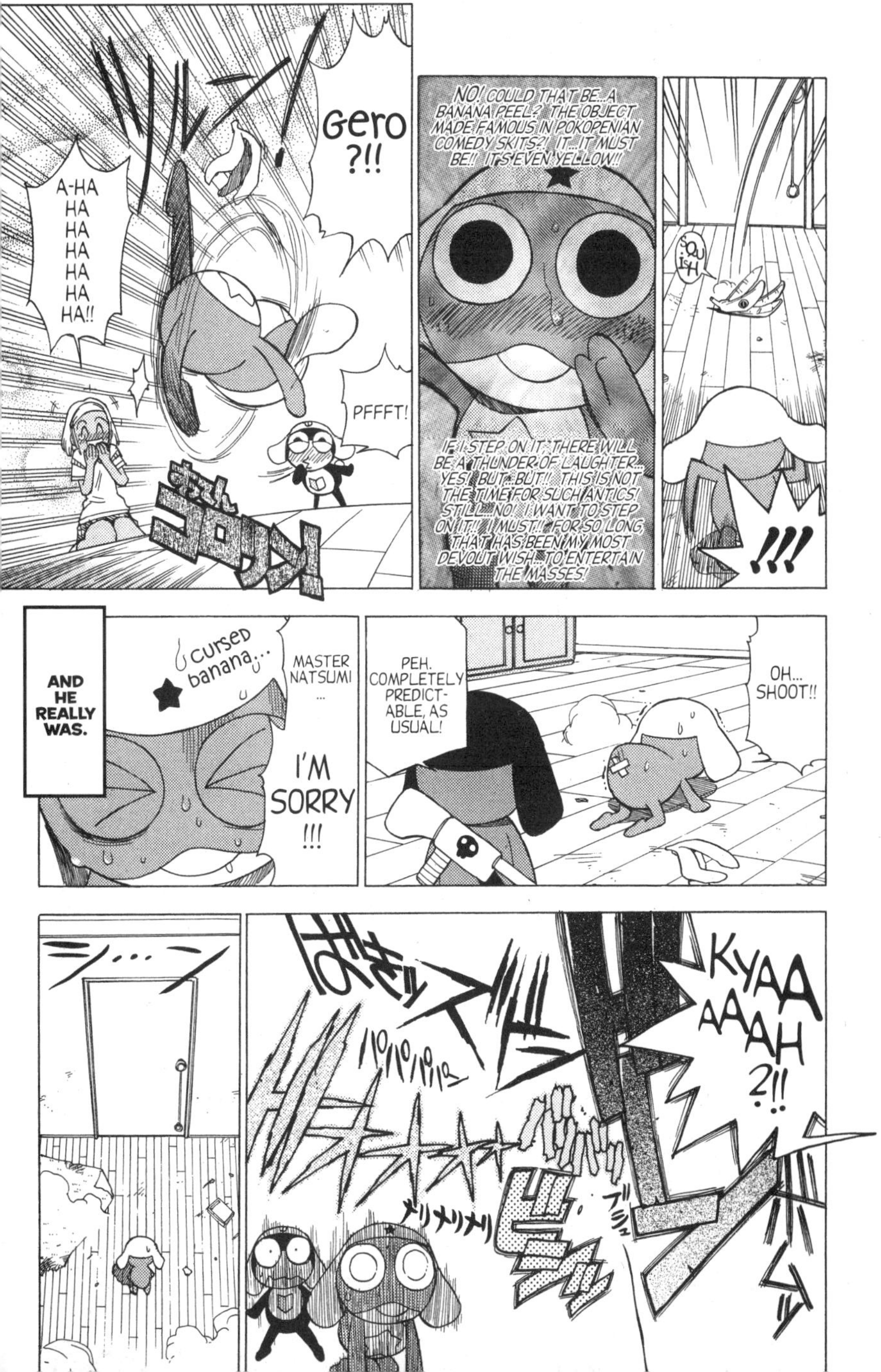
SQUISH
!!!
NO! COULD THAT BE...A BANANA PEEL? THE OBJECT MADE FAMOUS IN POKOPENIAN COMEDY SKITS?! IT...IT MUST BE!! IT'S EVEN YELLOW!!
IF I STEP ON IT, THERE WILL BE A THUNDER OF LAUGHTER... YES! BUT...BUT!! THIS IS NOT THE TIME FOR SUCH ANTICS! STILL...NO! I WANT TO STEP ON IT!! I MUST!! FOR SO LONG, THAT HAS BEEN MY MOST DEVOUT WISH...TO ENTERTAIN THE MASSES!
Gero ?!!
PFFFT!
A-HA HA HA HA HA HA HA HA!!
OH... SHOOT!!
PEH. COMPLETELY PREDICT-ABLE, AS USUAL!
MASTER NATSUMI ...
I'M SORRY !!!
cursed banana...
AND HE REALLY WAS.
KYAA AAAH ?!!

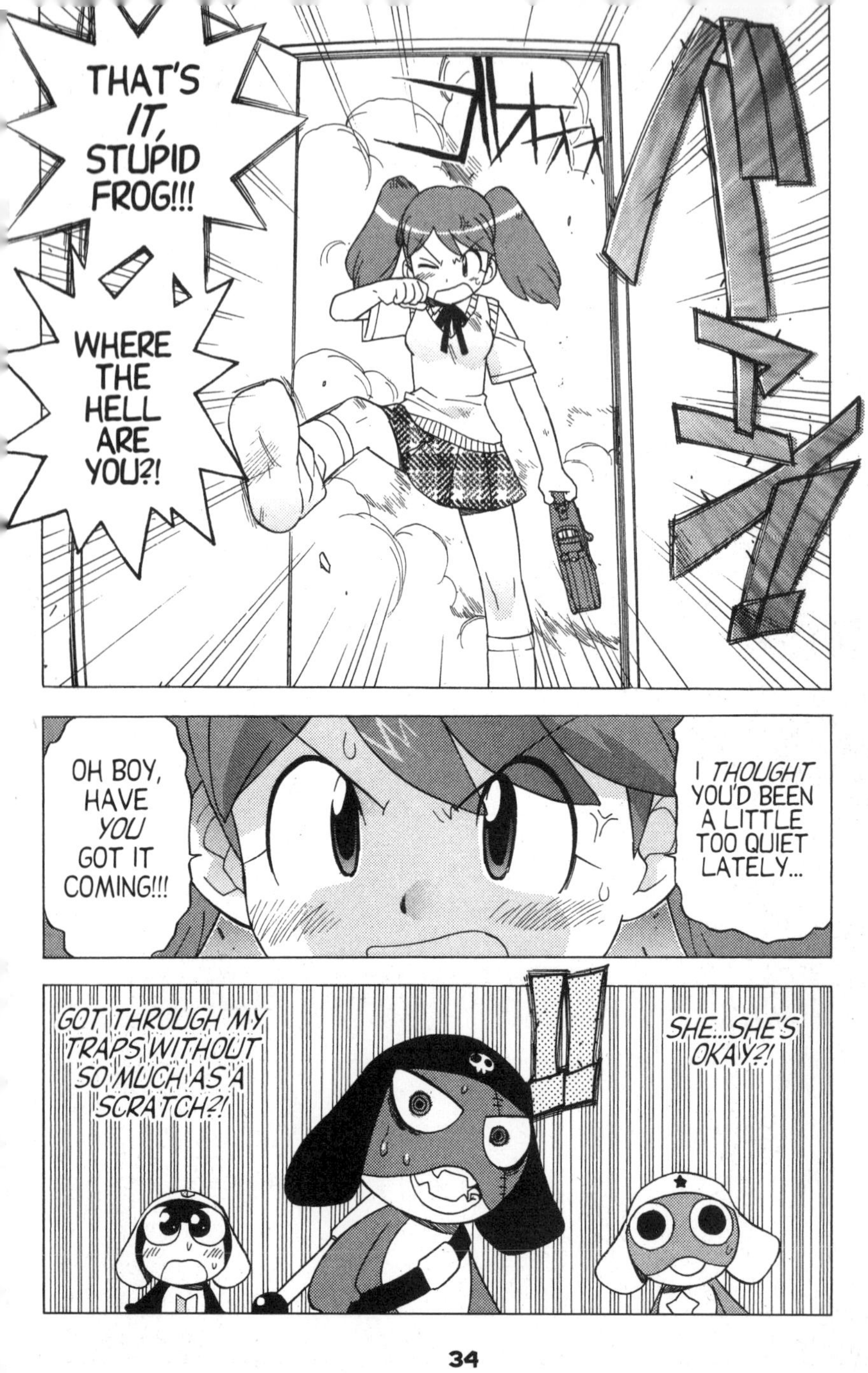
THAT'S IT, STUPID FROG!!!
WHERE THE HELL ARE YOU?!
I THOUGHT YOU'D BEEN A LITTLE TOO QUIET LATELY...
OH BOY, HAVE YOU GOT IT COMING!!!
SHE...SHE'S OKAY?!
GOT THROUGH MY TRAPS WITHOUT SO MUCH AS A SCRATCH?!

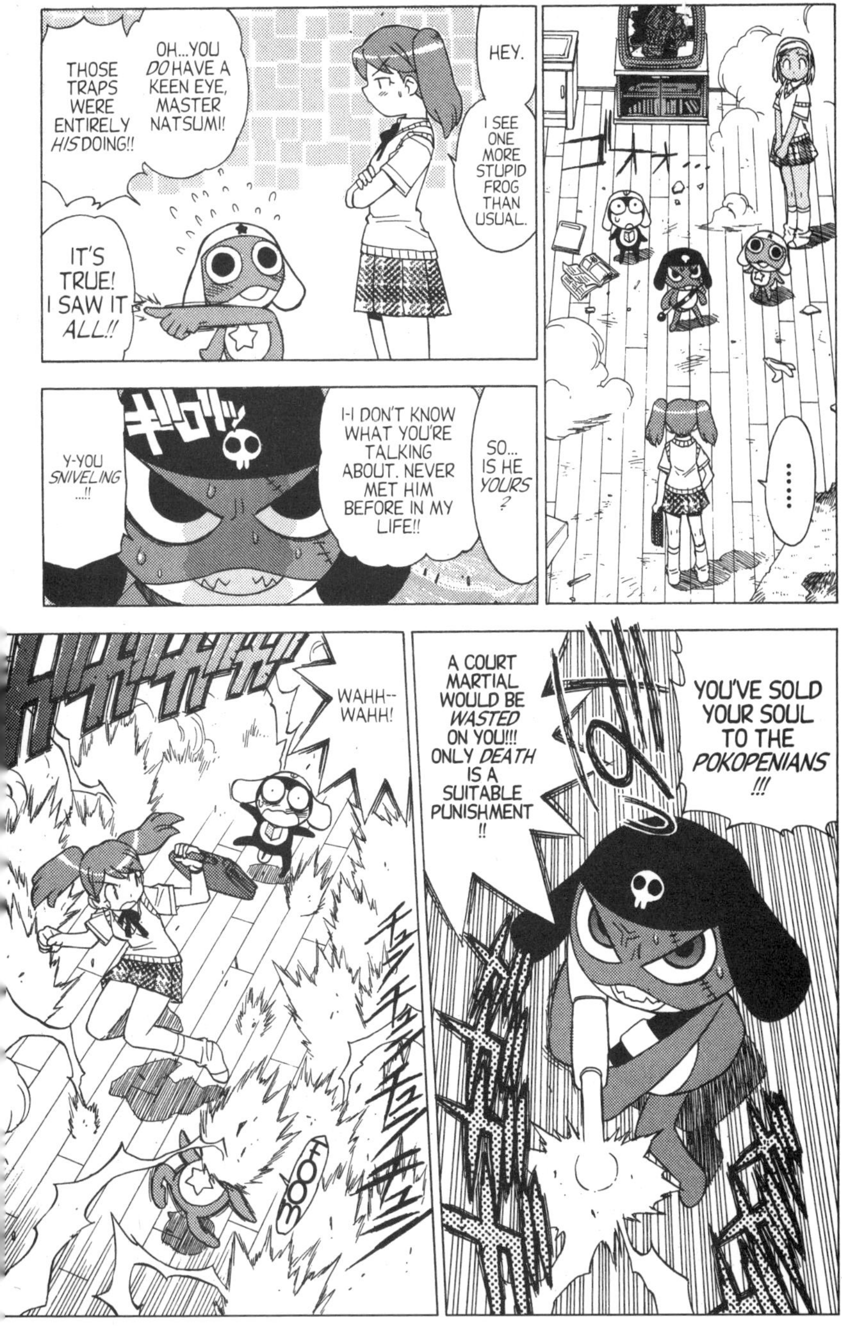
......
HEY.
I SEE ONE MORE STUPID FROG THAN USUAL.
OH...YOU *DO* HAVE A KEEN EYE, MASTER NATSUMI!
THOSE TRAPS WERE ENTIRELY *HIS* DOING!!
IT'S TRUE! I SAW IT *ALL!!*
SO... IS HE *YOURS*?
I-I DON'T KNOW WHAT YOU'RE TALKING ABOUT. NEVER MET HIM BEFORE IN MY LIFE!!
Y-YOU *SNIVELING* ...!!
YOU'VE SOLD YOUR SOUL TO THE *POKOPENIANS* !!!
A COURT MARTIAL WOULD BE *WASTED* ON YOU!!! ONLY *DEATH* IS A SUITABLE PUNISHMENT !!
WAHH-- WAHH!

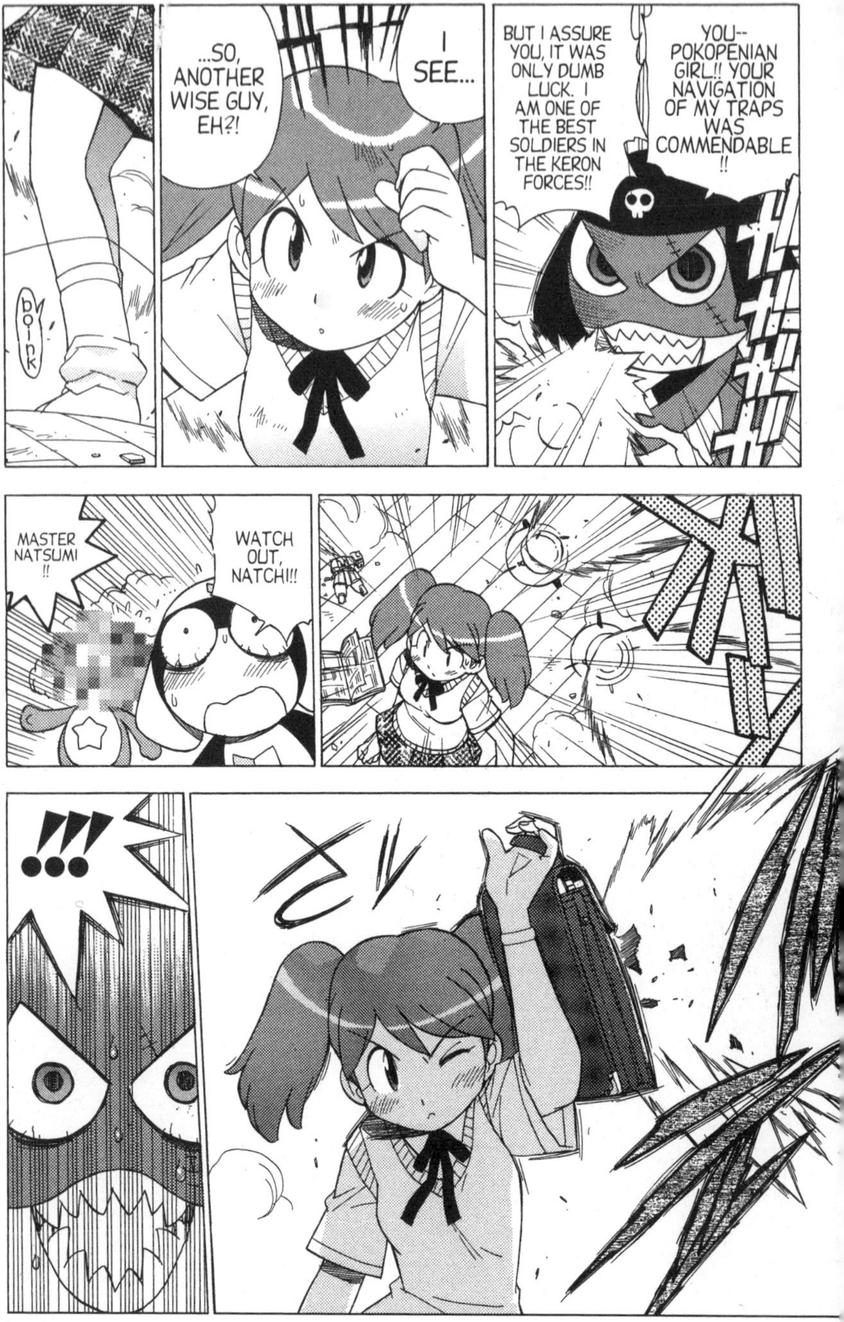
YOU-- POKOPENIAN GIRL!! YOUR NAVIGATION OF MY TRAPS WAS COMMENDABLE !!
BUT I ASSURE YOU, IT WAS ONLY DUMB LUCK. I AM ONE OF THE BEST SOLDIERS IN THE KERON FORCES!!
I SEE...
...SO, ANOTHER WISE GUY, EH?!
boink
WATCH OUT, NATCHI!!
MASTER NATSUMI !!
!!!

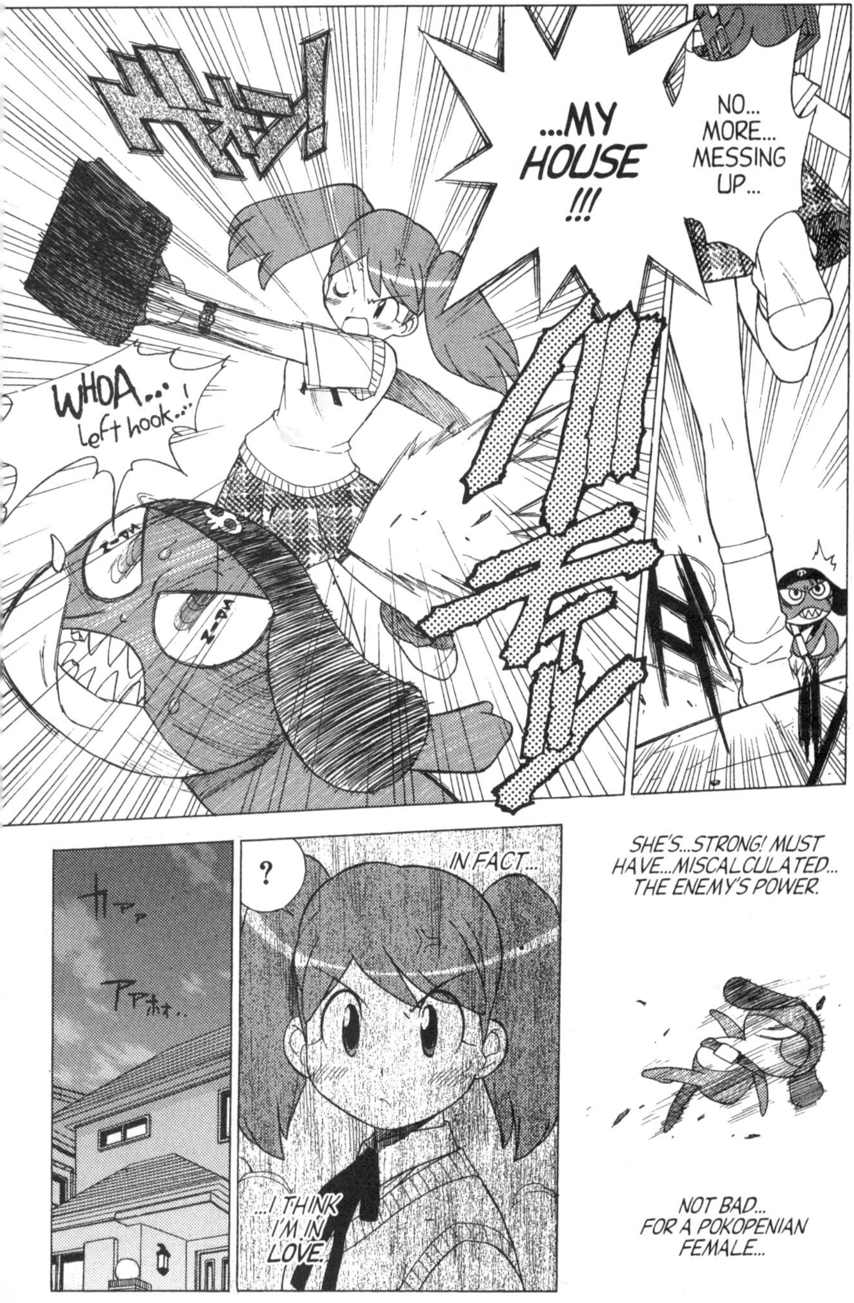
NO... MORE... MESSING UP...
...MY HOUSE !!!
WHOA... left hook...!
SHE'S...STRONG! MUST HAVE...MISCALCULATED... THE ENEMY'S POWER.
NOT BAD... FOR A POKOPENIAN FEMALE...
?
IN FACT...
...I THINK I'M IN LOVE.

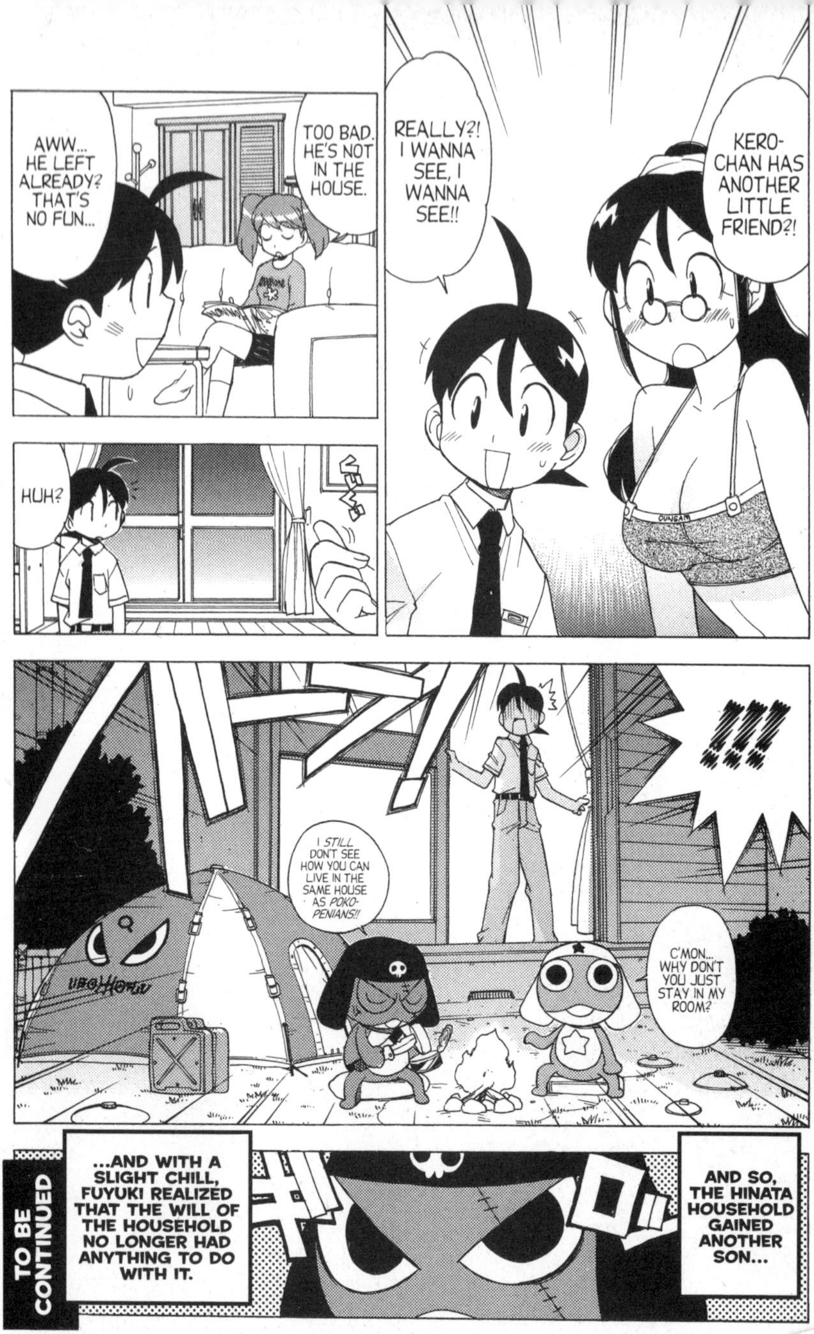
KERO-CHAN HAS ANOTHER LITTLE FRIEND?!
REALLY?! I WANNA SEE, I WANNA SEE!!
TOO BAD. HE'S NOT IN THE HOUSE.
AWW... HE LEFT ALREADY? THAT'S NO FUN...
HUH?
C'MON... WHY DON'T YOU JUST STAY IN MY ROOM?
I STILL DON'T SEE HOW YOU CAN LIVE IN THE SAME HOUSE AS POKO-PENIANS!!
AND SO, THE HINATA HOUSEHOLD GAINED ANOTHER SON...
...AND WITH A SLIGHT CHILL, FUYUKI REALIZED THAT THE WILL OF THE HOUSEHOLD NO LONGER HAD ANYTHING TO DO WITH IT.
TO BE CONTINUED

ENCOUNTER XIII

SERGEANT REACHES THE CRITICAL POINT

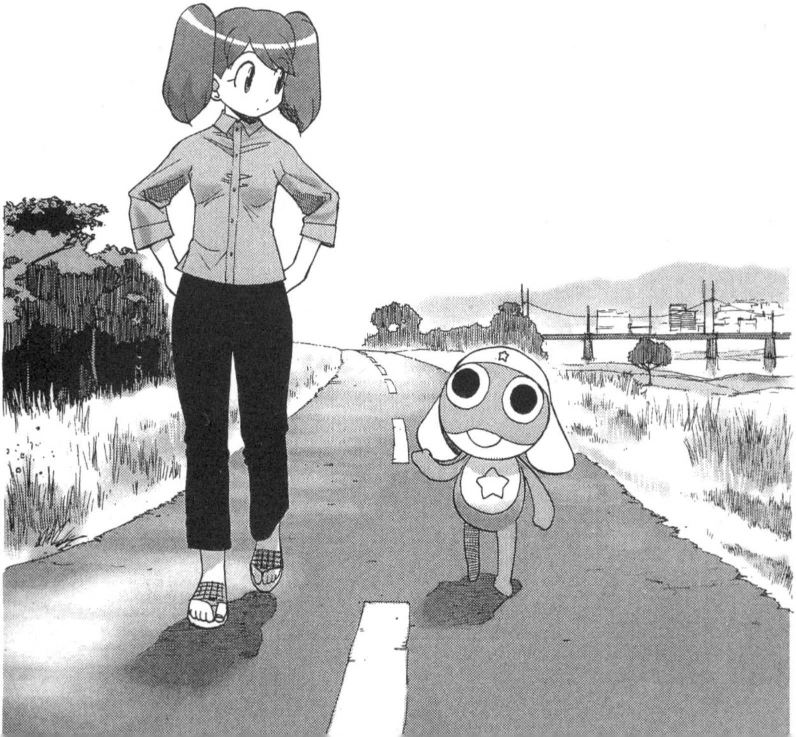

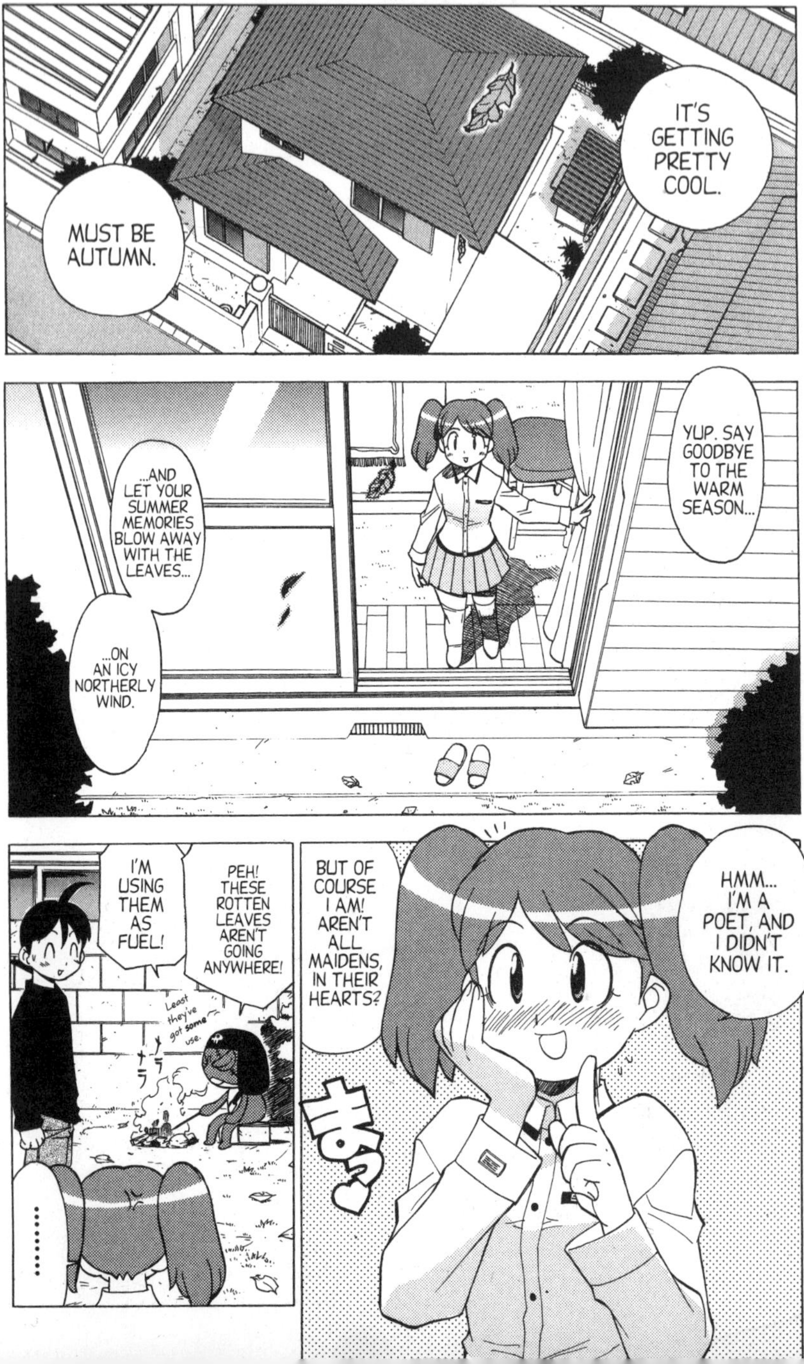
IT'S GETTING PRETTY COOL.
MUST BE AUTUMN.
YUP. SAY GOODBYE TO THE WARM SEASON...
...AND LET YOUR SUMMER MEMORIES BLOW AWAY WITH THE LEAVES...
...ON AN ICY NORTHERLY WIND.
HMM... I'M A POET, AND I DIDN'T KNOW IT.
BUT OF COURSE I AM! AREN'T ALL MAIDENS, IN THEIR HEARTS?
まっ
PEH! THESE ROTTEN LEAVES AREN'T GOING ANYWHERE!
I'M USING THEM AS FUEL!
Least they've got some use.
....

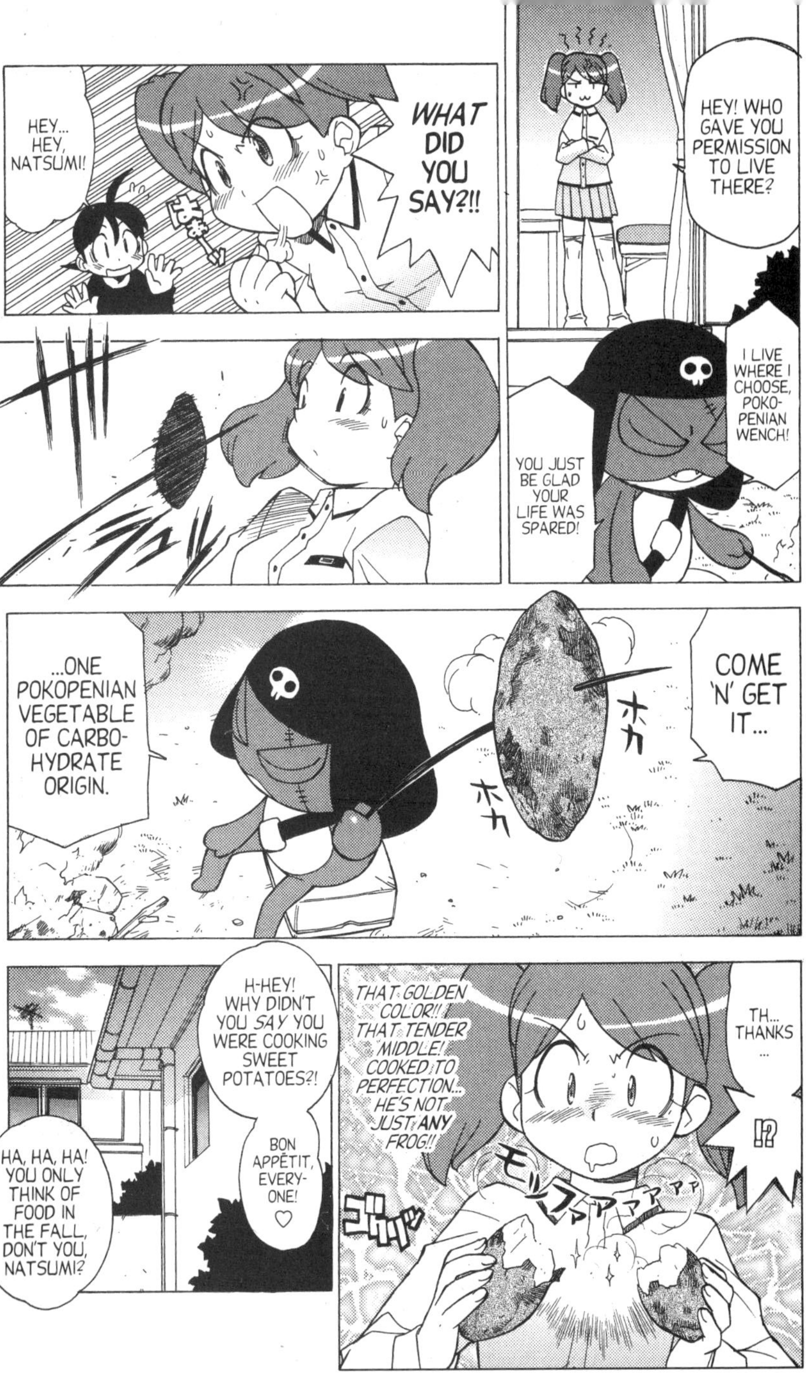
HEY! WHO GAVE YOU PERMISSION TO LIVE THERE?
WHAT DID YOU SAY?!!
HEY... HEY, NATSUMI!
I LIVE WHERE I CHOOSE, POKOPENIAN WENCH!
YOU JUST BE GLAD YOUR LIFE WAS SPARED!
COME 'N' GET IT...
ホカ
ホカ
...ONE POKOPENIAN VEGETABLE OF CARBO-HYDRATE ORIGIN.
TH... THANKS ...
!?
THAT GOLDEN COLOR!! THAT TENDER MIDDLE! COOKED TO PERFECTION... HE'S NOT JUST ANY FROG!!
H-HEY! WHY DIDN'T YOU *SAY* YOU WERE COOKING SWEET POTATOES?!
BON APPÊTIT, EVERYONE! ♡
HA, HA, HA! YOU ONLY THINK OF FOOD IN THE FALL, DON'T YOU, NATSUMI?

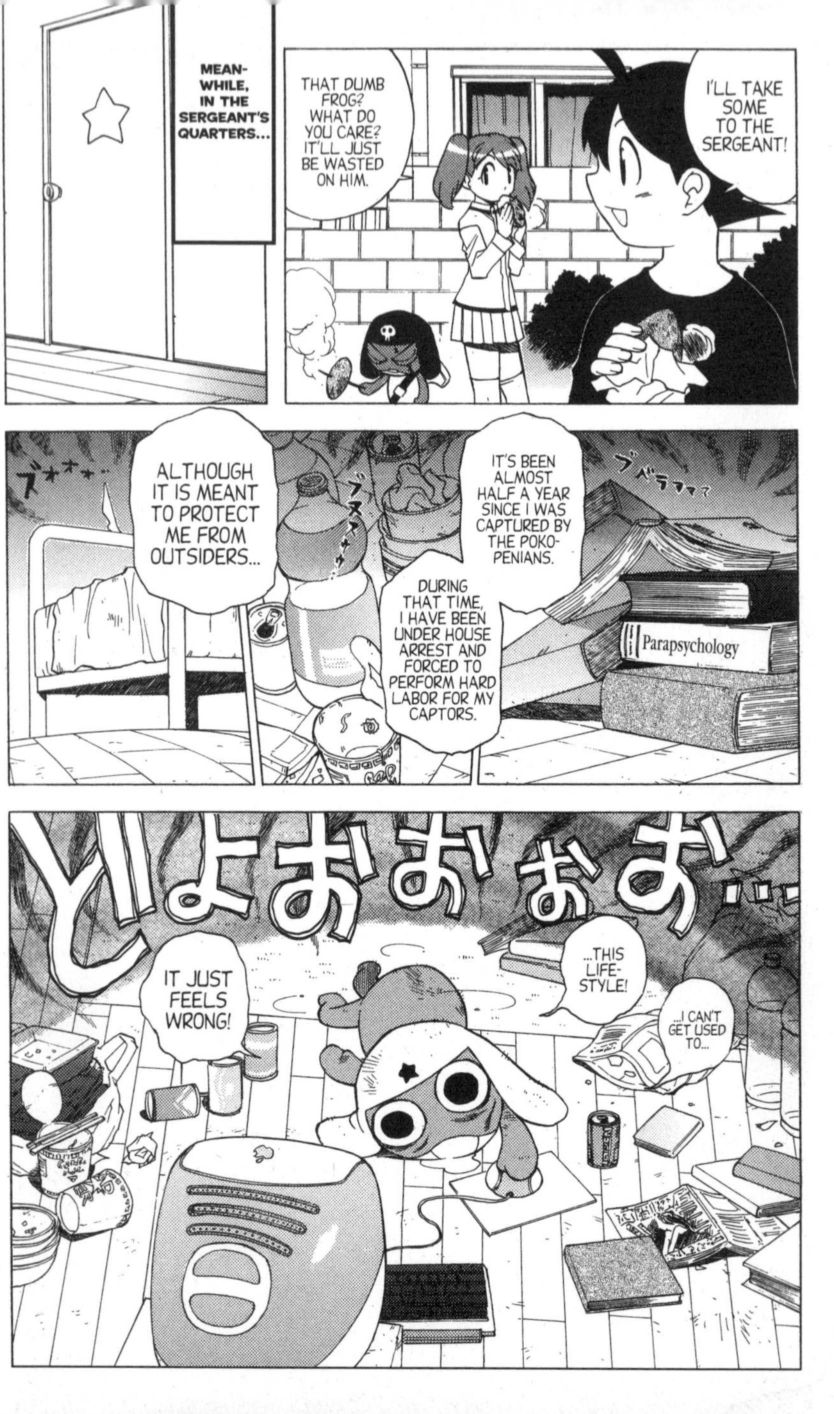
I'LL TAKE SOME TO THE SERGEANT!
THAT DUMB FROG? WHAT DO YOU CARE? IT'LL JUST BE WASTED ON HIM.
MEAN-WHILE, IN THE SERGEANT'S QUARTERS...
IT'S BEEN ALMOST HALF A YEAR SINCE I WAS CAPTURED BY THE POKO-PENIANS.
DURING THAT TIME, I HAVE BEEN UNDER HOUSE ARREST AND FORCED TO PERFORM HARD LABOR FOR MY CAPTORS.
Parapsychology
ALTHOUGH IT IS MEANT TO PROTECT ME FROM OUTSIDERS...
...I CAN'T GET USED TO...
...THIS LIFE-STYLE!
IT JUST FEELS WRONG!

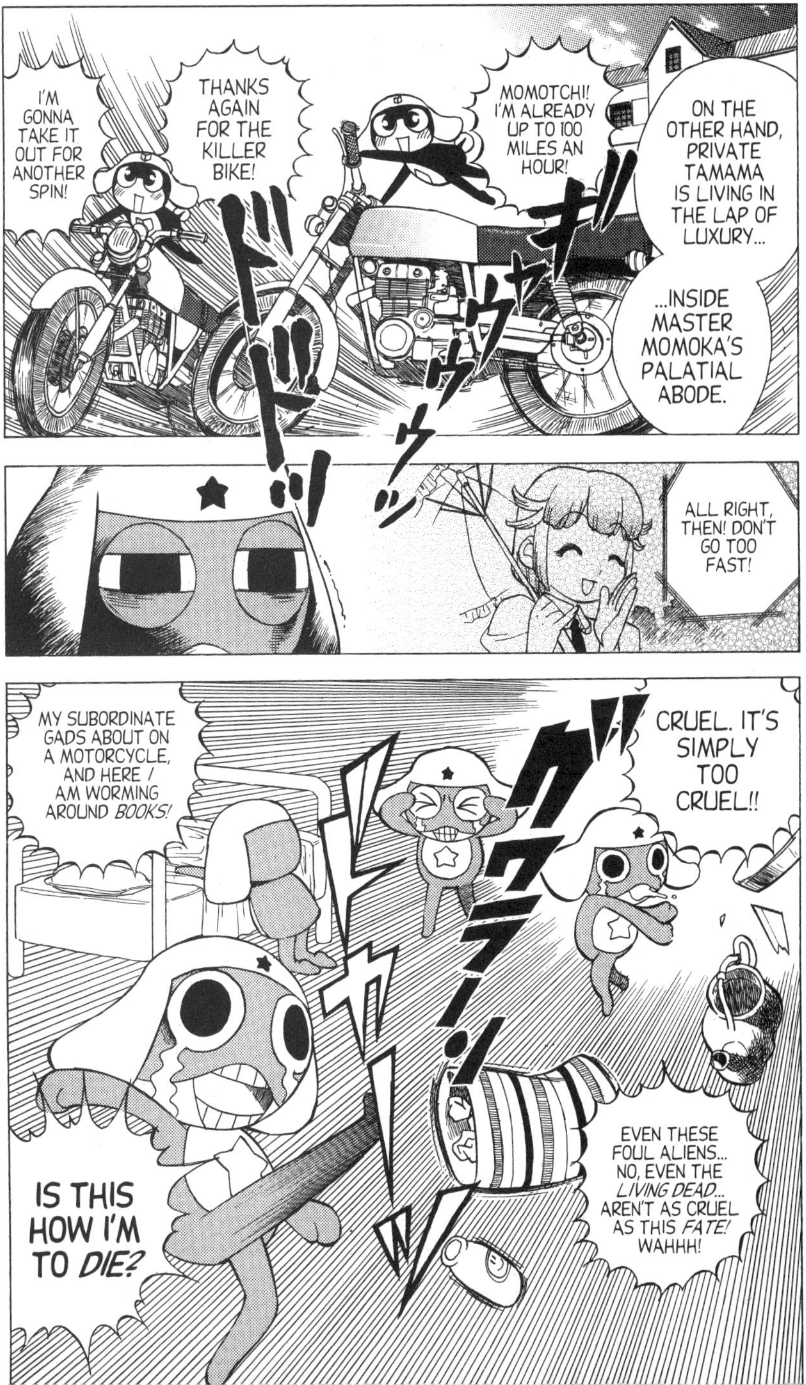
ON THE OTHER HAND, PRIVATE TAMAMA IS LIVING IN THE LAP OF LUXURY...
...INSIDE MASTER MOMOKA'S PALATIAL ABODE.
MOMOTCHI! I'M ALREADY UP TO 100 MILES AN HOUR!
THANKS AGAIN FOR THE KILLER BIKE!
I'M GONNA TAKE IT OUT FOR ANOTHER SPIN!
ALL RIGHT, THEN! DON'T GO TOO FAST!
CRUEL. IT'S SIMPLY TOO CRUEL!!
MY SUBORDINATE GADS ABOUT ON A MOTORCYCLE, AND HERE I AM WORMING AROUND BOOKS!
EVEN THESE FOUL ALIENS... NO, EVEN THE LIVING DEAD... AREN'T AS CRUEL AS THIS FATE! WAHHH!
IS THIS HOW I'M TO DIE?

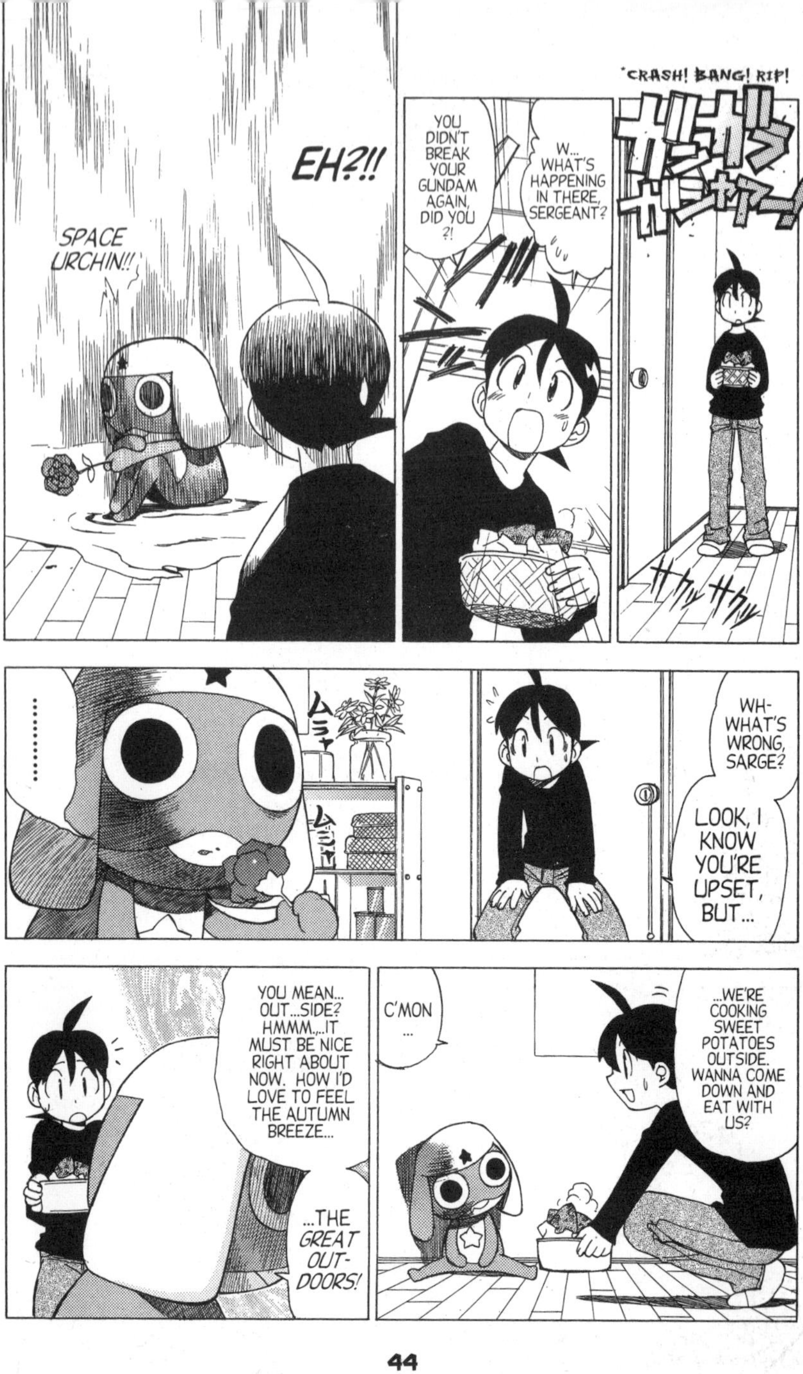
*CRASH! BANG! RIP!
W... WHAT'S HAPPENING IN THERE, SERGEANT?
YOU DIDN'T BREAK YOUR GUNDAM AGAIN, DID YOU ?!
EH?!!
SPACE URCHIN!!
WH-WHAT'S WRONG, SARGE?
LOOK, I KNOW YOU'RE UPSET, BUT...
....
...WE'RE COOKING SWEET POTATOES OUTSIDE. WANNA COME DOWN AND EAT WITH US?
C'MON ...
YOU MEAN... OUT...SIDE? HMMM...IT MUST BE NICE RIGHT ABOUT NOW. HOW I'D LOVE TO FEEL THE AUTUMN BREEZE...
...THE GREAT OUTDOORS!

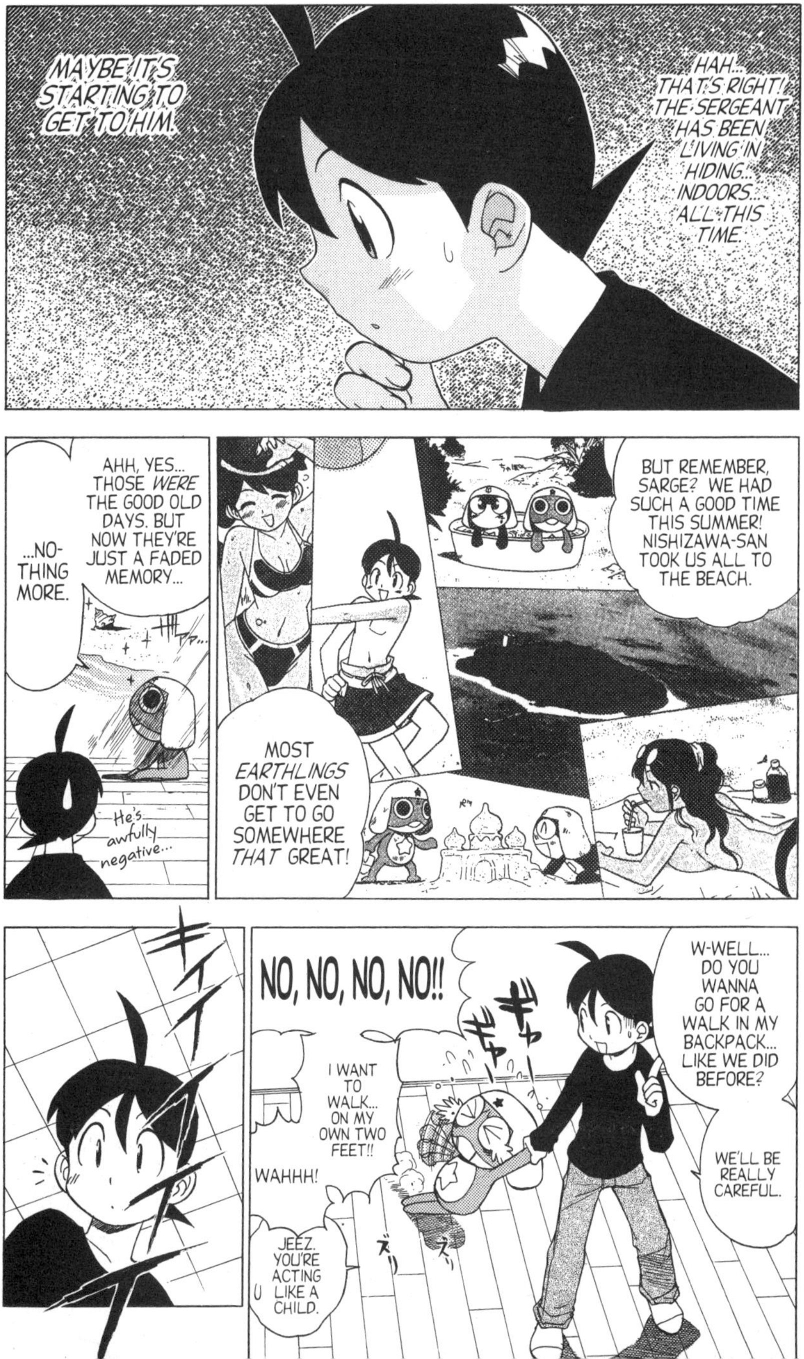
HAH... THAT'S RIGHT! THE SERGEANT HAS BEEN LIVING IN HIDING... INDOORS... ALL THIS TIME.
MAYBE IT'S STARTING TO GET TO HIM.
BUT REMEMBER, SARGE? WE HAD SUCH A GOOD TIME THIS SUMMER! NISHIZAWA-SAN TOOK US ALL TO THE BEACH.
MOST *EARTHLINGS* DON'T EVEN GET TO GO SOMEWHERE *THAT* GREAT!
AHH, YES... THOSE *WERE* THE GOOD OLD DAYS. BUT NOW THEY'RE JUST A FADED MEMORY...
...NO-THING MORE.
He's awfully negative...
W-WELL... DO YOU WANNA GO FOR A WALK IN MY BACKPACK... LIKE WE DID BEFORE?
WE'LL BE REALLY CAREFUL.
NO, NO, NO, NO!!
ギャー ギャー
I WANT TO WALK... ON MY OWN TWO FEET!!
WAHHH!
JEEZ. YOU'RE ACTING LIKE A CHILD.
ズリ ズリ

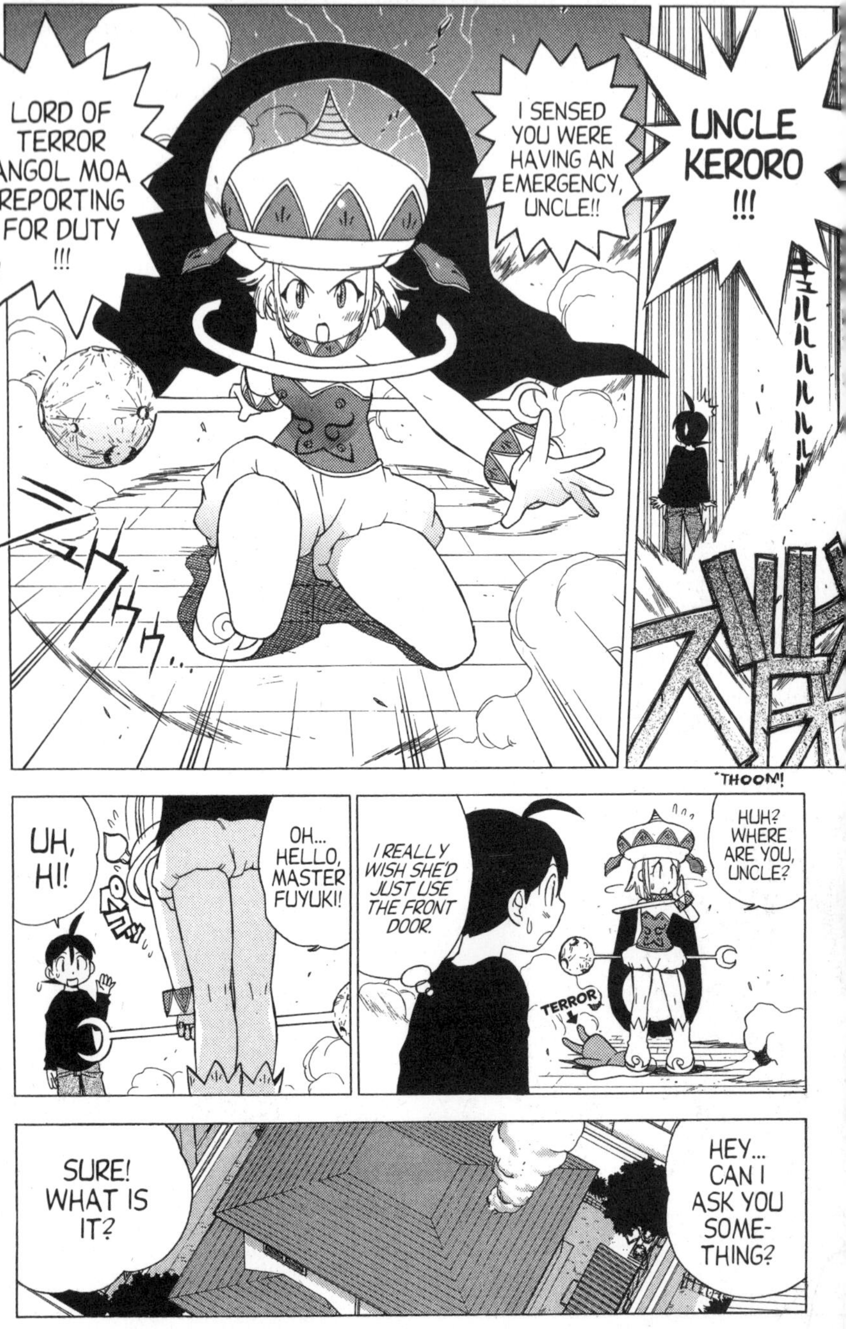
UNCLE KERORO !!!
I SENSED YOU WERE HAVING AN EMERGENCY, UNCLE!!
LORD OF TERROR ANGOL MOA REPORTING FOR DUTY !!!
*THOOM!
HUH? WHERE ARE YOU, UNCLE?
I REALLY WISH SHE'D JUST USE THE FRONT DOOR.
TERROR
OH... HELLO, MASTER FUYUKI!
UH, HI!
HEY... CAN I ASK YOU SOME-THING?
SURE! WHAT IS IT?

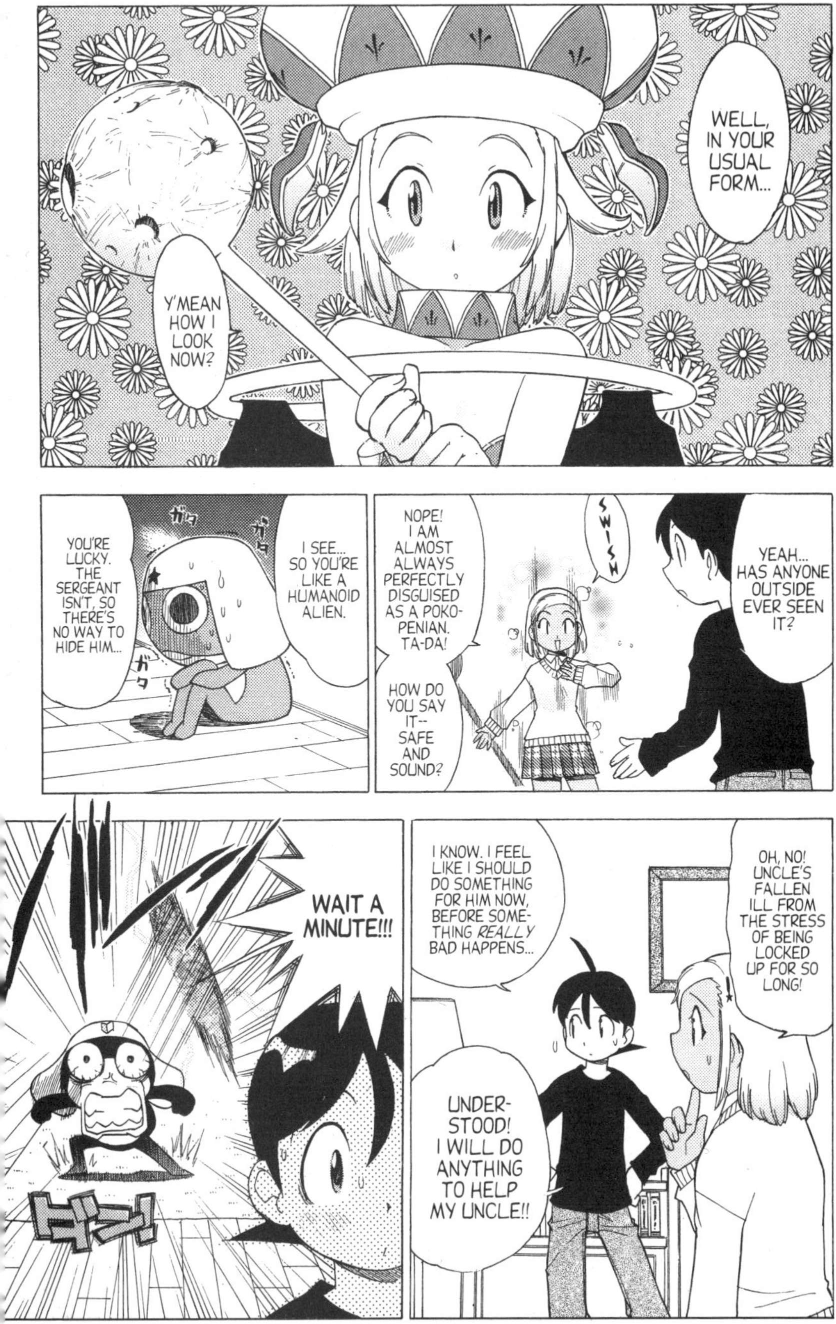
WELL, IN YOUR USUAL FORM...
Y'MEAN HOW I LOOK NOW?
YEAH... HAS ANYONE OUTSIDE EVER SEEN IT?
SWISH
NOPE! I AM ALMOST ALWAYS PERFECTLY DISGUISED AS A POKO-PENIAN. TA-DA!
HOW DO YOU SAY IT-- SAFE AND SOUND?
I SEE... SO YOU'RE LIKE A HUMANOID ALIEN.
YOU'RE LUCKY. THE SERGEANT ISN'T, SO THERE'S NO WAY TO HIDE HIM...
OH, NO! UNCLE'S FALLEN ILL FROM THE STRESS OF BEING LOCKED UP FOR SO LONG!
I KNOW. I FEEL LIKE I SHOULD DO SOMETHING FOR HIM NOW, BEFORE SOME-THING *REALLY* BAD HAPPENS...
UNDER-STOOD! I WILL DO ANYTHING TO HELP MY UNCLE!!
WAIT A MINUTE!!!

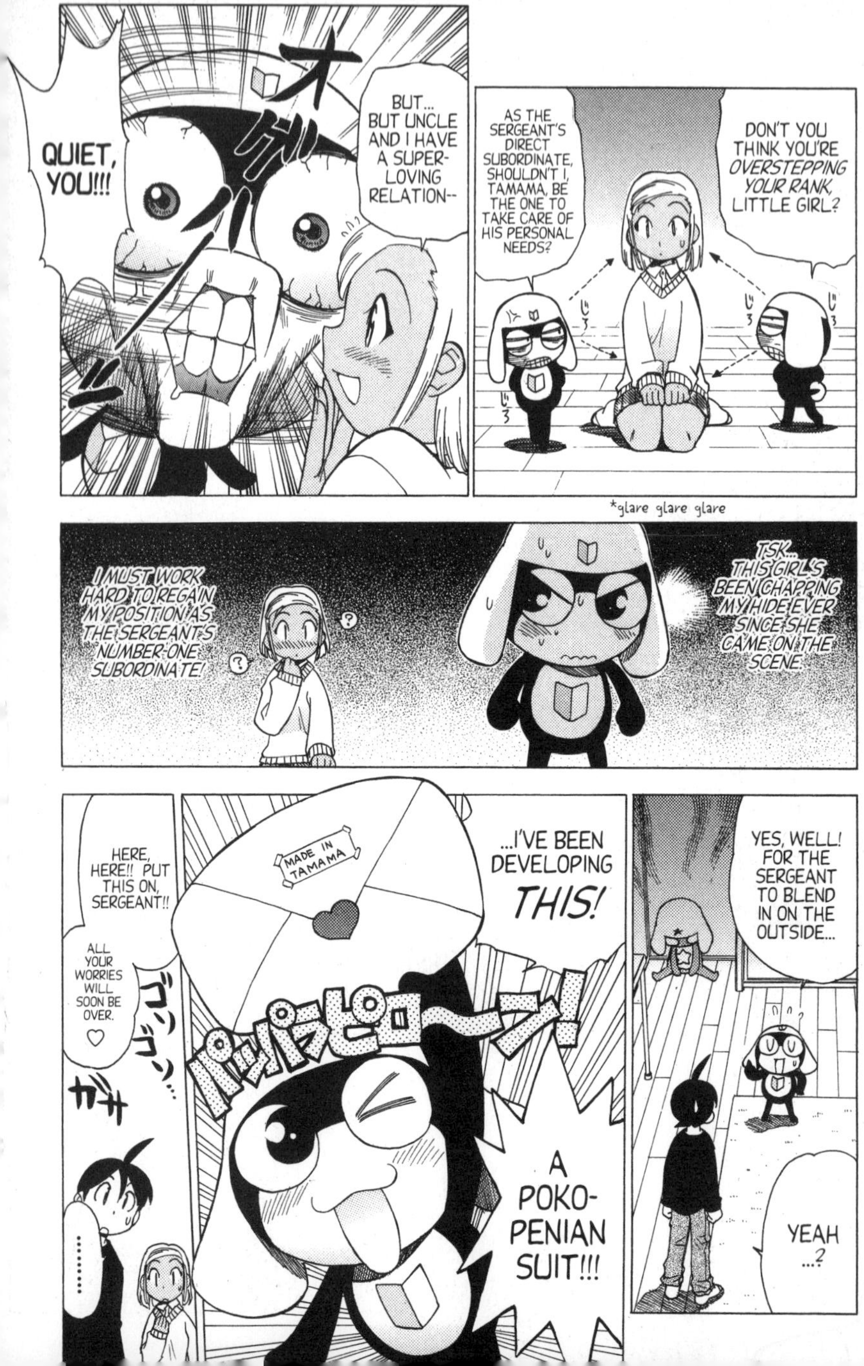
DON'T YOU THINK YOU'RE OVERSTEPPING YOUR RANK, LITTLE GIRL?
AS THE SERGEANT'S DIRECT SUBORDINATE, SHOULDN'T I, TAMAMA, BE THE ONE TO TAKE CARE OF HIS PERSONAL NEEDS?
*glare glare glare
BUT... BUT UNCLE AND I HAVE A SUPER-LOVING RELATION--
QUIET, YOU!!!
TSK... THIS GIRL'S BEEN CHAPPING MY HIDE EVER SINCE SHE CAME ON THE SCENE.
I MUST WORK HARD TO REGAIN MY POSITION AS THE SERGEANT'S NUMBER-ONE SUBORDINATE!
YES, WELL! FOR THE SERGEANT TO BLEND IN ON THE OUTSIDE...
YEAH ...?
...I'VE BEEN DEVELOPING THIS!
MADE IN TAMAMA
A POKO-PENIAN SUIT!!!
HERE, HERE!! PUT THIS ON, SERGEANT!!
ALL YOUR WORRIES WILL SOON BE OVER. ♡
....

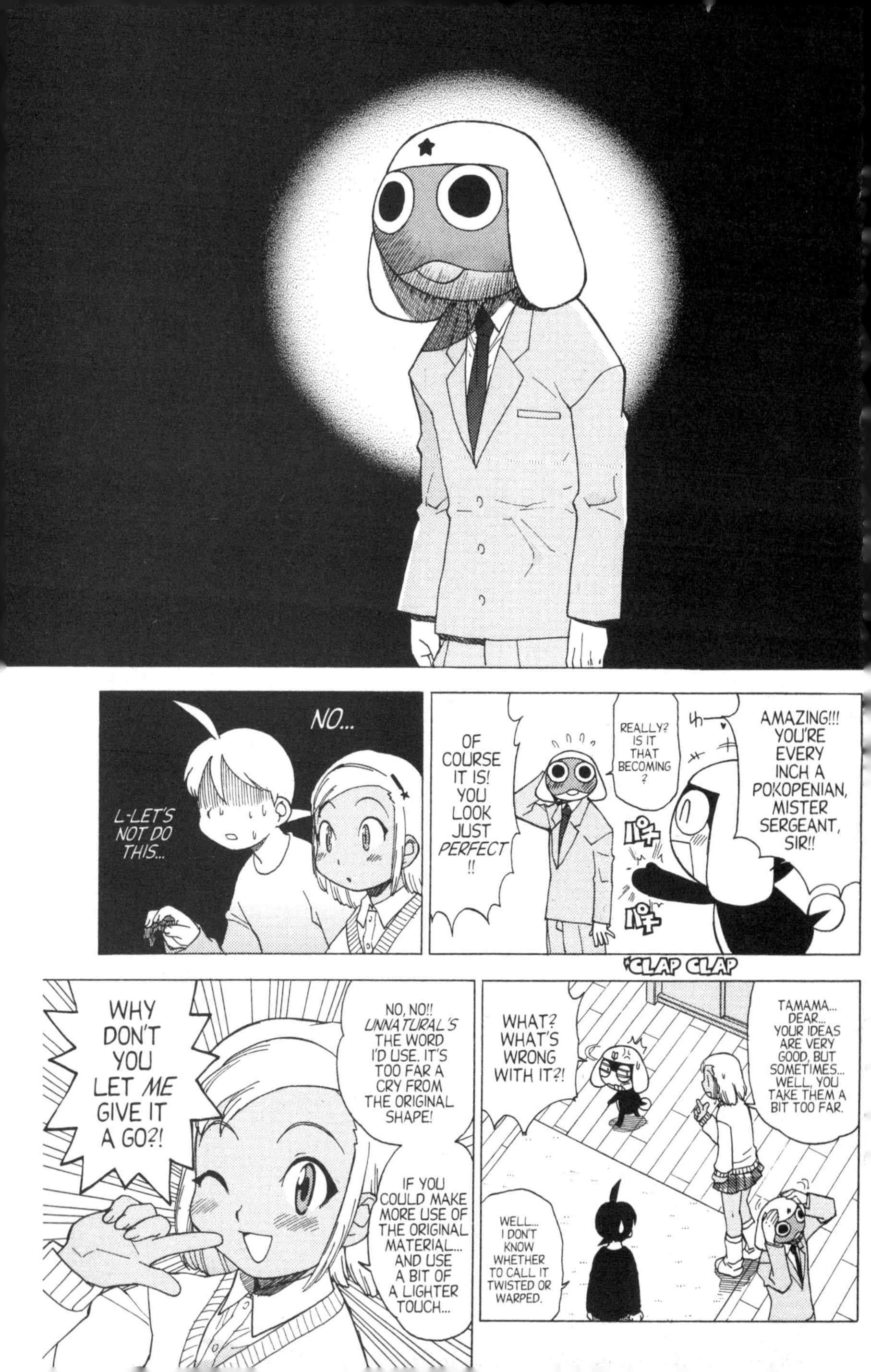
AMAZING!!! YOU'RE EVERY INCH A POKOPENIAN, MISTER SERGEANT, SIR!!
REALLY? IS IT THAT BECOMING?
OF COURSE IT IS! YOU LOOK JUST PERFECT!!
CLAP CLAP
NO...
L-LET'S NOT DO THIS...
TAMAMA... DEAR... YOUR IDEAS ARE VERY GOOD, BUT SOMETIMES... WELL, YOU TAKE THEM A BIT TOO FAR.
WHAT? WHAT'S WRONG WITH IT?!
WELL... I DON'T KNOW WHETHER TO CALL IT TWISTED OR WARPED.
NO, NO!! UNNATURAL'S THE WORD I'D USE. IT'S TOO FAR A CRY FROM THE ORIGINAL SHAPE!
IF YOU COULD MAKE MORE USE OF THE ORIGINAL MATERIAL... AND USE A BIT OF A LIGHTER TOUCH...
WHY DON'T YOU LET ME GIVE IT A GO?!

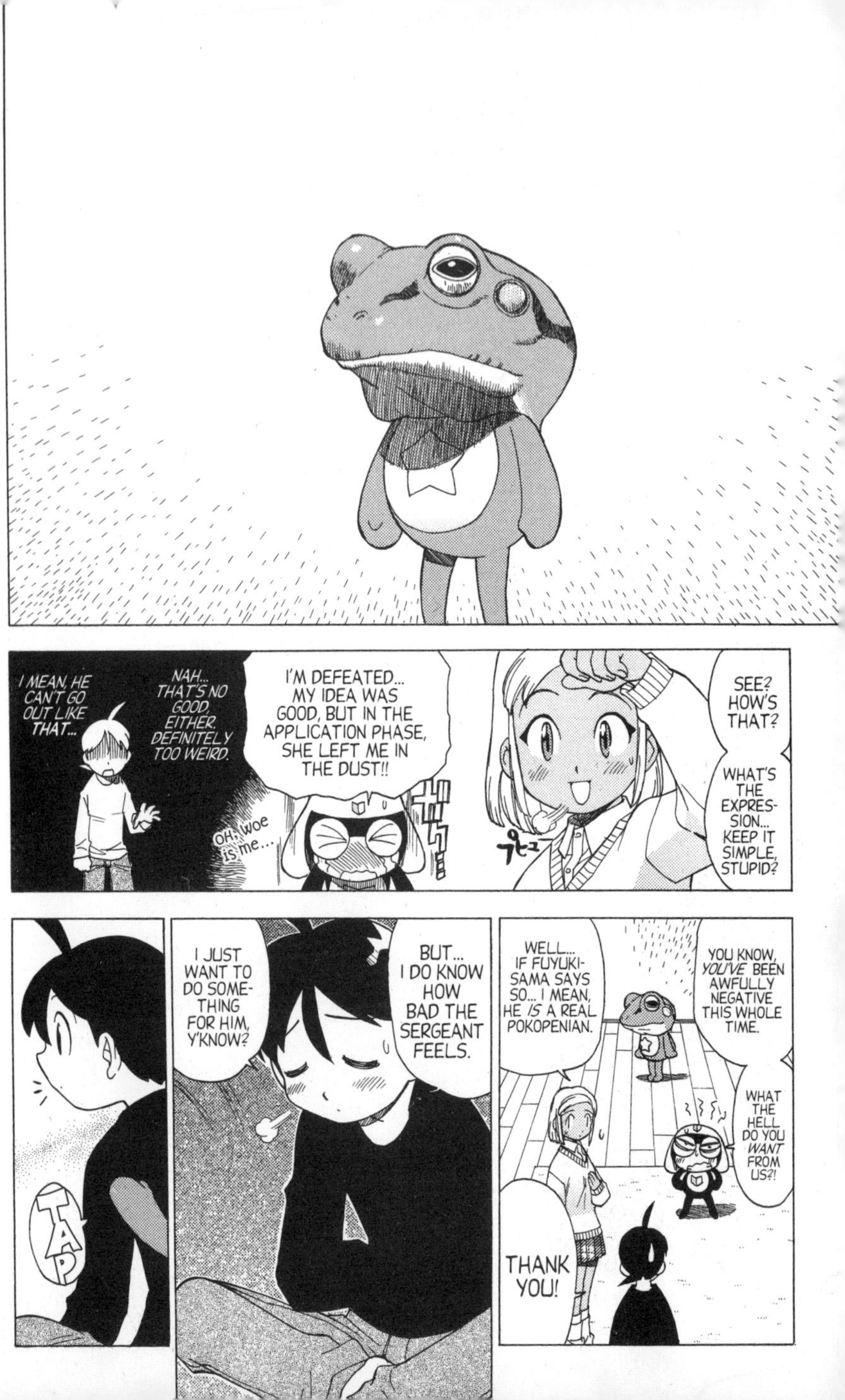
SEE? HOW'S THAT?
WHAT'S THE EXPRESSION... KEEP IT SIMPLE, STUPID?
I'M DEFEATED... MY IDEA WAS GOOD, BUT IN THE APPLICATION PHASE, SHE LEFT ME IN THE DUST!!
OH, woe is me...
NAH... THAT'S NO GOOD, EITHER. DEFINITELY TOO WEIRD.
I MEAN, HE CAN'T GO OUT LIKE THAT...
YOU KNOW, YOU'VE BEEN AWFULLY NEGATIVE THIS WHOLE TIME.
WELL... IF FUYUKI-SAMA SAYS SO... I MEAN, HE IS A REAL POKOPENIAN.
WHAT THE HELL DO YOU WANT FROM US?!
THANK YOU!
BUT... I DO KNOW HOW BAD THE SERGEANT FEELS.
I JUST WANT TO DO SOMETHING FOR HIM, Y'KNOW?
TAP

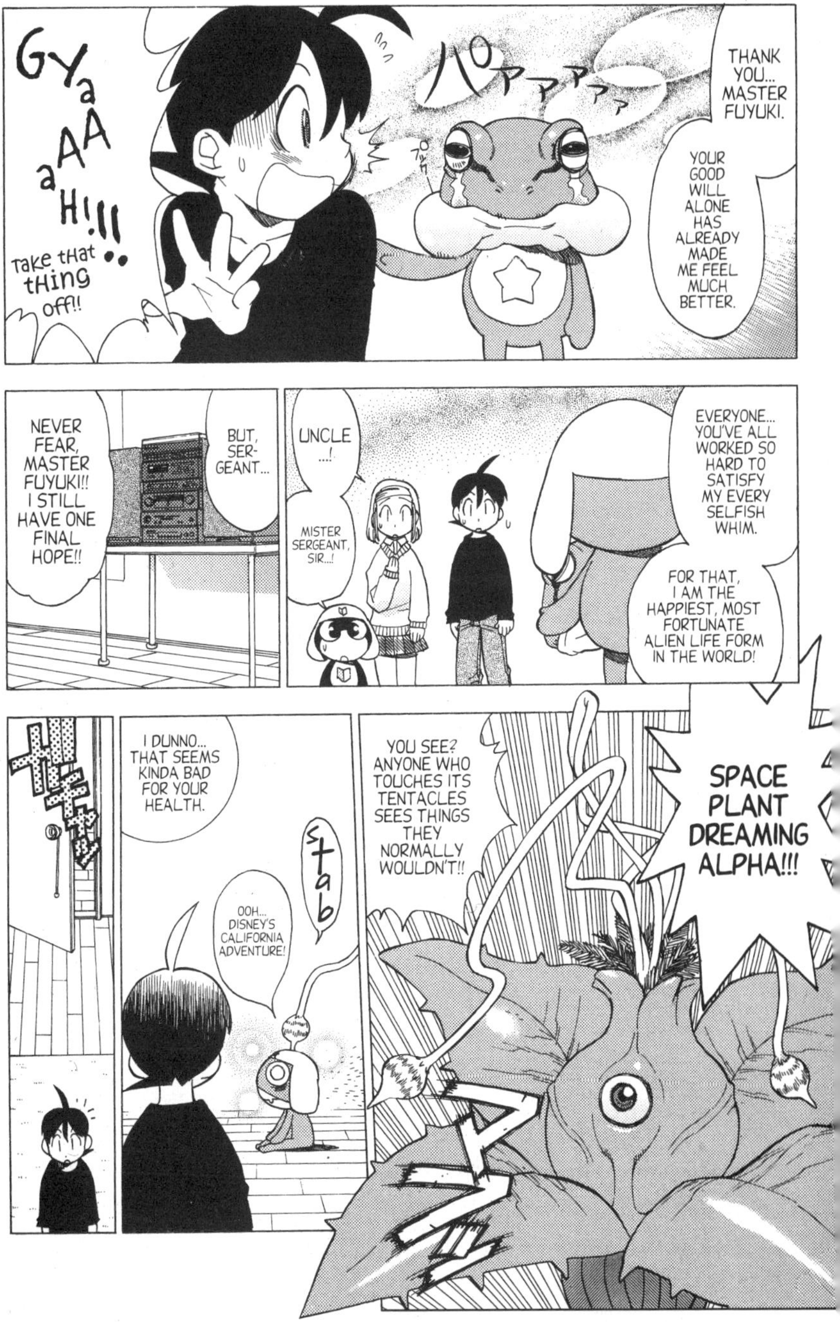
THANK YOU... MASTER FUYUKI.
YOUR GOOD WILL ALONE HAS ALREADY MADE ME FEEL MUCH BETTER.
GYaaAAH!!!!
Take that thing off!!
EVERYONE... YOU'VE ALL WORKED SO HARD TO SATISFY MY EVERY SELFISH WHIM.
FOR THAT, I AM THE HAPPIEST, MOST FORTUNATE ALIEN LIFE FORM IN THE WORLD!
UNCLE...!
MISTER SERGEANT, SIR...!
BUT, SER-GEANT...
NEVER FEAR, MASTER FUYUKI!! I STILL HAVE ONE FINAL HOPE!!
SPACE PLANT DREAMING ALPHA!!!
YOU SEE? ANYONE WHO TOUCHES ITS TENTACLES SEES THINGS THEY NORMALLY WOULDN'T!!
stab
OOH... DISNEY'S CALIFORNIA ADVENTURE!
I DUNNO... THAT SEEMS KINDA BAD FOR YOUR HEALTH.

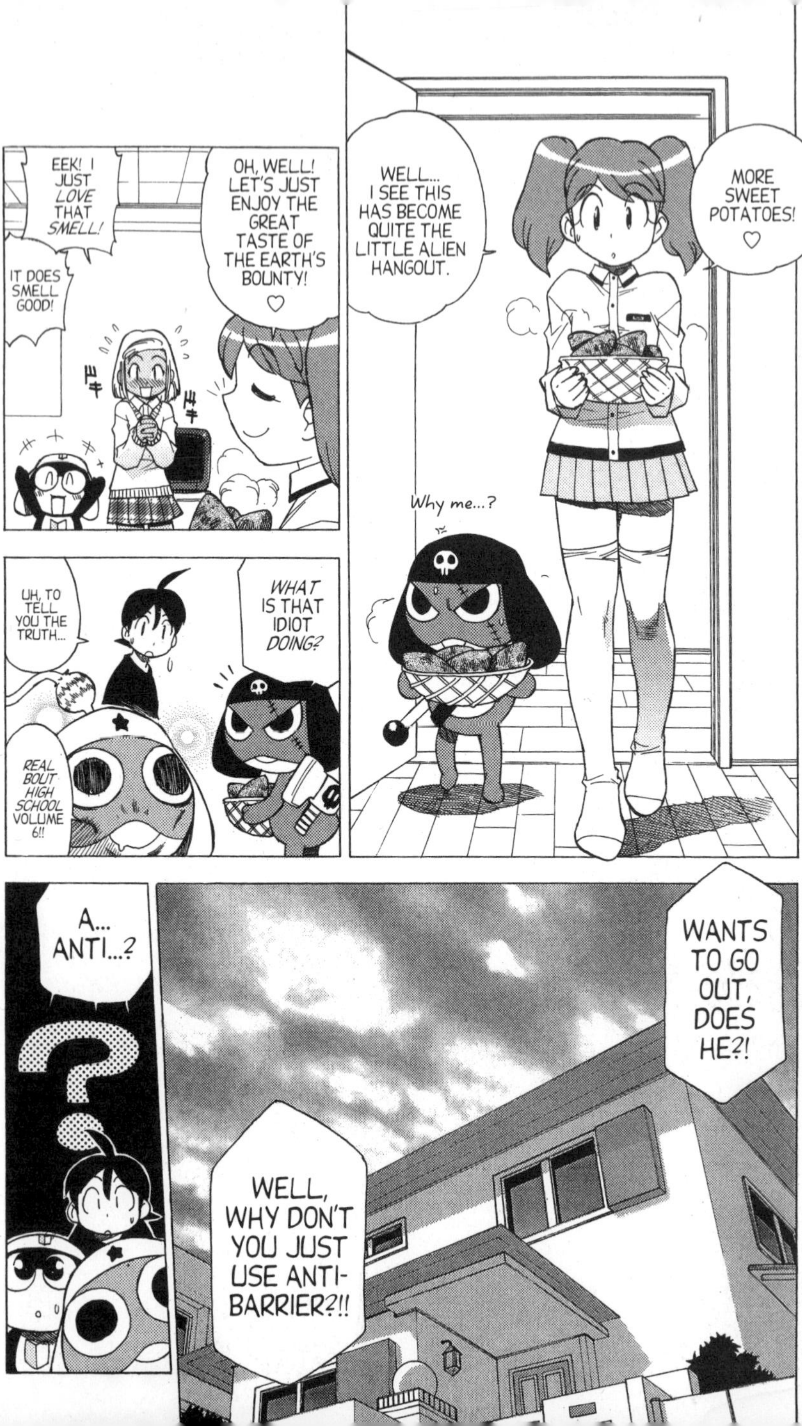
MORE SWEET POTATOES! ♡
WELL... I SEE THIS HAS BECOME QUITE THE LITTLE ALIEN HANGOUT.
Why me...?
OH, WELL! LET'S JUST ENJOY THE GREAT TASTE OF THE EARTH'S BOUNTY! ♡
EEK! I JUST *LOVE* THAT *SMELL!*
IT DOES SMELL GOOD!
WHAT IS THAT IDIOT *DOING?*
UH, TO TELL YOU THE TRUTH...
REAL BOUT HIGH SCHOOL VOLUME 6!!
WANTS TO GO OUT, DOES HE?!
WELL, WHY DON'T YOU JUST USE ANTI-BARRIER?!!
A... ANTI...?

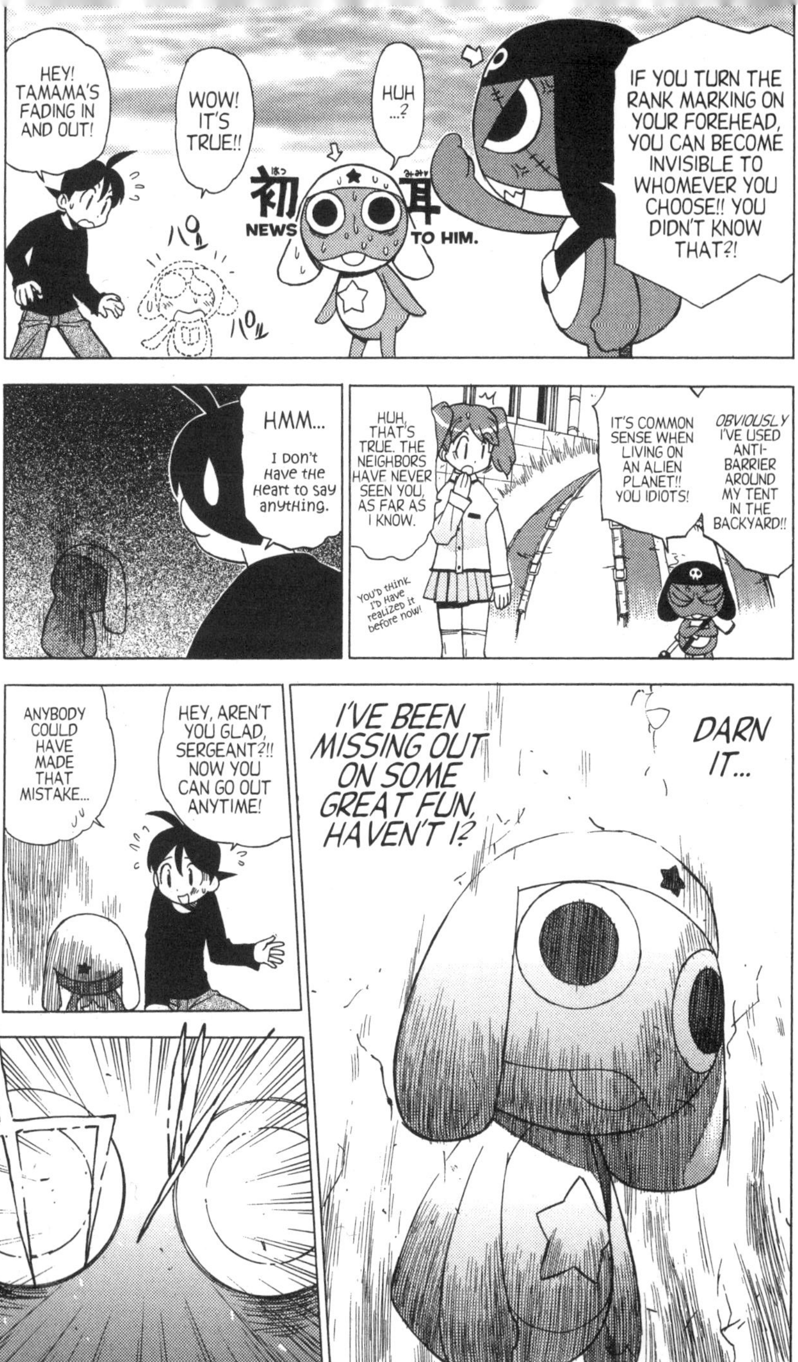
IF YOU TURN THE RANK MARKING ON YOUR FOREHEAD, YOU CAN BECOME INVISIBLE TO WHOMEVER YOU CHOOSE!! YOU DIDN'T KNOW THAT?!
HUH ...?
初耳 NEWS TO HIM.
WOW! IT'S TRUE!!
HEY! TAMAMA'S FADING IN AND OUT!
OBVIOUSLY I'VE USED ANTI-BARRIER AROUND MY TENT IN THE BACKYARD!!
IT'S COMMON SENSE WHEN LIVING ON AN ALIEN PLANET!! YOU IDIOTS!
HUH, THAT'S TRUE. THE NEIGHBORS HAVE NEVER SEEN YOU, AS FAR AS I KNOW.
You'd think I'd have realized it before now!
HMM...
I don't have the heart to say anything.
DARN IT...
I'VE BEEN MISSING OUT ON SOME GREAT FUN, HAVEN'T I?
HEY, AREN'T YOU GLAD, SERGEANT?!! NOW YOU CAN GO OUT ANYTIME!
ANYBODY COULD HAVE MADE THAT MISTAKE...

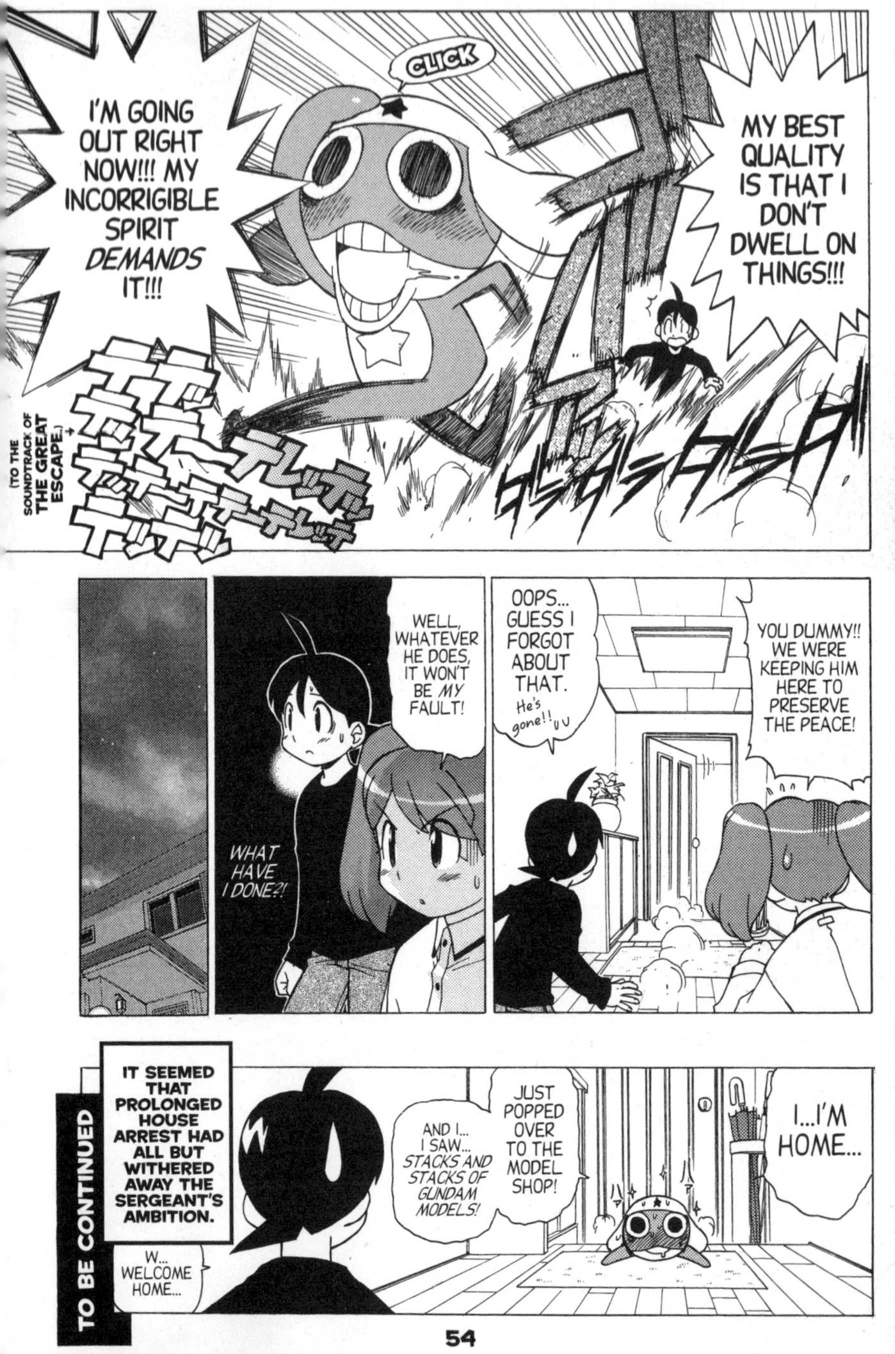
MY BEST QUALITY IS THAT I DON'T DWELL ON THINGS!!!
CLICK
I'M GOING OUT RIGHT NOW!!! MY INCORRIGIBLE SPIRIT *DEMANDS* IT!!!
(TO THE SOUNDTRACK OF THE GREAT ESCAPE.)
YOU DUMMY!! WE WERE KEEPING HIM HERE TO PRESERVE THE PEACE!
OOPS... GUESS I FORGOT ABOUT THAT.
He's gone!!
WELL, WHATEVER HE DOES, IT WON'T BE *MY* FAULT!
WHAT HAVE I DONE?!
I...I'M HOME...
JUST POPPED OVER TO THE MODEL SHOP!
AND I... I SAW... *STACKS AND STACKS OF GUNDAM MODELS!*
IT SEEMED THAT PROLONGED HOUSE ARREST HAD ALL BUT WITHERED AWAY THE SERGEANT'S AMBITION.
W... WELCOME HOME...
TO BE CONTINUED

SPECIAL BLACK-AND-WHITE BONUS 1

AN ILLUMINATING INTERVIEW WITH PRIVATE TAMAMA

"EVEN WHEN I WAS YOUNG, I KNEW I WAS DIFFERENT FROM OTHER TADPOLES."

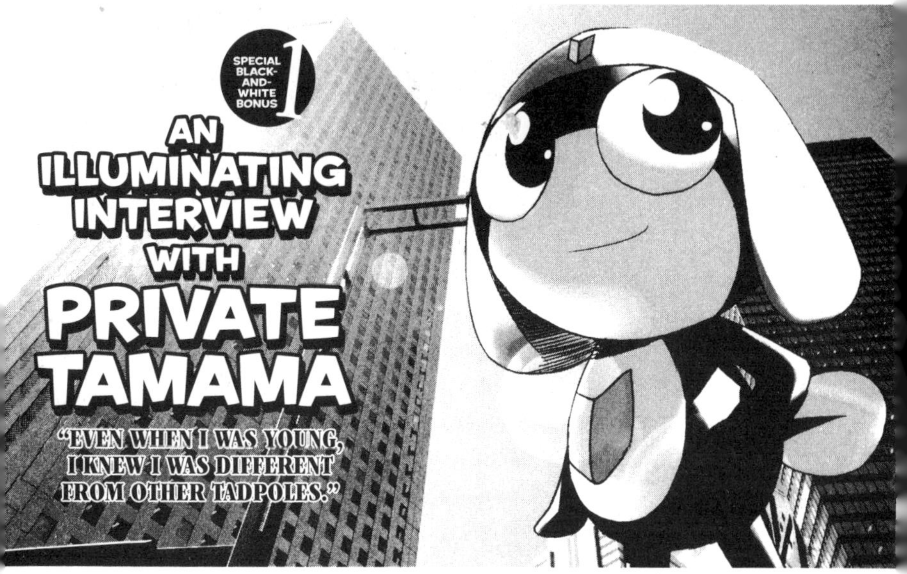

HIS DARK, FORMATIVE YEARS

-- When people think of you, they think of the tail.

Tamama: This old thing? (wry smile) Yeah, I guess it has become my selling point… even if it *is* full of bad memories.

-- Bad memories, huh? That's surprising.

Tamama: Well, normally, members of the Keron Tribe don't have a tail. Keroro and Giroro have smooth bottoms, you may have noticed.

-- That's right. But I always assumed it just meant that you were not yet fully grown.

Tamama: Yeah, I just let everybody think that. (laughs) I can't really go into the details, but I guess I always knew I was special. Eventually, this tail got me respect. My youth may have been a little rough, but it built character.

-- Your road to becoming a Private wasn't always easy, was it, Tamama?

Tamama: Well, I was never dissatisfied with my rank. I figured this is just how we all start out. Like how humans start out with "Ga ga" and progress to "Goo goo." (laughs)

-- "Ga ga" to "Goo goo," huh? That's a very Tamama response. Any insights on that "new driver" sign on your stomach? (The symbol on Tamama's stomach is the same one as a sticker given to new drivers in Japan when they first get their licenses.) **Or is that getting a bit too personal?**

Tamama: Oh, no problem. (laughs) In fact, I only recently learned that this mark has its own meaning on Pokopen. I was, like, really? But you know, I can't give it up just because it has different associations here-- I gotta be who I am.

-- And you certainly are, Tamama. So…any parting words on your hopes for the future?

Tamama: Well, obviously I'd like to strengthen our collaborative efforts on… you know. But then, as our next step to the big time, I'd like start working on our first album. I just hope everything always stays this exciting, you know? I don't think I'll outgrow the glamour anytime soon.

PICTURE ABOVE:
At Takizawa Bekkan Bldg., Shinjuku Station's East Exit.

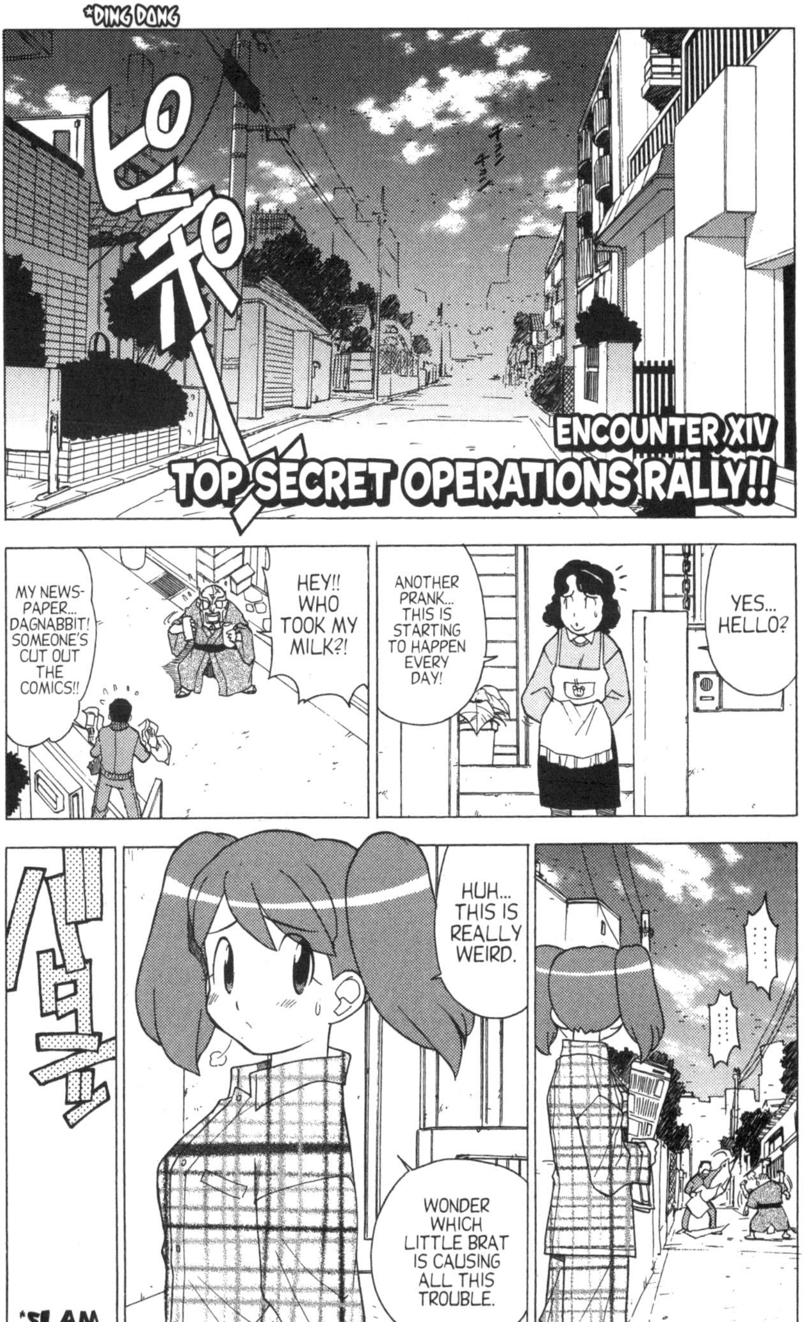
*DING DONG
ENCOUNTER XIV
TOP SECRET OPERATIONS RALLY!!
YES... HELLO?
ANOTHER PRANK... THIS IS STARTING TO HAPPEN EVERY DAY!
HEY!! WHO TOOK MY MILK?!
MY NEWS-PAPER... DAGNABBIT! SOMEONE'S CUT OUT THE COMICS!!
HUH... THIS IS REALLY WEIRD.
WONDER WHICH LITTLE BRAT IS CAUSING ALL THIS TROUBLE.
*SLAM

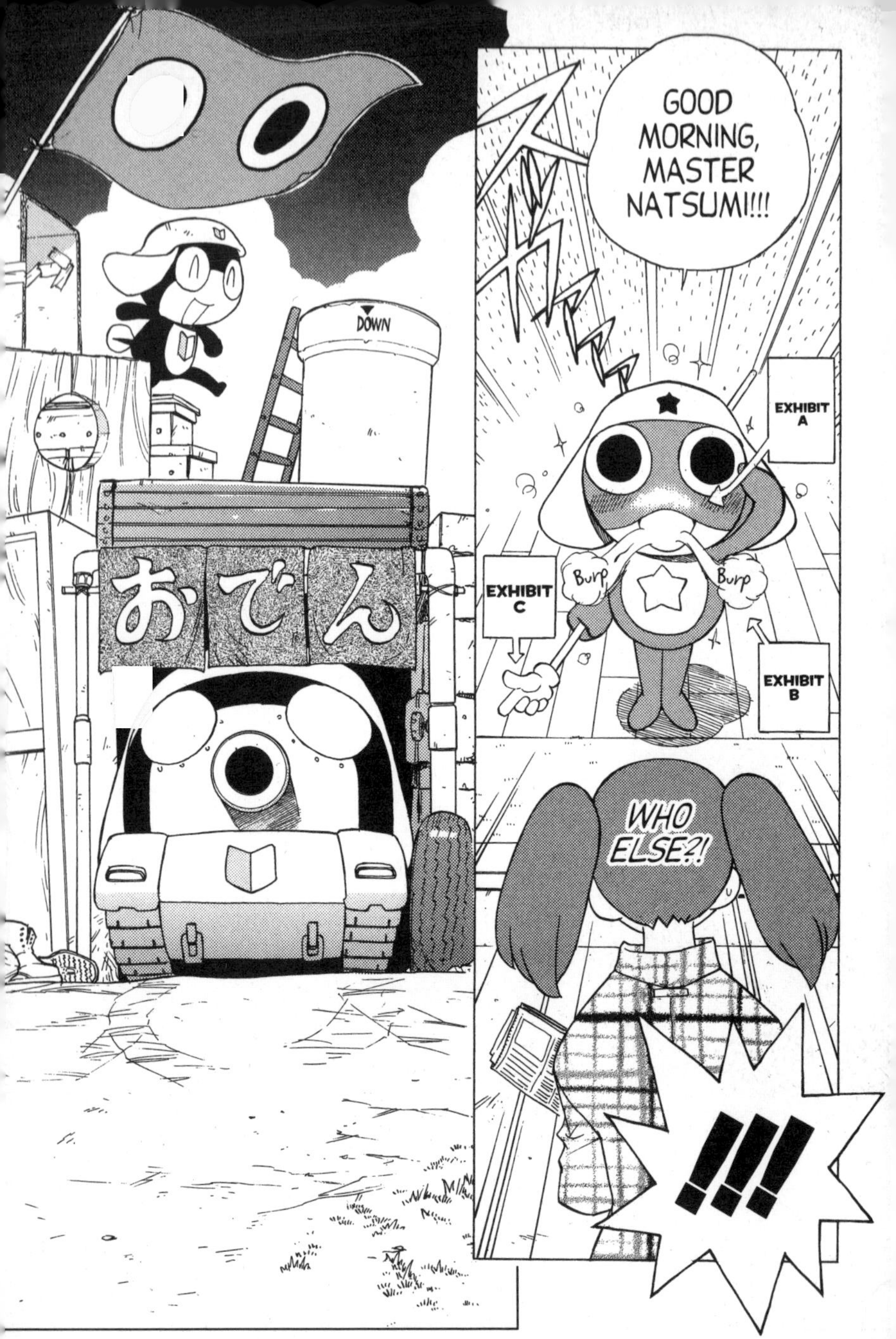
GOOD MORNING, MASTER NATSUMI!!!
EXHIBIT A
Burp
Burp
EXHIBIT C
EXHIBIT B
WHO ELSE?!
!!!
DOWN
おでん

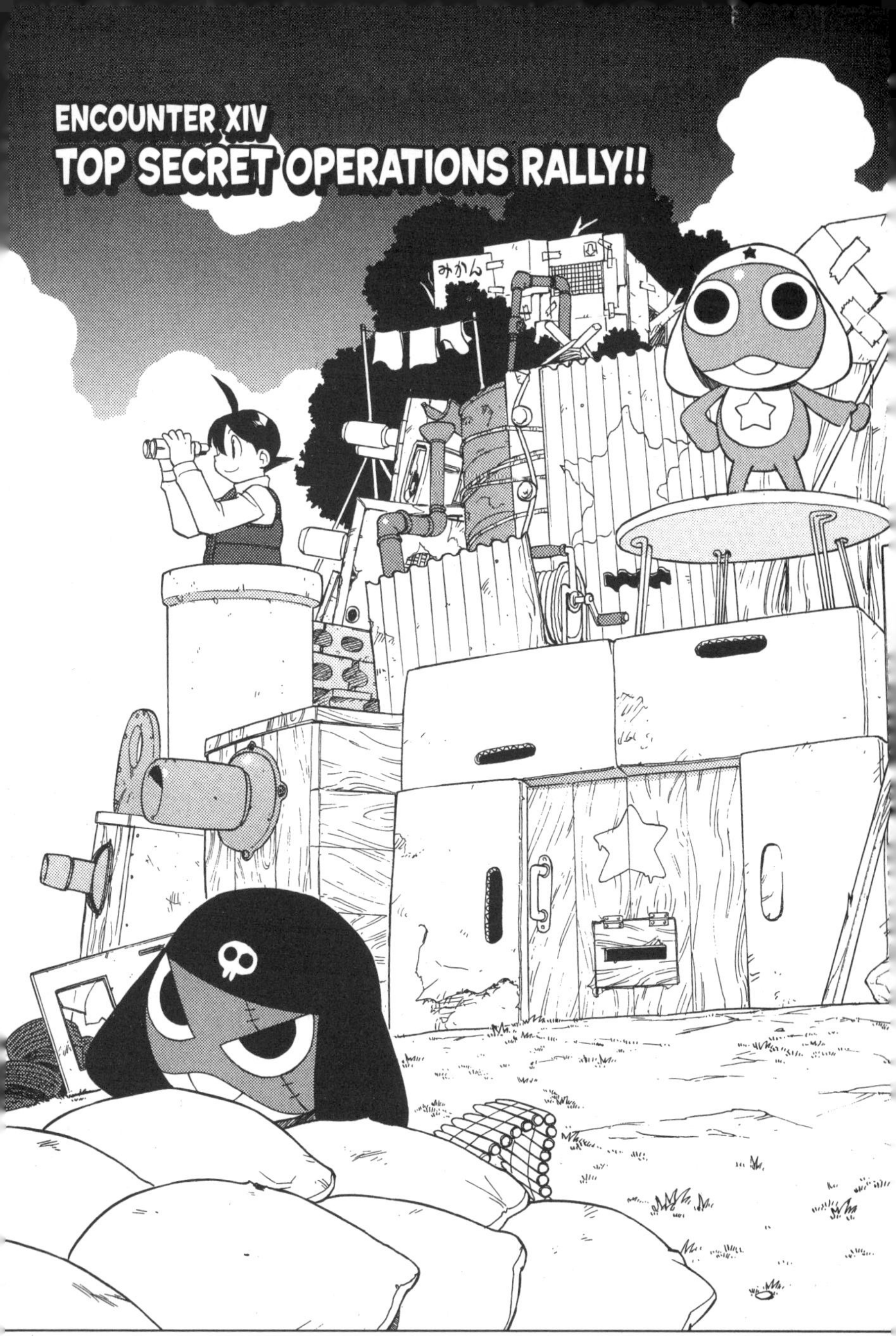
ENCOUNTER XIV
TOP SECRET OPERATIONS RALLY!!
みかん

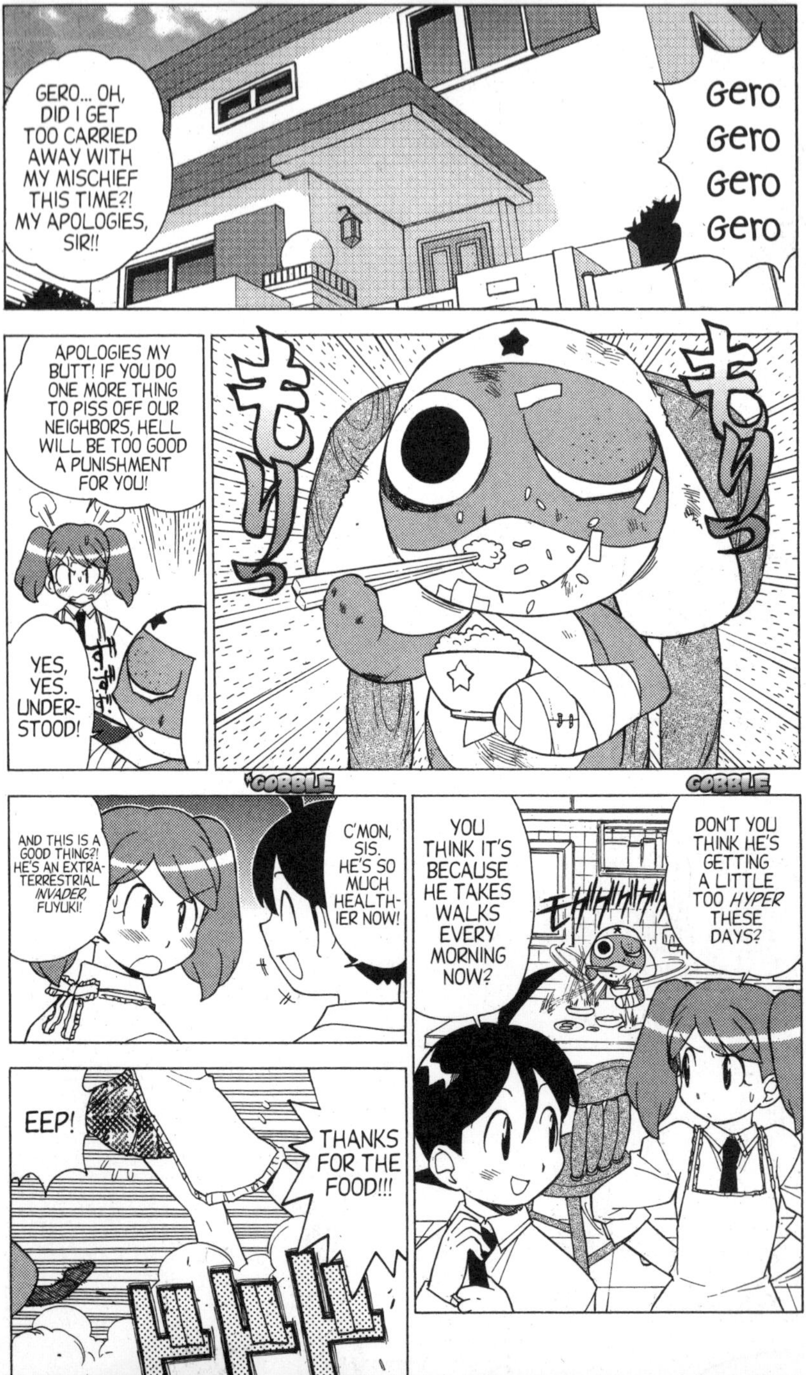

Gero Gero Gero Gero
GERO... OH, DID I GET TOO CARRIED AWAY WITH MY MISCHIEF THIS TIME?! MY APOLOGIES, SIR!!
もりっ
もりっ
APOLOGIES MY BUTT! IF YOU DO ONE MORE THING TO PISS OFF OUR NEIGHBORS, HELL WILL BE TOO GOOD A PUNISHMENT FOR YOU!
YES, YES. UNDER-STOOD!
GOBBLE
*GOBBLE
DON'T YOU THINK HE'S GETTING A LITTLE TOO *HYPER* THESE DAYS?
YOU THINK IT'S BECAUSE HE TAKES WALKS EVERY MORNING NOW?
C'MON, SIS. HE'S SO MUCH HEALTH-IER NOW!
AND THIS IS A GOOD THING?! HE'S AN EXTRA-TERRESTRIAL *INVADER*, FUYUKI!
THANKS FOR THE FOOD!!!
EEP!

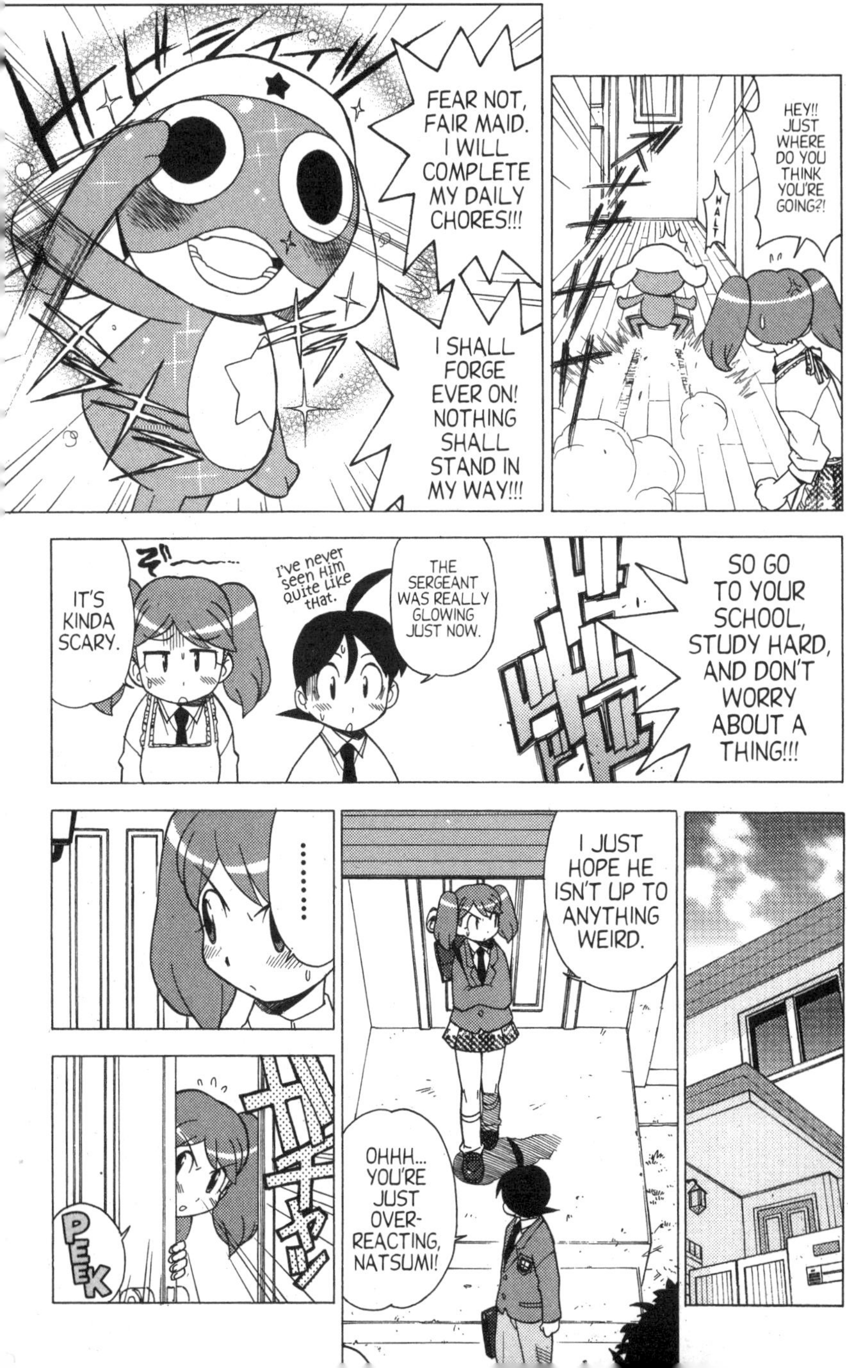
HEY!! JUST WHERE DO YOU THINK YOU'RE GOING?!
WAIT
FEAR NOT, FAIR MAID. I WILL COMPLETE MY DAILY CHORES!!!
I SHALL FORGE EVER ON! NOTHING SHALL STAND IN MY WAY!!!
SO GO TO YOUR SCHOOL, STUDY HARD, AND DON'T WORRY ABOUT A THING!!!
THE SERGEANT WAS REALLY GLOWING JUST NOW.
I've never seen him quite like that.
IT'S KINDA SCARY.
I JUST HOPE HE ISN'T UP TO ANYTHING WEIRD.
OHHH... YOU'RE JUST OVER-REACTING, NATSUMI!
....
PEEK

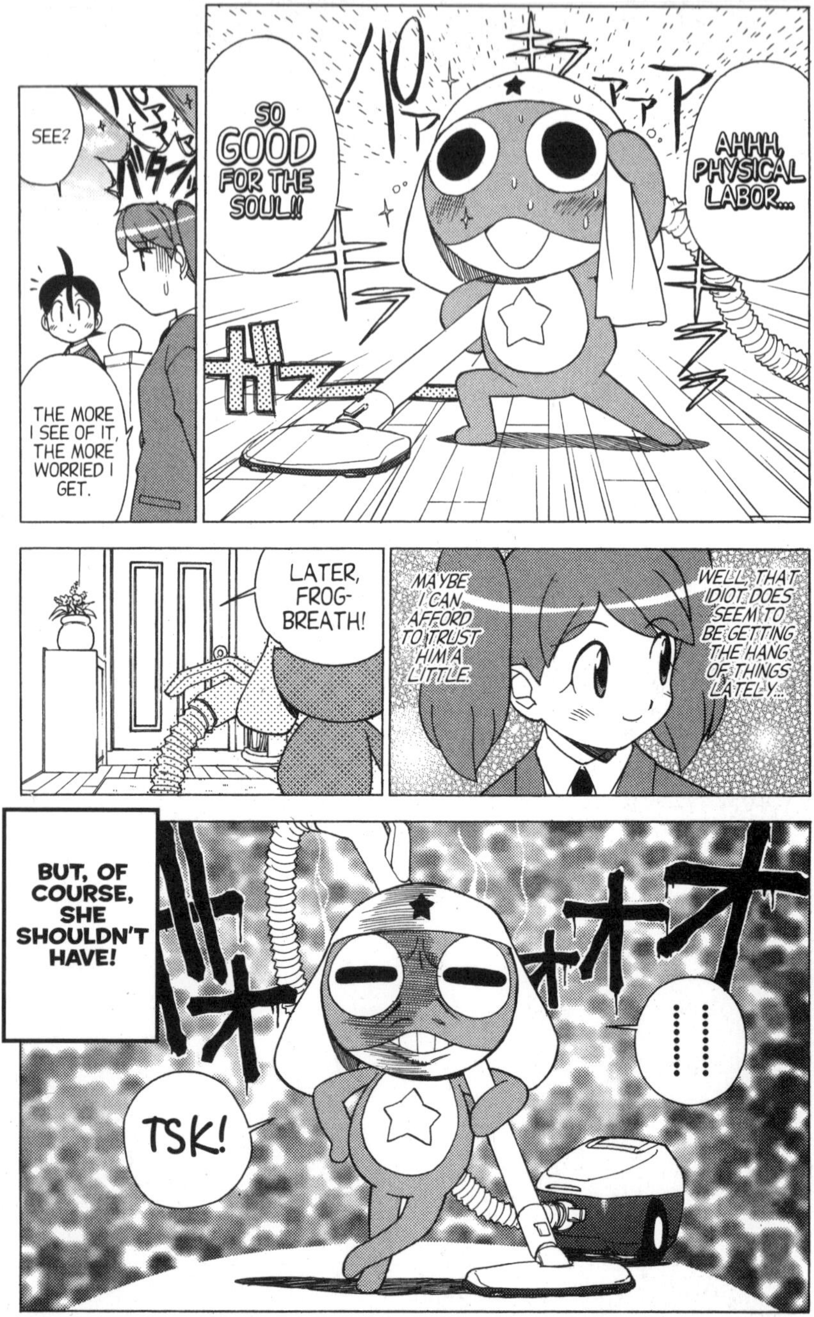

AHHH, PHYSICAL LABOR...
SO GOOD FOR THE SOUL!!
SEE?
THE MORE I SEE OF IT, THE MORE WORRIED I GET.
WELL, THAT IDIOT DOES SEEM TO BE GETTING THE HANG OF THINGS LATELY...
MAYBE I CAN AFFORD TO TRUST HIM A LITTLE.
LATER, FROG-BREATH!
BUT, OF COURSE, SHE SHOULDN'T HAVE!
......
TSK!

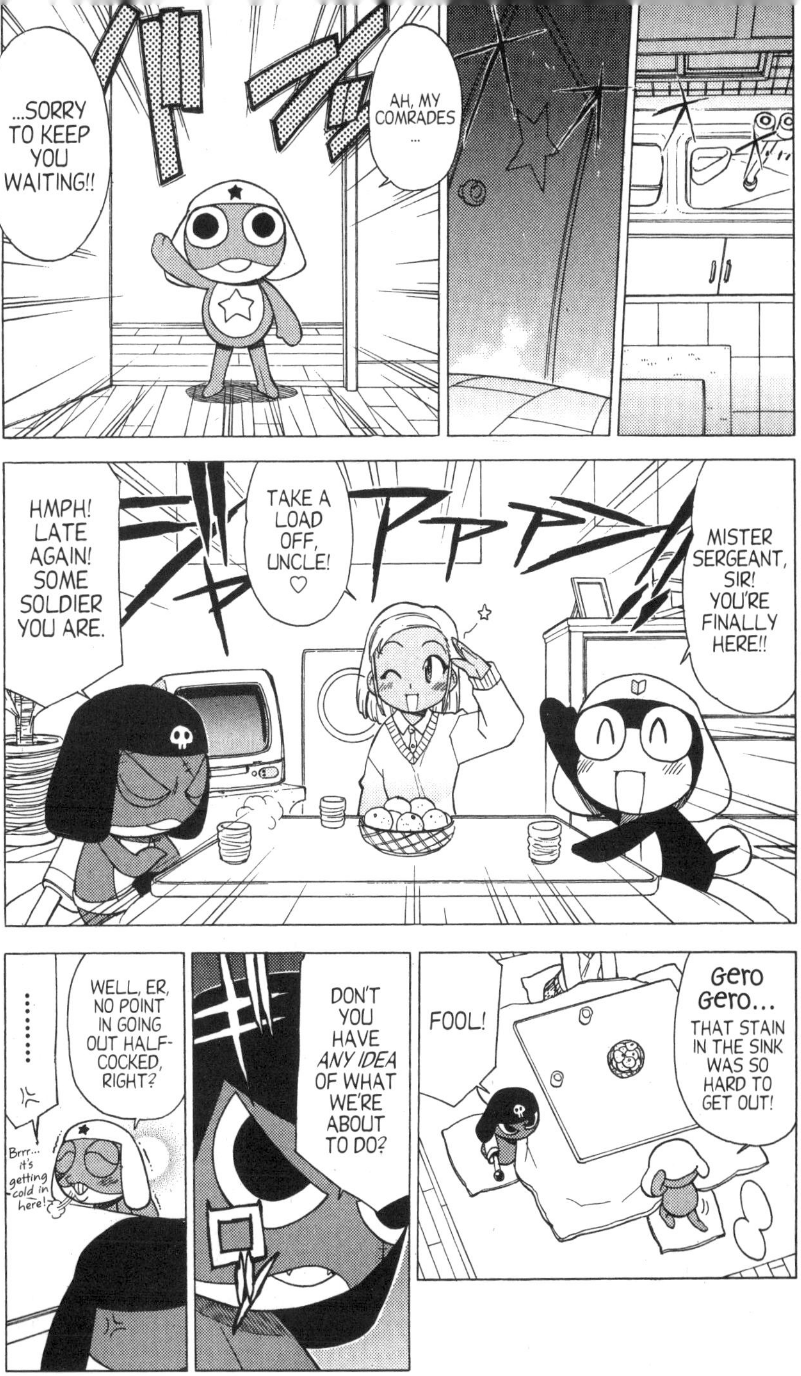
AH, MY COMRADES ...
...SORRY TO KEEP YOU WAITING!!
MISTER SERGEANT, SIR! YOU'RE FINALLY HERE!!
TAKE A LOAD OFF, UNCLE! ♡
HMPH! LATE AGAIN! SOME SOLDIER YOU ARE.
Gero Gero... THAT STAIN IN THE SINK WAS SO HARD TO GET OUT!
FOOL!
DON'T YOU HAVE *ANY IDEA* OF WHAT WE'RE ABOUT TO DO?
WELL, ER, NO POINT IN GOING OUT HALF-COCKED, RIGHT?
....
Brrr... it's getting cold in here!

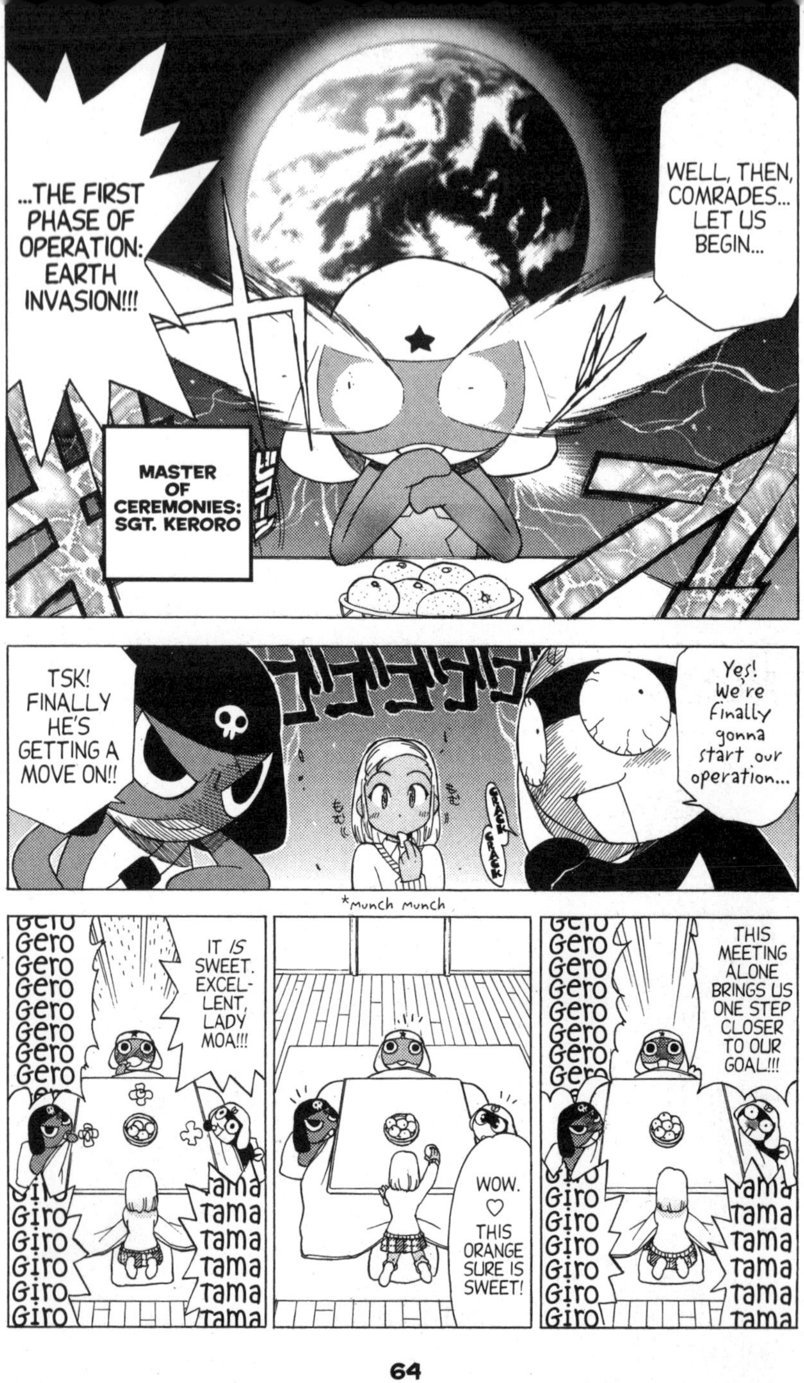
WELL, THEN, COMRADES... LET US BEGIN...
...THE FIRST PHASE OF OPERATION: EARTH INVASION!!!
MASTER OF CEREMONIES: SGT. KERORO
Yes! We're finally gonna start our operation...
TSK! FINALLY HE'S GETTING A MOVE ON!!
CRACK CRACK
*munch munch
THIS MEETING ALONE BRINGS US ONE STEP CLOSER TO OUR GOAL!!!
Gero Gero Gero Gero Gero Gero Gero Gero
Giro Giro Giro Giro Giro Giro
Tama Tama Tama Tama Tama Tama
WOW. ♡ THIS ORANGE SURE IS SWEET!
IT IS SWEET. EXCEL-LENT, LADY MOA!!!
Gero Gero Gero Gero Gero Gero Gero Gero
Giro Giro Giro Giro Giro Giro
Tama Tama Tama Tama Tama Tama

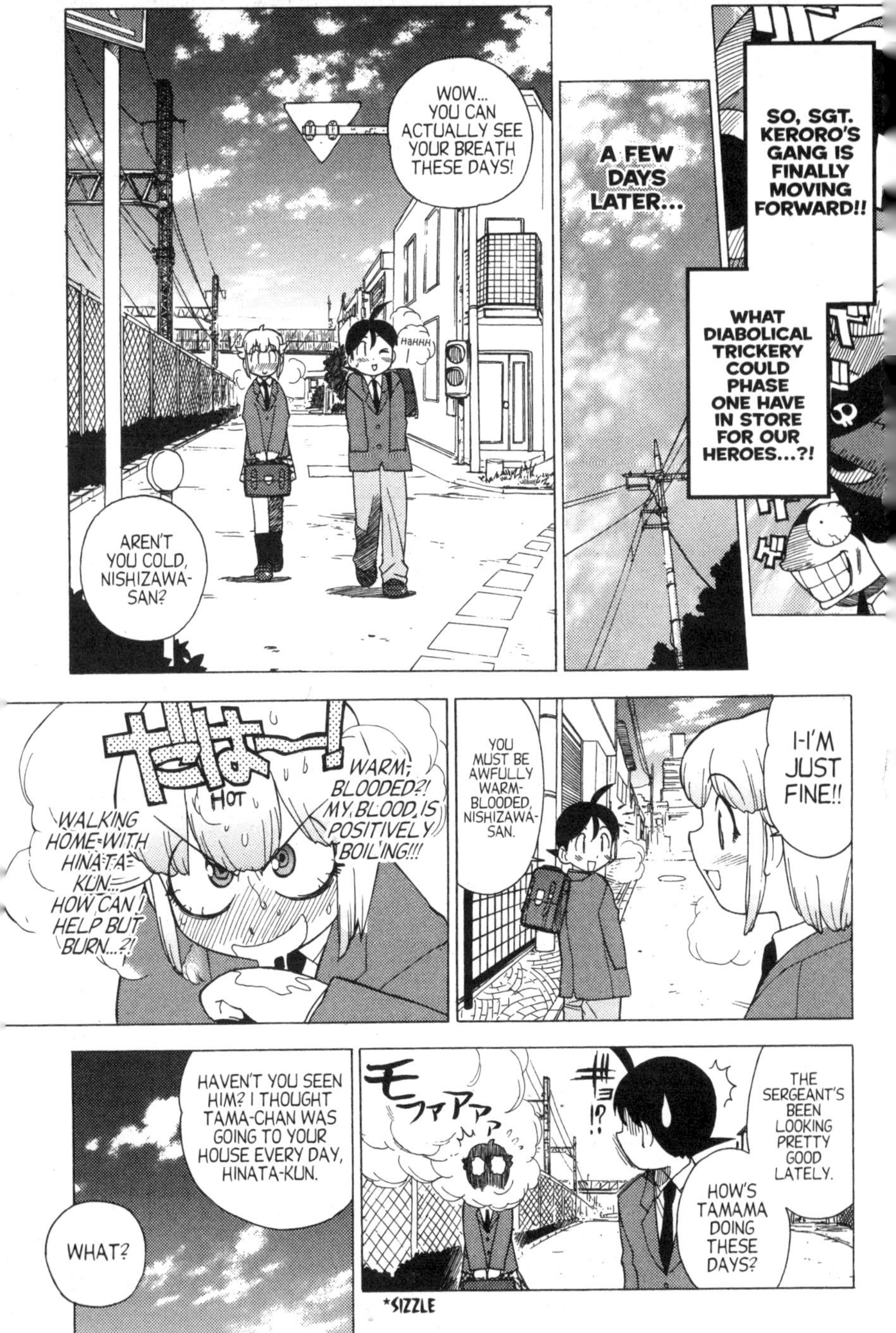

SO, SGT. KERORO'S GANG IS FINALLY MOVING FORWARD!!
WHAT DIABOLICAL TRICKERY COULD PHASE ONE HAVE IN STORE FOR OUR HEROES...?!
A FEW DAYS LATER...
WOW... YOU CAN ACTUALLY SEE YOUR BREATH THESE DAYS!
HAHHH
AREN'T YOU COLD, NISHIZAWA-SAN?
I-I'M JUST FINE!!
YOU MUST BE AWFULLY WARM-BLOODED, NISHIZAWA-SAN.
だはー!
HOT
WARM-BLOODED?! MY BLOOD IS POSITIVELY BOILING!!!
WALKING HOME WITH HINATA-KUN... HOW CAN I HELP BUT BURN...?!
THE SERGEANT'S BEEN LOOKING PRETTY GOOD LATELY.
HOW'S TAMAMA DOING THESE DAYS?
!?
モファアアア
HAVEN'T YOU SEEN HIM? I THOUGHT TAMA-CHAN WAS GOING TO YOUR HOUSE EVERY DAY, HINATA-KUN.
WHAT?

*SIZZLE

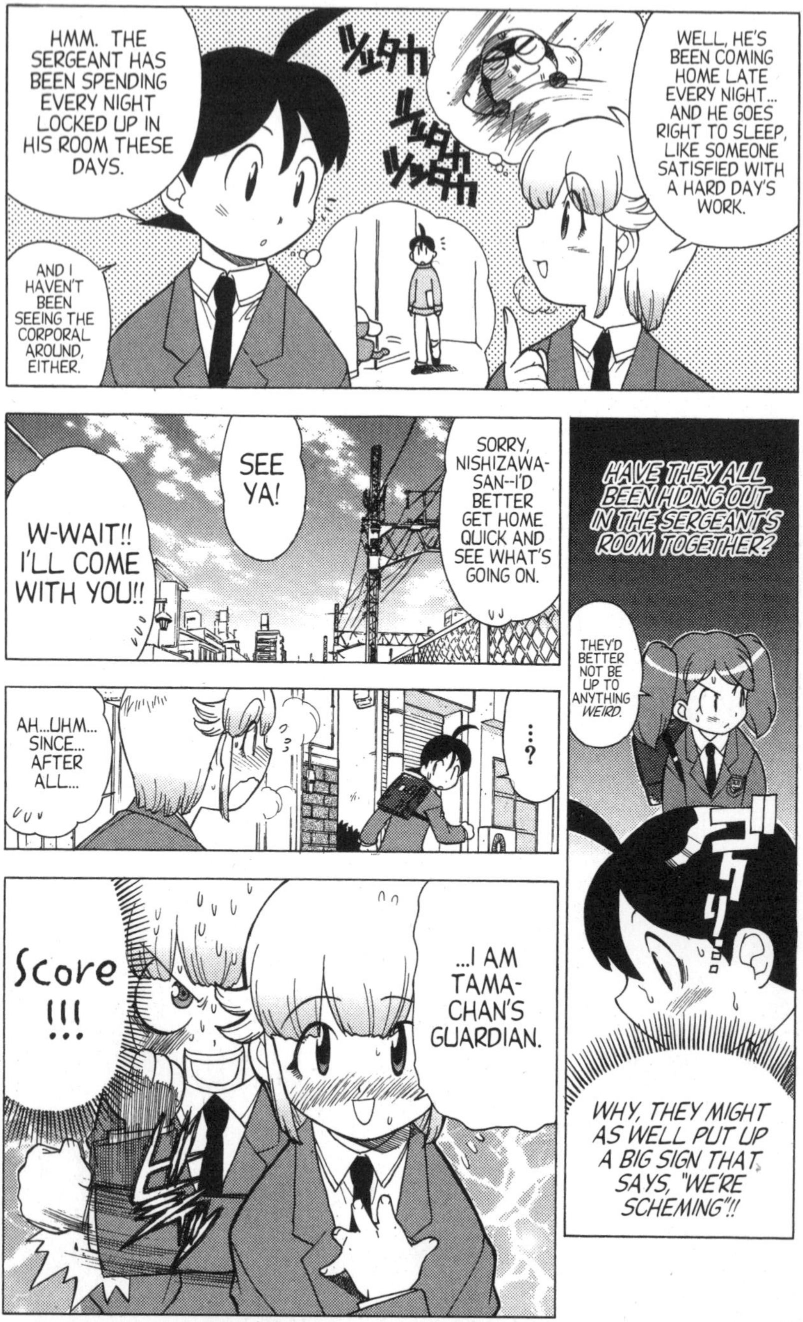
WELL, HE'S BEEN COMING HOME LATE EVERY NIGHT... AND HE GOES RIGHT TO SLEEP, LIKE SOMEONE SATISFIED WITH A HARD DAY'S WORK.
HMM. THE SERGEANT HAS BEEN SPENDING EVERY NIGHT LOCKED UP IN HIS ROOM THESE DAYS.
AND I HAVEN'T BEEN SEEING THE CORPORAL AROUND, EITHER.
HAVE THEY ALL BEEN HIDING OUT IN THE SERGEANT'S ROOM TOGETHER?
THEY'D BETTER NOT BE UP TO ANYTHING *WEIRD.*
WHY, THEY MIGHT AS WELL PUT UP A BIG SIGN THAT SAYS, "WE'RE SCHEMING"!!
SORRY, NISHIZAWA-SAN--I'D BETTER GET HOME QUICK AND SEE WHAT'S GOING ON.
SEE YA!
W-WAIT!! I'LL COME WITH YOU!!
...?
AH...UHM... SINCE... AFTER ALL...
...I AM TAMA-CHAN'S GUARDIAN.
Score !!! ...

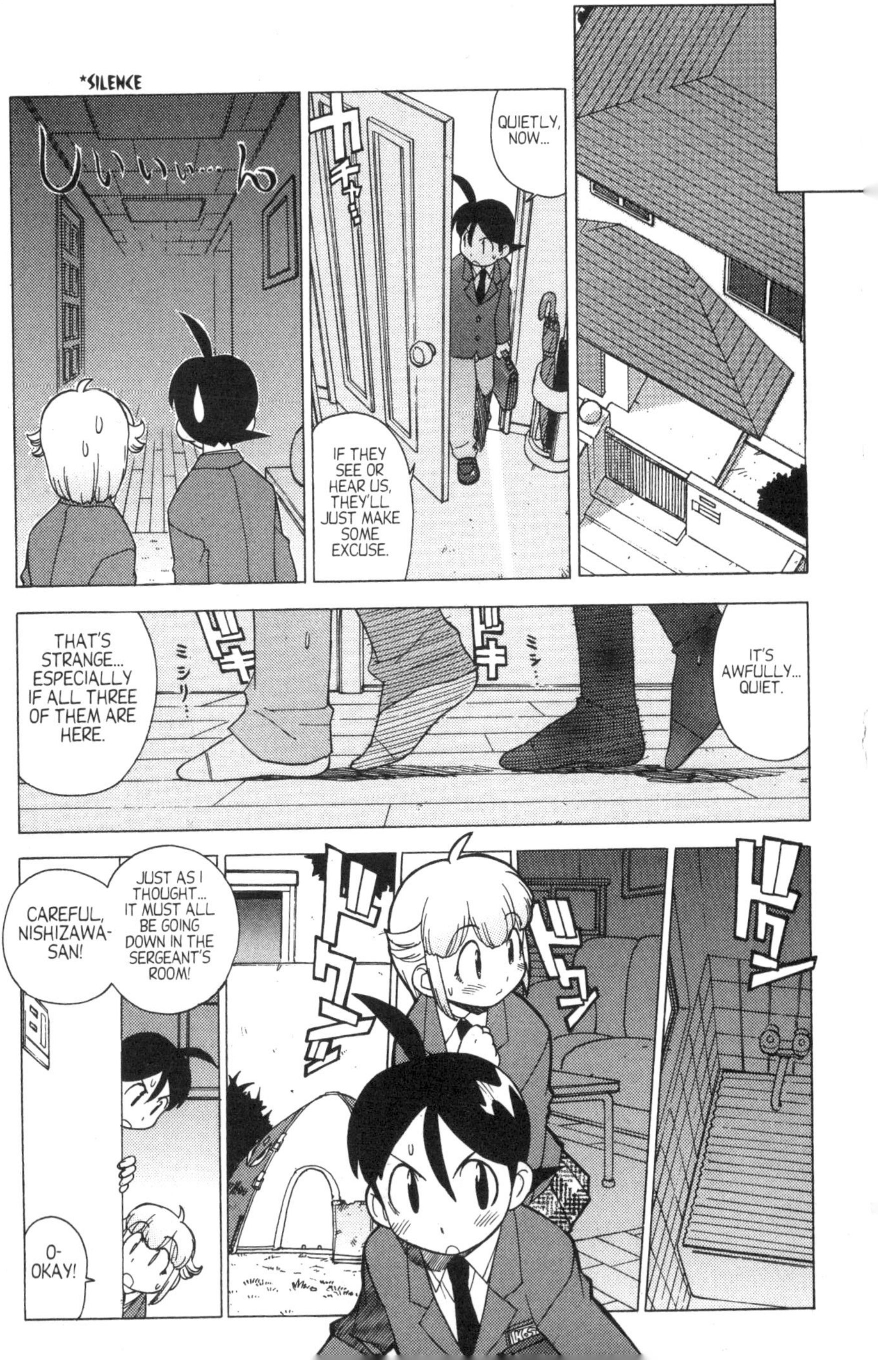

QUIETLY, NOW...
IF THEY SEE OR HEAR US, THEY'LL JUST MAKE SOME EXCUSE.
*SILENCE
IT'S AWFULLY... QUIET.
THAT'S STRANGE... ESPECIALLY IF ALL THREE OF THEM ARE HERE.
JUST AS I THOUGHT... IT MUST ALL BE GOING DOWN IN THE SERGEANT'S ROOM!
CAREFUL, NISHIZAWA-SAN!
O-OKAY!

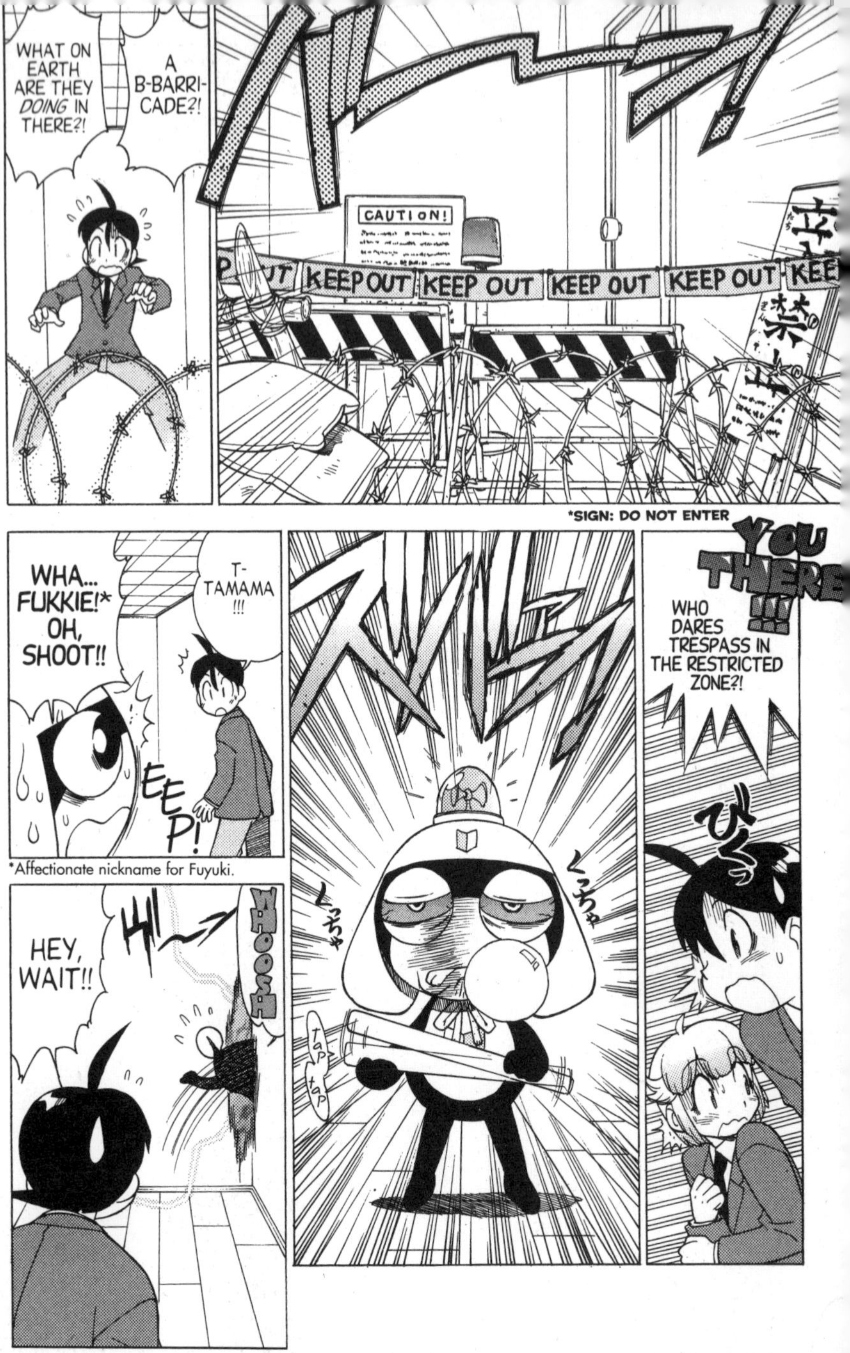
CAUTION!
KEEP OUT KEEP OUT KEEP OUT KEEP OUT
A B-BARRICADE?!
WHAT ON EARTH ARE THEY *DOING* IN THERE?!
YOU THERE!!!
WHO DARES TRESPASS IN THE RESTRICTED ZONE?!
びくっ
くっちゃ
くっちゃ
tap tap
T-TAMAMA!!!
WHA... FUKKIE!* OH, SHOOT!!
EEP!
WHOOSH
HEY, WAIT!!

*SIGN: DO NOT ENTER

*Affectionate nickname for Fuyuki.

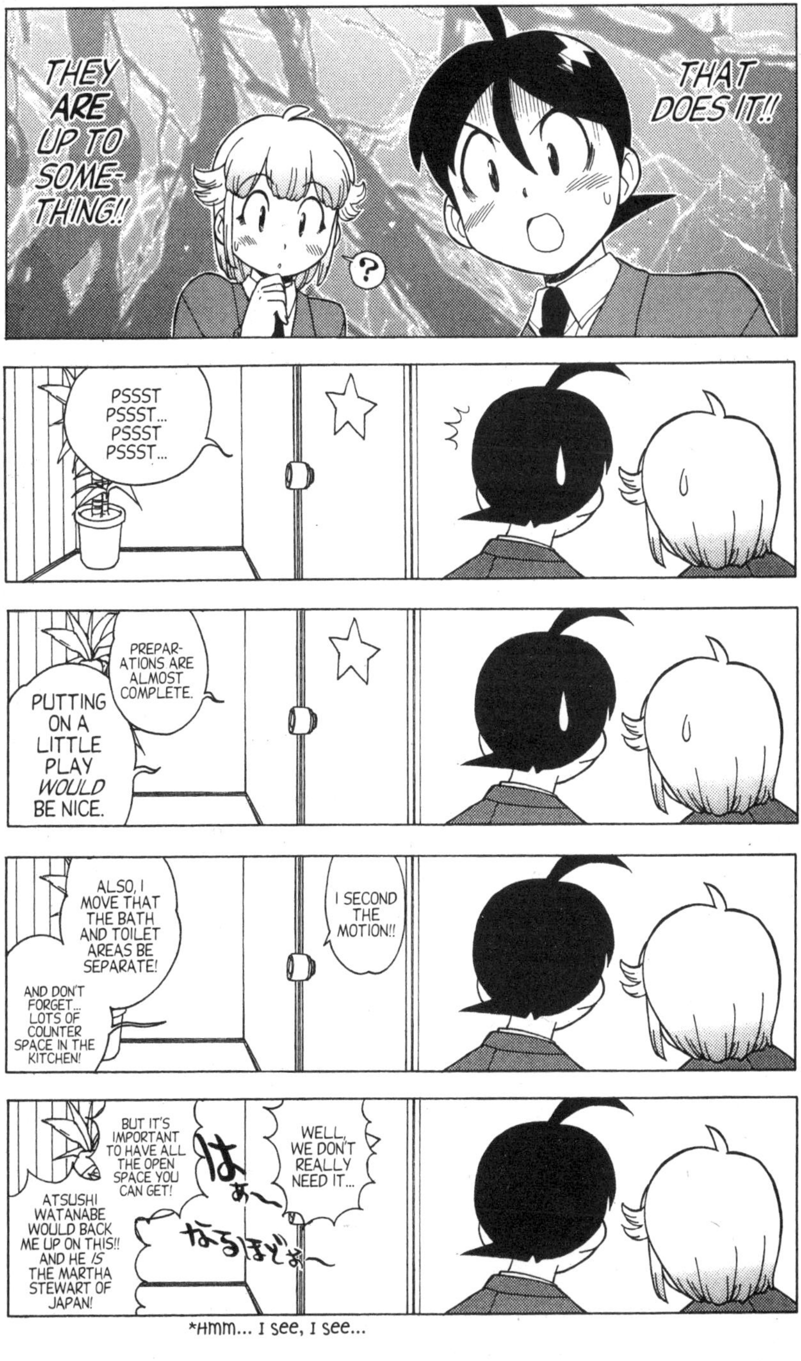
THAT DOES IT!!
THEY ARE UP TO SOME-THING!!
?
PSSST PSSST... PSSST PSSST...
PREPAR-ATIONS ARE ALMOST COMPLETE.
PUTTING ON A LITTLE PLAY *WOULD* BE NICE.
I SECOND THE MOTION!!
ALSO, I MOVE THAT THE BATH AND TOILET AREAS BE SEPARATE!
AND DON'T FORGET... LOTS OF COUNTER SPACE IN THE KITCHEN!
WELL, WE DON'T REALLY NEED IT...
BUT IT'S IMPORTANT TO HAVE ALL THE OPEN SPACE YOU CAN GET!
はぁ〜
なるほどなぁ〜
ATSUSHI WATANABE WOULD BACK ME UP ON THIS!! AND HE *IS* THE MARTHA STEWART OF JAPAN!

*Hmm... I see, I see...

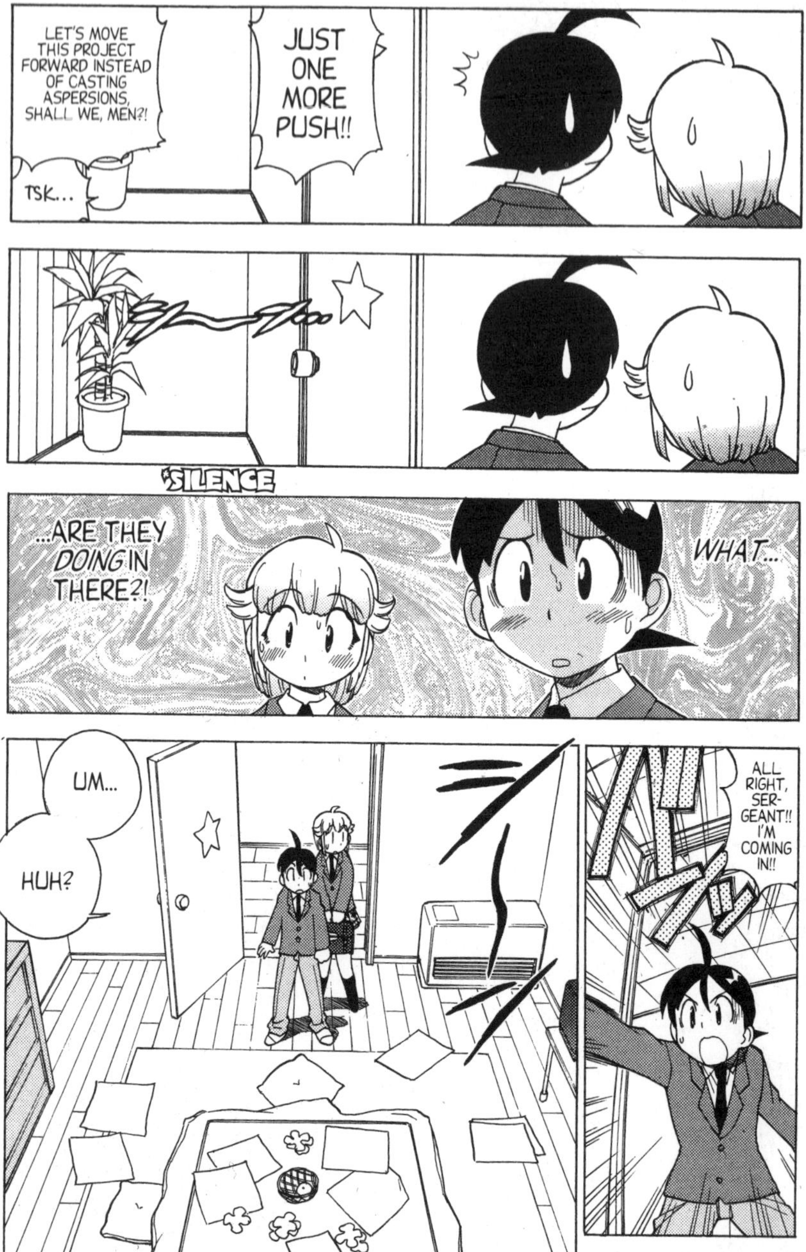
JUST ONE MORE PUSH!!
LET'S MOVE THIS PROJECT FORWARD INSTEAD OF CASTING ASPERSIONS, SHALL WE, MEN?!
TSK...
*SILENCE
WHAT...
...ARE THEY DOING IN THERE?!
ALL RIGHT, SER-GEANT!! I'M COMING IN!!
UM...
HUH?

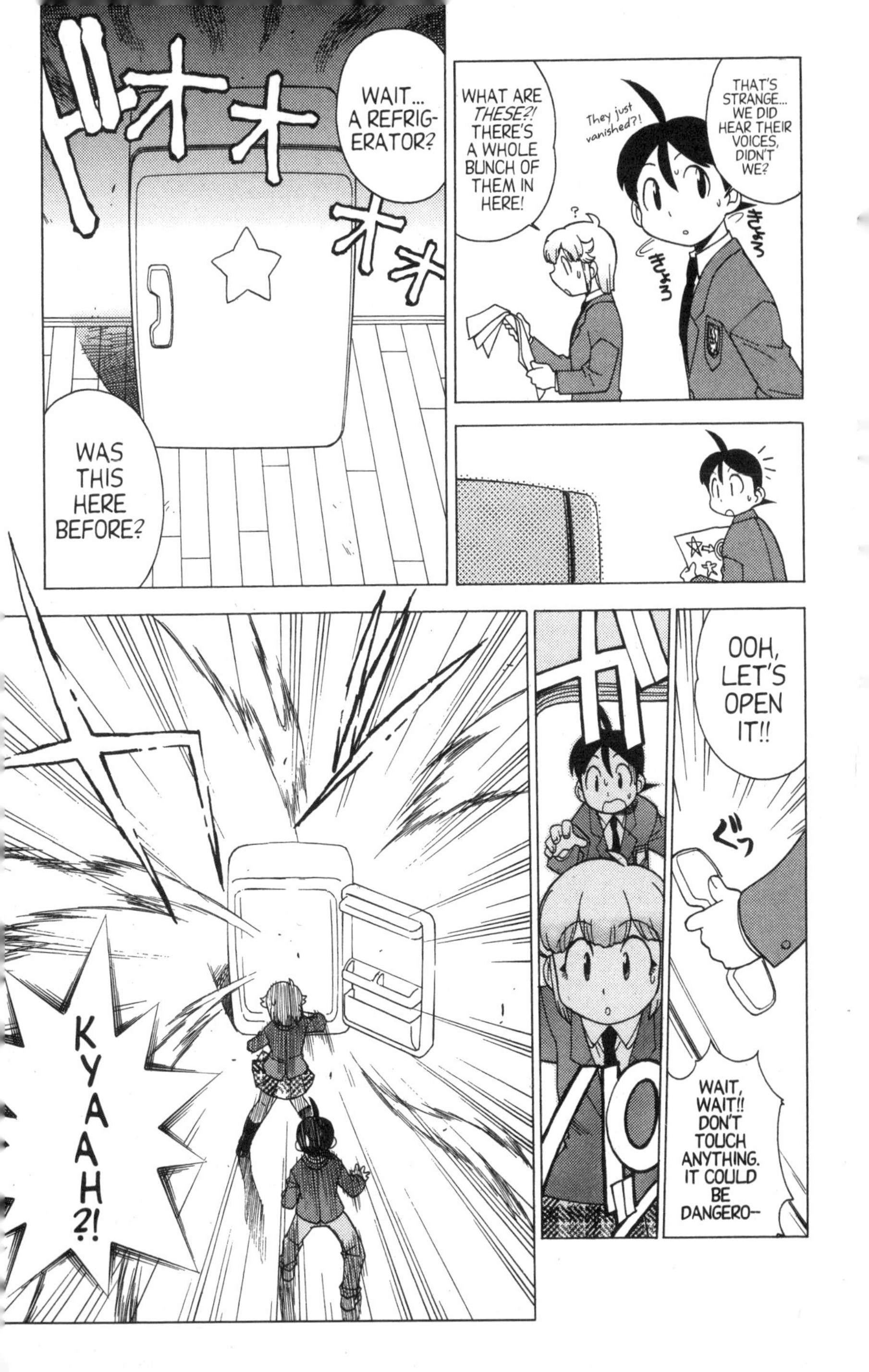
THAT'S STRANGE... WE DID HEAR THEIR VOICES, DIDN'T WE?
They just vanished?!
WHAT ARE THESE?! THERE'S A WHOLE BUNCH OF THEM IN HERE!
WAIT... A REFRIG-ERATOR?
WAS THIS HERE BEFORE?
OOH, LET'S OPEN IT!!
ぐっ
WAIT, WAIT!! DON'T TOUCH ANYTHING. IT COULD BE DANGERO--
KYAAH?!

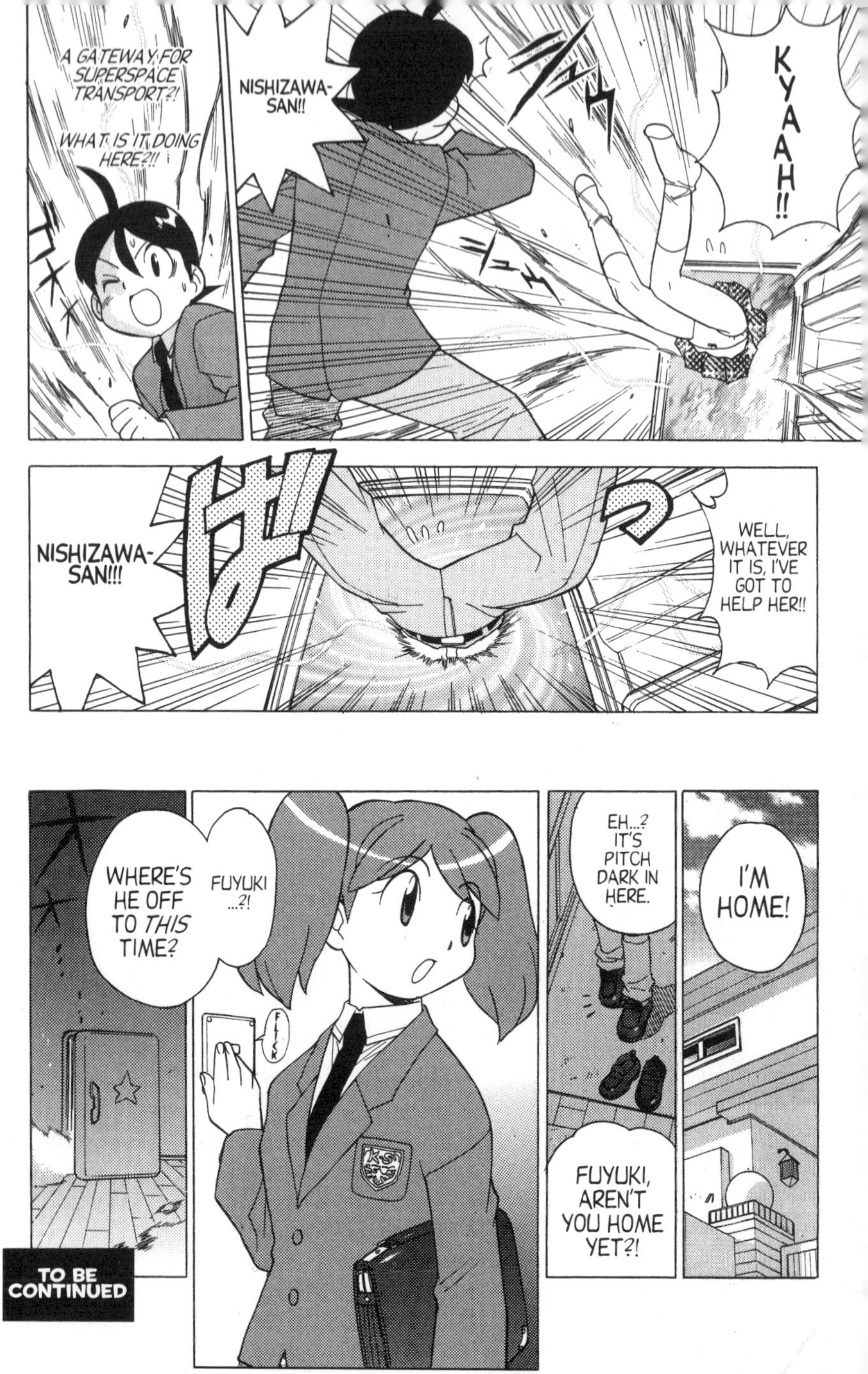
KYAAH!!
NISHIZAWA-SAN!!
A GATEWAY FOR SUPERSPACE TRANSPORT?!
WHAT IS IT DOING HERE?!!
WELL, WHATEVER IT IS, I'VE GOT TO HELP HER!!
NISHIZAWA-SAN!!!
I'M HOME!
EH...? IT'S PITCH DARK IN HERE.
FUYUKI, AREN'T YOU HOME YET?!
FUYUKI ...?!
FLICK
WHERE'S HE OFF TO *THIS* TIME?
TO BE CONTINUED

ENCOUNTER XV
MOMOKA'S LOVE: A NARROW ESCAPE!

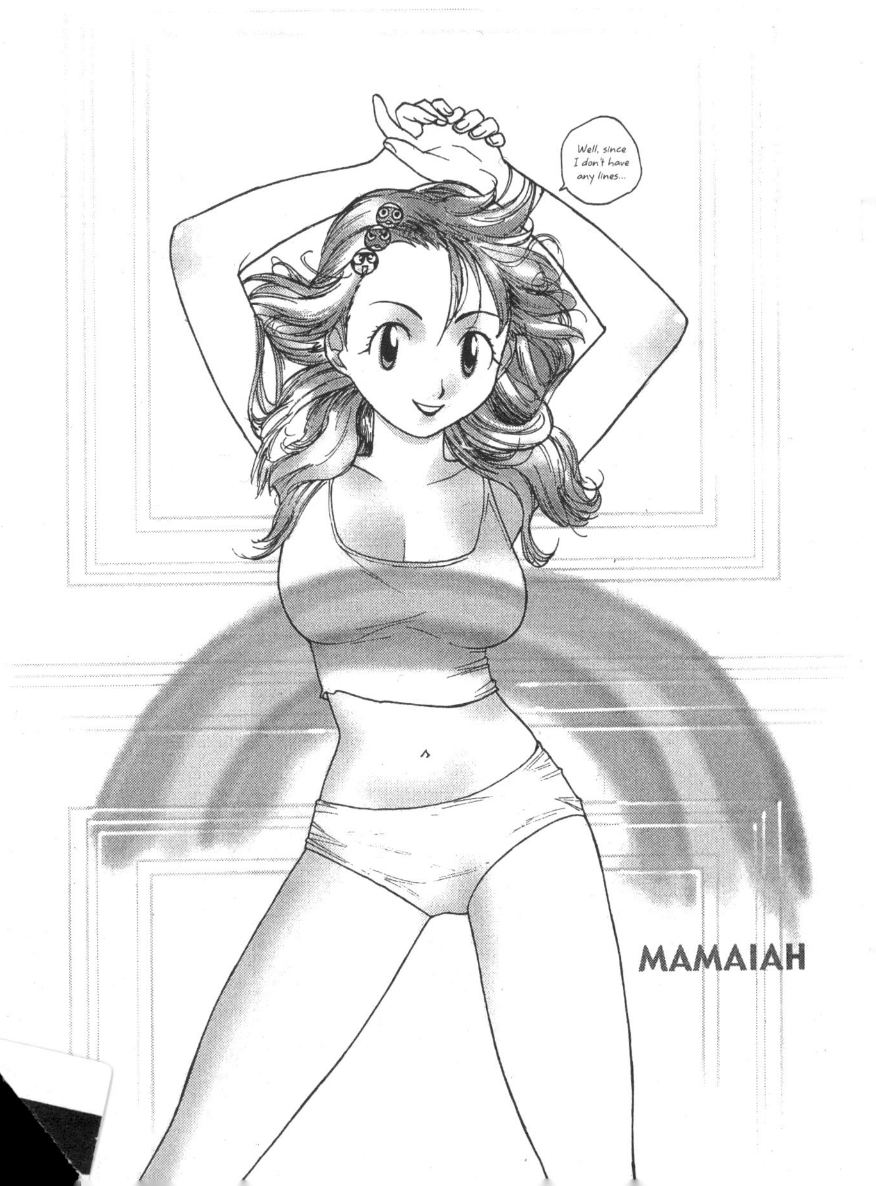
Well, since I don't have any lines...
MAMAIAH

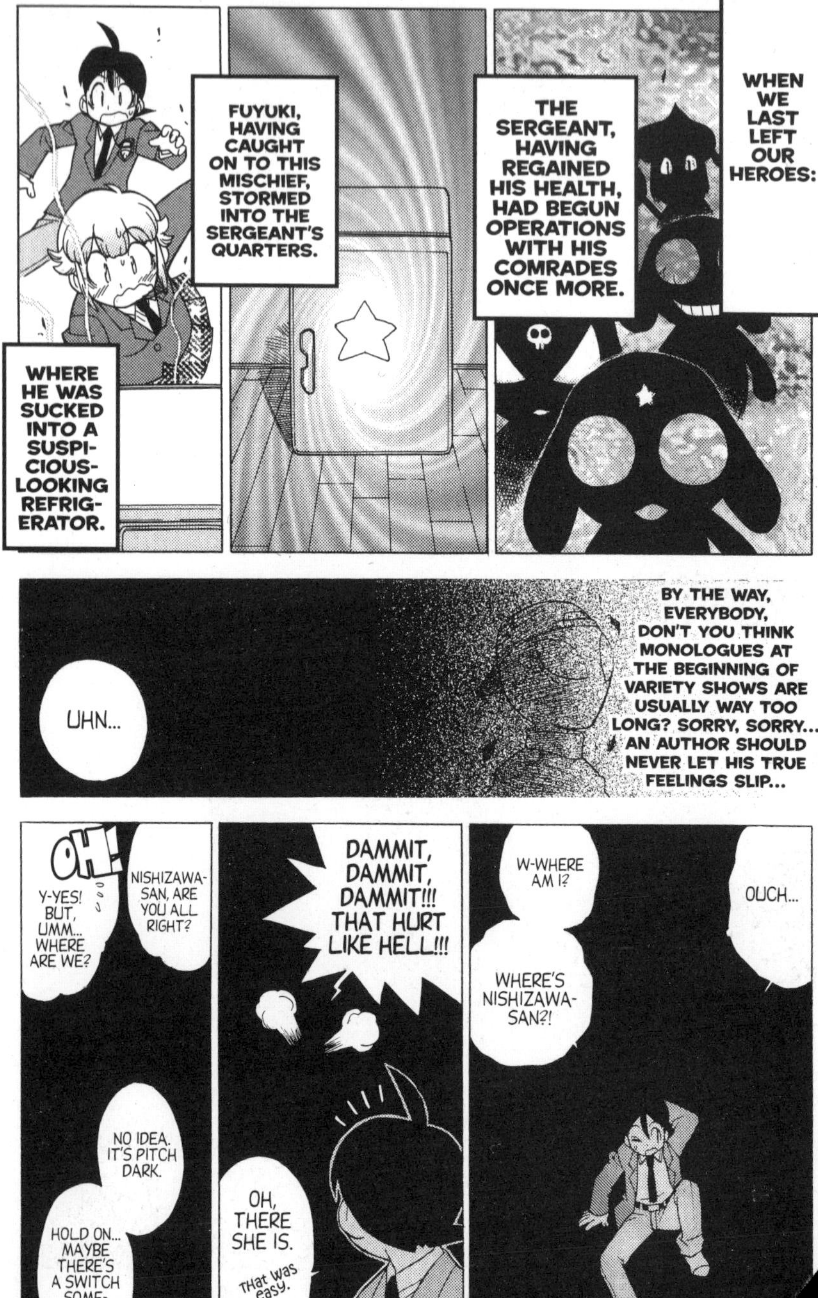
WHEN WE LAST LEFT OUR HEROES:
THE SERGEANT, HAVING REGAINED HIS HEALTH, HAD BEGUN OPERATIONS WITH HIS COMRADES ONCE MORE.
FUYUKI, HAVING CAUGHT ON TO THIS MISCHIEF, STORMED INTO THE SERGEANT'S QUARTERS.
WHERE HE WAS SUCKED INTO A SUSPICIOUS-LOOKING REFRIGERATOR.
BY THE WAY, EVERYBODY, DON'T YOU THINK MONOLOGUES AT THE BEGINNING OF VARIETY SHOWS ARE USUALLY WAY TOO LONG? SORRY, SORRY... AN AUTHOR SHOULD NEVER LET HIS TRUE FEELINGS SLIP...
UHN...
OUCH...
W-WHERE AM I?
WHERE'S NISHIZAWA-SAN?!
DAMMIT, DAMMIT, DAMMIT!!! THAT HURT LIKE HELL!!!
OH, THERE SHE IS.
That was easy.
OH!
NISHIZAWA-SAN, ARE YOU ALL RIGHT?
Y-YES! BUT, UMM... WHERE ARE WE?
NO IDEA. IT'S PITCH DARK.
HOLD ON... MAYBE THERE'S A SWITCH SOMEWHERE...

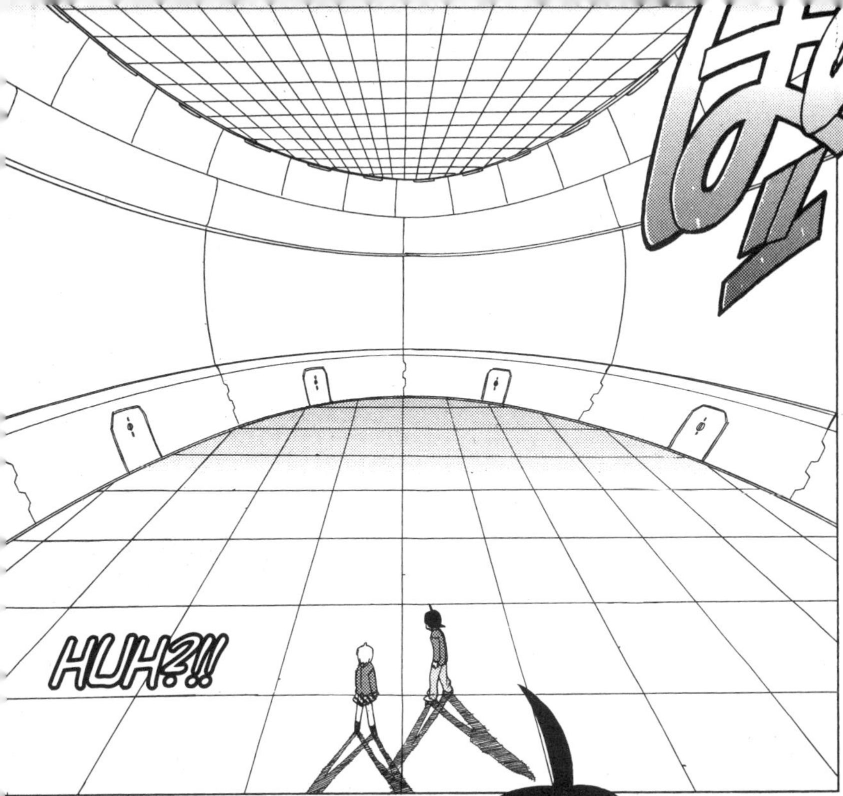
HUH?!!
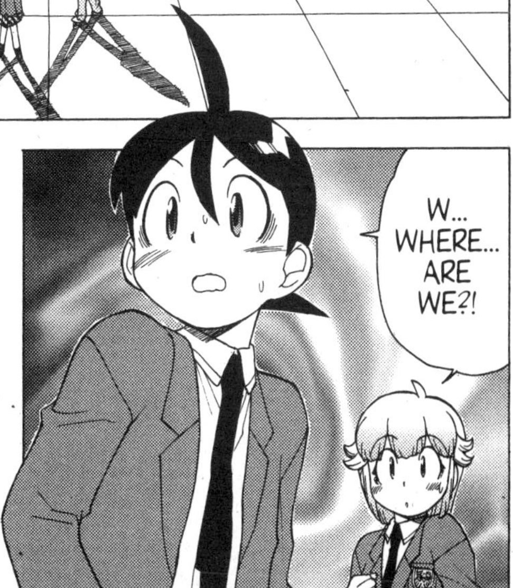
W... WHERE... ARE WE?!
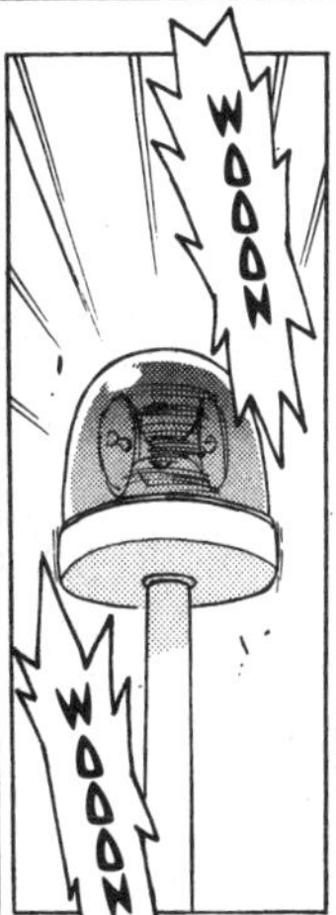
WOOON
WOOON
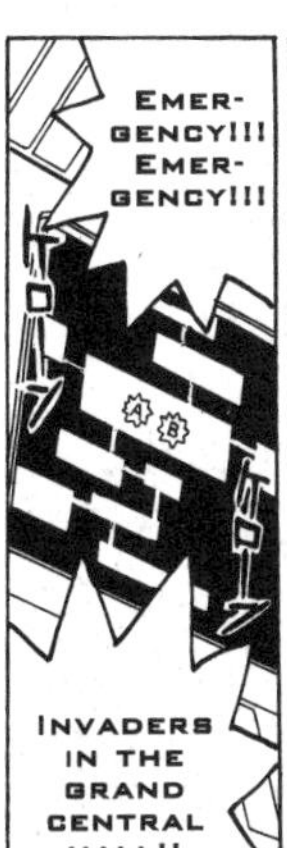
EMERGENCY!!! EMERGENCY!!!
INVADERS IN THE GRAND CENTRAL HALL!!

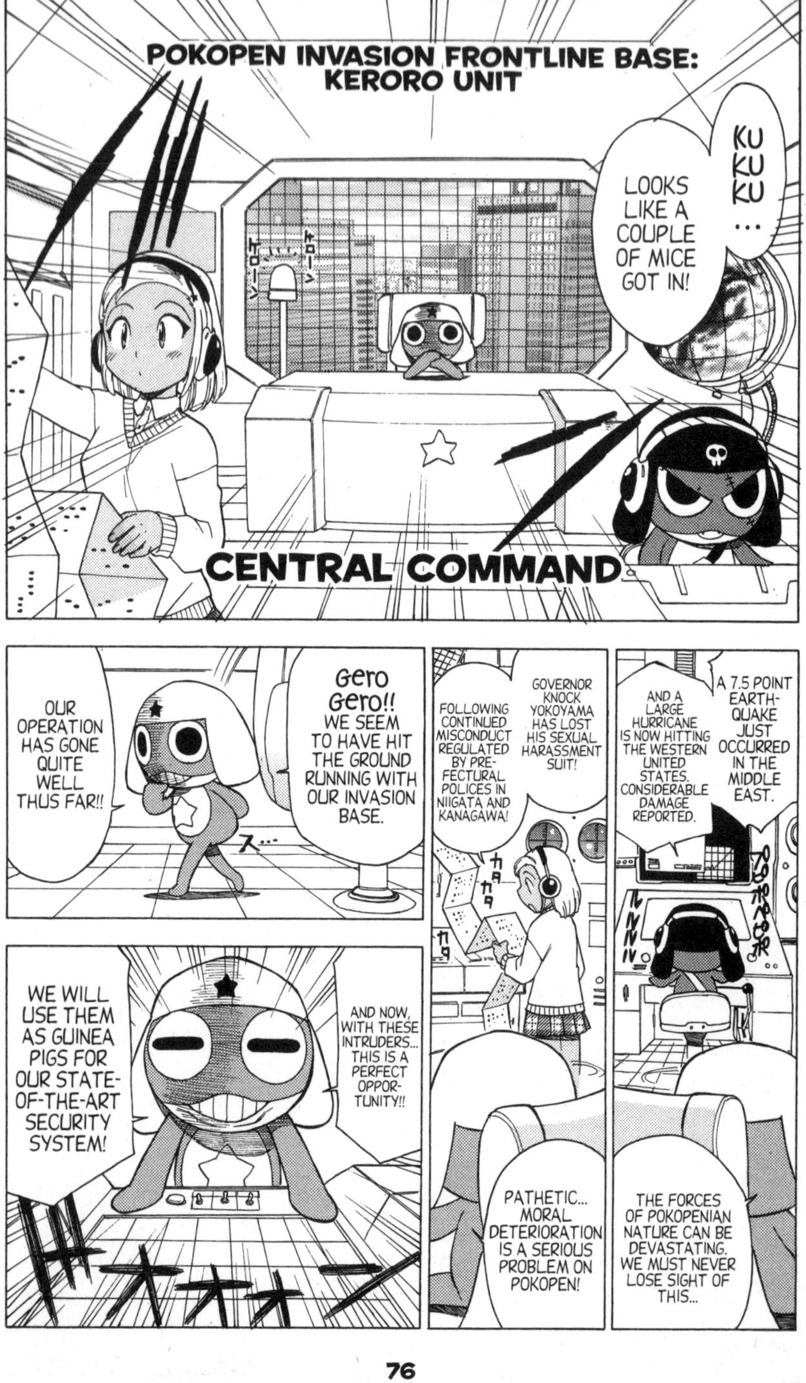
POKOPEN INVASION FRONTLINE BASE: KERORO UNIT
KU KU KU...
LOOKS LIKE A COUPLE OF MICE GOT IN!
CENTRAL COMMAND
A 7.5 POINT EARTHQUAKE JUST OCCURRED IN THE MIDDLE EAST.
AND A LARGE HURRICANE IS NOW HITTING THE WESTERN UNITED STATES. CONSIDERABLE DAMAGE REPORTED.
THE FORCES OF POKOPENIAN NATURE CAN BE DEVASTATING. WE MUST NEVER LOSE SIGHT OF THIS...
GOVERNOR KNOCK YOKOYAMA HAS LOST HIS SEXUAL HARASSMENT SUIT!
FOLLOWING CONTINUED MISCONDUCT REGULATED BY PREFECTURAL POLICES IN NIIGATA AND KANAGAWA!
PATHETIC... MORAL DETERIORATION IS A SERIOUS PROBLEM ON POKOPEN!
Gero Gero!! WE SEEM TO HAVE HIT THE GROUND RUNNING WITH OUR INVASION BASE.
OUR OPERATION HAS GONE QUITE WELL THUS FAR!!
AND NOW, WITH THESE INTRUDERS... THIS IS A PERFECT OPPORTUNITY!!
WE WILL USE THEM AS GUINEA PIGS FOR OUR STATE-OF-THE-ART SECURITY SYSTEM!

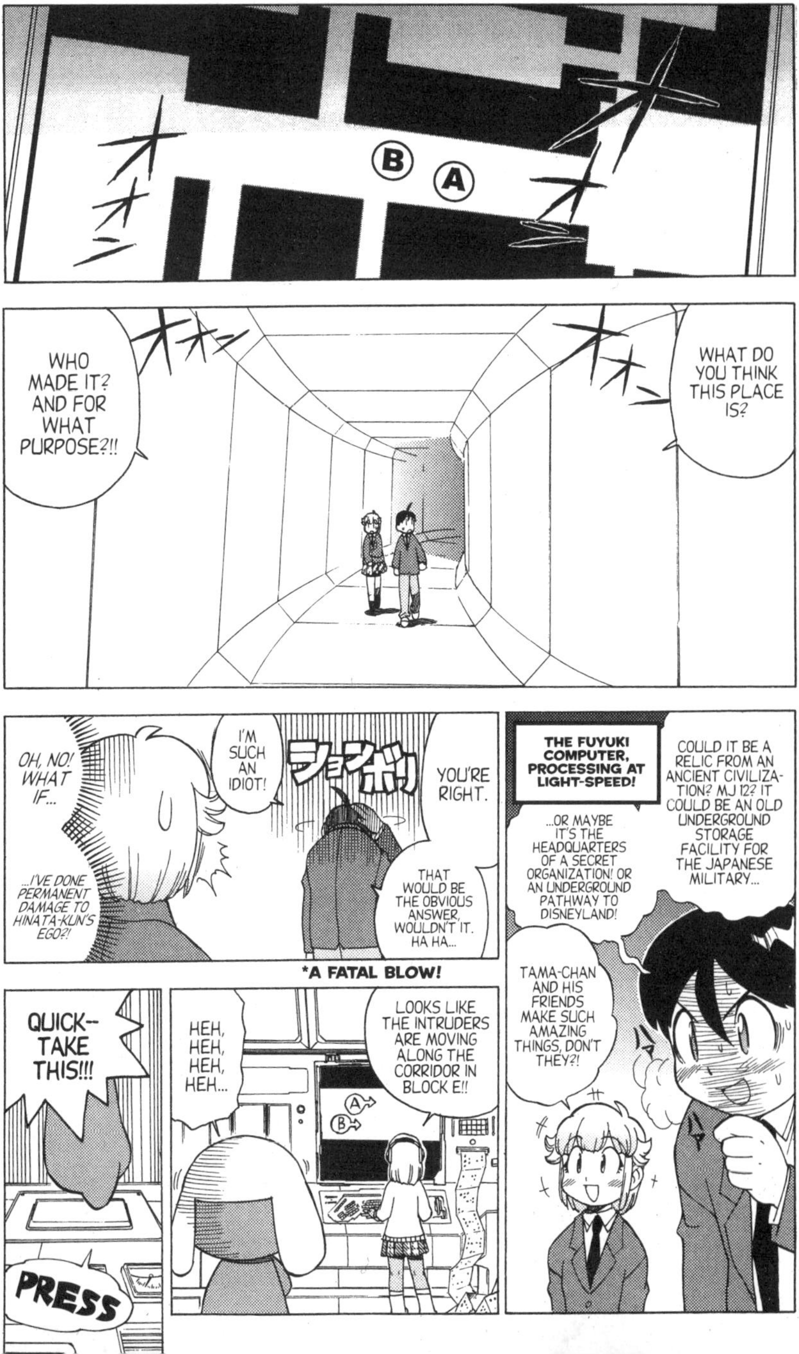
B
A
WHAT DO YOU THINK THIS PLACE IS?
WHO MADE IT? AND FOR WHAT PURPOSE?!!
THE FUYUKI COMPUTER, PROCESSING AT LIGHT-SPEED!
COULD IT BE A RELIC FROM AN ANCIENT CIVILIZATION? MJ 12? IT COULD BE AN OLD UNDERGROUND STORAGE FACILITY FOR THE JAPANESE MILITARY...
...OR MAYBE IT'S THE HEADQUARTERS OF A SECRET ORGANIZATION! OR AN UNDERGROUND PATHWAY TO DISNEYLAND!
TAMA-CHAN AND HIS FRIENDS MAKE SUCH AMAZING THINGS, DON'T THEY?!
YOU'RE RIGHT.
ションボリ
THAT WOULD BE THE OBVIOUS ANSWER, WOULDN'T IT. HA HA...
I'M SUCH AN IDIOT!
OH, NO! WHAT IF...
...I'VE DONE PERMANENT DAMAGE TO HINATA-KUN'S EGO?!
*A FATAL BLOW!
LOOKS LIKE THE INTRUDERS ARE MOVING ALONG THE CORRIDOR IN BLOCK E!!
HEH, HEH, HEH, HEH...
QUICK-- TAKE THIS!!!
PRESS

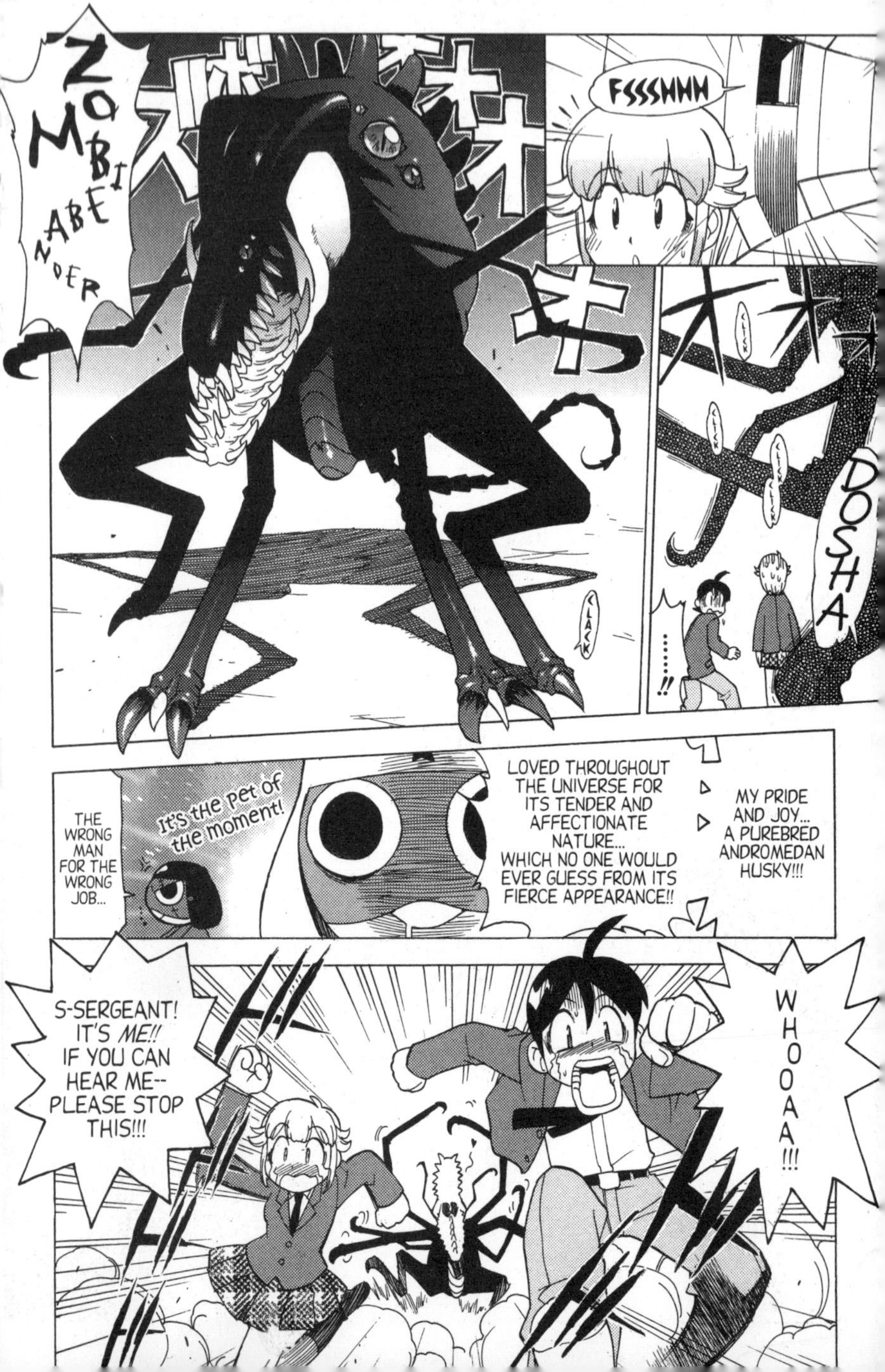
FSSSHHH
CLICK
CLICK
CLICK
CLICK
DOSHA
......!!
ZOMBIZABENDER
CLACK
MY PRIDE AND JOY... A PUREBRED ANDROMEDAN HUSKY!!!
LOVED THROUGHOUT THE UNIVERSE FOR ITS TENDER AND AFFECTIONATE NATURE... WHICH NO ONE WOULD EVER GUESS FROM ITS FIERCE APPEARANCE!!
It's the pet of the moment!
THE WRONG MAN FOR THE WRONG JOB...
WHOOAA!!!
S-SERGEANT! IT'S *ME!!* IF YOU CAN HEAR ME-- PLEASE STOP THIS!!!

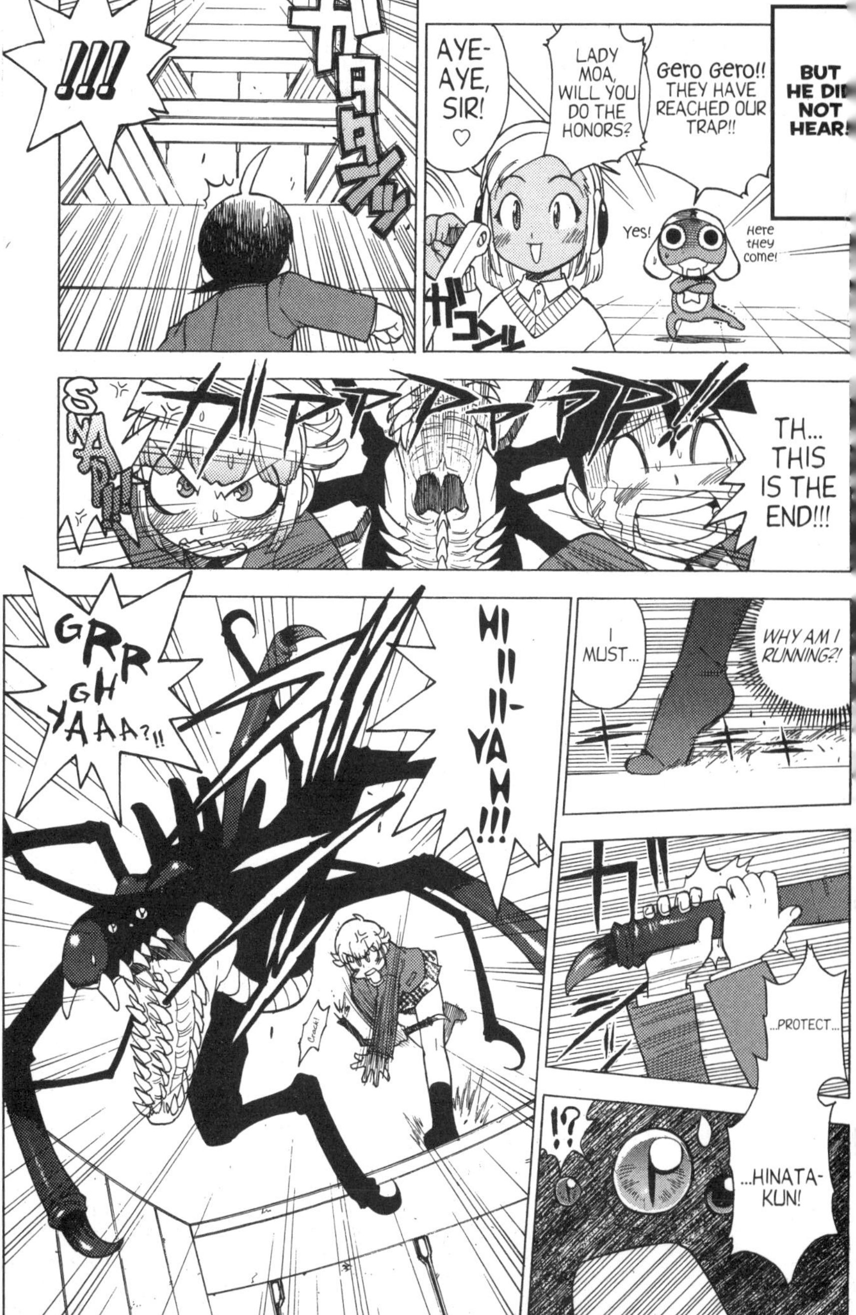

BUT HE DI NOT HEAR!
Gero Gero!! THEY HAVE REACHED OUR TRAP!!
LADY MOA, WILL YOU DO THE HONORS?
AYE-AYE, SIR! ♡
Here they come!
Yes!
!!!
TH... THIS IS THE END!!!
SNAP!!
WHY AM I RUNNING?!
I MUST...
...PROTECT...
!?
...HINATA-KUN!
HI-II-II-YAH!!!
GRRGH YAAA?!!
Crack!

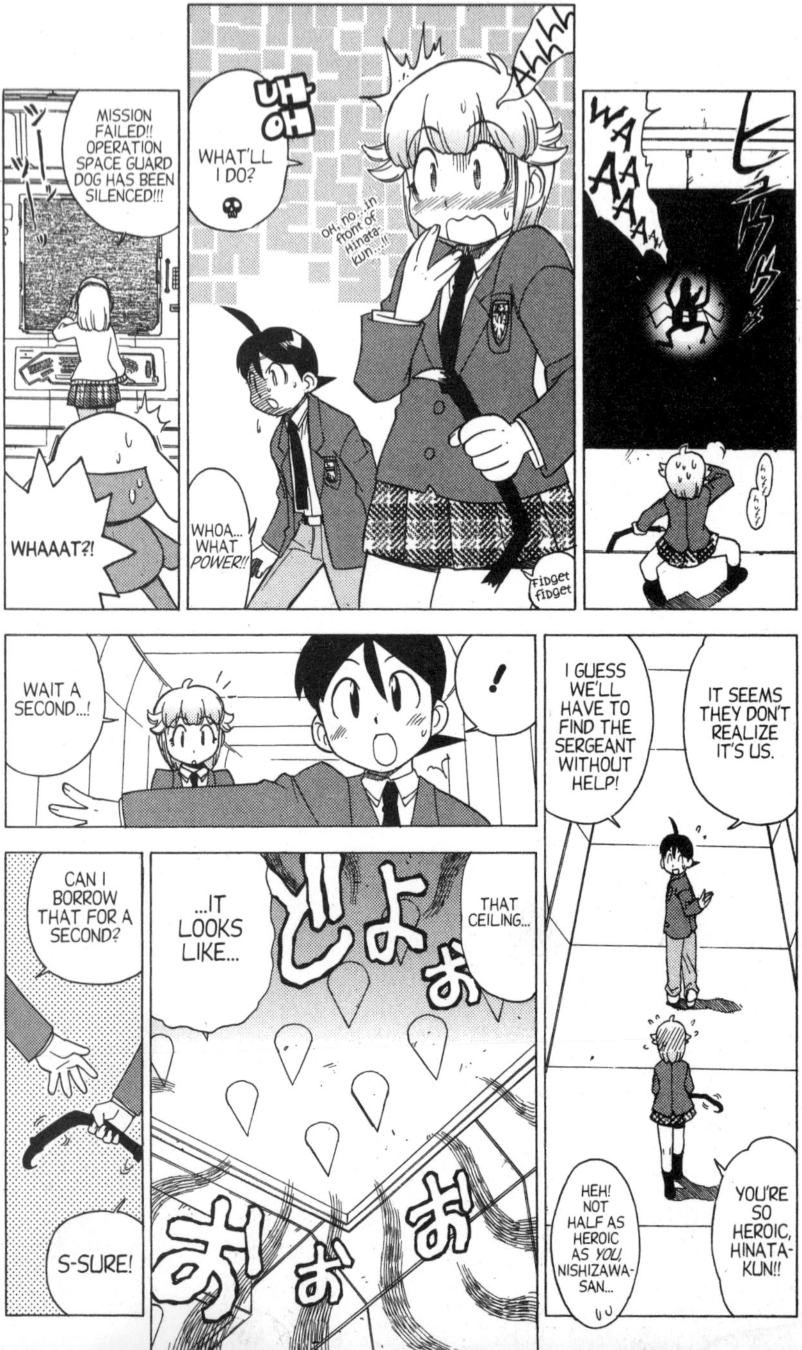
WAAAAAAAAH
Ahhhh
UH-OH
WHAT'LL I DO?
OH, no... in front of Hinata-kun...!!
WHOA... WHAT POWER!!
Fidget fidget
MISSION FAILED!! OPERATION SPACE GUARD DOG HAS BEEN SILENCED!!!
WHAAAT?!
IT SEEMS THEY DON'T REALIZE IT'S US.
I GUESS WE'LL HAVE TO FIND THE SERGEANT WITHOUT HELP!
YOU'RE SO HEROIC, HINATA-KUN!!
HEH! NOT HALF AS HEROIC AS YOU, NISHIZAWA-SAN...
!
WAIT A SECOND...!
THAT CEILING...
...IT LOOKS LIKE...
CAN I BORROW THAT FOR A SECOND?
S-SURE!

*THOOM!!!

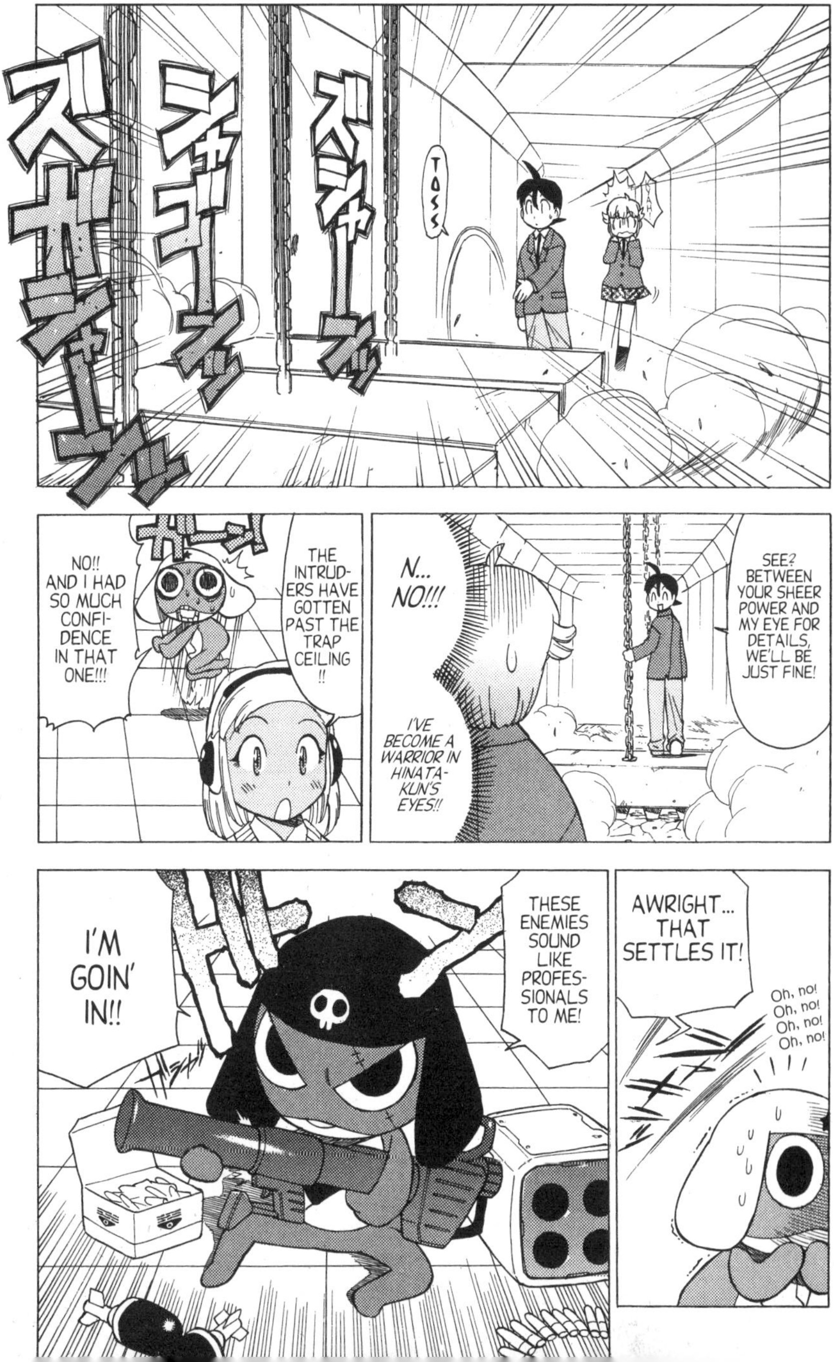
TOSS
SEE? BETWEEN YOUR SHEER POWER AND MY EYE FOR DETAILS, WE'LL BE JUST FINE!
N... NO!!!
I'VE BECOME A WARRIOR IN HINATA-KUN'S EYES!!
THE INTRUDERS HAVE GOTTEN PAST THE TRAP CEILING !!
NO!! AND I HAD SO MUCH CONFIDENCE IN THAT ONE!!!
AWRIGHT... THAT SETTLES IT!
Oh, no! Oh, no! Oh, no! Oh, no!
THESE ENEMIES SOUND LIKE PROFESSIONALS TO ME!
I'M GOIN' IN!!

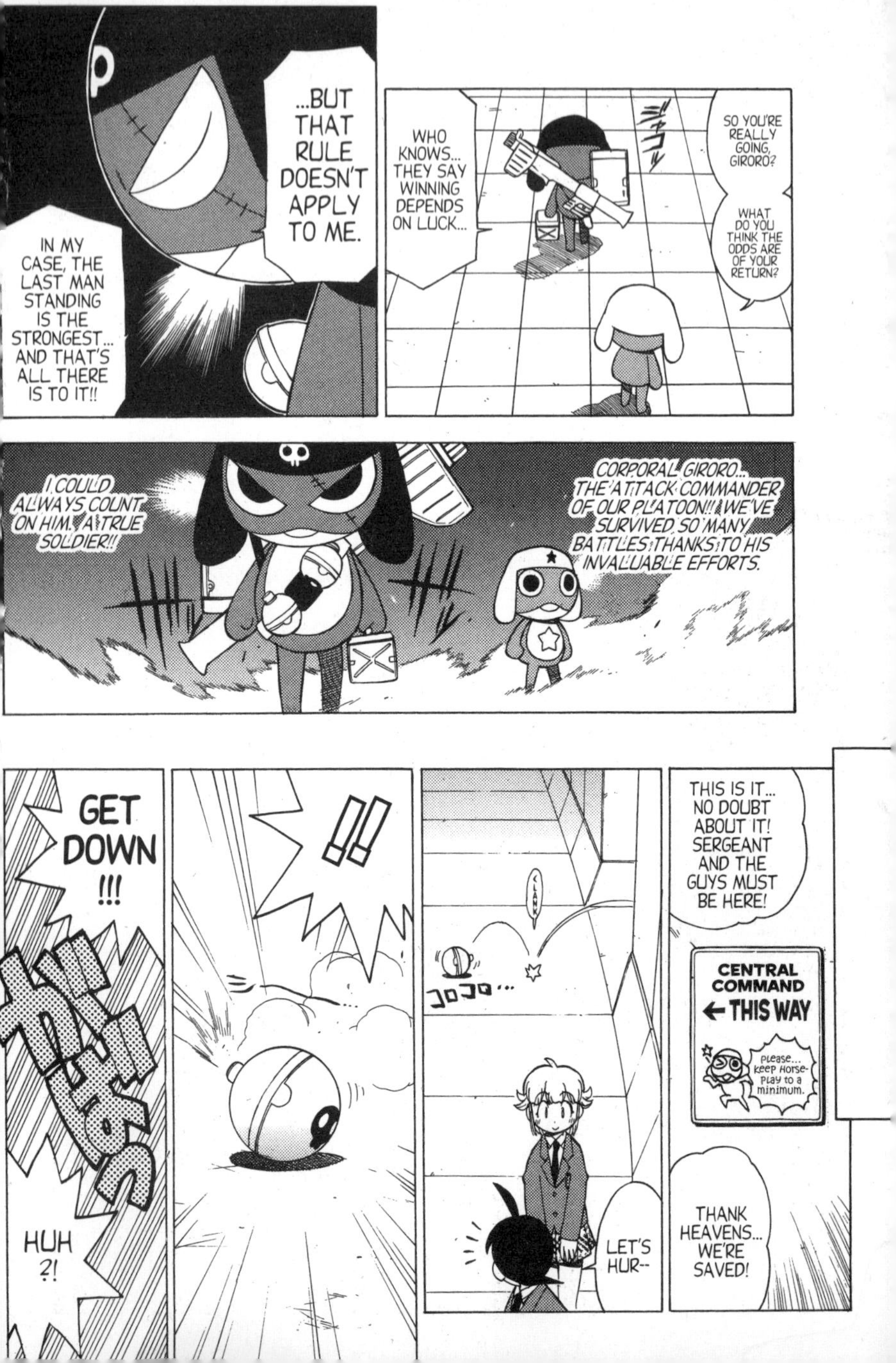
SO YOU'RE REALLY GOING, GIRORO?
WHAT DO YOU THINK THE ODDS ARE OF YOUR RETURN?
WHO KNOWS... THEY SAY WINNING DEPENDS ON LUCK...
...BUT THAT RULE DOESN'T APPLY TO ME.
IN MY CASE, THE LAST MAN STANDING IS THE STRONGEST... AND THAT'S ALL THERE IS TO IT!!
CORPORAL GIRORO... THE ATTACK COMMANDER OF OUR PLATOON!! WE'VE SURVIVED SO MANY BATTLES THANKS TO HIS INVALUABLE EFFORTS.
I COULD ALWAYS COUNT ON HIM. A TRUE SOLDIER!!
THIS IS IT... NO DOUBT ABOUT IT! SERGEANT AND THE GUYS MUST BE HERE!
CENTRAL COMMAND
← THIS WAY
Please... keep Horse-play to a minimum.
THANK HEAVENS... WE'RE SAVED!
LET'S HUR--
CLANK
コロコロ...
!!
GET DOWN !!!
HUH ?!

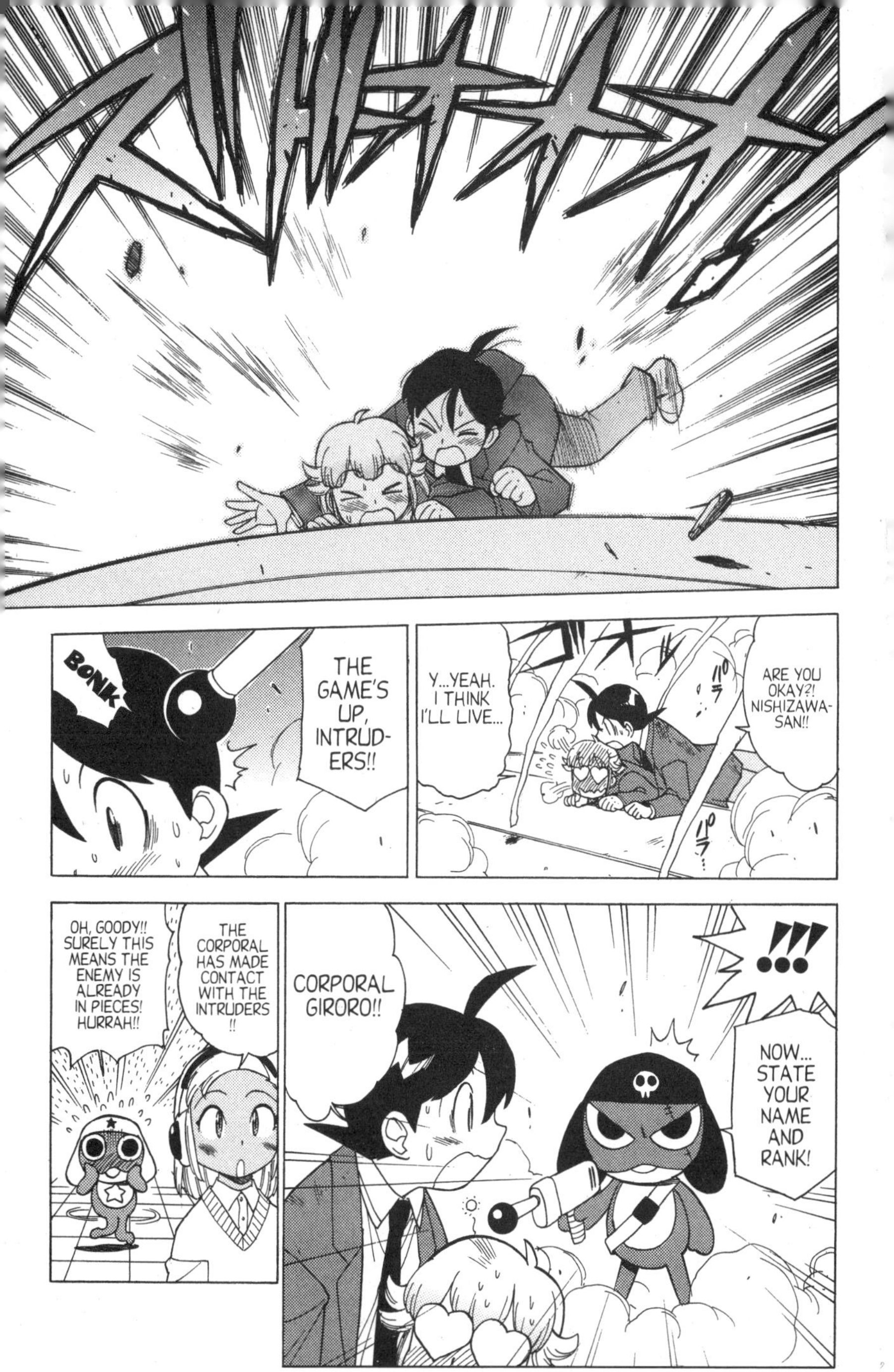
ARE YOU OKAY?! NISHIZAWA-SAN!!
Y...YEAH. I THINK I'LL LIVE...
BONK
THE GAME'S UP, INTRUD-ERS!!
!!!
NOW... STATE YOUR NAME AND RANK!
CORPORAL GIRORO!!
THE CORPORAL HAS MADE CONTACT WITH THE INTRUDERS!!
OH, GOODY!! SURELY THIS MEANS THE ENEMY IS ALREADY IN PIECES! HURRAH!!

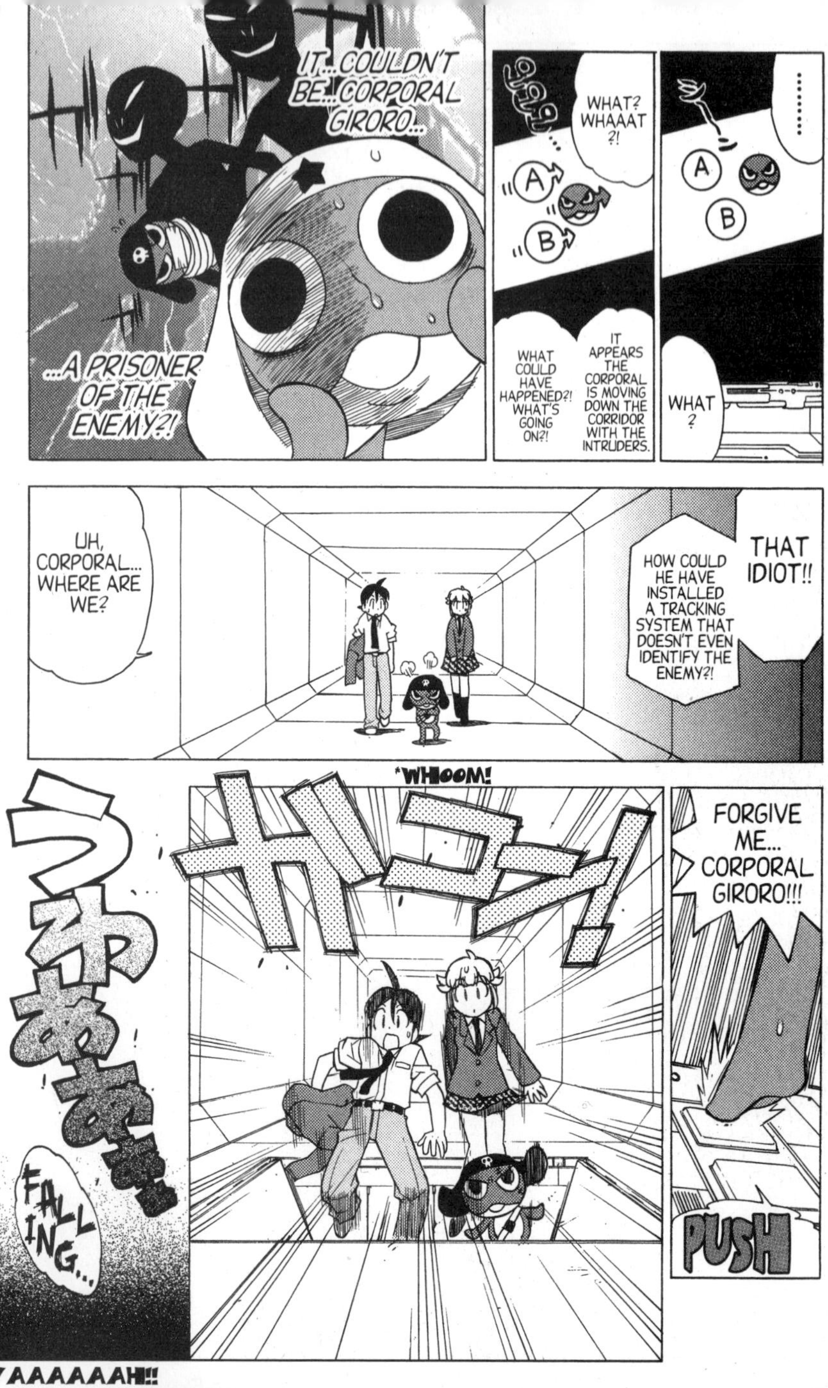
....
WHAT ?
WHAT? WHAAAT ?!
IT APPEARS THE CORPORAL IS MOVING DOWN THE CORRIDOR WITH THE INTRUDERS.
WHAT COULD HAVE HAPPENED?! WHAT'S GOING ON?!
IT... COULDN'T BE... CORPORAL GIRORO...
...A PRISONER OF THE ENEMY?!
THAT IDIOT!!
HOW COULD HE HAVE INSTALLED A TRACKING SYSTEM THAT DOESN'T EVEN IDENTIFY THE ENEMY?!
UH, CORPORAL... WHERE ARE WE?
FORGIVE ME... CORPORAL GIRORO!!!
PUSH
*WHOOM!
ガコン!
うわあああ
FALLING...
*YAAAAAAH!!

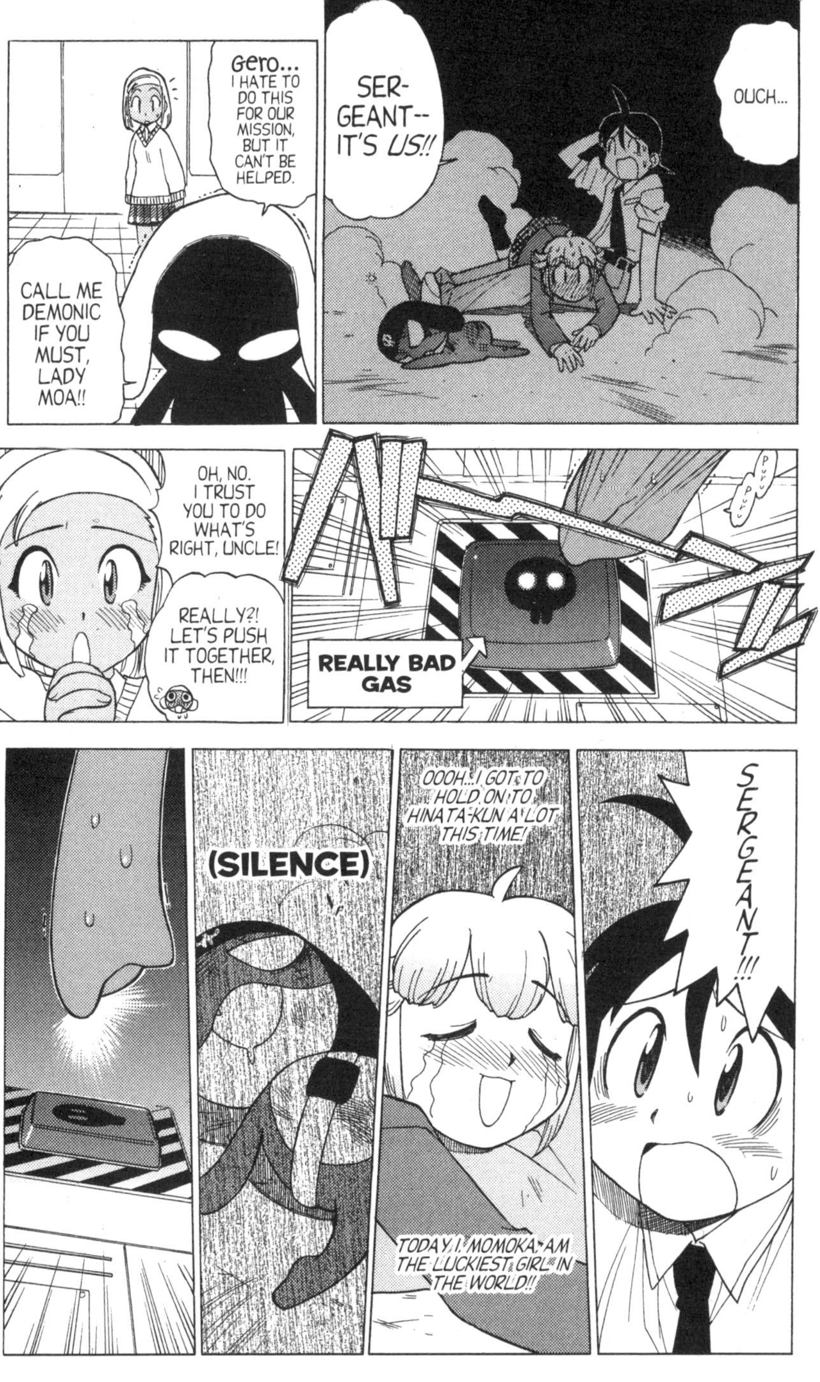
OUCH...
SER-GEANT-- IT'S *US!!*
Gero... I HATE TO DO THIS FOR OUR MISSION, BUT IT CAN'T BE HELPED.
CALL ME DEMONIC IF YOU MUST, LADY MOA!!
Puru Puru
REALLY BAD GAS
OH, NO. I TRUST YOU TO DO WHAT'S RIGHT, UNCLE!
REALLY?! LET'S PUSH IT TOGETHER, THEN!!!
SERGEANT!!!
OOOH...I GOT TO HOLD ON TO HINATA-KUN A LOT THIS TIME!
TODAY I, MOMOKA, AM THE LUCKIEST GIRL IN THE WORLD!!
(SILENCE)

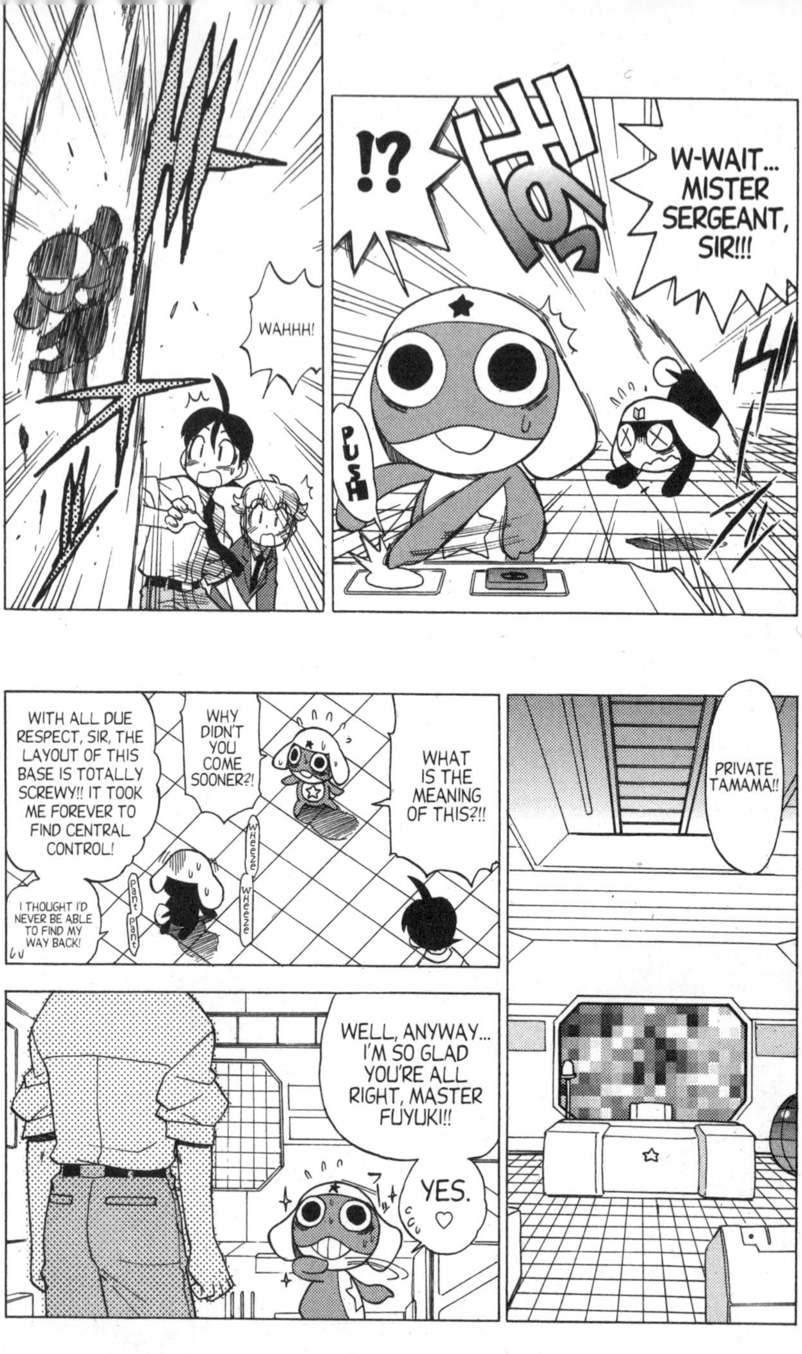

W-WAIT... MISTER SERGEANT, SIR!!!
!?
PUSH
WAHHH!
PRIVATE TAMAMA!!
WHAT IS THE MEANING OF THIS?!!
WHY DIDN'T YOU COME SOONER?!
Wheeze Wheeze
Pant Pant
WITH ALL DUE RESPECT, SIR, THE LAYOUT OF THIS BASE IS TOTALLY SCREWY!! IT TOOK ME FOREVER TO FIND CENTRAL CONTROL!
I THOUGHT I'D NEVER BE ABLE TO FIND MY WAY BACK!
WELL, ANYWAY... I'M SO GLAD YOU'RE ALL RIGHT, MASTER FUYUKI!!
YES. ♡

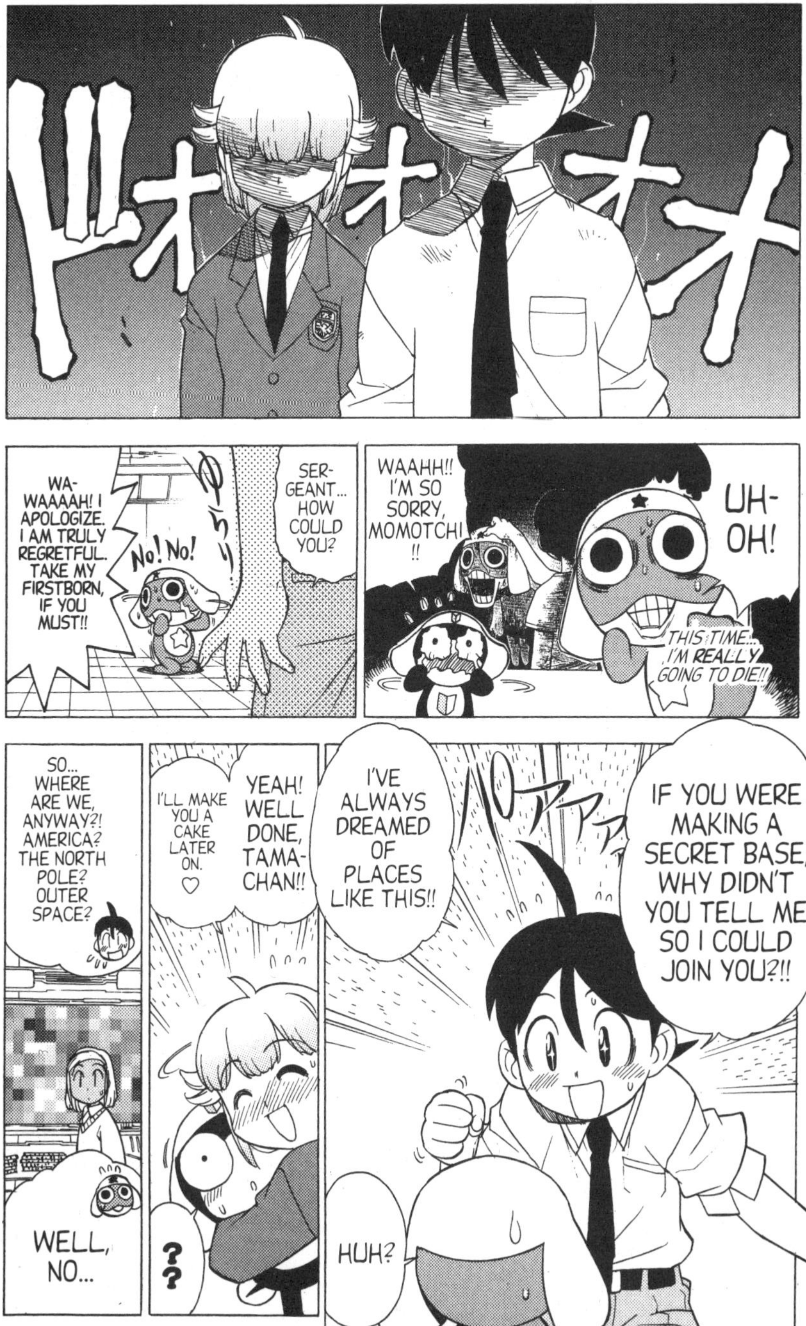
ドオオオオ
UH-OH!
WAAHH!! I'M SO SORRY, MOMOTCHI!!
THIS TIME... I'M REALLY GOING TO DIE!!
SER-GEANT... HOW COULD YOU?
ゆらり
WA-WAAAAH! I APOLOGIZE. I AM TRULY REGRETFUL. TAKE MY FIRSTBORN, IF YOU MUST!!
No! No!
IF YOU WERE MAKING A SECRET BASE, WHY DIDN'T YOU TELL ME SO I COULD JOIN YOU?!!
I'VE ALWAYS DREAMED OF PLACES LIKE THIS!!
HUH?
YEAH! WELL DONE, TAMA-CHAN!!
I'LL MAKE YOU A CAKE LATER ON. ♡
??
SO... WHERE ARE WE, ANYWAY?! AMERICA? THE NORTH POLE? OUTER SPACE?
WELL, NO...

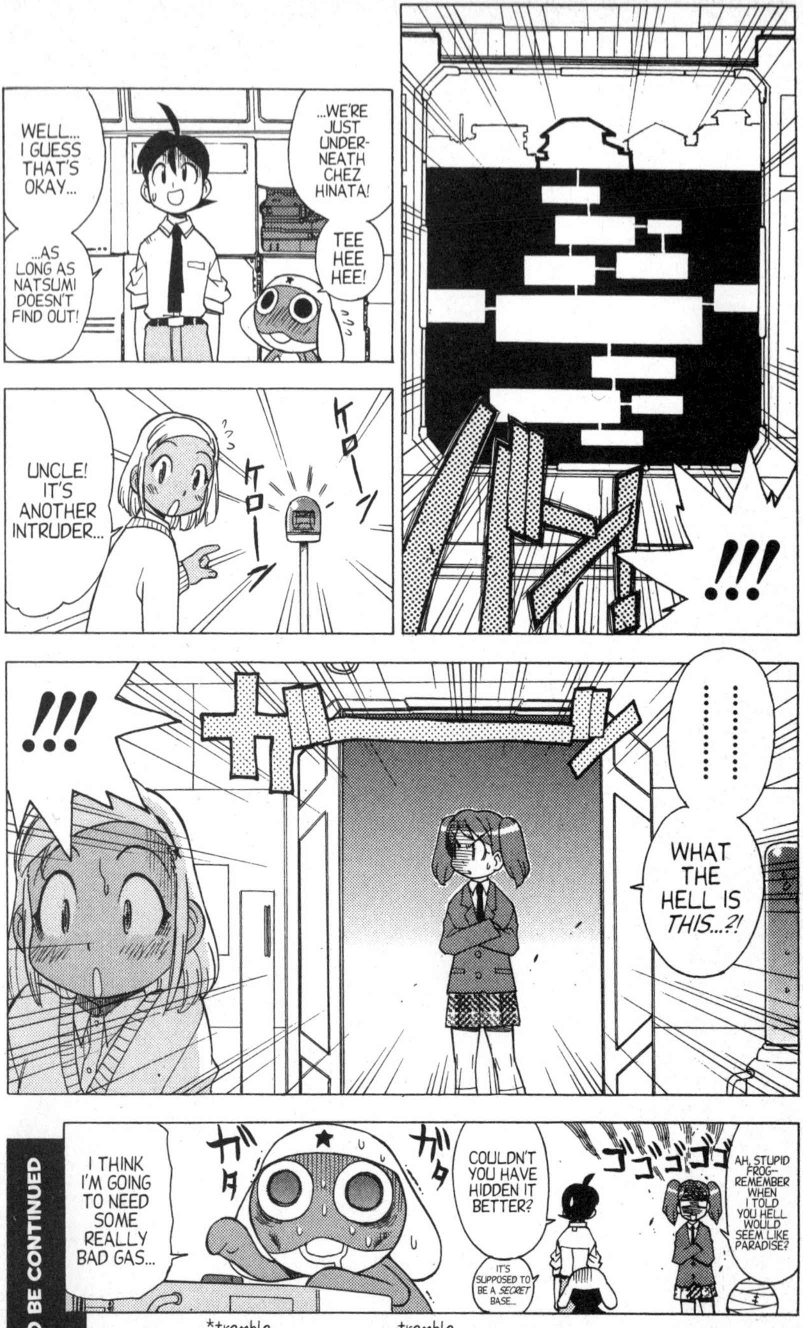
!!!
...WE'RE JUST UNDERNEATH CHEZ HINATA!
WELL... I GUESS THAT'S OKAY...
TEE HEE HEE!
...AS LONG AS NATSUMI DOESN'T FIND OUT!
ケローン
ケローン
UNCLE! IT'S ANOTHER INTRUDER...
......
WHAT THE HELL IS *THIS...?!*
!!!
ゴゴゴゴゴ
AH, STUPID FROG-- REMEMBER WHEN I TOLD YOU HELL WOULD SEEM LIKE PARADISE?
COULDN'T YOU HAVE HIDDEN IT BETTER?
IT'S SUPPOSED TO BE A *SECRET* BASE...
ガタ
I THINK I'M GOING TO NEED SOME REALLY BAD GAS...
ガタ
TO BE CONTINUED

*tremble tremble

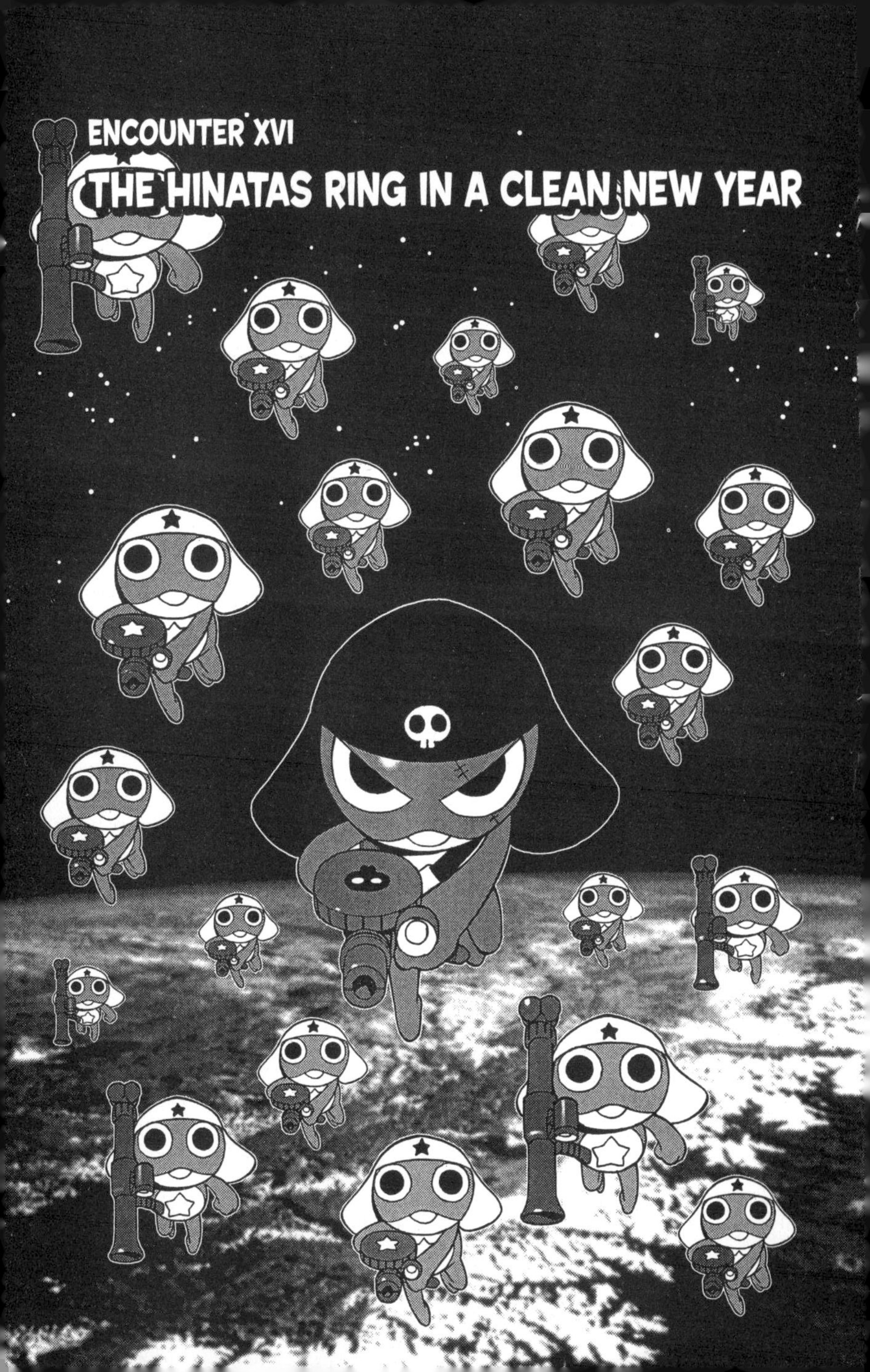
ENCOUNTER XVI
THE HINATAS RING IN A CLEAN NEW YEAR

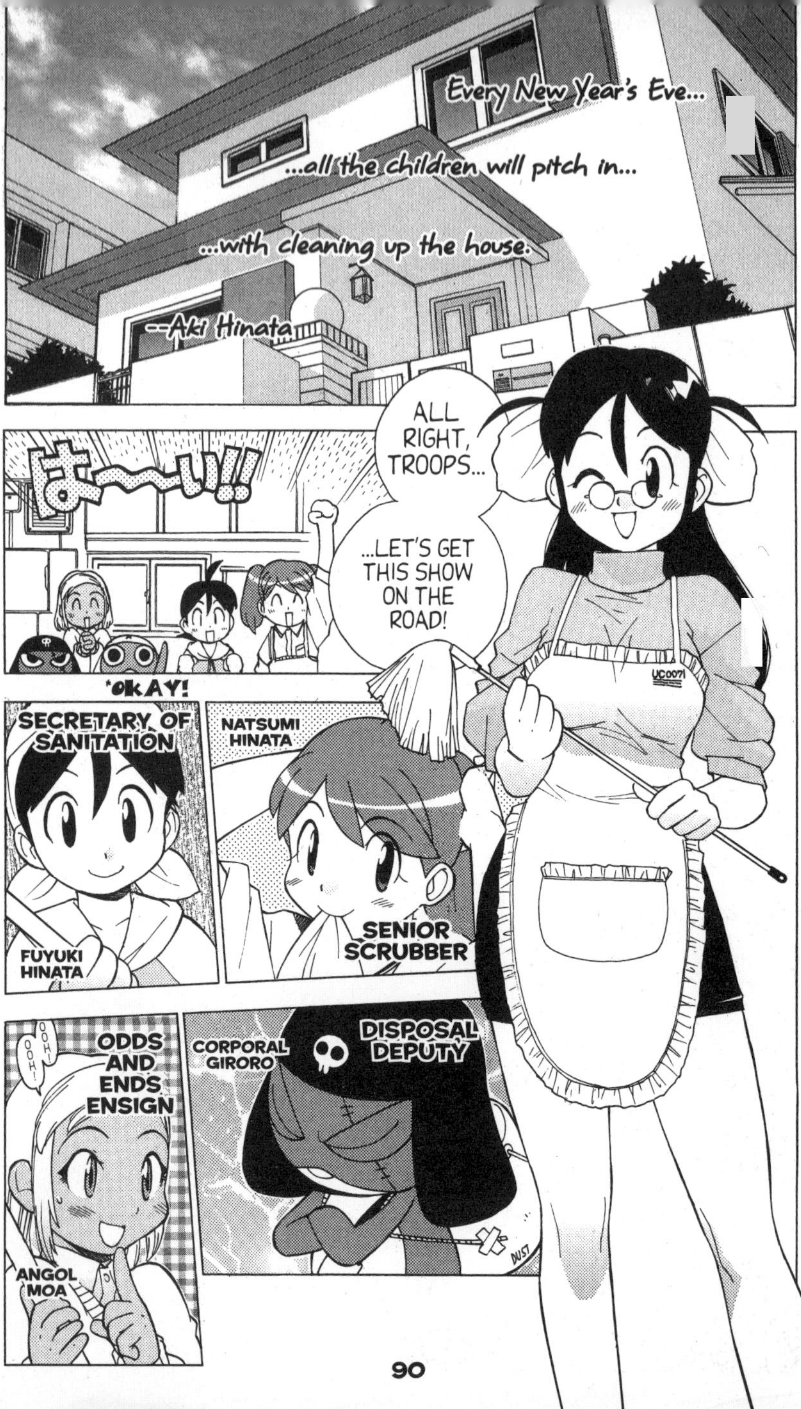
Every New Year's Eve...
...all the children will pitch in...
...with cleaning up the house.
--Aki Hinata
ALL RIGHT, TROOPS...
...LET'S GET THIS SHOW ON THE ROAD!
はーーい!!
*OKAY!
NATSUMI HINATA
SENIOR SCRUBBER
SECRETARY OF SANITATION
FUYUKI HINATA
DISPOSAL DEPUTY
CORPORAL GIRORO
DUST
ODDS AND ENDS ENSIGN
OOH! OOH!
ANGOL MOA

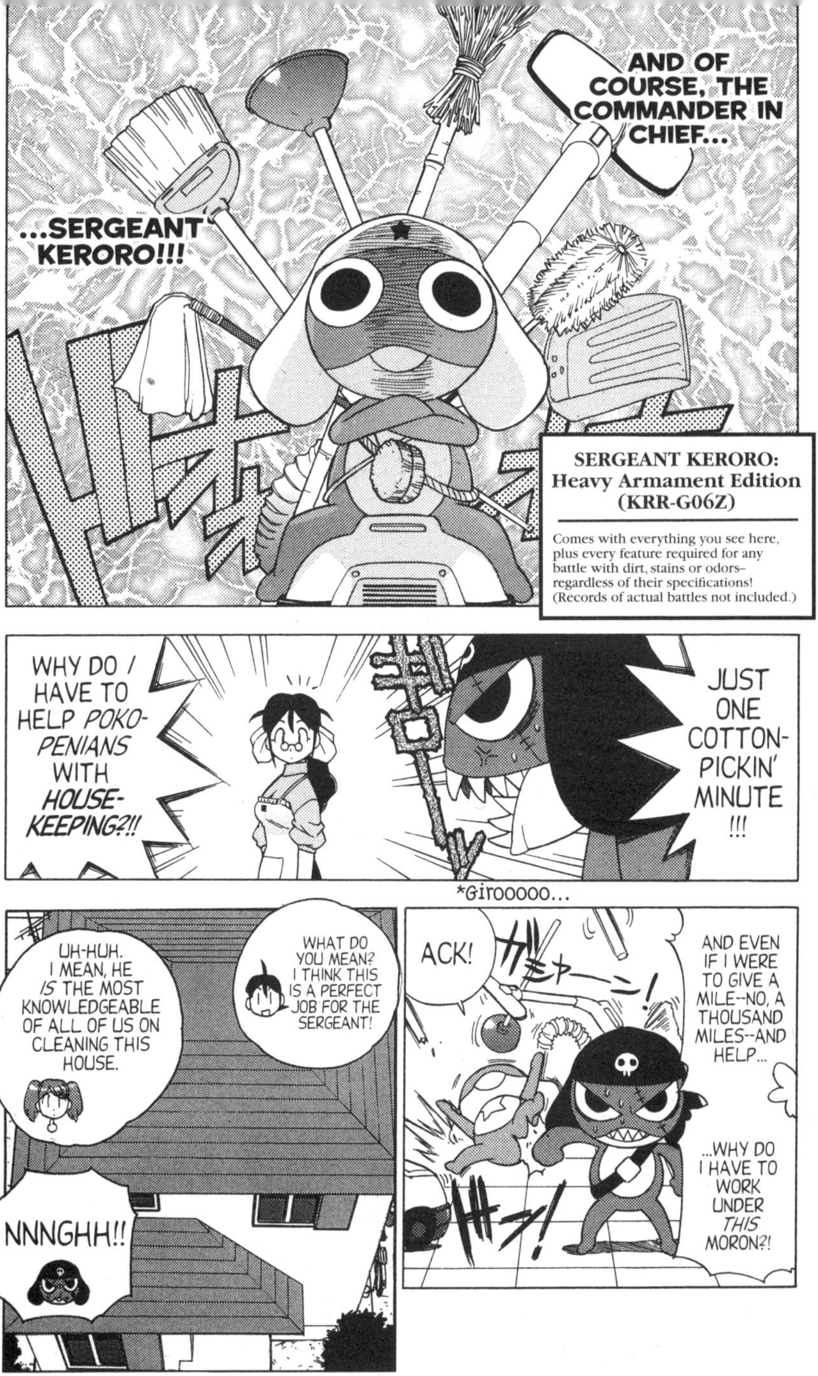
AND OF COURSE, THE COMMANDER IN CHIEF...
...SERGEANT KERORO!!!
SERGEANT KERORO: Heavy Armament Edition (KRR-G06Z)
Comes with everything you see here, plus every feature required for any battle with dirt, stains or odors– regardless of their specifications! (Records of actual battles not included.)
JUST ONE COTTON-PICKIN' MINUTE!!!
WHY DO I HAVE TO HELP POKOPENIANS WITH HOUSEKEEPING?!!
*Giroooooo...
AND EVEN IF I WERE TO GIVE A MILE--NO, A THOUSAND MILES--AND HELP...
ACK!
...WHY DO I HAVE TO WORK UNDER THIS MORON?!
WHAT DO YOU MEAN? I THINK THIS IS A PERFECT JOB FOR THE SERGEANT!
UH-HUH. I MEAN, HE IS THE MOST KNOWLEDGEABLE OF ALL OF US ON CLEANING THIS HOUSE.
NNNGHH!!

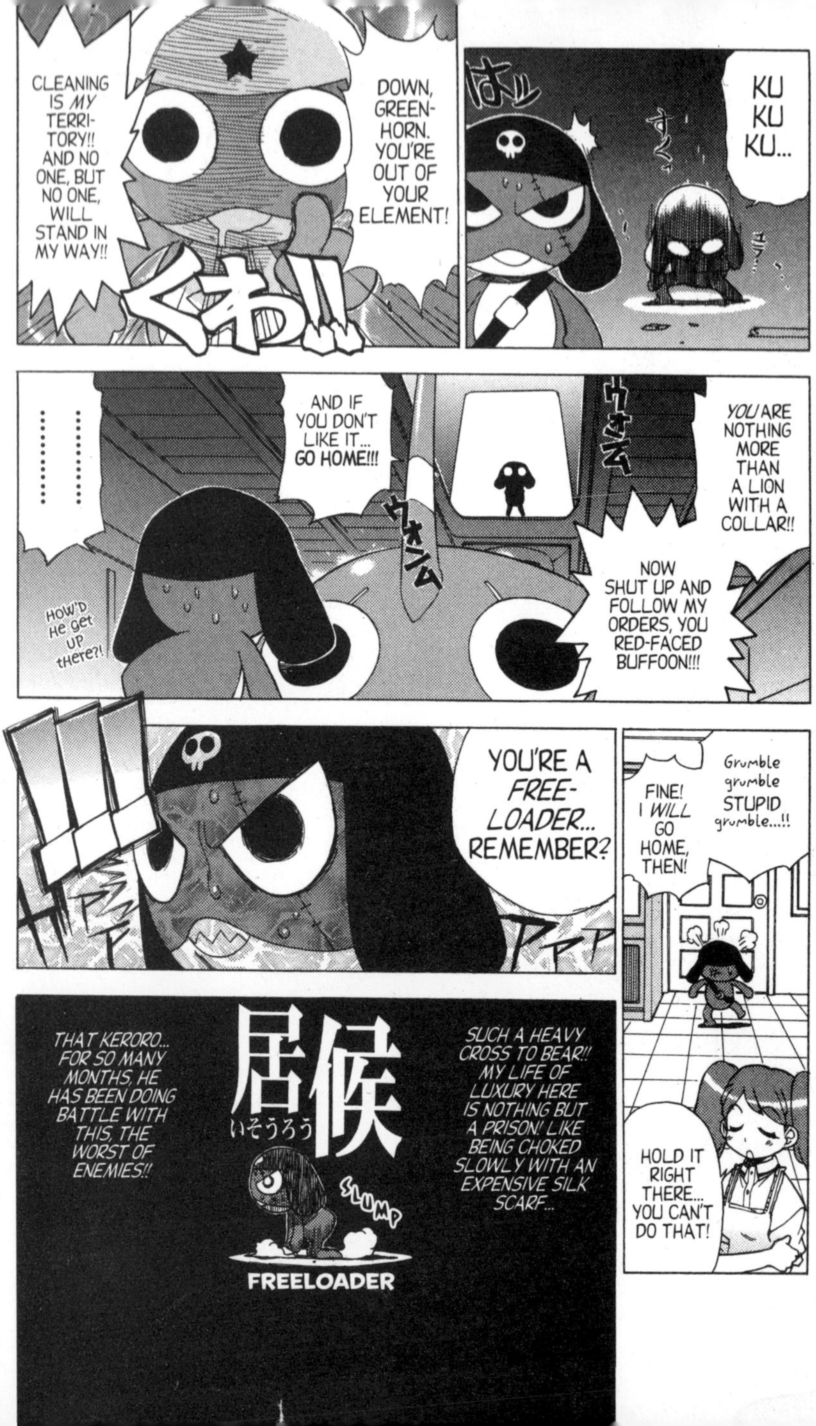
KU KU KU...
はッ
DOWN, GREEN-HORN. YOU'RE OUT OF YOUR ELEMENT!
CLEANING IS *MY* TERRI-TORY!! AND NO ONE, BUT NO ONE, WILL STAND IN MY WAY!!
くわ!!
YOU ARE NOTHING MORE THAN A LION WITH A COLLAR!!
NOW SHUT UP AND FOLLOW MY ORDERS, YOU RED-FACED BUFFOON!!!
AND IF YOU DON'T LIKE IT... **GO HOME!!!**
......
HOW'D He get UP there?!
Grumble grumble STUPID grumble...!!
FINE! I *WILL* GO HOME, THEN!
YOU'RE A *FREE-LOADER*... REMEMBER?
HOLD IT RIGHT THERE... YOU CAN'T DO THAT!
SUCH A HEAVY CROSS TO BEAR!! MY LIFE OF LUXURY HERE IS NOTHING BUT A PRISON! LIKE BEING CHOKED SLOWLY WITH AN EXPENSIVE SILK SCARF...
居候
いそうろう
SLUMP
FREELOADER
THAT KERORO... FOR SO MANY MONTHS, HE HAS BEEN DOING BATTLE WITH THIS, THE WORST OF ENEMIES!!

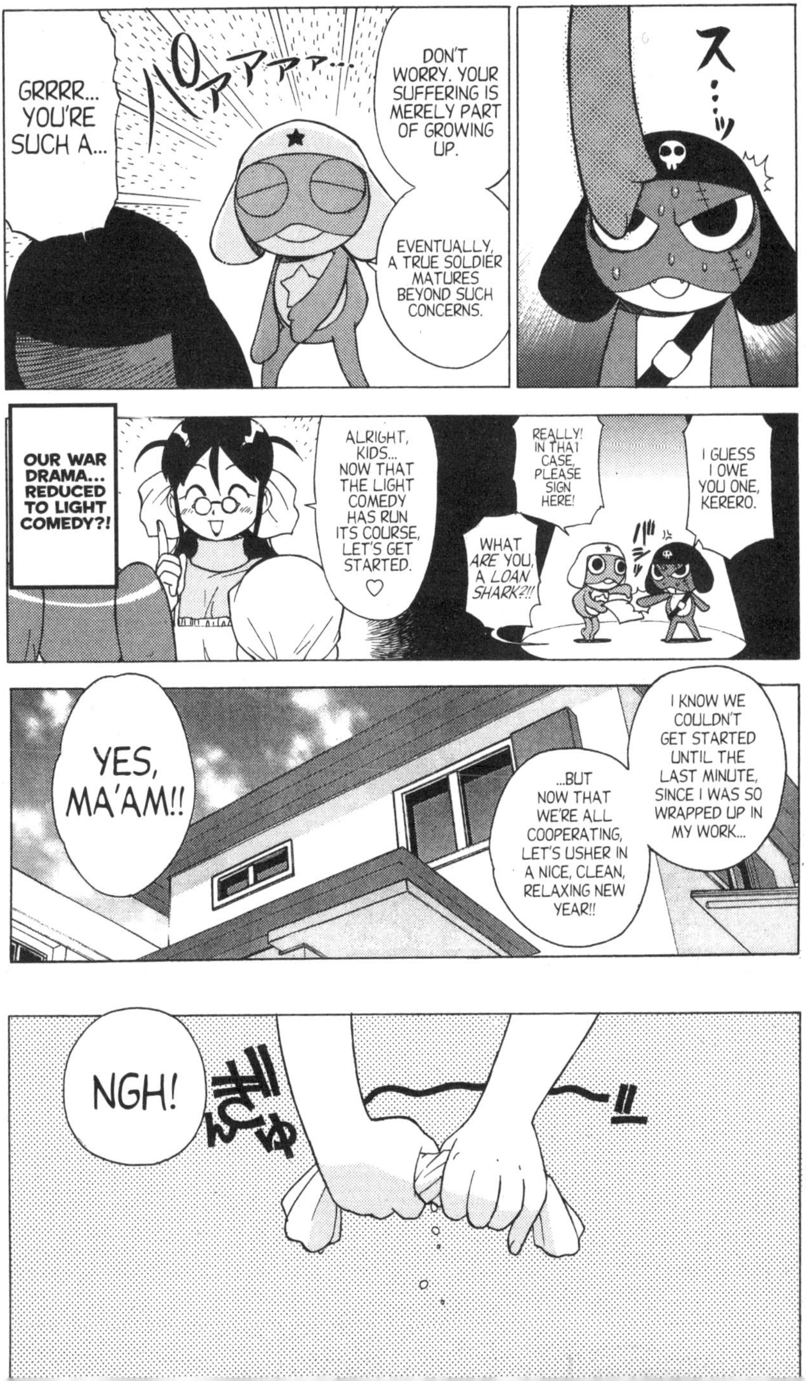
ス…ッ
DON'T WORRY. YOUR SUFFERING IS MERELY PART OF GROWING UP.
EVENTUALLY, A TRUE SOLDIER MATURES BEYOND SUCH CONCERNS.
GRRRR... YOU'RE SUCH A...
I GUESS I OWE YOU ONE, KERERO.
REALLY! IN THAT CASE, PLEASE SIGN HERE!
WHAT *ARE* YOU, A *LOAN SHARK?!!*
ALRIGHT, KIDS... NOW THAT THE LIGHT COMEDY HAS RUN ITS COURSE, LET'S GET STARTED. ♡
OUR WAR DRAMA... REDUCED TO LIGHT COMEDY?!
I KNOW WE COULDN'T GET STARTED UNTIL THE LAST MINUTE, SINCE I WAS SO WRAPPED UP IN MY WORK...
...BUT NOW THAT WE'RE ALL COOPERATING, LET'S USHER IN A NICE, CLEAN, RELAXING NEW YEAR!!
YES, MA'AM!!
NGH!

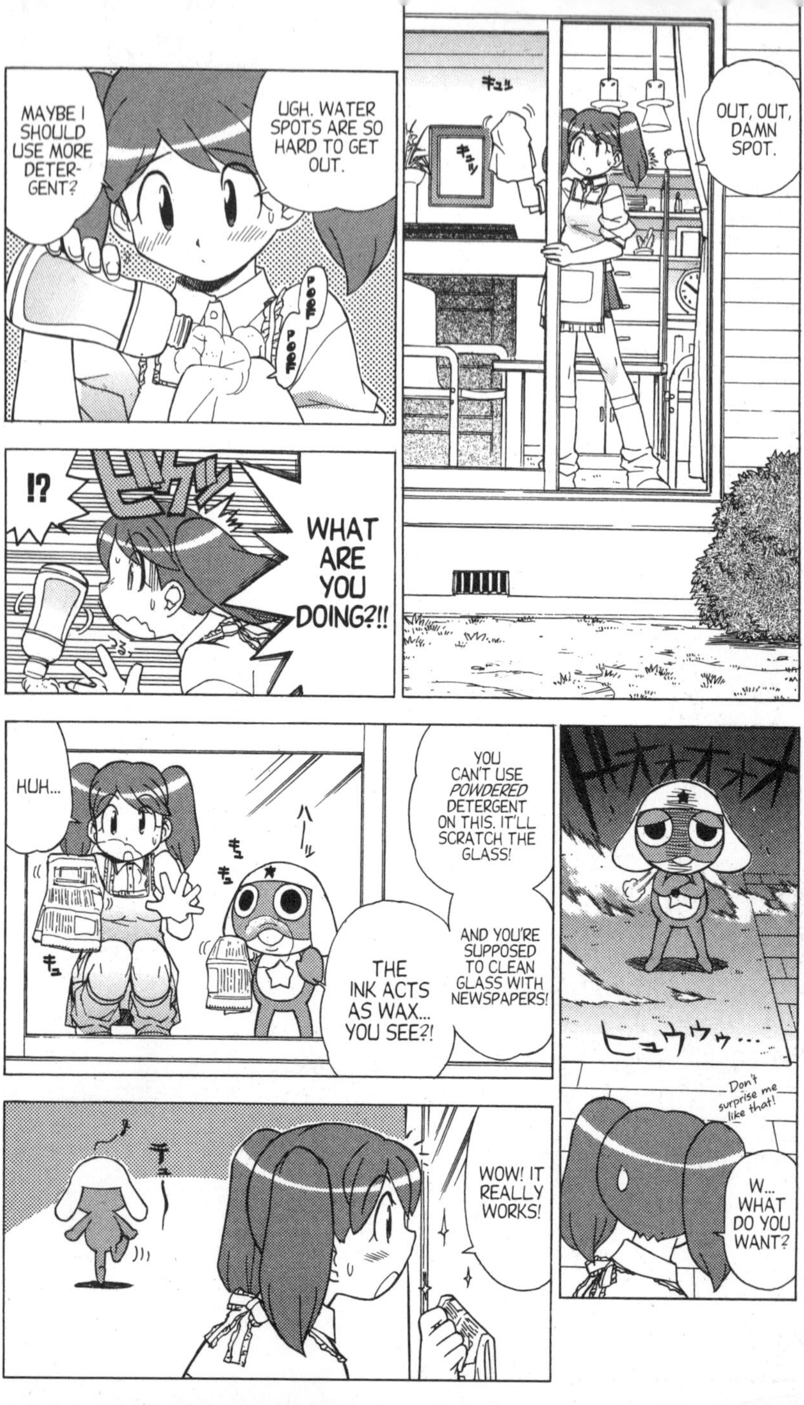
OUT, OUT, DAMN SPOT.
UGH. WATER SPOTS ARE SO HARD TO GET OUT.
MAYBE I SHOULD USE MORE DETER-GENT?
POOF
POOF
!?
WHAT ARE YOU DOING?!!
ヒュウウゥ…
Don't surprise me like that!
W... WHAT DO YOU WANT?
YOU CAN'T USE *POWDERED* DETERGENT ON THIS. IT'LL SCRATCH THE GLASS!
AND YOU'RE SUPPOSED TO CLEAN GLASS WITH NEWSPAPERS!
THE INK ACTS AS WAX... YOU SEE?!
HUH...
WOW! IT REALLY WORKS!

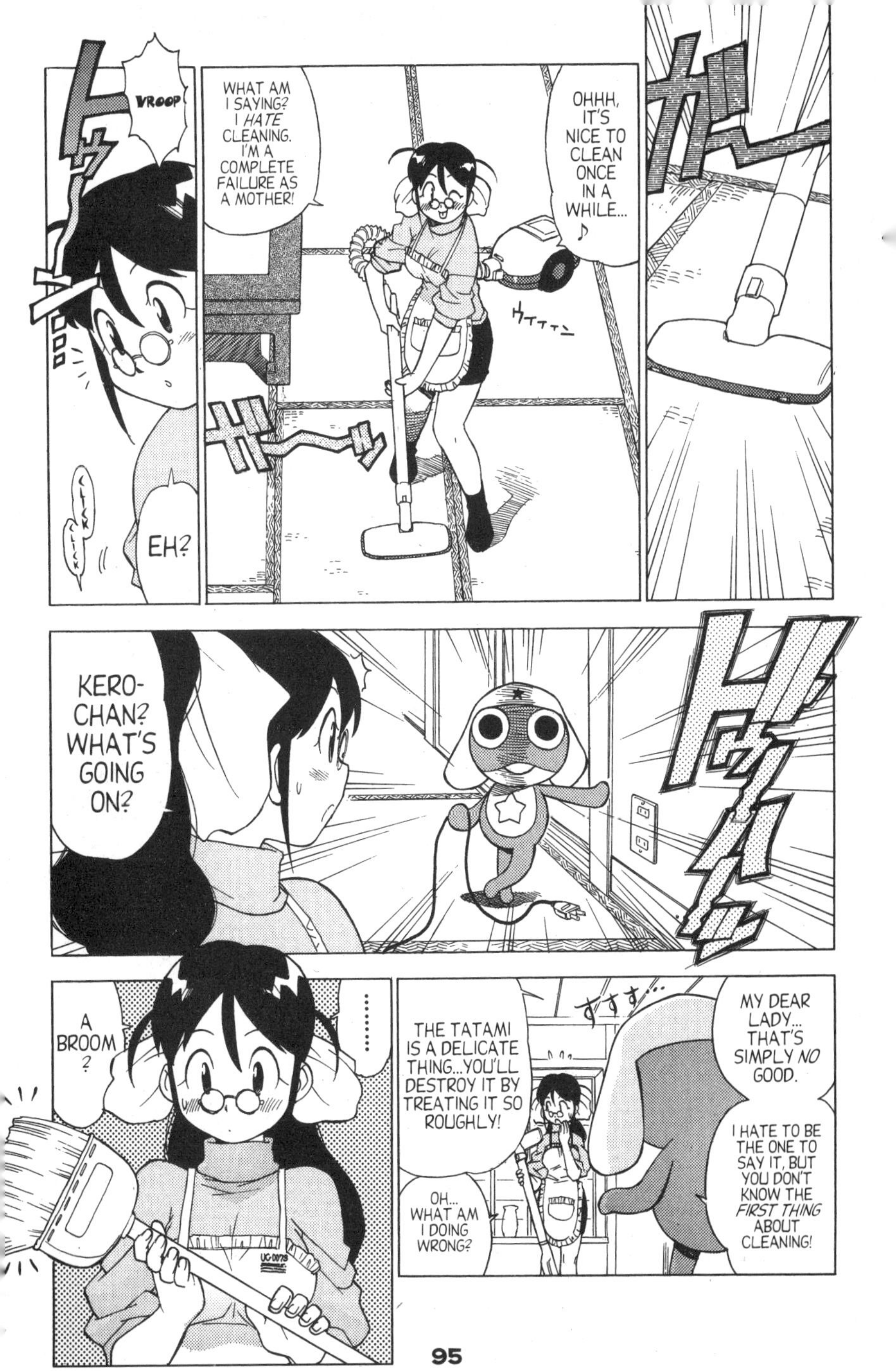
OHHH, IT'S NICE TO CLEAN ONCE IN A WHILE... ♪
WHAT AM I SAYING? I *HATE* CLEANING. I'M A COMPLETE FAILURE AS A MOTHER!
VROOP
CLICK CLICK
EH?
KERO-CHAN? WHAT'S GOING ON?
すすす…
MY DEAR LADY... THAT'S SIMPLY *NO* GOOD.
I HATE TO BE THE ONE TO SAY IT, BUT YOU DON'T KNOW THE *FIRST THING* ABOUT CLEANING!
THE TATAMI IS A DELICATE THING...YOU'LL DESTROY IT BY TREATING IT SO ROUGHLY!
OH... WHAT AM I DOING WRONG?
......
A BROOM?

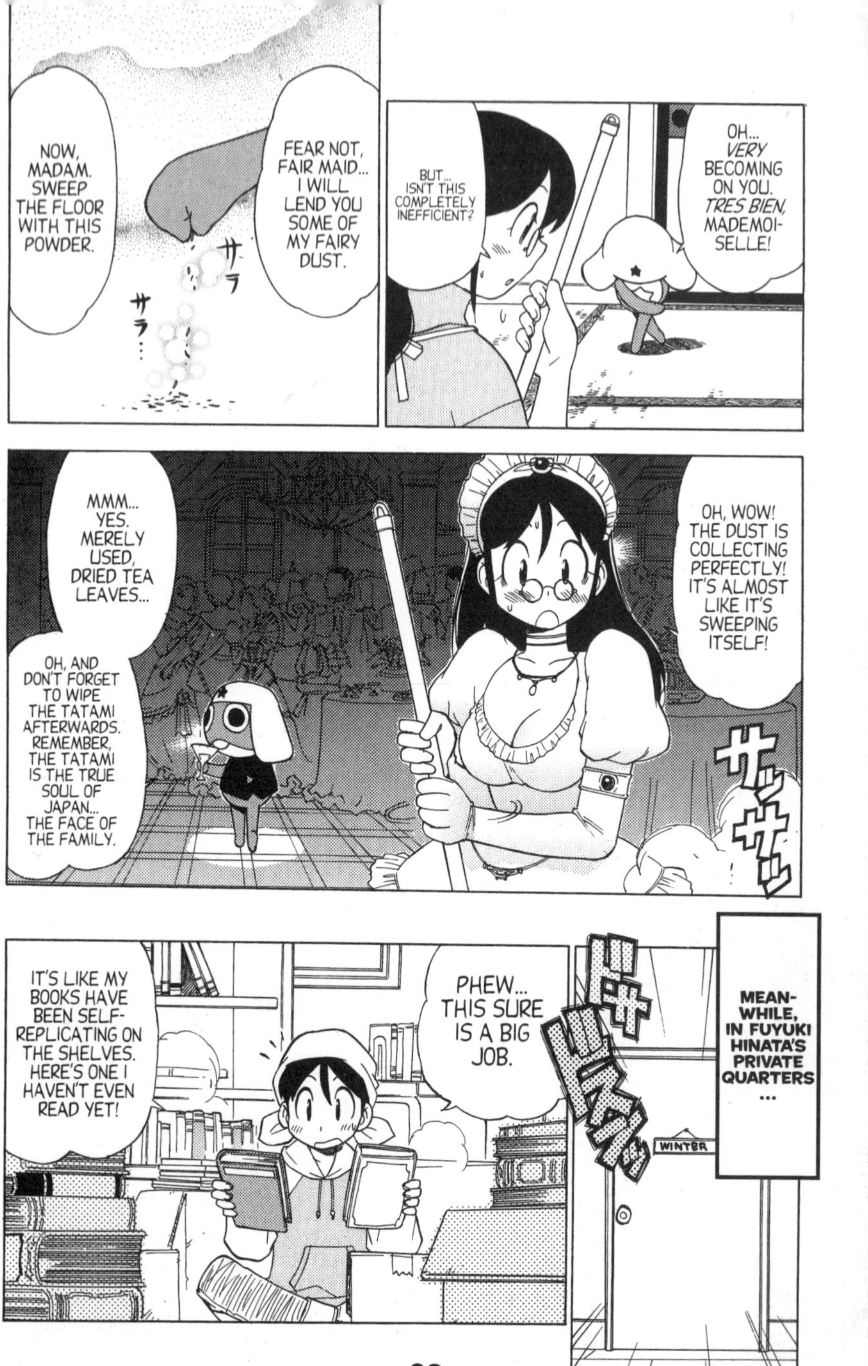
OH... *VERY* BECOMING ON YOU. *TRES BIEN,* MADEMOISELLE!
BUT... ISN'T THIS COMPLETELY INEFFICIENT?
FEAR NOT, FAIR MAID... I WILL LEND YOU SOME OF MY FAIRY DUST.
サラ
サラ…
NOW, MADAM. SWEEP THE FLOOR WITH THIS POWDER.
OH, WOW! THE DUST IS COLLECTING PERFECTLY! IT'S ALMOST LIKE IT'S SWEEPING ITSELF!
サッサッ
MMM... YES. MERELY USED, DRIED TEA LEAVES...
OH, AND DON'T FORGET TO WIPE THE TATAMI AFTERWARDS. REMEMBER, THE TATAMI IS THE TRUE SOUL OF JAPAN... THE FACE OF THE FAMILY.
MEANWHILE, IN FUYUKI HINATA'S PRIVATE QUARTERS...
WINTER
PHEW... THIS SURE IS A BIG JOB.
IT'S LIKE MY BOOKS HAVE BEEN SELF-REPLICATING ON THE SHELVES. HERE'S ONE I HAVEN'T EVEN READ YET!

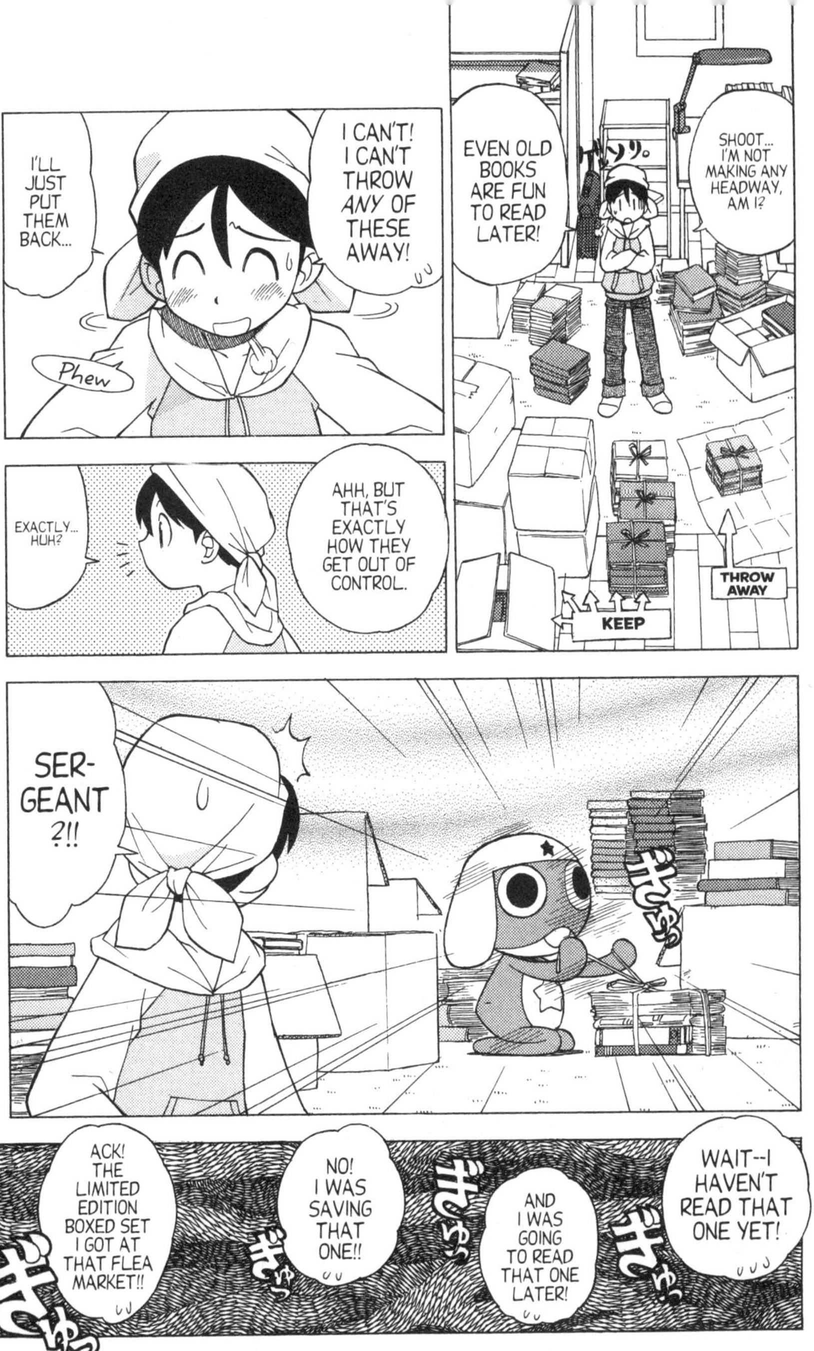

SHOOT... I'M NOT MAKING ANY HEADWAY, AM I!?
EVEN OLD BOOKS ARE FUN TO READ LATER!
THROW AWAY
KEEP
I CAN'T! I CAN'T THROW *ANY* OF THESE AWAY!
I'LL JUST PUT THEM BACK...
Phew
AHH, BUT THAT'S EXACTLY HOW THEY GET OUT OF CONTROL.
EXACTLY... HUH?
ぎゅっ
SER-GEANT ?!!
WAIT--I HAVEN'T READ THAT ONE YET!
ぎゅっ
AND I WAS GOING TO READ THAT ONE LATER!
ぎゅっ
NO! I WAS SAVING THAT ONE!!
ぎゅっ
ACK! THE LIMITED EDITION BOXED SET I GOT AT THAT FLEA MARKET!!
ぎゅっ

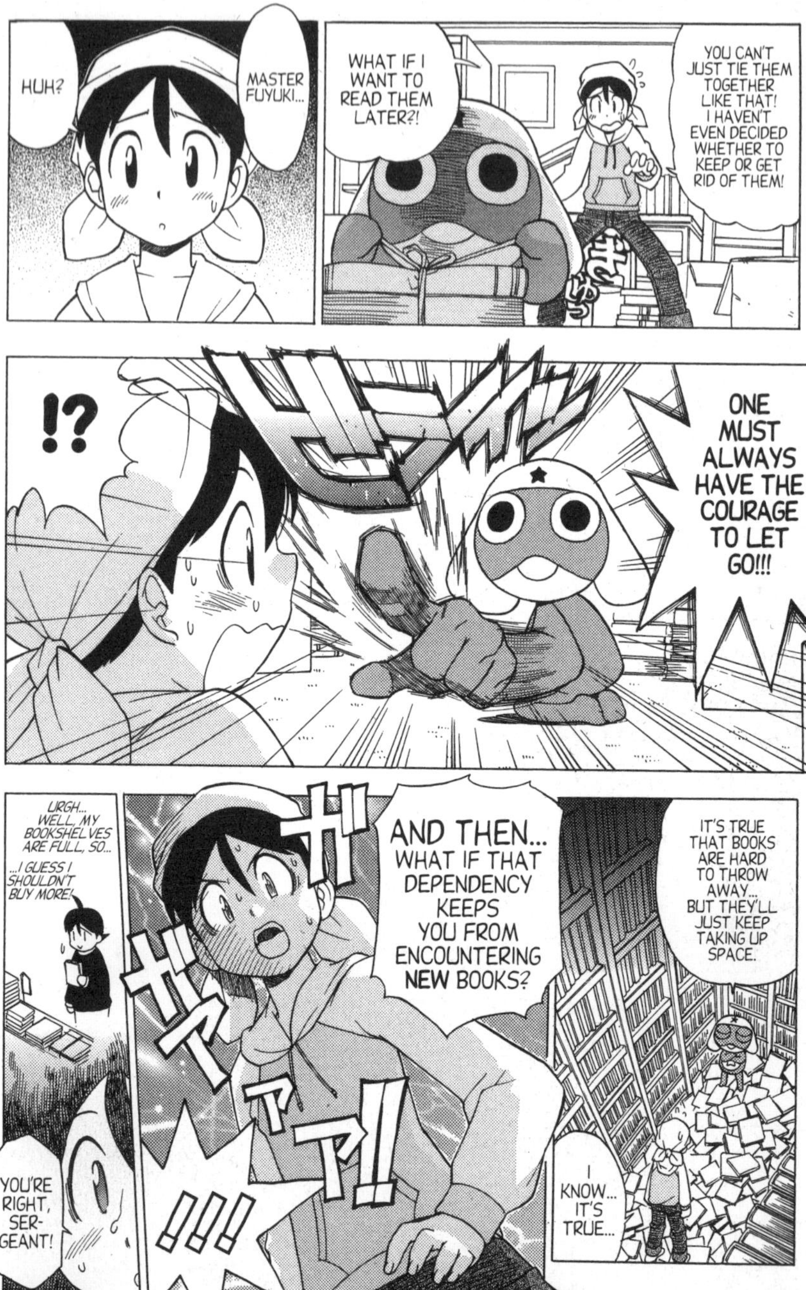
YOU CAN'T JUST TIE THEM TOGETHER LIKE THAT! I HAVEN'T EVEN DECIDED WHETHER TO KEEP OR GET RID OF THEM!
WHAT IF I WANT TO READ THEM LATER?!
MASTER FUYUKI...
HUH?
ONE MUST ALWAYS HAVE THE COURAGE TO LET GO!!!
!?
IT'S TRUE THAT BOOKS ARE HARD TO THROW AWAY... BUT THEY'LL JUST KEEP TAKING UP SPACE.
I KNOW... IT'S TRUE...
AND THEN... WHAT IF THAT DEPENDENCY KEEPS YOU FROM ENCOUNTERING NEW BOOKS?
!!!
URGH... WELL, MY BOOKSHELVES ARE FULL, SO...
...I GUESS I SHOULDN'T BUY MORE!
YOU'RE RIGHT, SERGEANT!

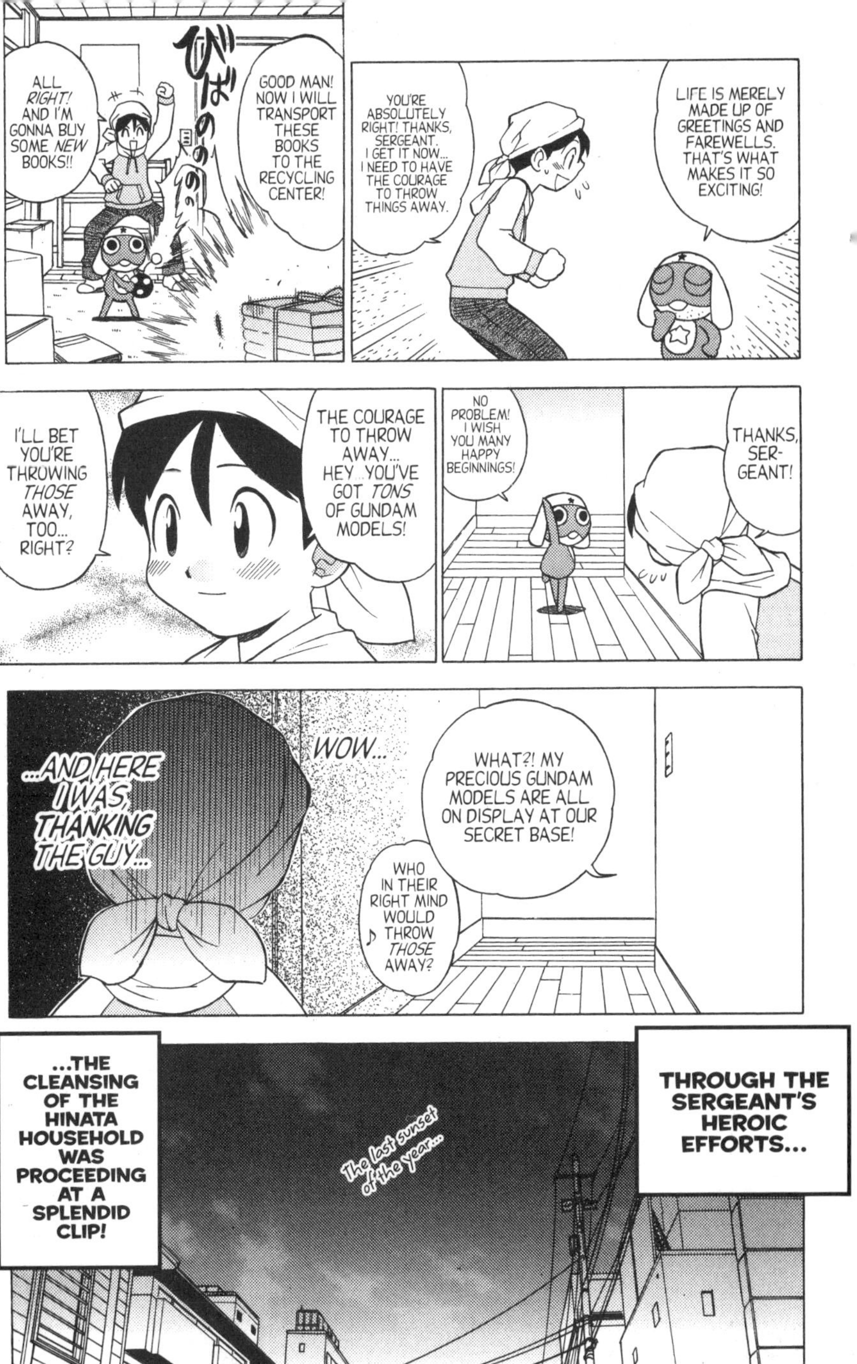
LIFE IS MERELY MADE UP OF GREETINGS AND FAREWELLS. THAT'S WHAT MAKES IT SO EXCITING!
YOU'RE ABSOLUTELY RIGHT! THANKS, SERGEANT. I GET IT NOW... I NEED TO HAVE THE COURAGE TO THROW THINGS AWAY.
GOOD MAN! NOW I WILL TRANSPORT THESE BOOKS TO THE RECYCLING CENTER!
ALL *RIGHT!* AND I'M GONNA BUY SOME *NEW* BOOKS!!
THANKS, SERGEANT!
NO PROBLEM! I WISH YOU MANY HAPPY BEGINNINGS!
THE COURAGE TO THROW AWAY... HEY...YOU'VE GOT *TONS* OF GUNDAM MODELS!
I'LL BET YOU'RE THROWING *THOSE* AWAY, TOO... RIGHT?
WHAT?! MY PRECIOUS GUNDAM MODELS ARE ALL ON DISPLAY AT OUR SECRET BASE!
WHO IN THEIR RIGHT MIND WOULD THROW *THOSE* AWAY? ♪
WOW...
...AND HERE I WAS, THANKING THE GUY...
THROUGH THE SERGEANT'S HEROIC EFFORTS...
The last sunset of the year...
...THE CLEANSING OF THE HINATA HOUSEHOLD WAS PROCEEDING AT A SPLENDID CLIP!

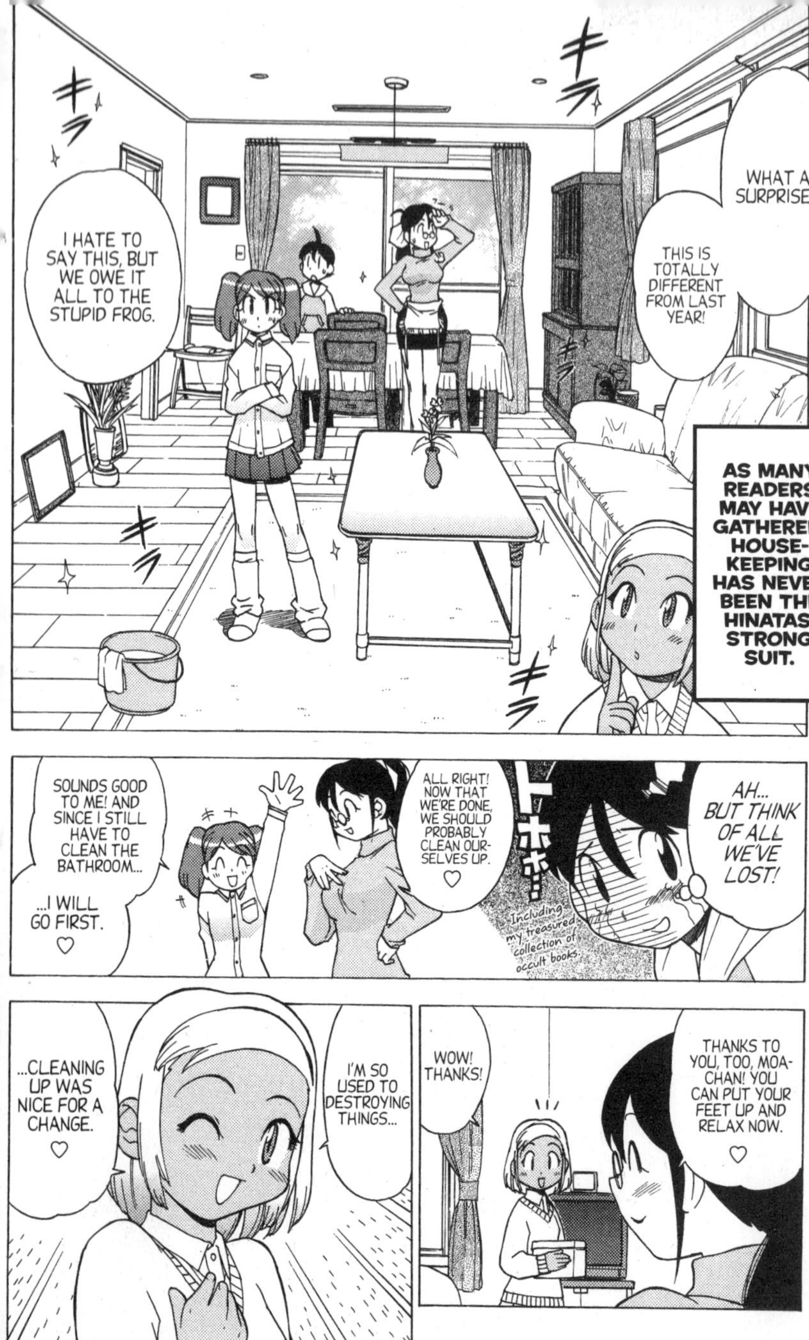
WHAT A SURPRISE...
THIS IS TOTALLY DIFFERENT FROM LAST YEAR!
AS MANY READERS MAY HAVE GATHERED, HOUSE-KEEPING HAS NEVER BEEN THE HINATAS' STRONG SUIT.
I HATE TO SAY THIS, BUT WE OWE IT ALL TO THE STUPID FROG.
AH... BUT THINK OF ALL WE'VE LOST!
Including my treasured collection of occult books.
ALL RIGHT! NOW THAT WE'RE DONE, WE SHOULD PROBABLY CLEAN OUR-SELVES UP. ♡
SOUNDS GOOD TO ME! AND SINCE I STILL HAVE TO CLEAN THE BATHROOM...
...I WILL GO FIRST. ♡
THANKS TO YOU, TOO, MOA-CHAN! YOU CAN PUT YOUR FEET UP AND RELAX NOW. ♡
WOW! THANKS!
I'M SO USED TO DESTROYING THINGS...
...CLEANING UP WAS NICE FOR A CHANGE. ♡

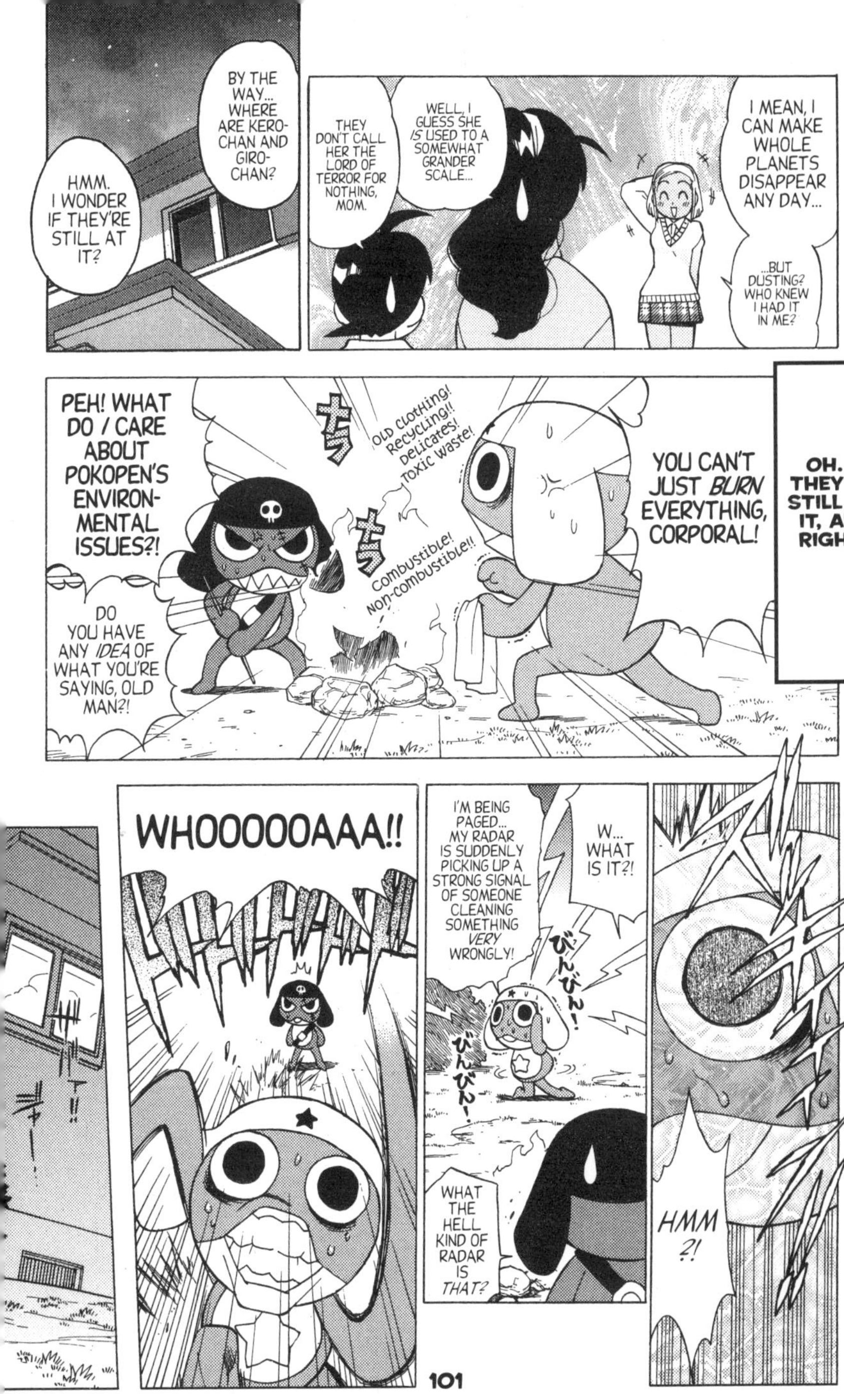

I MEAN, I CAN MAKE WHOLE PLANETS DISAPPEAR ANY DAY...
...BUT DUSTING? WHO KNEW I HAD IT IN ME?
WELL, I GUESS SHE *IS* USED TO A SOMEWHAT GRANDER SCALE...
THEY DON'T CALL HER THE LORD OF TERROR FOR NOTHING, MOM.
BY THE WAY... WHERE ARE KERO-CHAN AND GIRO-CHAN?
HMM. I WONDER IF THEY'RE STILL AT IT?
OH... THEY'RE STILL AT IT, ALL RIGHT.
YOU CAN'T JUST *BURN* EVERYTHING, CORPORAL!
Old clothing! Recycling!! Delicates! Toxic Waste!
Combustible! Non-combustible!!
PEH! WHAT DO *I* CARE ABOUT POKOPEN'S ENVIRONMENTAL ISSUES?!
DO YOU HAVE ANY *IDEA* OF WHAT YOU'RE SAYING, OLD MAN?!
HMM?!
W... WHAT IS IT?!
I'M BEING PAGED... MY RADAR IS SUDDENLY PICKING UP A STRONG SIGNAL OF SOMEONE CLEANING SOMETHING *VERY* WRONGLY!
WHAT THE HELL KIND OF RADAR IS *THAT*?
WHOOOOOAAA!!

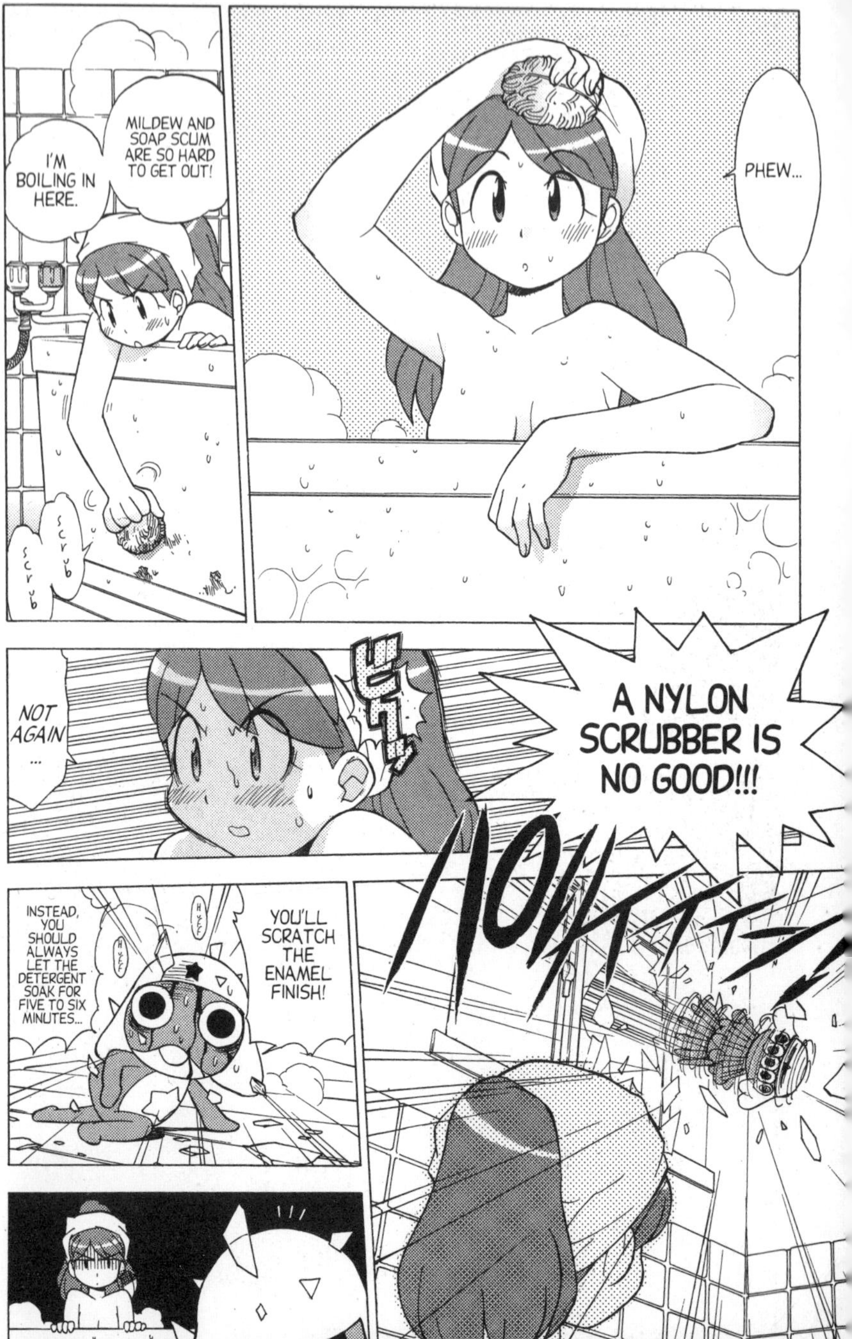
PHEW...
MILDEW AND SOAP SCUM ARE SO HARD TO GET OUT!
I'M BOILING IN HERE.
scrub
scrub
NOT AGAIN ...
A NYLON SCRUBBER IS NO GOOD!!!
YOU'LL SCRATCH THE ENAMEL FINISH!
INSTEAD, YOU SHOULD ALWAYS LET THE DETERGENT SOAK FOR FIVE TO SIX MINUTES...

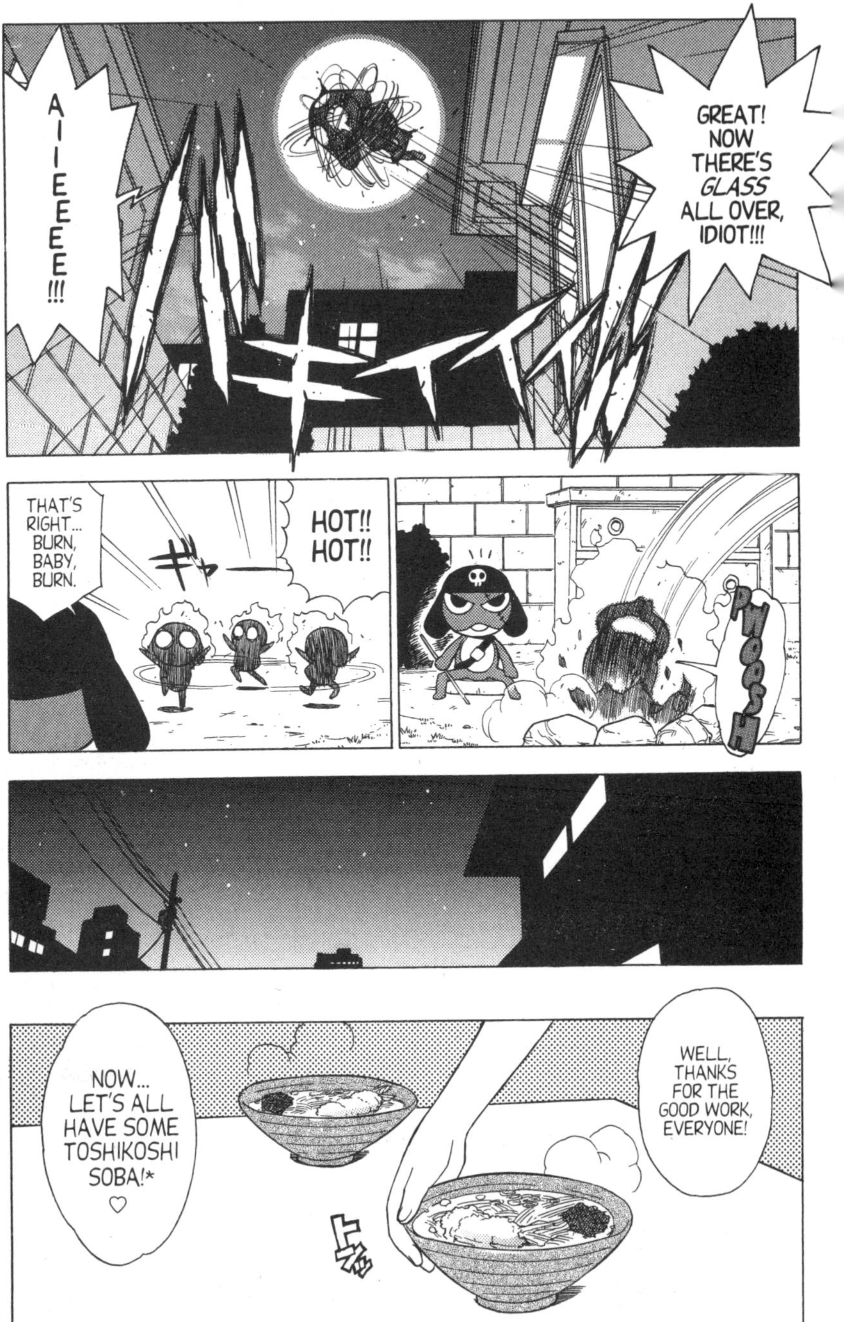
GREAT! NOW THERE'S *GLASS* ALL OVER, IDIOT!!!
AIIEEEEE!!!
PHOOSH
HOT!! HOT!!
ギャー
THAT'S RIGHT... BURN, BABY, BURN.
WELL, THANKS FOR THE GOOD WORK, EVERYONE!
NOW... LET'S ALL HAVE SOME TOSHIKOSHI SOBA!* ♡

*** In Japan, Toshikoshi soba is traditionally eaten on New Year's Eve for good luck.**

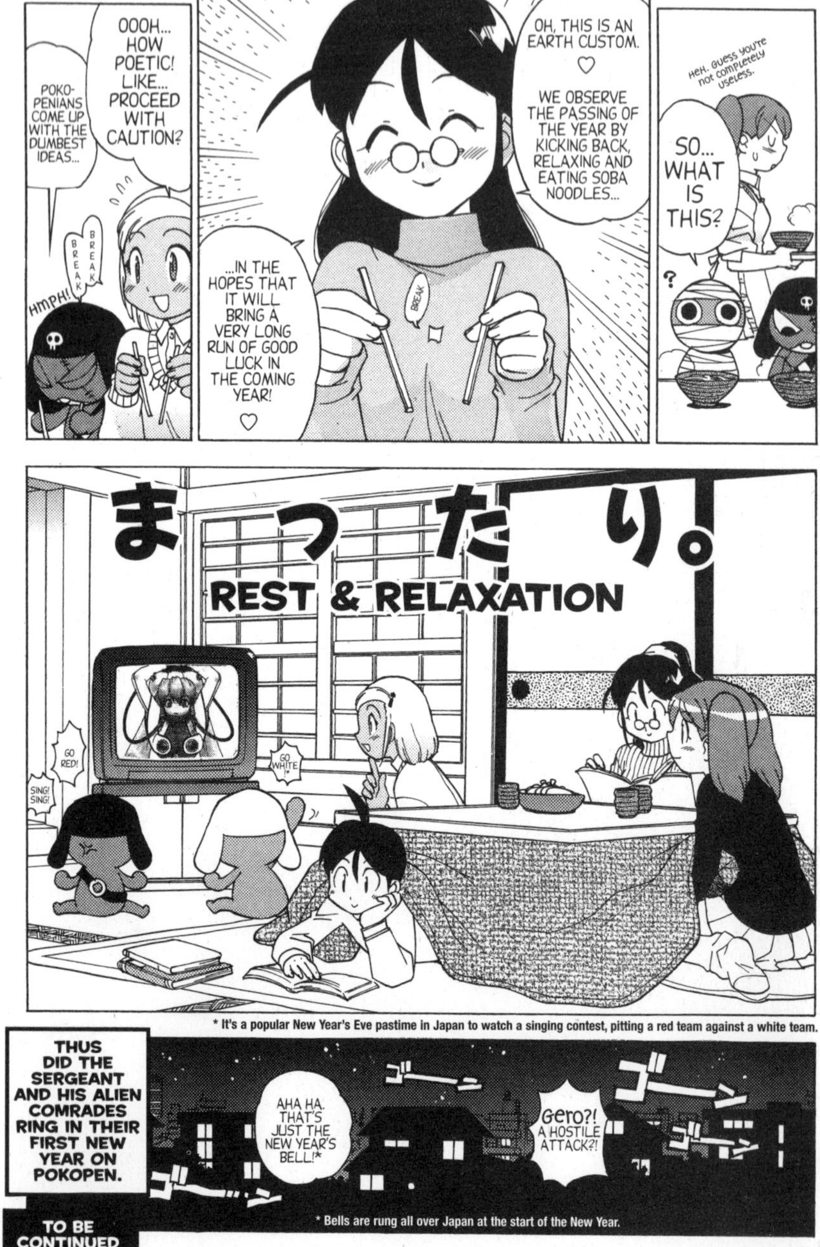
HEH. GUESS YOU'RE NOT COMPLETELY USELESS.
SO... WHAT IS THIS?
?
OH, THIS IS AN EARTH CUSTOM. ♡
WE OBSERVE THE PASSING OF THE YEAR BY KICKING BACK, RELAXING AND EATING SOBA NOODLES...
BREAK
...IN THE HOPES THAT IT WILL BRING A VERY LONG RUN OF GOOD LUCK IN THE COMING YEAR! ♡
OOOH... HOW POETIC! LIKE... PROCEED WITH CAUTION?
POKO-PENIANS COME UP WITH THE DUMBEST IDEAS...
BREAK BREAK
HMPH!
まったり。
REST & RELAXATION
GO WHITE!*
GO RED!
SING! SING!
* It's a popular New Year's Eve pastime in Japan to watch a singing contest, pitting a red team against a white team.
ゴーン
Gero?! A HOSTILE ATTACK?!
AHA HA. THAT'S JUST THE NEW YEAR'S BELL!*
THUS DID THE SERGEANT AND HIS ALIEN COMRADES RING IN THEIR FIRST NEW YEAR ON POKOPEN.
* Bells are rung all over Japan at the start of the New Year.
TO BE CONTINUED

ENCOUNTER XVII
OPERATION: RELATIVE INTERCEPTION!

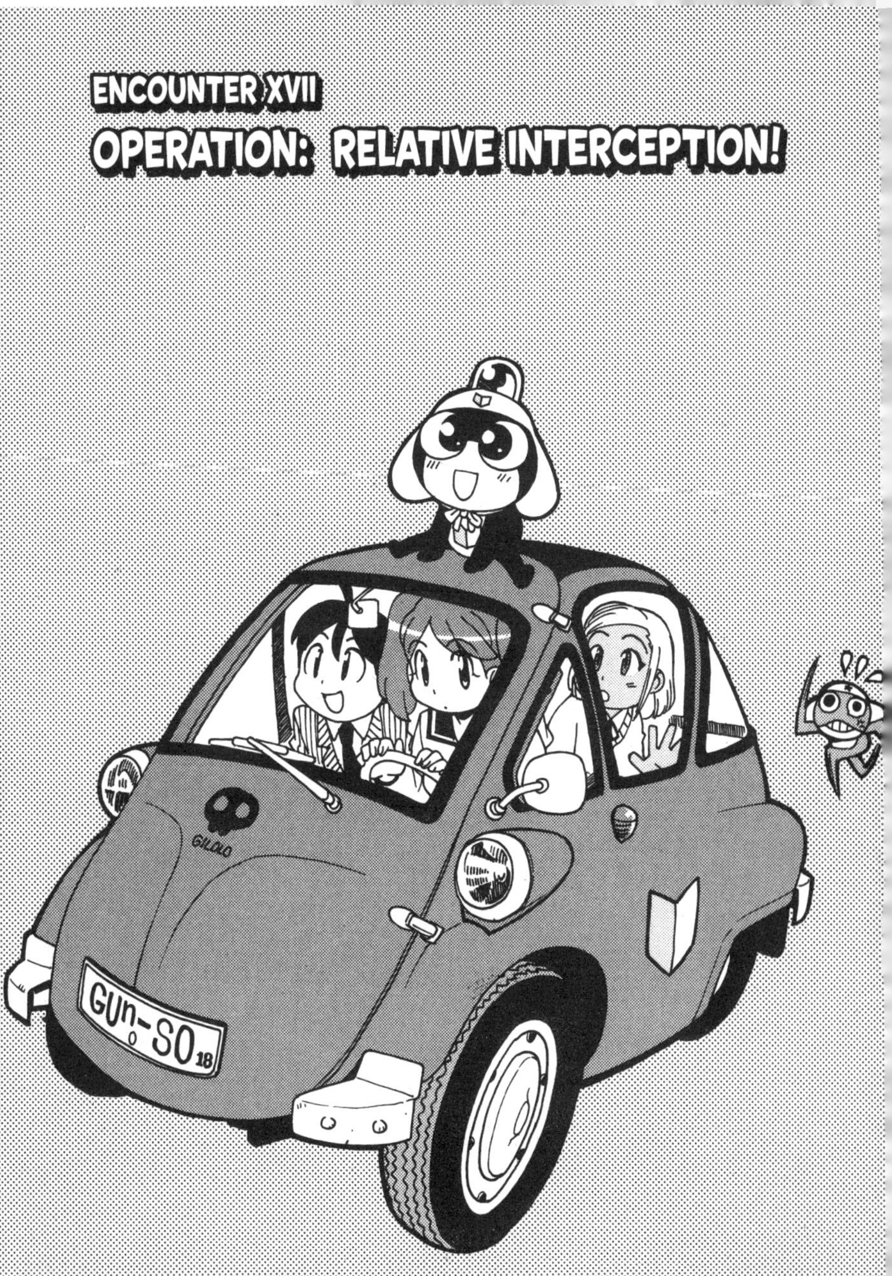

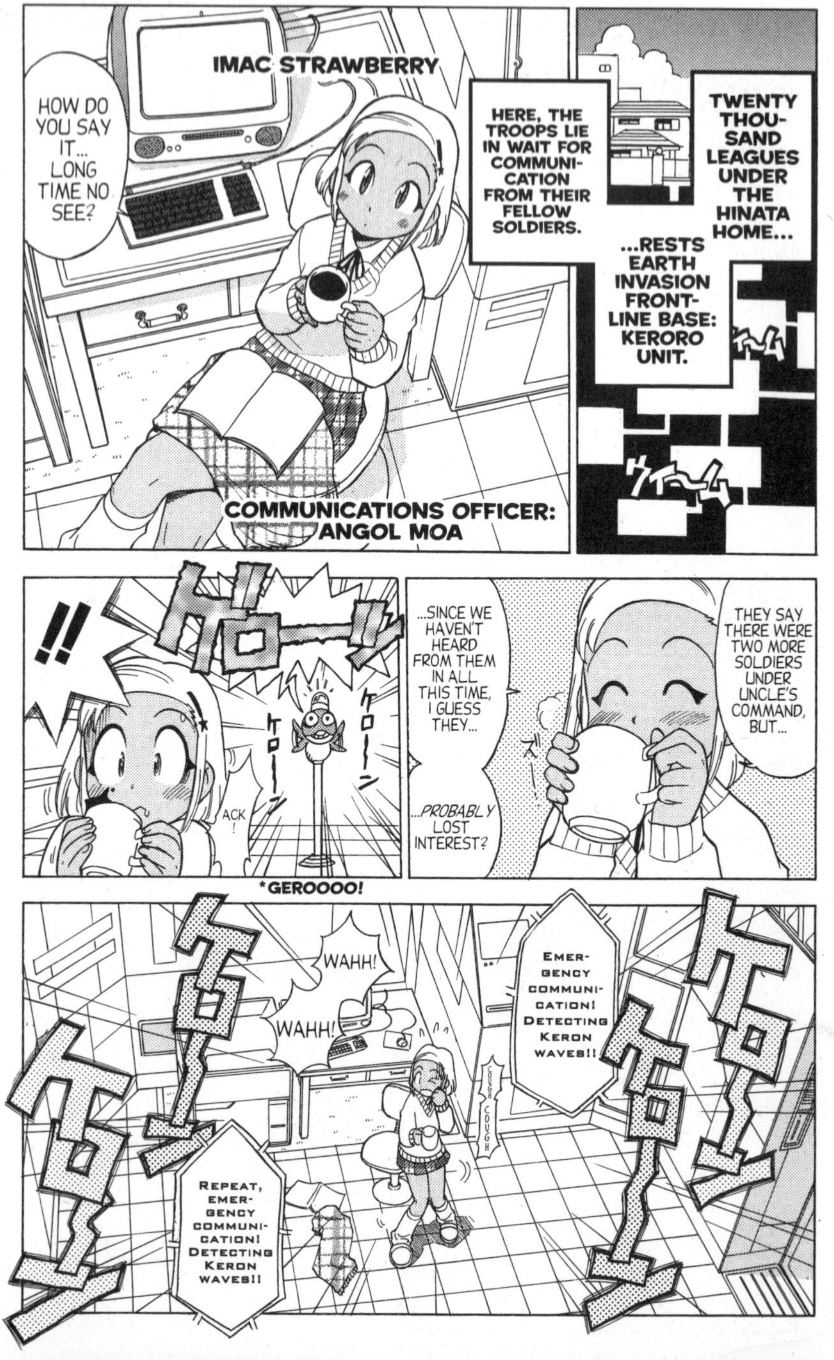
TWENTY THOUSAND LEAGUES UNDER THE HINATA HOME...
...RESTS EARTH INVASION FRONT-LINE BASE: KERORO UNIT.
HERE, THE TROOPS LIE IN WAIT FOR COMMUNICATION FROM THEIR FELLOW SOLDIERS.
IMAC STRAWBERRY
HOW DO YOU SAY IT... LONG TIME NO SEE?
COMMUNICATIONS OFFICER: ANGOL MOA
THEY SAY THERE WERE TWO MORE SOLDIERS UNDER UNCLE'S COMMAND, BUT...
...SINCE WE HAVEN'T HEARD FROM THEM IN ALL THIS TIME, I GUESS THEY...
...PROBABLY LOST INTEREST?
!!
ACK!
*GEROOOO!
Emergency communication! Detecting Keron waves!!
WAHH!
WAHH!
COUGH COUGH
Repeat, emergency communication! Detecting Keron waves!!

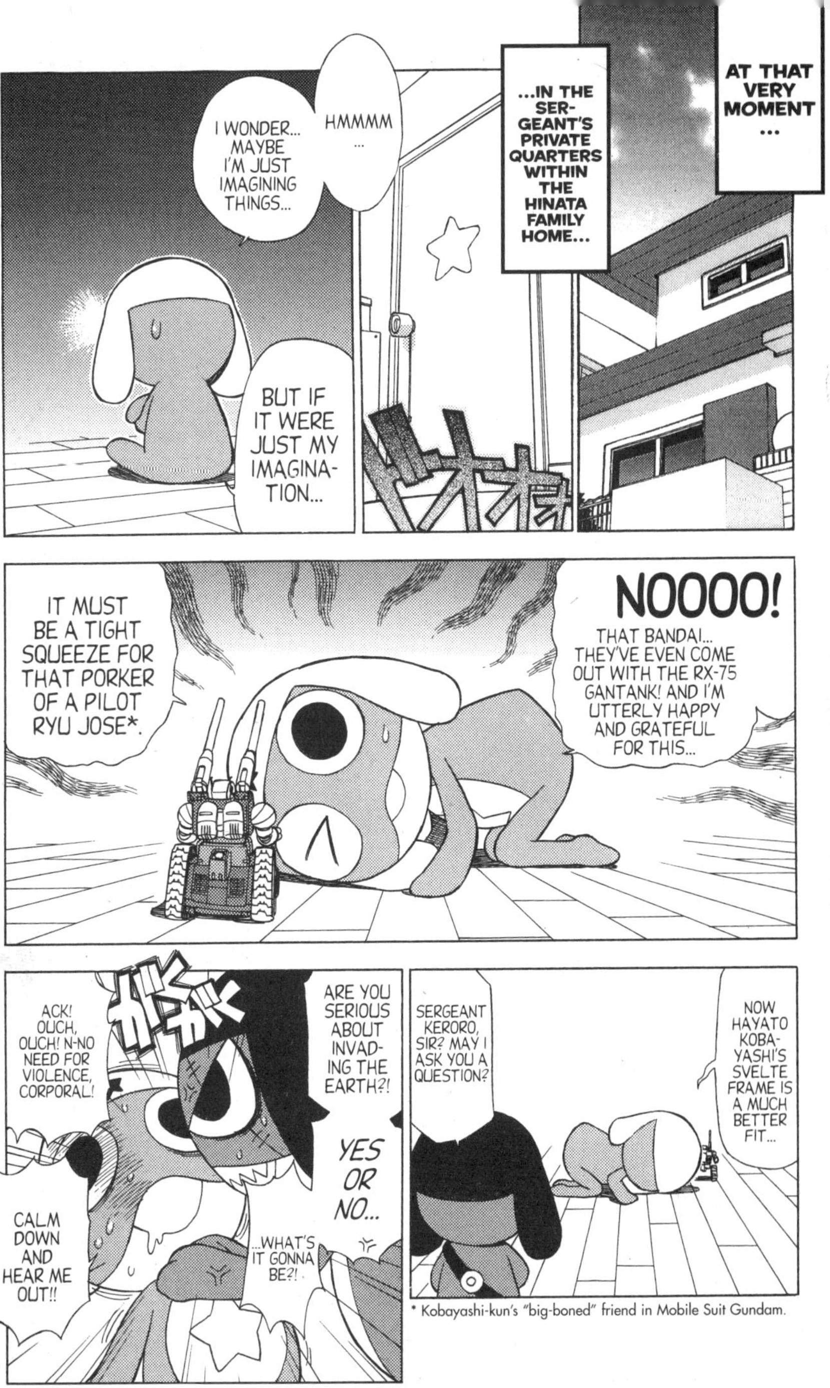
AT THAT VERY MOMENT...
...IN THE SER-GEANT'S PRIVATE QUARTERS WITHIN THE HINATA FAMILY HOME...
HMMMM...
I WONDER... MAYBE I'M JUST IMAGINING THINGS...
BUT IF IT WERE JUST MY IMAGINA-TION...
NOOOO!
THAT BANDAI... THEY'VE EVEN COME OUT WITH THE RX-75 GANTANK! AND I'M UTTERLY HAPPY AND GRATEFUL FOR THIS...
IT MUST BE A TIGHT SQUEEZE FOR THAT PORKER OF A PILOT RYU JOSE*.
NOW HAYATO KOBA-YASHI'S SVELTE FRAME IS A MUCH BETTER FIT...
SERGEANT KERORO, SIR? MAY I ASK YOU A QUESTION?
ARE YOU SERIOUS ABOUT INVAD-ING THE EARTH?!
YES OR NO...
...WHAT'S IT GONNA BE?!
ACK! OUCH, OUCH! N-NO NEED FOR VIOLENCE, CORPORAL!
CALM DOWN AND HEAR ME OUT!!

* Kobayashi-kun's "big-boned" friend in Mobile Suit Gundam.

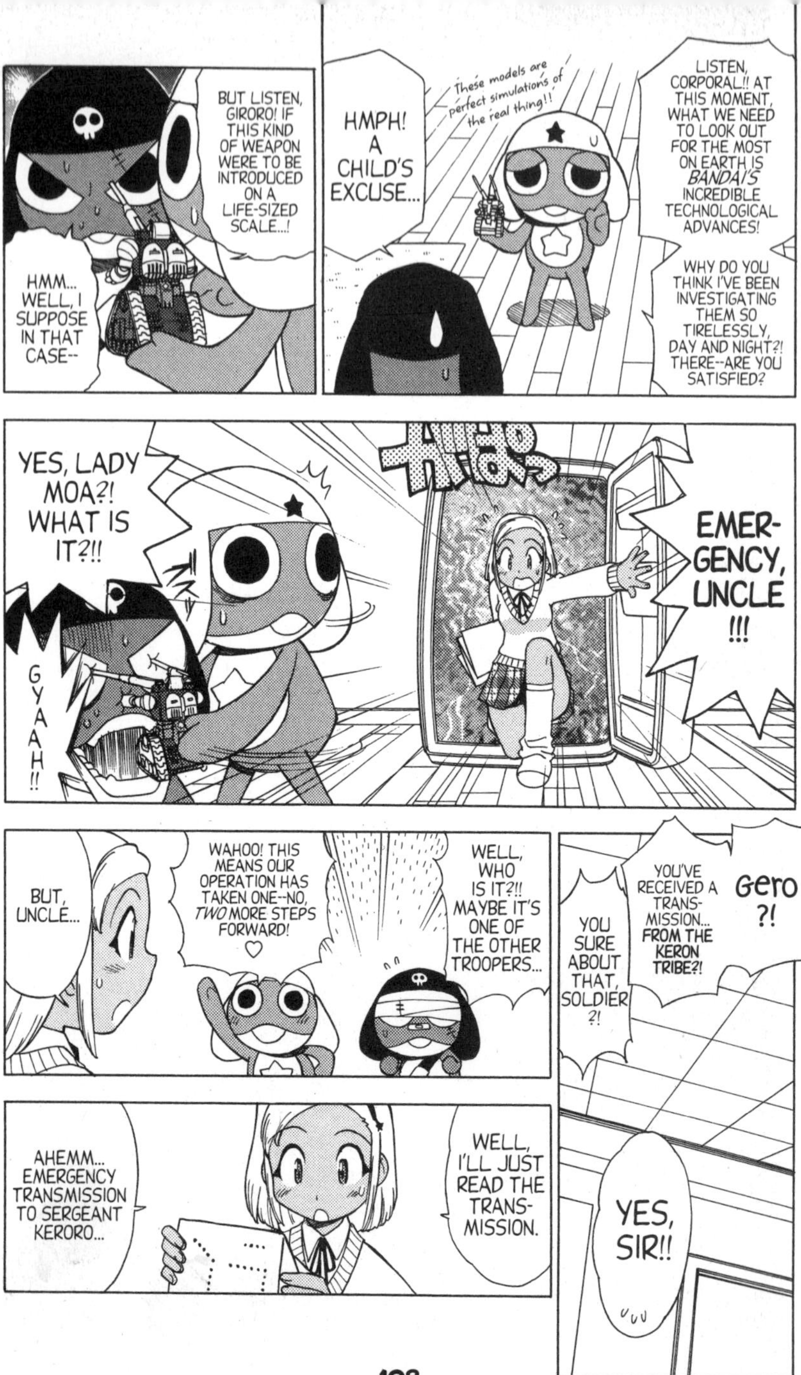
LISTEN, CORPORAL!! AT THIS MOMENT, WHAT WE NEED TO LOOK OUT FOR THE MOST ON EARTH IS *BANDAI'S* INCREDIBLE TECHNOLOGICAL ADVANCES!
WHY DO YOU THINK I'VE BEEN INVESTIGATING THEM SO TIRELESSLY, DAY AND NIGHT?! THERE--ARE YOU SATISFIED?
These models are perfect simulations of the real thing!!
HMPH! A CHILD'S EXCUSE...
BUT LISTEN, GIRORO! IF THIS KIND OF WEAPON WERE TO BE INTRODUCED ON A LIFE-SIZED SCALE...!
HMM... WELL, I SUPPOSE IN THAT CASE--
EMERGENCY, UNCLE!!!
YES, LADY MOA?! WHAT IS IT?!!
GYAAAH!!
Gero?!
YOU'VE RECEIVED A TRANSMISSION... FROM THE KERON TRIBE?!
YOU SURE ABOUT THAT, SOLDIER?!
YES, SIR!!
WELL, WHO IS IT?!! MAYBE IT'S ONE OF THE OTHER TROOPERS...
WAHOO! THIS MEANS OUR OPERATION HAS TAKEN ONE--NO, *TWO* MORE STEPS FORWARD! ♡
BUT, UNCLE...
WELL, I'LL JUST READ THE TRANSMISSION.
AHEMM... EMERGENCY TRANSMISSION TO SERGEANT KERORO...

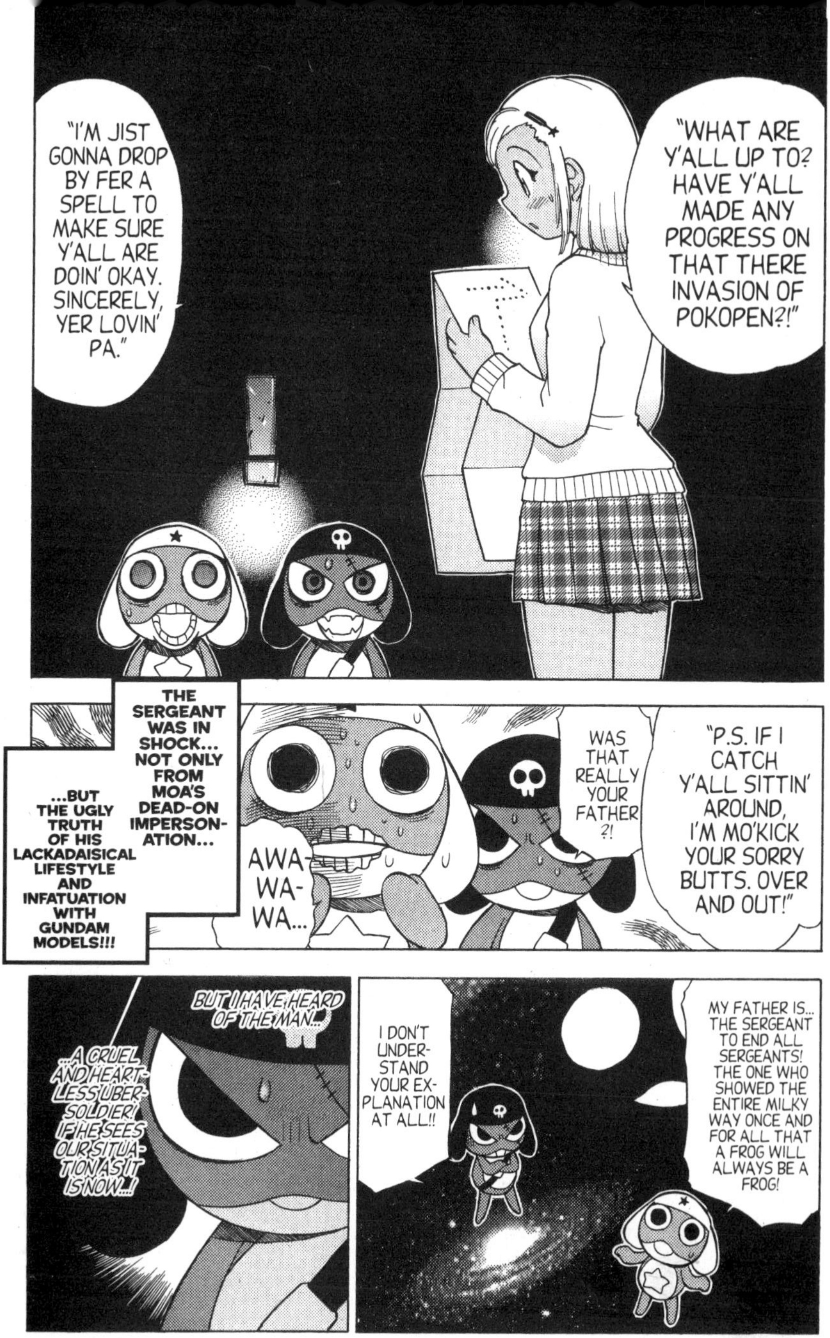
"WHAT ARE Y'ALL UP TO? HAVE Y'ALL MADE ANY PROGRESS ON THAT THERE INVASION OF POKOPEN?!"
"I'M JIST GONNA DROP BY FER A SPELL TO MAKE SURE Y'ALL ARE DOIN' OKAY. SINCERELY, YER LOVIN' PA."
"P.S. IF I CATCH Y'ALL SITTIN' AROUND, I'M MO'KICK YOUR SORRY BUTTS. OVER AND OUT!"
WAS THAT REALLY YOUR FATHER?!
AWA-WA-WA...
THE SERGEANT WAS IN SHOCK... NOT ONLY FROM MOA'S DEAD-ON IMPERSONATION...
...BUT THE UGLY TRUTH OF HIS LACKADAISICAL LIFESTYLE AND INFATUATION WITH GUNDAM MODELS!!!
MY FATHER IS... THE SERGEANT TO END ALL SERGEANTS! THE ONE WHO SHOWED THE ENTIRE MILKY WAY ONCE AND FOR ALL THAT A FROG WILL ALWAYS BE A FROG!
I DON'T UNDERSTAND YOUR EXPLANATION AT ALL!!
BUT I HAVE HEARD OF THE MAN...
...A CRUEL AND HEARTLESS ÜBER-SOLDIER! IF HE SEES OUR SITUATION AS IT IS NOW...!

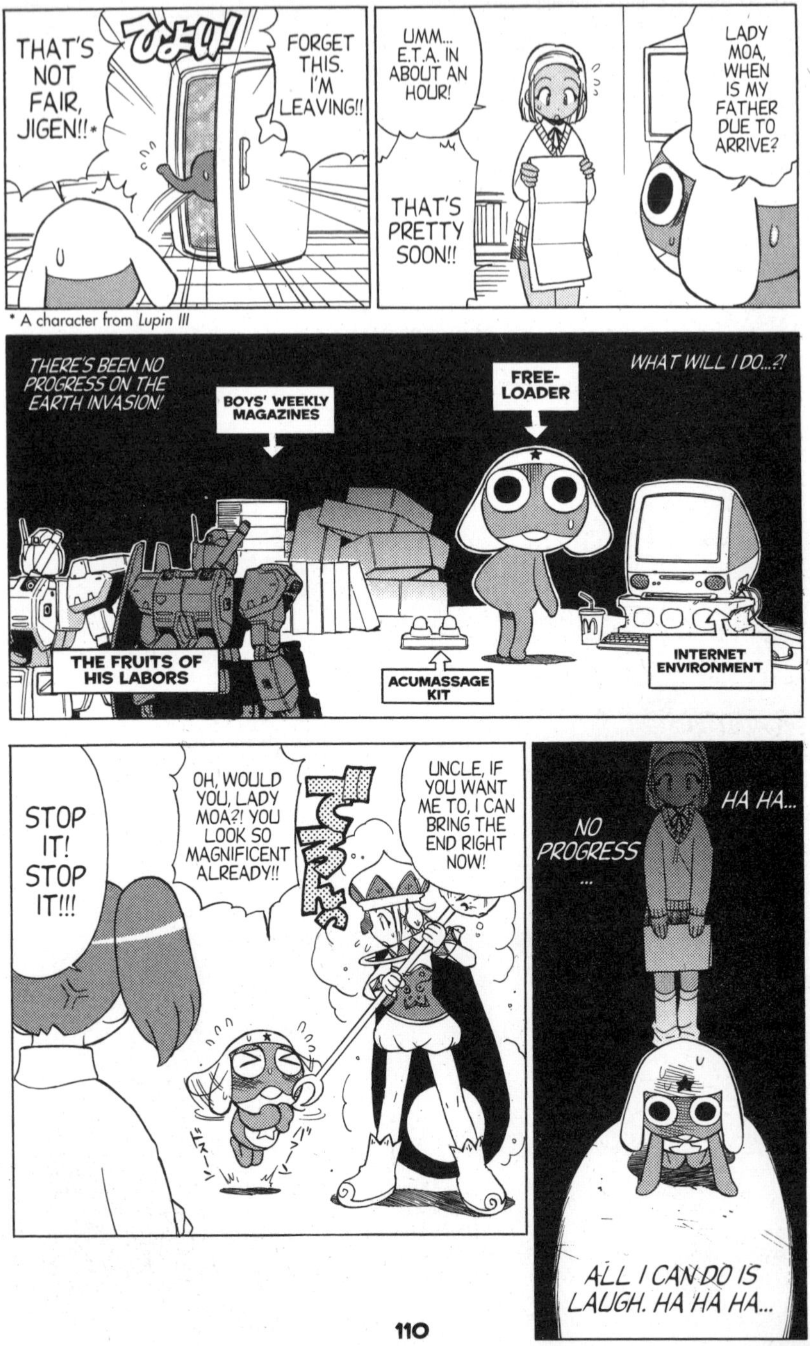

LADY MOA, WHEN IS MY FATHER DUE TO ARRIVE?
UMM... E.T.A. IN ABOUT AN HOUR!
THAT'S PRETTY SOON!!
FORGET THIS. I'M LEAVING!!
THAT'S NOT FAIR, JIGEN!!*
WHAT WILL I DO...?!
FREE-LOADER
BOYS' WEEKLY MAGAZINES
THERE'S BEEN NO PROGRESS ON THE EARTH INVASION!
INTERNET ENVIRONMENT
ACUMASSAGE KIT
THE FRUITS OF HIS LABORS
HA HA...
NO PROGRESS ...
ALL I CAN DO IS LAUGH. HA HA HA...
UNCLE, IF YOU WANT ME TO, I CAN BRING THE END RIGHT NOW!
OH, WOULD YOU, LADY MOA?! YOU LOOK SO MAGNIFICENT ALREADY!!
STOP IT! STOP IT!!!

* A character from *Lupin III*

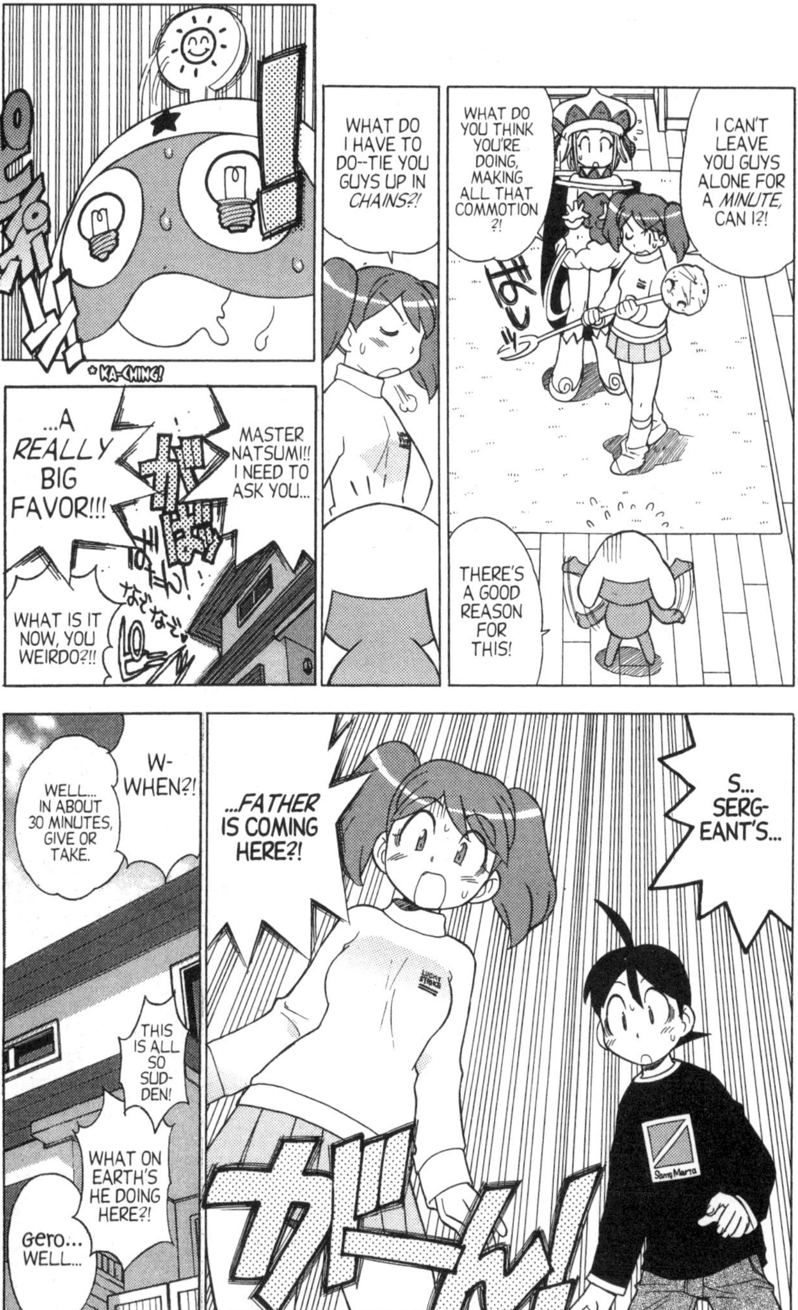
I CAN'T LEAVE YOU GUYS ALONE FOR A *MINUTE,* CAN I?!
WHAT DO YOU THINK YOU'RE DOING, MAKING ALL THAT COMMOTION?!
THERE'S A GOOD REASON FOR THIS!
WHAT DO I HAVE TO DO--TIE YOU GUYS UP IN *CHAINS?!*
* KA-CHING!
MASTER NATSUMI!! I NEED TO ASK YOU...
...A *REALLY* BIG FAVOR!!!
WHAT IS IT NOW, YOU WEIRDO?!!
S... SERG-EANT'S...
...*FATHER* IS COMING HERE?!
W-WHEN?!
WELL... IN ABOUT 30 MINUTES, GIVE OR TAKE.
THIS IS ALL SO SUD-DEN!
WHAT ON EARTH'S HE DOING HERE?!
Gero... WELL...

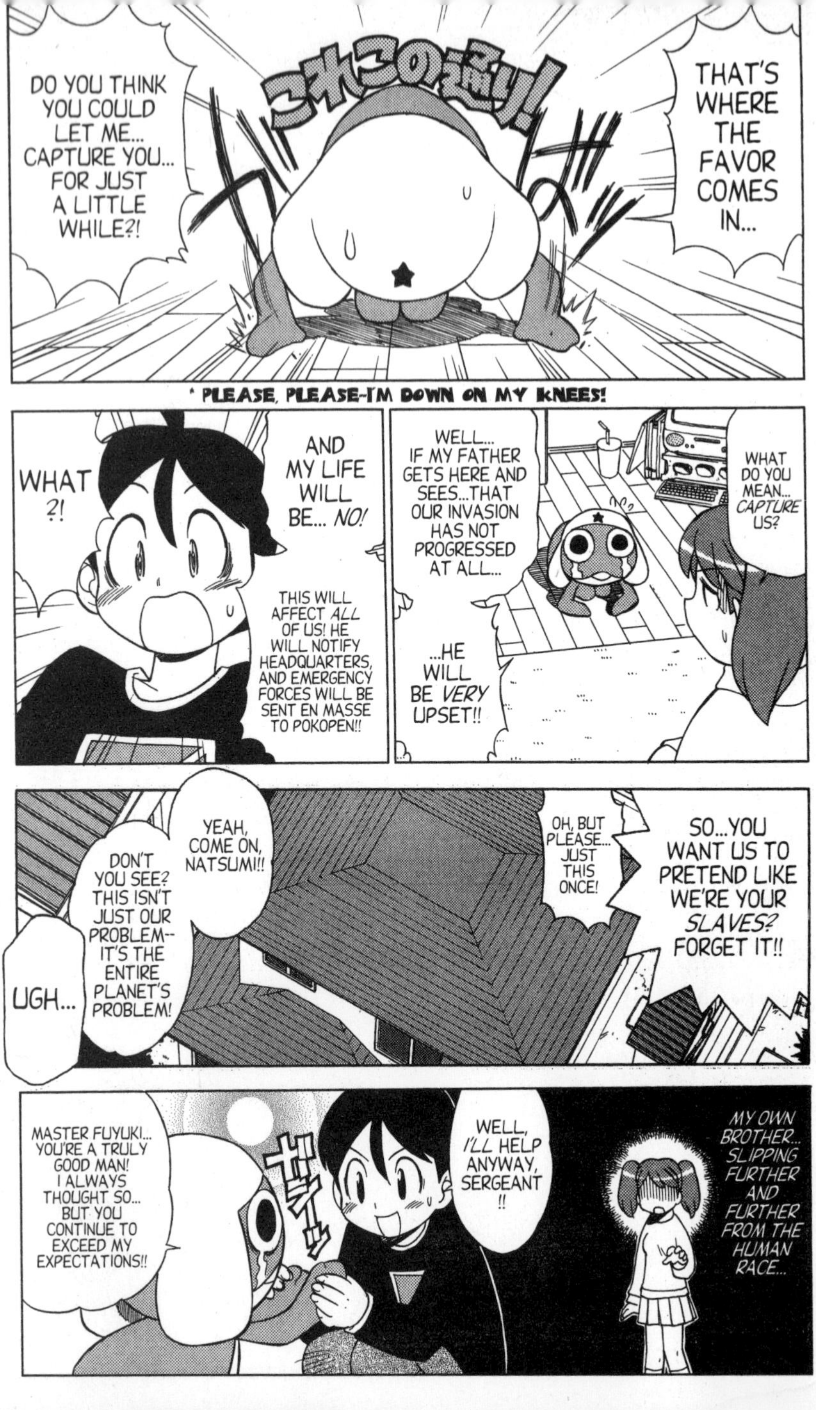
THAT'S WHERE THE FAVOR COMES IN...
これこの通り!!
DO YOU THINK YOU COULD LET ME... CAPTURE YOU... FOR JUST A LITTLE WHILE?!
* PLEASE, PLEASE-I'M DOWN ON MY KNEES!
WHAT DO YOU MEAN... CAPTURE US?
WELL... IF MY FATHER GETS HERE AND SEES...THAT OUR INVASION HAS NOT PROGRESSED AT ALL...
...HE WILL BE VERY UPSET!!
AND MY LIFE WILL BE... NO!
THIS WILL AFFECT ALL OF US! HE WILL NOTIFY HEADQUARTERS, AND EMERGENCY FORCES WILL BE SENT EN MASSE TO POKOPEN!!
WHAT?!
SO...YOU WANT US TO PRETEND LIKE WE'RE YOUR SLAVES? FORGET IT!!
OH, BUT PLEASE... JUST THIS ONCE!
YEAH, COME ON, NATSUMI!!
DON'T YOU SEE? THIS ISN'T JUST OUR PROBLEM-- IT'S THE ENTIRE PLANET'S PROBLEM!
UGH...
MY OWN BROTHER... SLIPPING FURTHER AND FURTHER FROM THE HUMAN RACE...
WELL, I'LL HELP ANYWAY, SERGEANT!!
MASTER FUYUKI... YOU'RE A TRULY GOOD MAN! I ALWAYS THOUGHT SO... BUT YOU CONTINUE TO EXCEED MY EXPECTATIONS!!

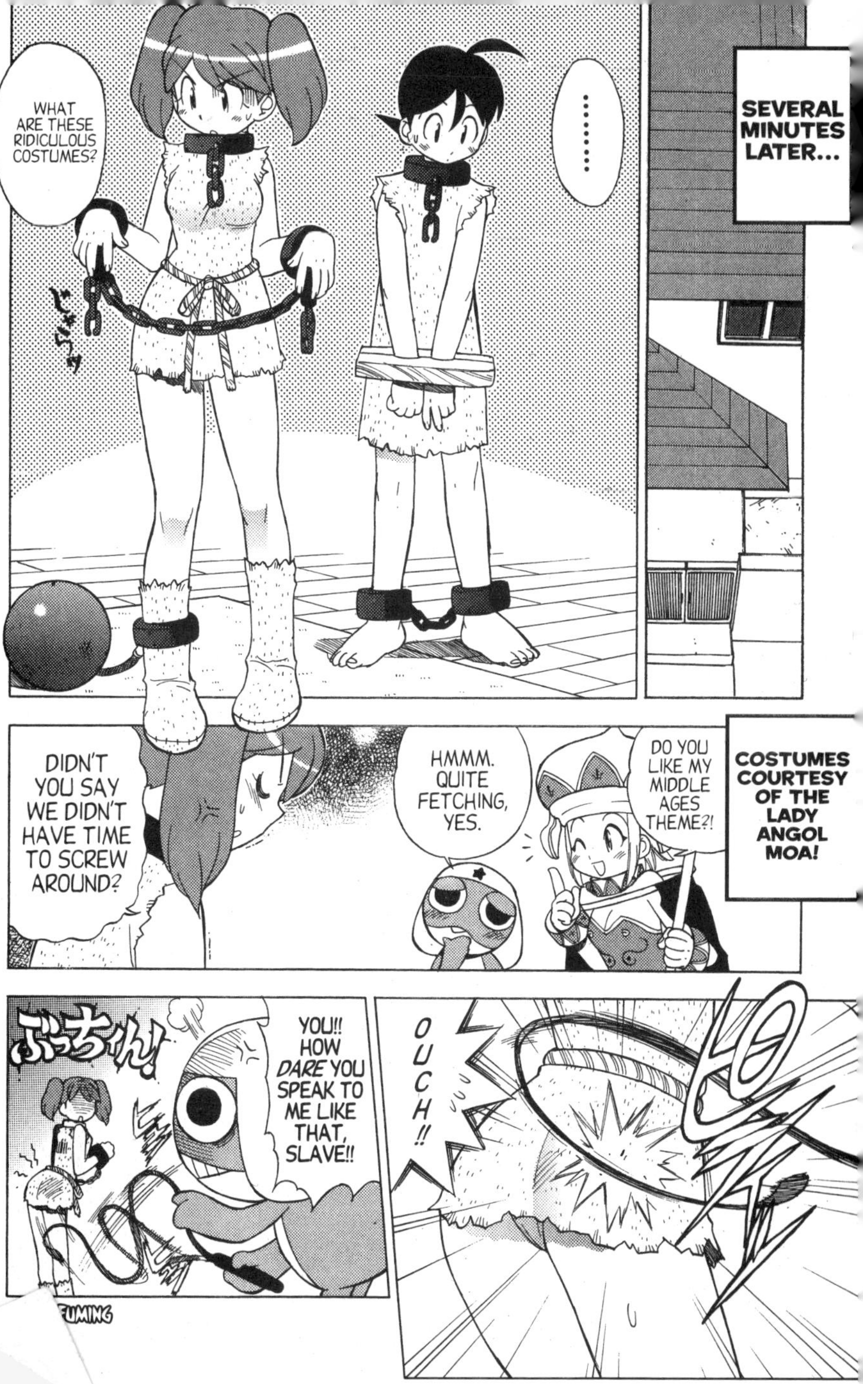
SEVERAL MINUTES LATER...
....
WHAT ARE THESE RIDICULOUS COSTUMES?
COSTUMES COURTESY OF THE LADY ANGOL MOA!
DO YOU LIKE MY MIDDLE AGES THEME?!
HMMM. QUITE FETCHING, YES.
DIDN'T YOU SAY WE DIDN'T HAVE TIME TO SCREW AROUND?
OUCH!!
YOU!! HOW *DARE* YOU SPEAK TO ME LIKE THAT, SLAVE!!
ぶっちん!
FUMING

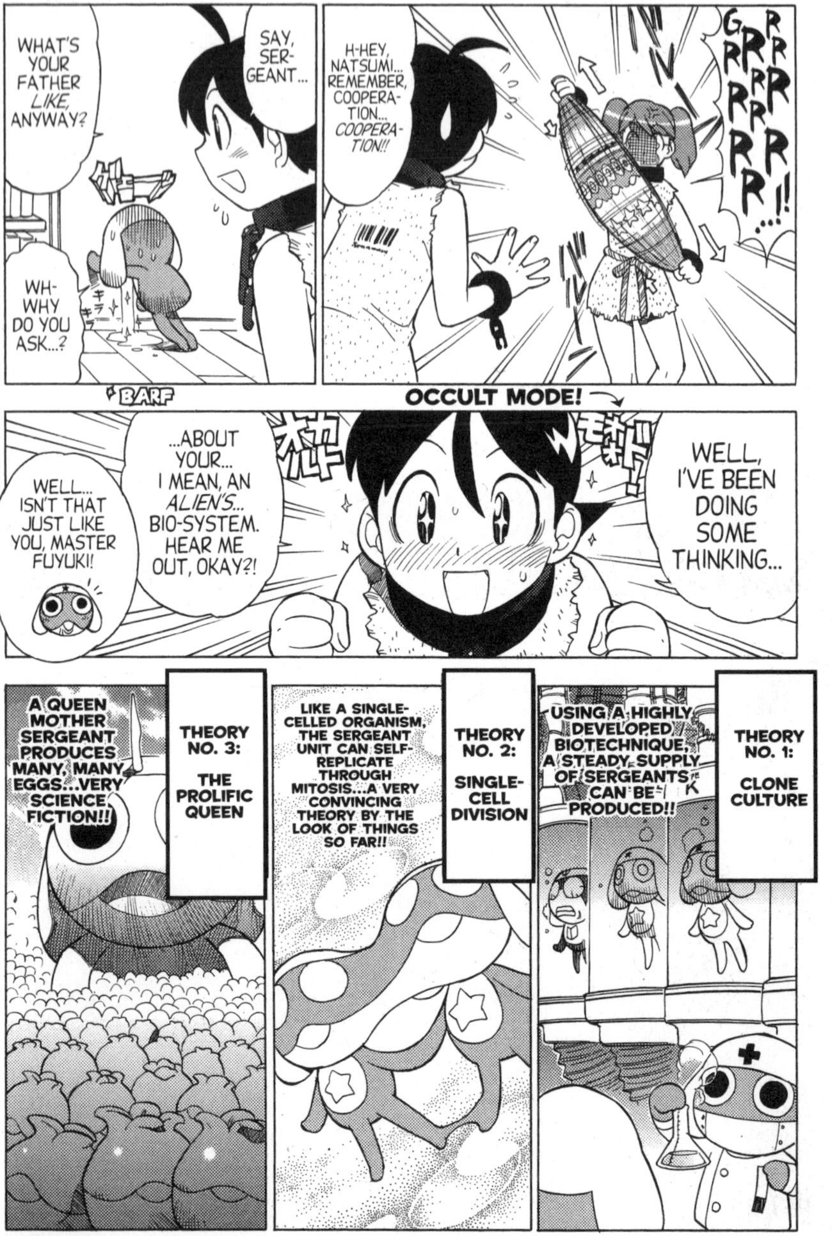
H-HEY, NATSUMI... REMEMBER, COOPERATION... COOPERATION!!
GRRRRRRRRRRRRR...!!
SAY, SERGEANT...
WHAT'S YOUR FATHER LIKE, ANYWAY?
WH-WHY DO YOU ASK...?
BARF
OCCULT MODE!
WELL, I'VE BEEN DOING SOME THINKING...
...ABOUT YOUR... I MEAN, AN ALIEN'S... BIO-SYSTEM. HEAR ME OUT, OKAY?!
WELL... ISN'T THAT JUST LIKE YOU, MASTER FUYUKI!
THEORY NO. 1: CLONE CULTURE
USING A HIGHLY DEVELOPED BIOTECHNIQUE, A STEADY SUPPLY OF SERGEANTS CAN BE PRODUCED!!
THEORY NO. 2: SINGLE-CELL DIVISION
LIKE A SINGLE-CELLED ORGANISM, THE SERGEANT UNIT CAN SELF-REPLICATE THROUGH MITOSIS...A VERY CONVINCING THEORY BY THE LOOK OF THINGS SO FAR!!
THEORY NO. 3: THE PROLIFIC QUEEN
A QUEEN MOTHER SERGEANT PRODUCES MANY, MANY EGGS...VERY SCIENCE FICTION!!

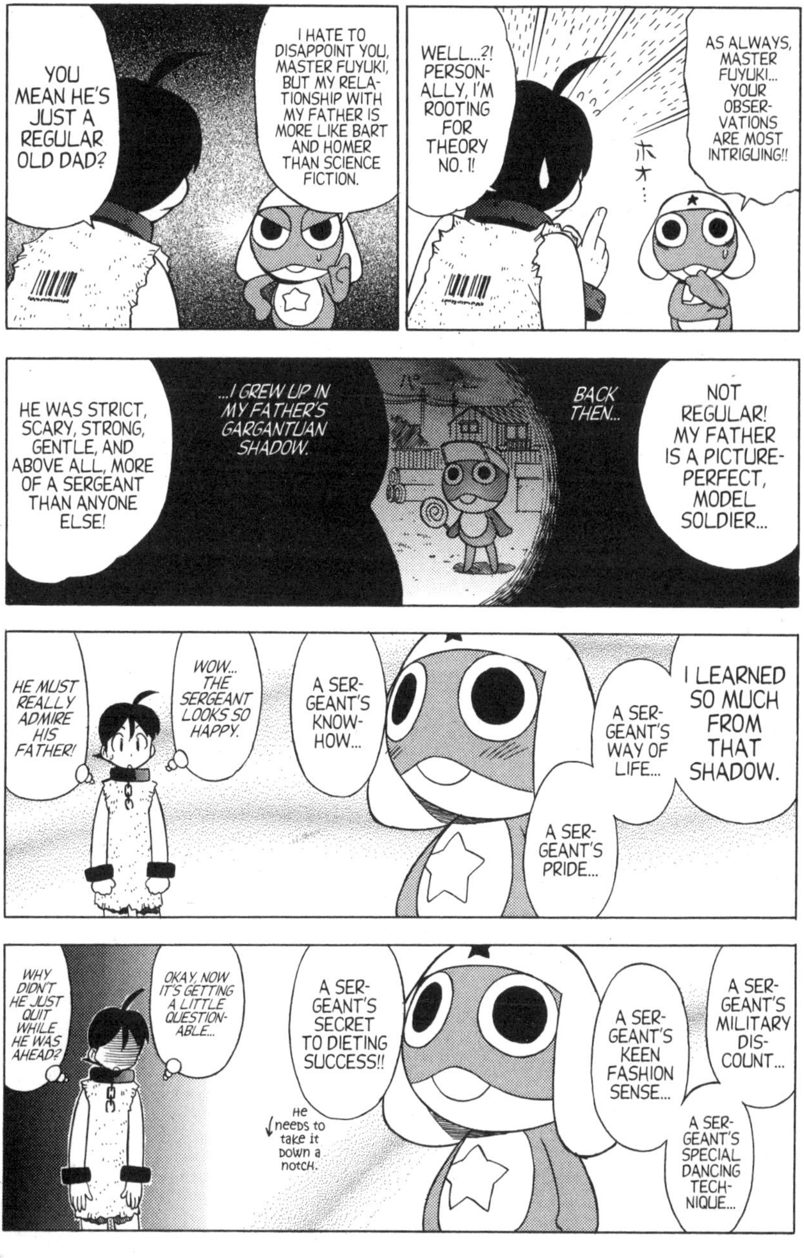
AS ALWAYS, MASTER FUYUKI... YOUR OBSERVATIONS ARE MOST INTRIGUING!!
ホオ…
WELL...?! PERSONALLY, I'M ROOTING FOR THEORY NO. 1!
I HATE TO DISAPPOINT YOU, MASTER FUYUKI, BUT MY RELATIONSHIP WITH MY FATHER IS MORE LIKE BART AND HOMER THAN SCIENCE FICTION.
YOU MEAN HE'S JUST A REGULAR OLD DAD?
NOT REGULAR! MY FATHER IS A PICTURE-PERFECT, MODEL SOLDIER...
BACK THEN...
...I GREW UP IN MY FATHER'S GARGANTUAN SHADOW.
HE WAS STRICT, SCARY, STRONG, GENTLE, AND ABOVE ALL, MORE OF A SERGEANT THAN ANYONE ELSE!
I LEARNED SO MUCH FROM THAT SHADOW.
A SERGEANT'S WAY OF LIFE...
A SERGEANT'S PRIDE...
A SERGEANT'S KNOW-HOW...
WOW... THE SERGEANT LOOKS SO HAPPY.
HE MUST REALLY ADMIRE HIS FATHER!
A SERGEANT'S MILITARY DISCOUNT...
A SERGEANT'S SPECIAL DANCING TECHNIQUE...
A SERGEANT'S KEEN FASHION SENSE...
A SERGEANT'S SECRET TO DIETING SUCCESS!!
He needs to take it down a notch.
OKAY, NOW IT'S GETTING A LITTLE QUESTIONABLE...
WHY DIDN'T HE JUST QUIT WHILE HE WAS AHEAD?

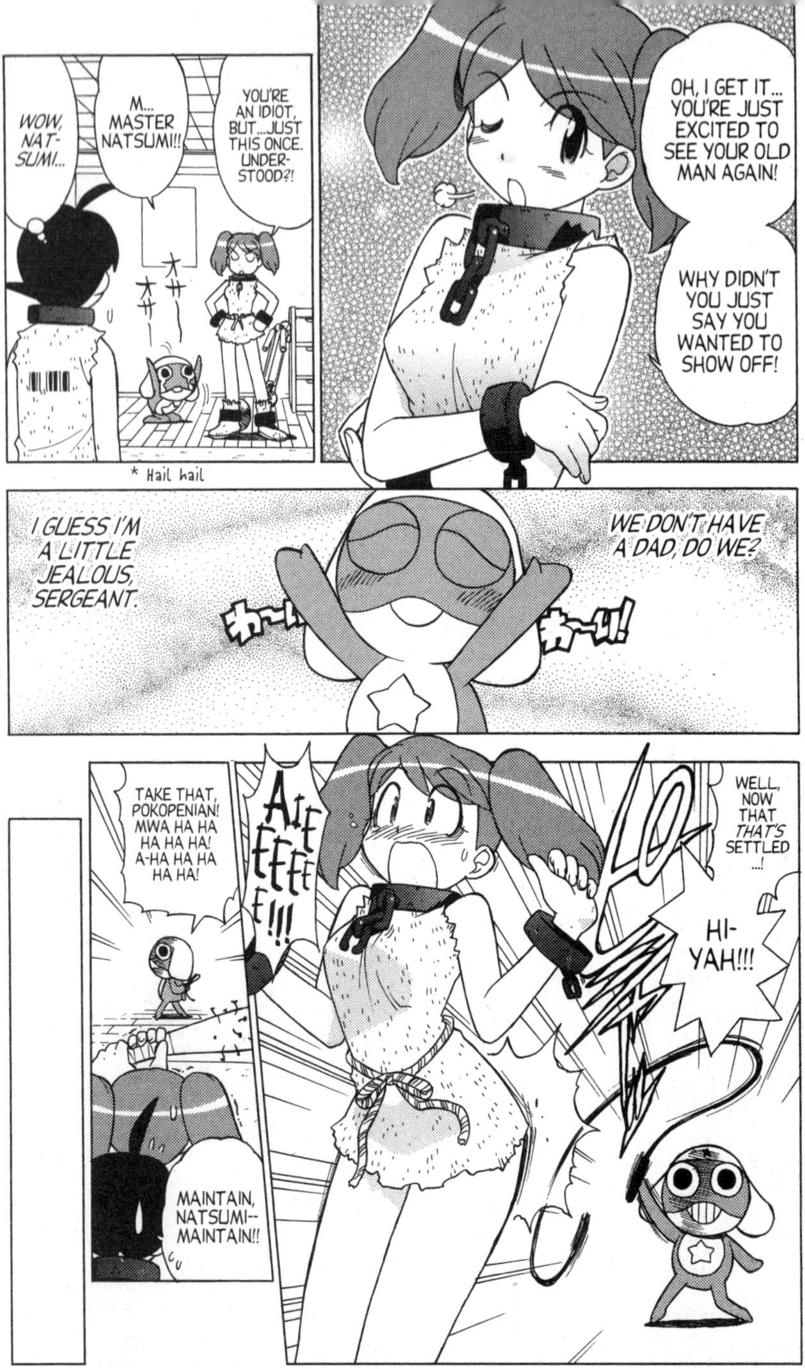
OH, I GET IT... YOU'RE JUST EXCITED TO SEE YOUR OLD MAN AGAIN!
WHY DIDN'T YOU JUST SAY YOU WANTED TO SHOW OFF!
YOU'RE AN IDIOT, BUT...JUST THIS ONCE. UNDERSTOOD?!
M... MASTER NATSUMI!!
WOW, NATSUMI...
オサー
オサー
* Hail hail
WE DON'T HAVE A DAD, DO WE?
I GUESS I'M A LITTLE JEALOUS, SERGEANT.
WELL, NOW THAT *THAT'S* SETTLED...!
HI-YAH!!!
AIEEEEEEE!!!
TAKE THAT, POKOPENIAN! MWA HA HA HA HA HA! A-HA HA HA HA HA!
MAINTAIN, NATSUMI-- MAINTAIN!!

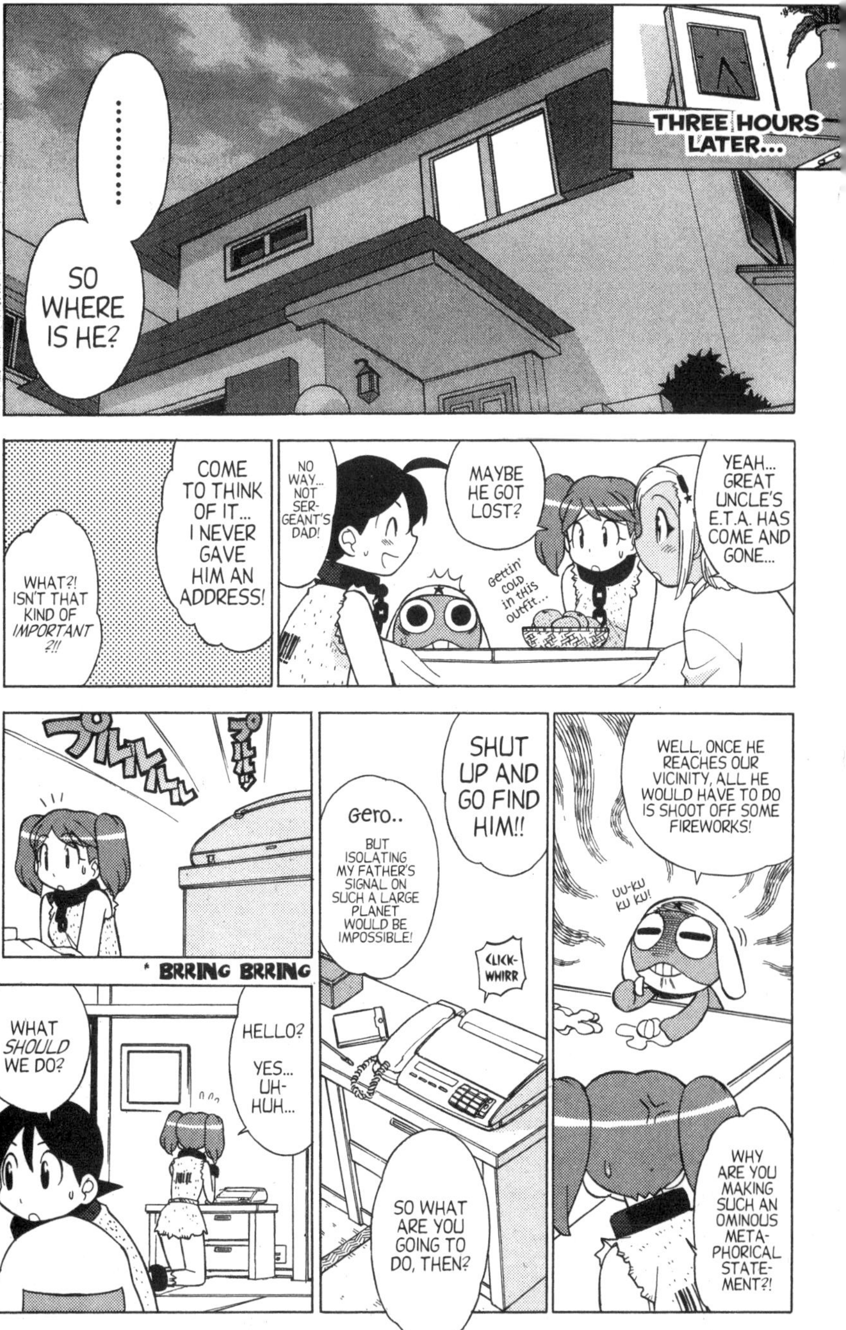
THREE HOURS LATER...
......
SO WHERE IS HE?
YEAH... GREAT UNCLE'S E.T.A. HAS COME AND GONE...
MAYBE HE GOT LOST?
Gettin' COLD in tHIS outfit...
NO WAY... NOT SERGEANT'S DAD!
COME TO THINK OF IT... I NEVER GAVE HIM AN ADDRESS!
WHAT?! ISN'T THAT KIND OF IMPORTANT?!!
WELL, ONCE HE REACHES OUR VICINITY, ALL HE WOULD HAVE TO DO IS SHOOT OFF SOME FIREWORKS!
UU-KU KU KU!
WHY ARE YOU MAKING SUCH AN OMINOUS METAPHORICAL STATEMENT?!
SHUT UP AND GO FIND HIM!!
Gero..
BUT ISOLATING MY FATHER'S SIGNAL ON SUCH A LARGE PLANET WOULD BE IMPOSSIBLE!
CLICK-WHIRR
SO WHAT ARE YOU GOING TO DO, THEN?
プルルルル
プルッ
BRRING BRRING
HELLO?
YES... UH-HUH...
WHAT SHOULD WE DO?

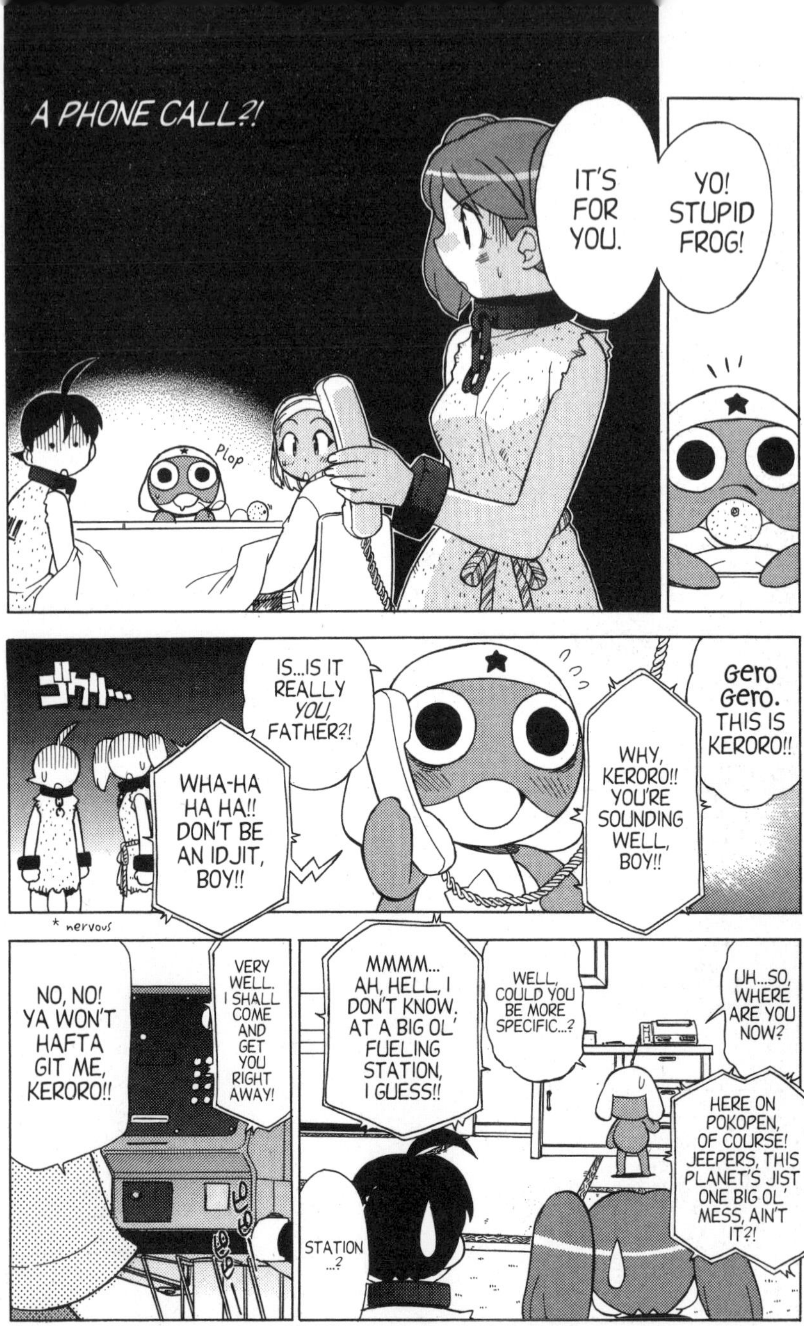
YO! STUPID FROG!
IT'S FOR YOU.
A PHONE CALL?!
Plop
Gero Gero. THIS IS KERORO!!
WHY, KERORO!! YOU'RE SOUNDING WELL, BOY!!
IS...IS IT REALLY YOU, FATHER?!
WHA-HA HA HA!! DON'T BE AN IDJIT, BOY!!
ゴクリ...
* nervous
UH...SO, WHERE ARE YOU NOW?
HERE ON POKOPEN, OF COURSE! JEEPERS, THIS PLANET'S JIST ONE BIG OL' MESS, AIN'T IT?!
WELL, COULD YOU BE MORE SPECIFIC...?
MMMM... AH, HELL, I DON'T KNOW. AT A BIG OL' FUELING STATION, I GUESS!!
STATION ...?
VERY WELL. I SHALL COME AND GET YOU RIGHT AWAY!
NO, NO! YA WON'T HAFTA GIT ME, KERORO!!

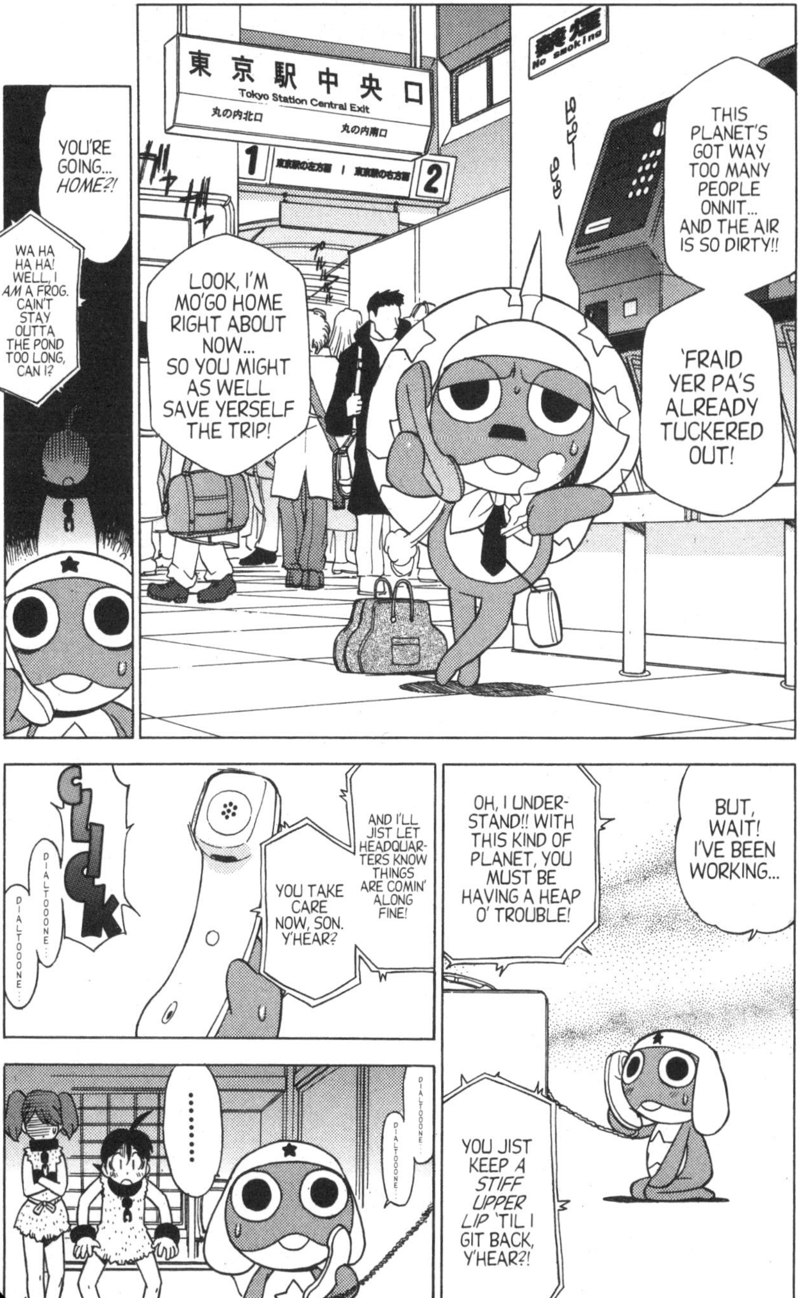
東京駅中央口
Tokyo Station Central Exit
丸の内北口
丸の内南口
No smoking
THIS PLANET'S GOT WAY TOO MANY PEOPLE ONNIT... AND THE AIR IS SO DIRTY!!
'FRAID YER PA'S ALREADY TUCKERED OUT!
LOOK, I'M MO'GO HOME RIGHT ABOUT NOW... SO YOU MIGHT AS WELL SAVE YERSELF THE TRIP!
YOU'RE GOING... *HOME?!*
WA HA HA HA! WELL, I *AM* A FROG. CAIN'T STAY OUTTA THE POND TOO LONG, CAN I?
BUT, WAIT! I'VE BEEN WORKING...
OH, I UNDERSTAND!! WITH THIS KIND OF PLANET, YOU MUST BE HAVING A HEAP O' TROUBLE!
YOU JIST KEEP *A STIFF UPPER LIP* 'TIL I GIT BACK, Y'HEAR?!
AND I'LL JIST LET HEADQUARTERS KNOW THINGS ARE COMIN' ALONG FINE!
YOU TAKE CARE NOW, SON. Y'HEAR?
CLICK
DIALTOOOONE...
DIALTOOOONE...
DIALTOOOONE...
DIALTOOOONE...
....

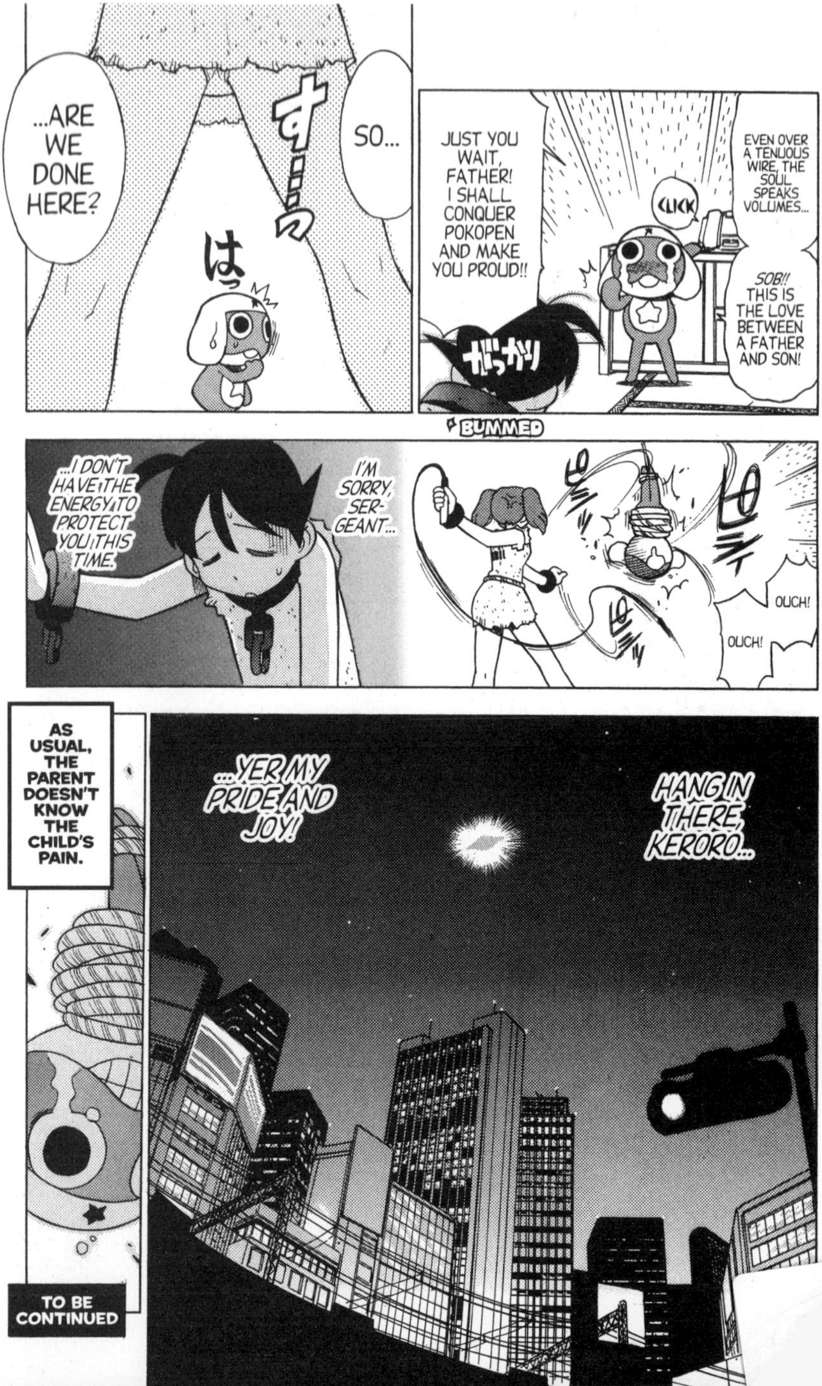
EVEN OVER A TENUOUS WIRE, THE SOUL SPEAKS VOLUMES...
CLICK
SOB!! THIS IS THE LOVE BETWEEN A FATHER AND SON!
JUST YOU WAIT, FATHER! I SHALL CONQUER POKOPEN AND MAKE YOU PROUD!!
がっかり
BUMMED
SO...
...ARE WE DONE HERE?
はっ
OUCH!
OUCH!
I'M SORRY, SERGEANT...
...I DON'T HAVE THE ENERGY TO PROTECT YOU THIS TIME.
HANG IN THERE, KERORO...
...YER MY PRIDE AND JOY!
AS USUAL, THE PARENT DOESN'T KNOW THE CHILD'S PAIN.
TO BE CONTINUED

BLACK AND WHITE SPECIAL BONUS 2

EVERYTHING YOU NEVER WANTED TO KNOW ABOUT CORPORAL GIRORO!

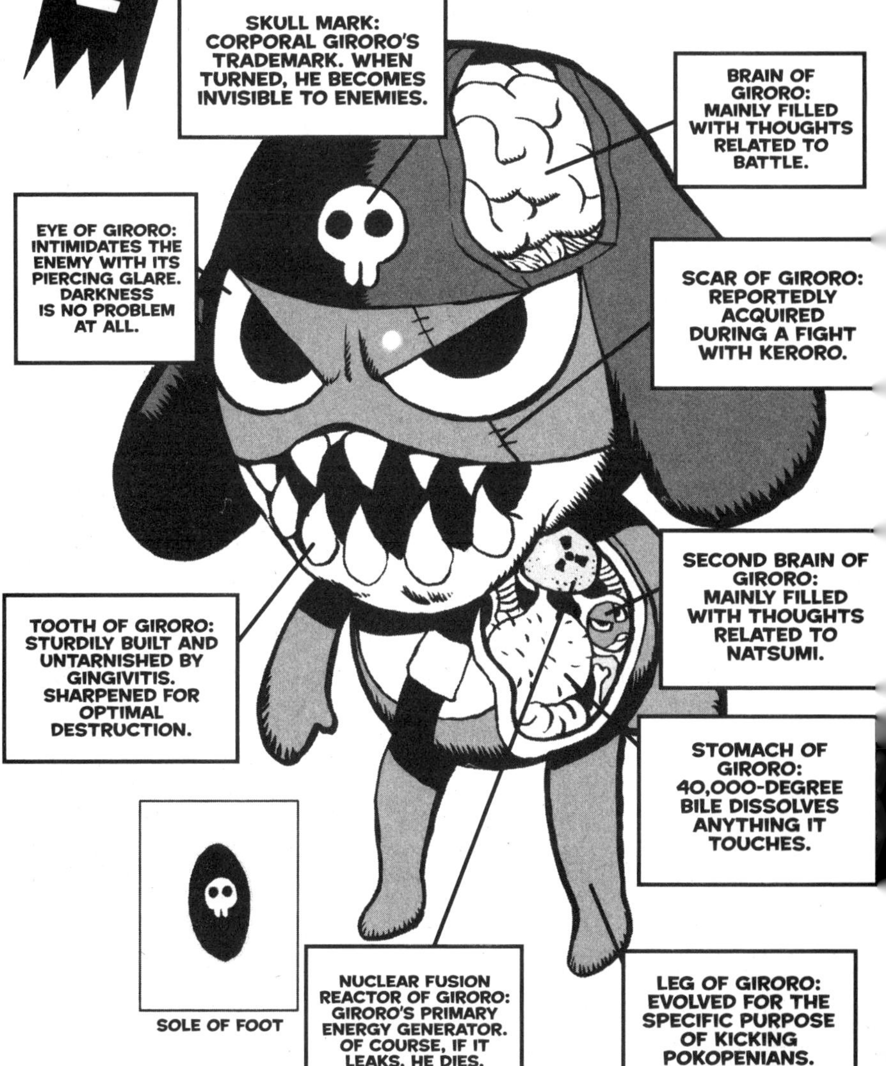
SKULL MARK: CORPORAL GIRORO'S TRADEMARK. WHEN TURNED, HE BECOMES INVISIBLE TO ENEMIES.
BRAIN OF GIRORO: MAINLY FILLED WITH THOUGHTS RELATED TO BATTLE.
EYE OF GIRORO: INTIMIDATES THE ENEMY WITH ITS PIERCING GLARE. DARKNESS IS NO PROBLEM AT ALL.
SCAR OF GIRORO: REPORTEDLY ACQUIRED DURING A FIGHT WITH KERORO.
SECOND BRAIN OF GIRORO: MAINLY FILLED WITH THOUGHTS RELATED TO NATSUMI.
TOOTH OF GIRORO: STURDILY BUILT AND UNTARNISHED BY GINGIVITIS. SHARPENED FOR OPTIMAL DESTRUCTION.
STOMACH OF GIRORO: 40,000-DEGREE BILE DISSOLVES ANYTHING IT TOUCHES.
SOLE OF FOOT
NUCLEAR FUSION REACTOR OF GIRORO: GIRORO'S PRIMARY ENERGY GENERATOR. OF COURSE, IF IT LEAKS, HE DIES.
LEG OF GIRORO: EVOLVED FOR THE SPECIFIC PURPOSE OF KICKING POKOPENIANS.

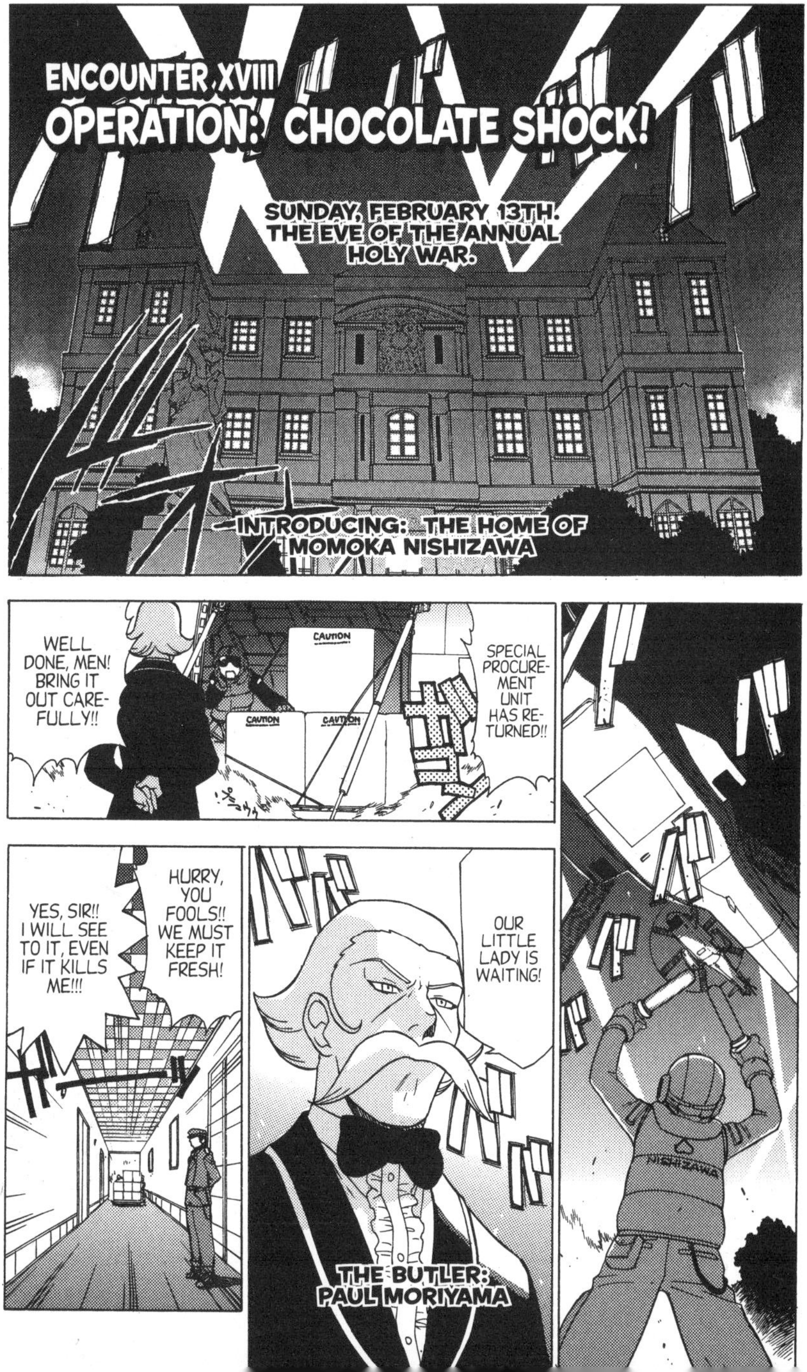
ENCOUNTER XVIII
OPERATION: CHOCOLATE SHOCK!
SUNDAY, FEBRUARY 13TH. THE EVE OF THE ANNUAL HOLY WAR.
INTRODUCING: THE HOME OF MOMOKA NISHIZAWA
SPECIAL PROCUREMENT UNIT HAS RETURNED!!
WELL DONE, MEN! BRING IT OUT CAREFULLY!!
CAUTION
CAUTION
CAUTION
HURRY, YOU FOOLS!! WE MUST KEEP IT FRESH!
OUR LITTLE LADY IS WAITING!
THE BUTLER: PAUL MORIYAMA
YES, SIR!! I WILL SEE TO IT, EVEN IF IT KILLS ME!!!
NISHIZAWA

ENCOUNTER XVIII
OPERATION: CHOCOLATE SHOCK!

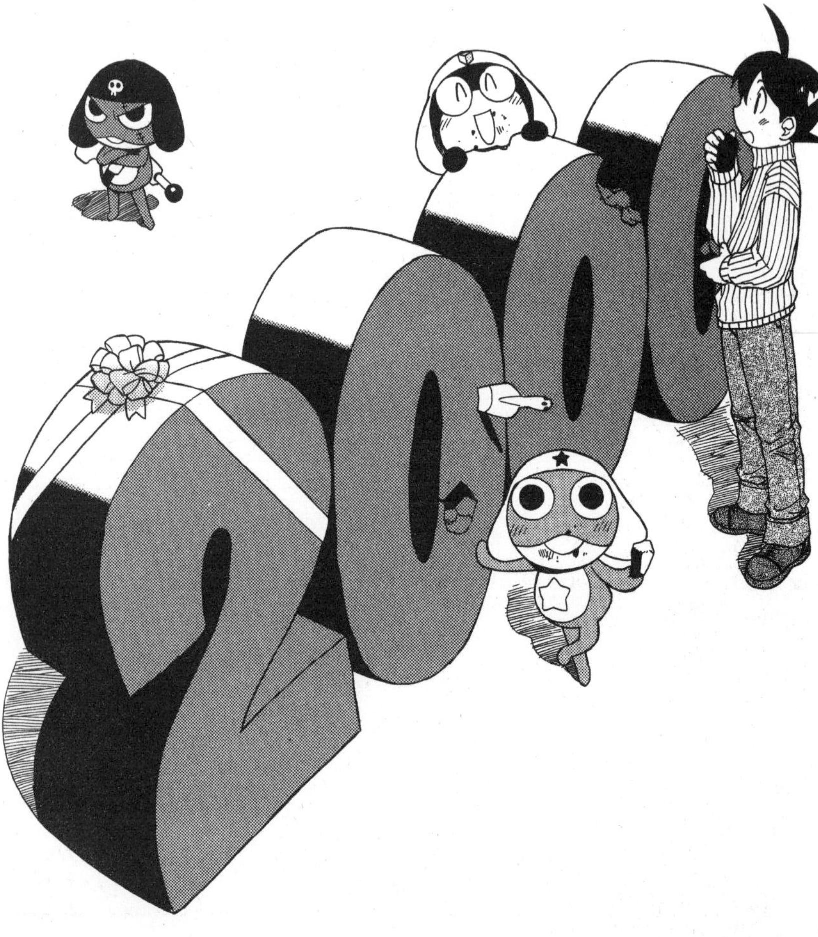

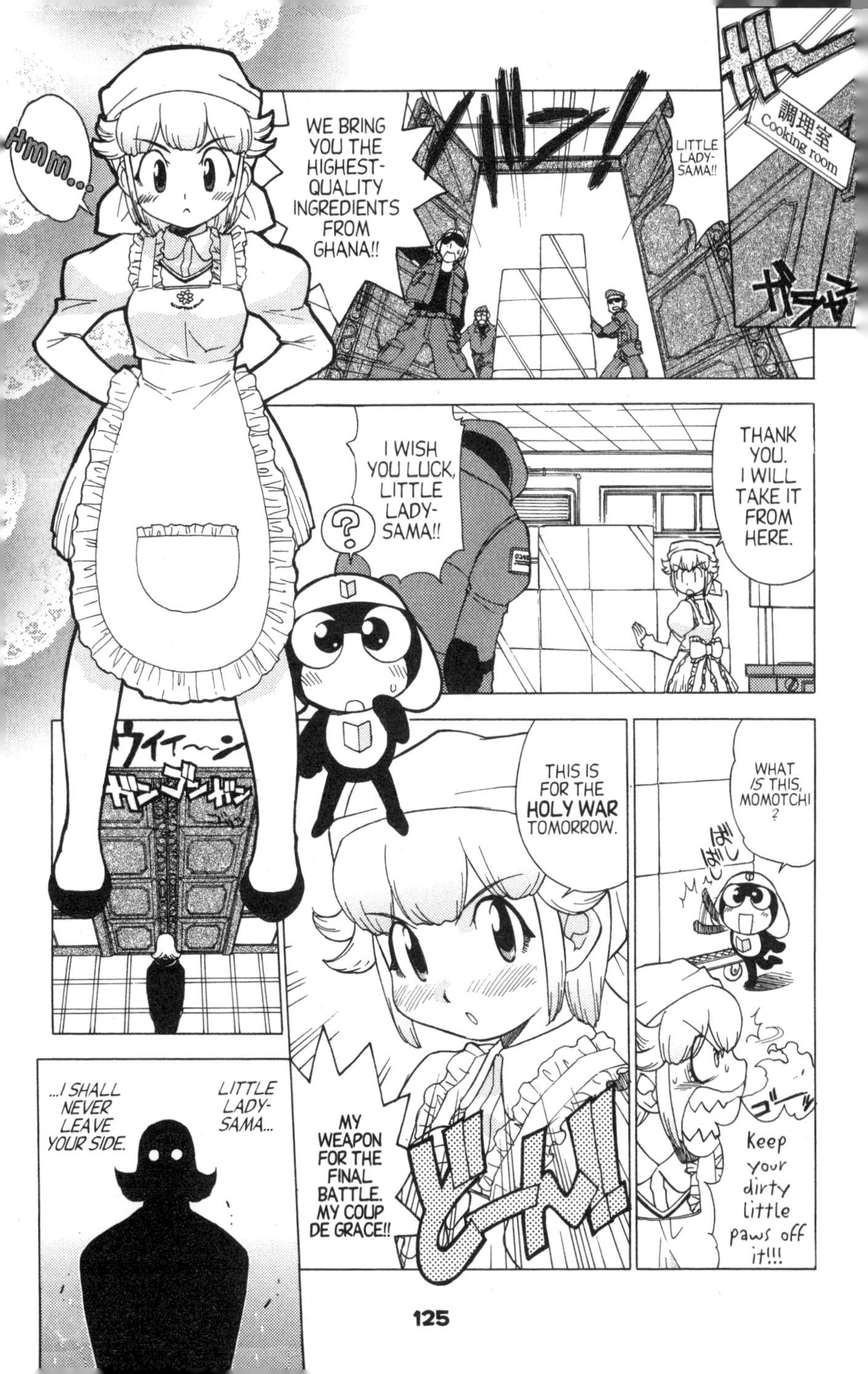

調理室
Cooking room
LITTLE LADY-SAMA!!
WE BRING YOU THE HIGHEST-QUALITY INGREDIENTS FROM GHANA!!
THANK YOU. I WILL TAKE IT FROM HERE.
I WISH YOU LUCK, LITTLE LADY-SAMA!!
?
Hmm...
WHAT IS THIS, MOMOTCHI?
Keep your dirty little paws off it!!!
THIS IS FOR THE HOLY WAR TOMORROW.
MY WEAPON FOR THE FINAL BATTLE. MY COUP DE GRACE!!
LITTLE LADY-SAMA...
...I SHALL NEVER LEAVE YOUR SIDE.

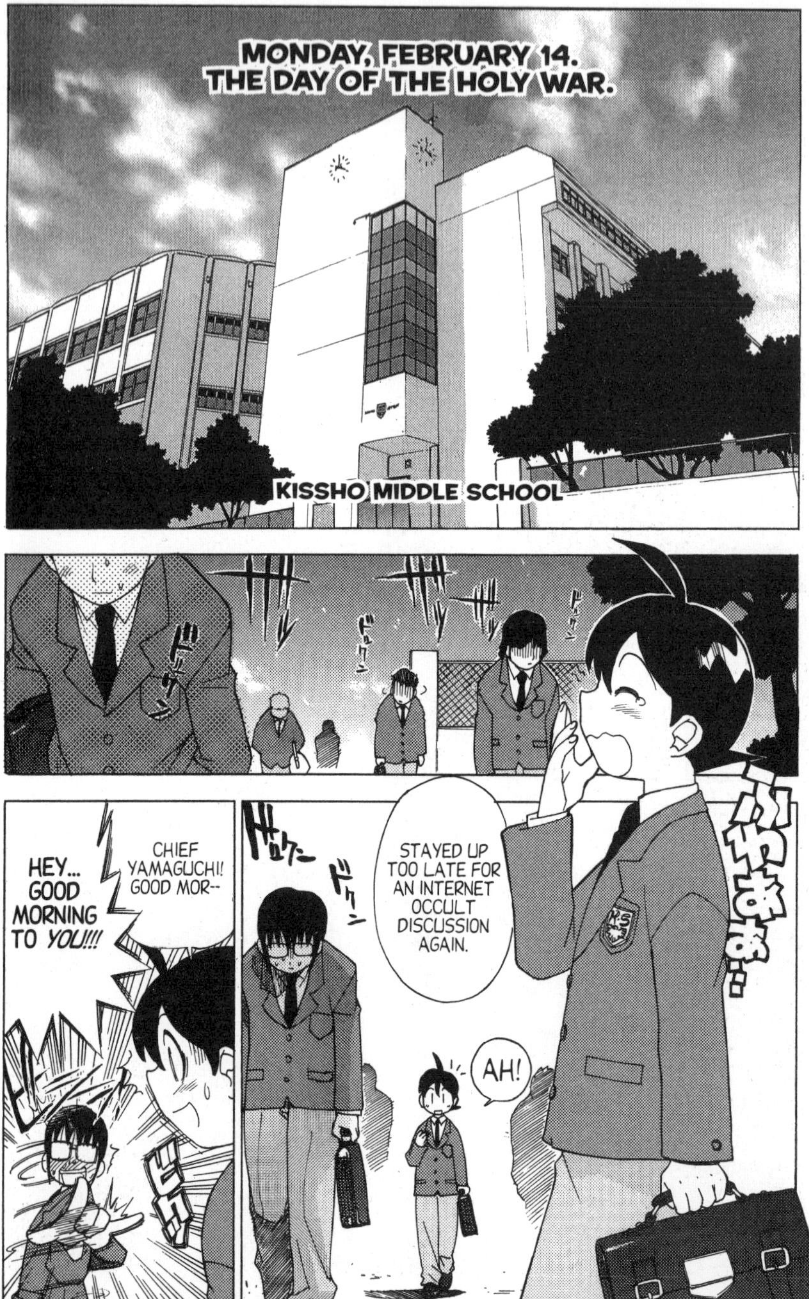
MONDAY, FEBRUARY 14.
THE DAY OF THE HOLY WAR.
KISSHO MIDDLE SCHOOL
STAYED UP TOO LATE FOR AN INTERNET OCCULT DISCUSSION AGAIN.
AH!
CHIEF YAMAGUCHI! GOOD MOR--
HEY... GOOD MORNING TO *YOU*!!!

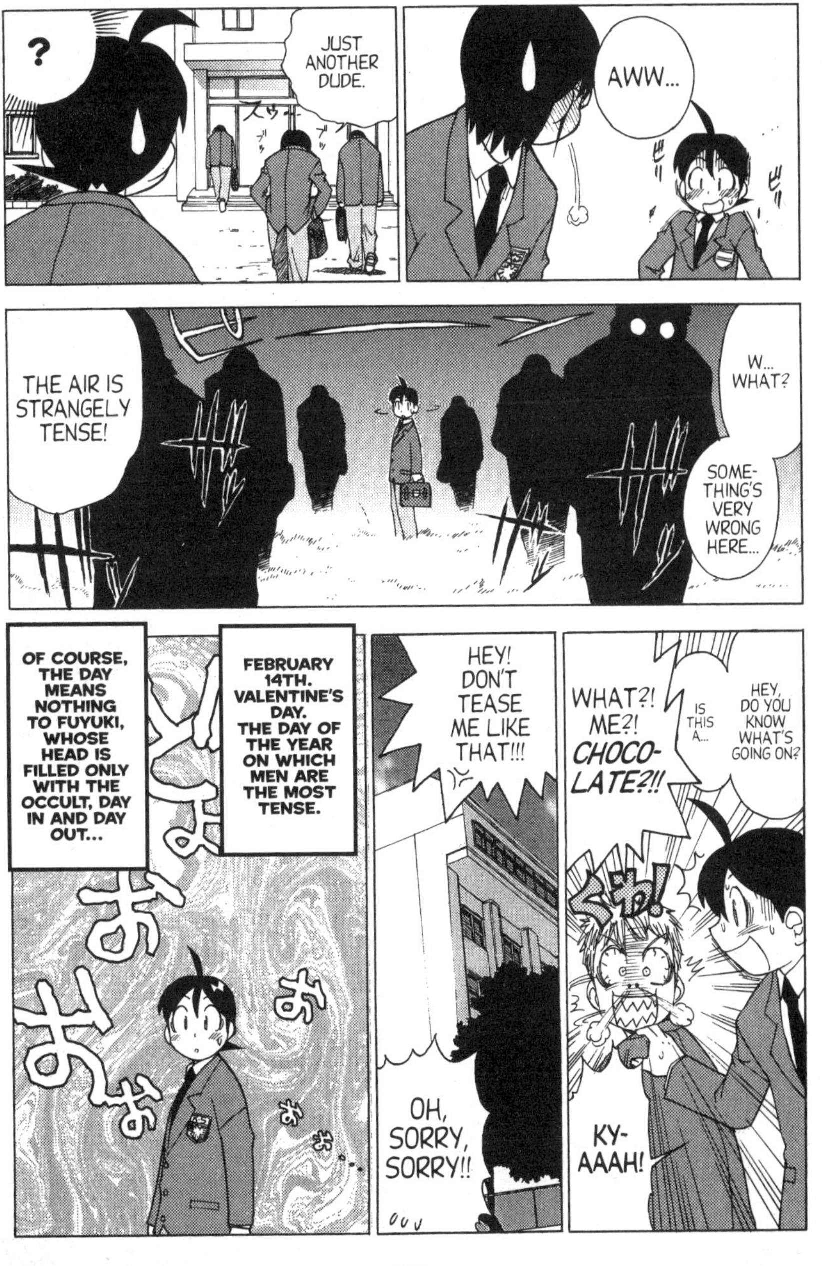
AWW...
?
JUST ANOTHER DUDE.
W... WHAT?
SOME-THING'S VERY WRONG HERE...
THE AIR IS STRANGELY TENSE!
HEY, DO YOU KNOW WHAT'S GOING ON?
IS THIS A...
WHAT?! ME?! CHOCO-LATE?!!
KY-AAAH!
HEY! DON'T TEASE ME LIKE THAT!!!
OH, SORRY, SORRY!!
FEBRUARY 14TH. VALENTINE'S DAY. THE DAY OF THE YEAR ON WHICH MEN ARE THE MOST TENSE.
OF COURSE, THE DAY MEANS NOTHING TO FUYUKI, WHOSE HEAD IS FILLED ONLY WITH THE OCCULT, DAY IN AND DAY OUT...

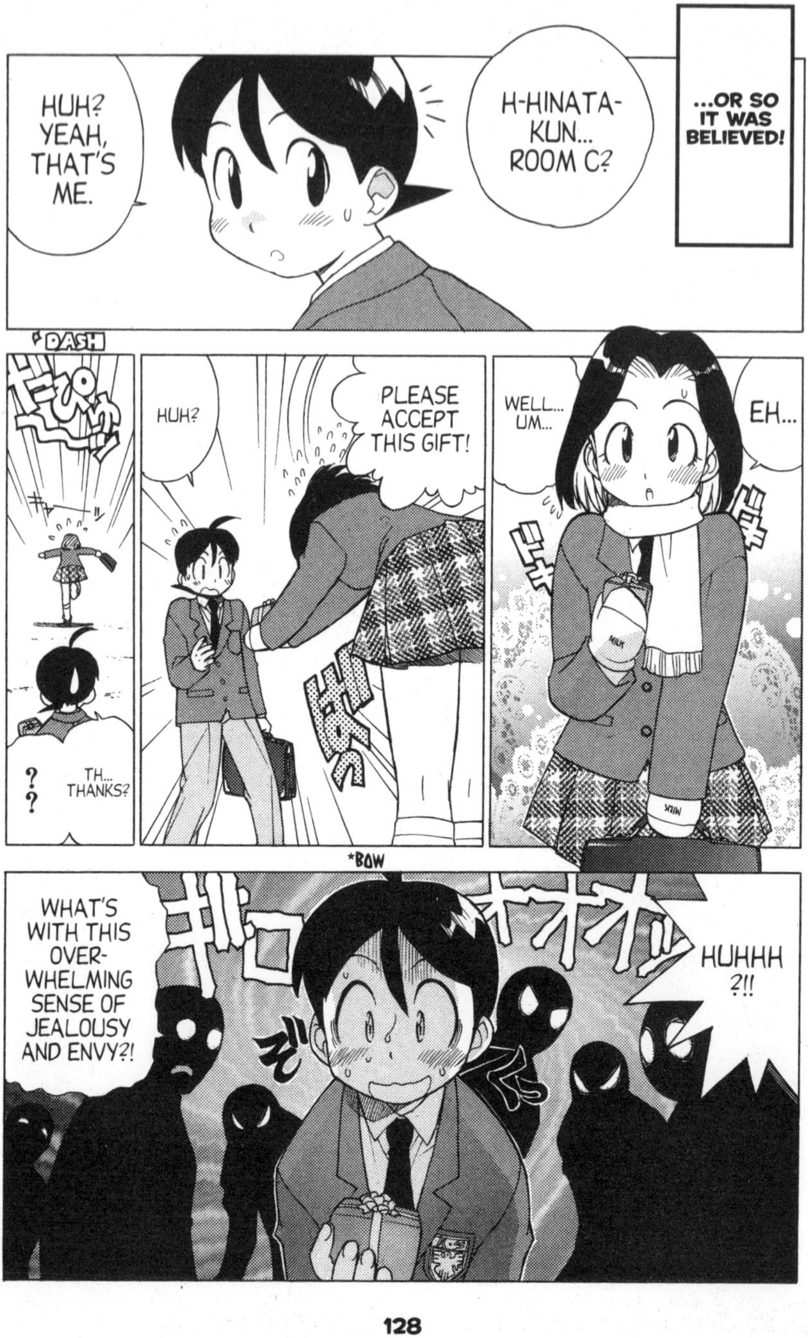
...OR SO IT WAS BELIEVED!
H-HINATA-KUN... ROOM C?
HUH? YEAH, THAT'S ME.
EH...
WELL... UM...
PLEASE ACCEPT THIS GIFT!
HUH?
*BOW
*DASH
TH... THANKS?
??
HUHHH ?!!
WHAT'S WITH THIS OVERWHELMING SENSE OF JEALOUSY AND ENVY?!

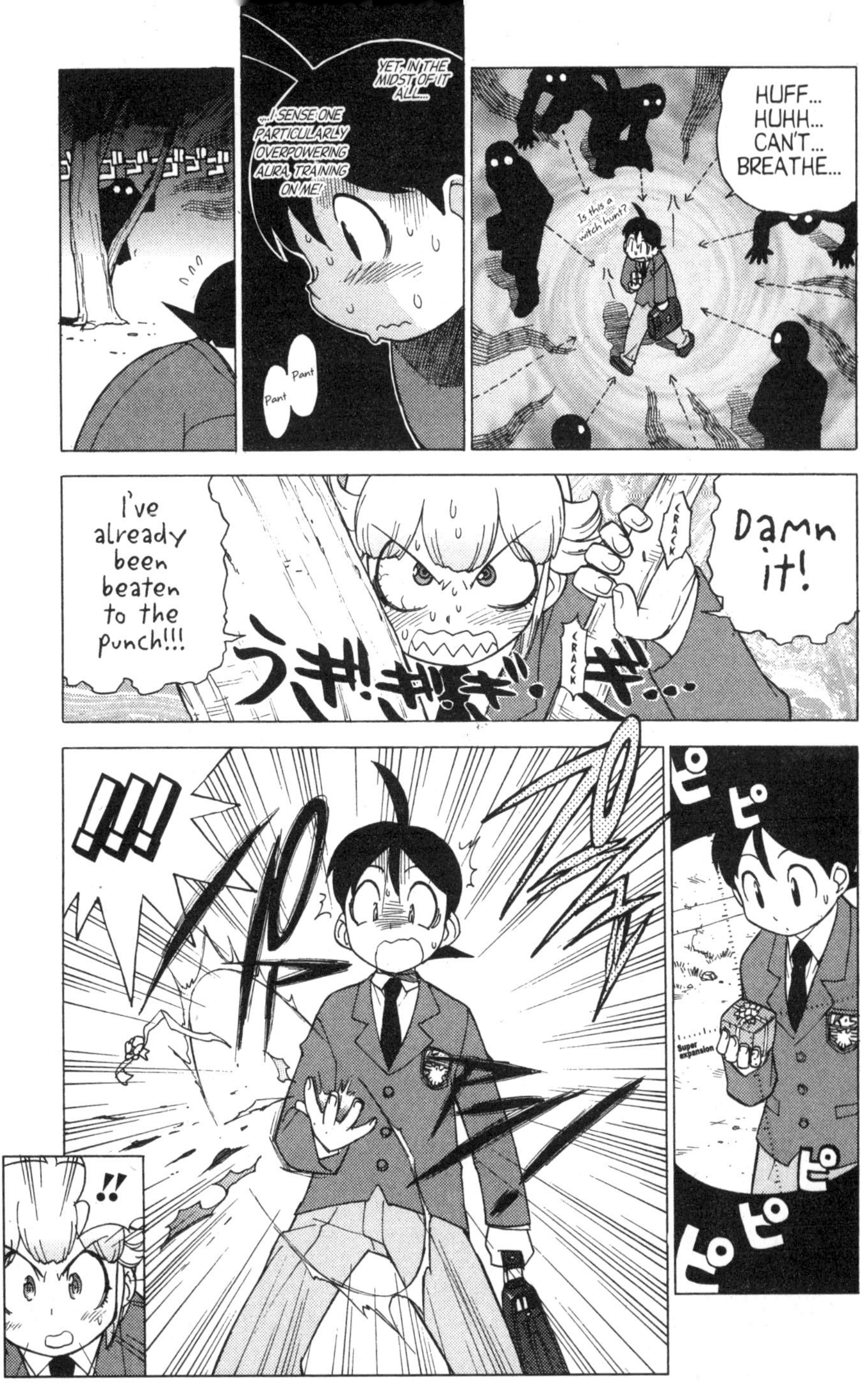

HUFF... HUHH... CAN'T... BREATHE...
Is this a witch hunt?
YET, IN THE MIDST OF IT ALL...
...I SENSE ONE PARTICULARLY OVERPOWERING AURA, TRAINING ON ME!
Pant
Pant
Damn it!
CRACK
CRACK
I've already been beaten to the punch!!!
Super expansion
!!!
!!

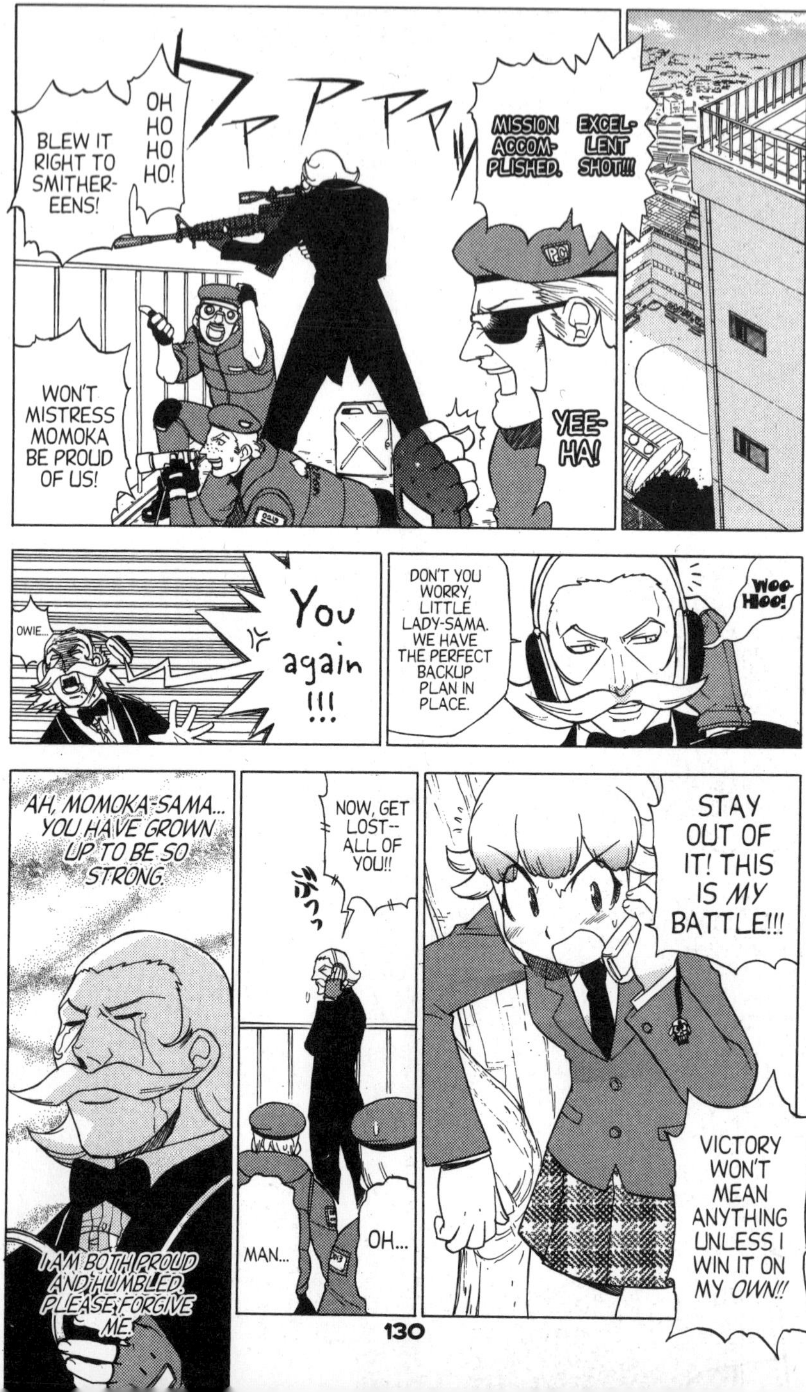

MISSION ACCOMPLISHED. EXCELLENT SHOT!!!
OH HO HO HO!
BLEW IT RIGHT TO SMITHEREENS!
YEE-HA!
WON'T MISTRESS MOMOKA BE PROUD OF US!
WOO-HOO!
DON'T YOU WORRY, LITTLE LADY-SAMA. WE HAVE THE PERFECT BACKUP PLAN IN PLACE.
You again!!!
OWIE...
STAY OUT OF IT! THIS IS *MY* BATTLE!!!
VICTORY WON'T MEAN ANYTHING UNLESS I WIN IT ON MY *OWN*!!
NOW, GET LOST-- ALL OF YOU!!
OH...
MAN...
AH, MOMOKA-SAMA... YOU HAVE GROWN UP TO BE SO STRONG.
I AM BOTH PROUD AND HUMBLED. PLEASE FORGIVE ME.

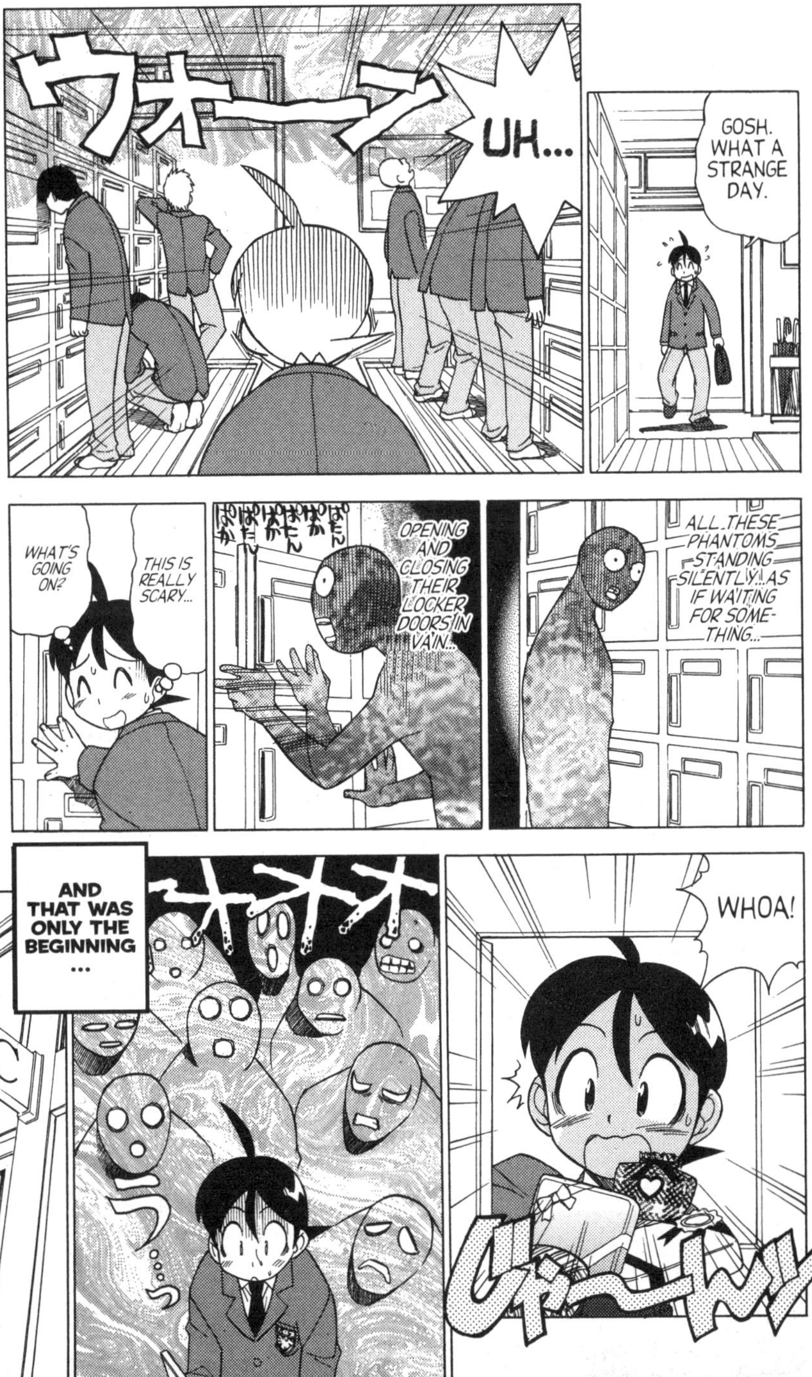
GOSH. WHAT A STRANGE DAY.
ウオーン
UH...
ALL THESE PHANTOMS STANDING SILENTLY... AS IF WAITING FOR SOMETHING...
OPENING AND CLOSING THEIR LOCKER DOORS IN VAIN...
THIS IS REALLY SCARY...
WHAT'S GOING ON?
WHOA!
AND THAT WAS ONLY THE BEGINNING...

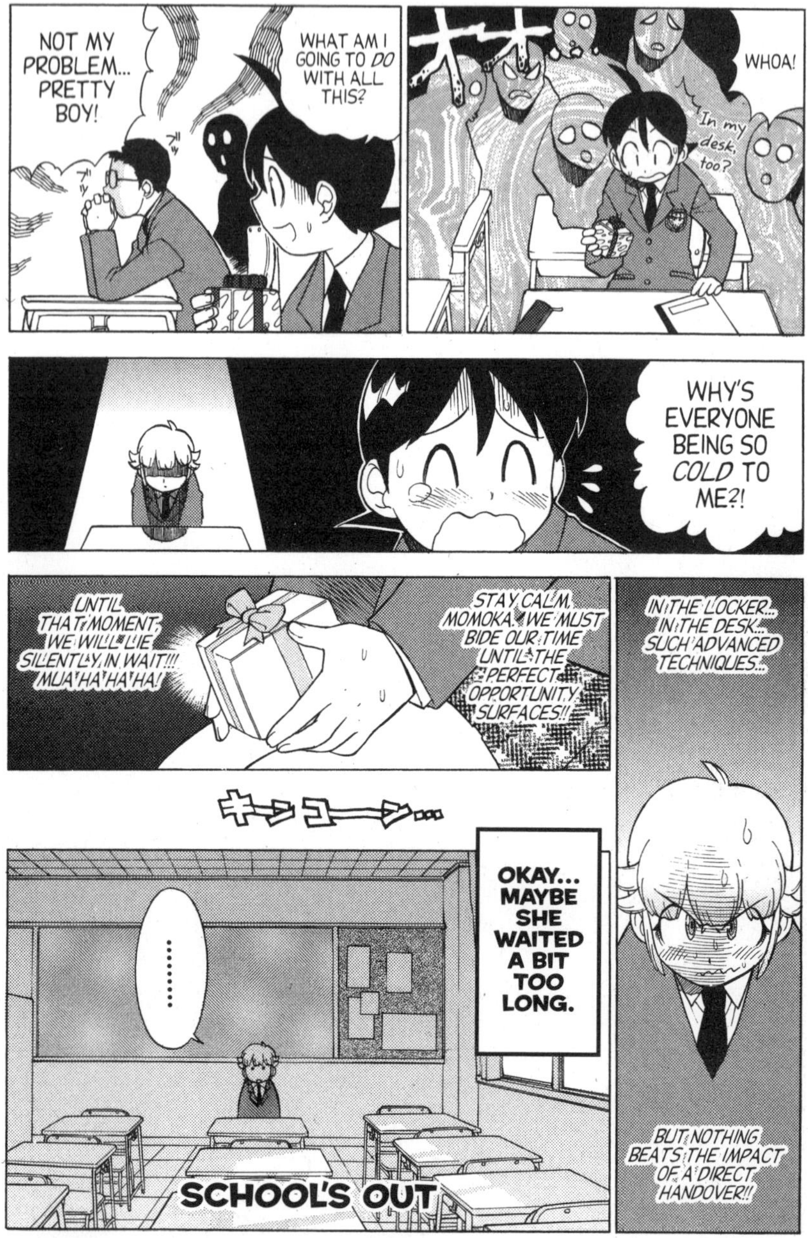
WHOA!
In my desk, too?
WHAT AM I GOING TO *DO* WITH ALL THIS?
NOT MY PROBLEM... PRETTY BOY!
WHY'S EVERYONE BEING SO *COLD* TO ME?!
IN THE LOCKER... IN THE DESK... SUCH ADVANCED TECHNIQUES...
BUT NOTHING BEATS THE IMPACT OF A DIRECT HANDOVER!!
STAY CALM, MOMOKA. WE MUST BIDE OUR TIME UNTIL THE PERFECT OPPORTUNITY SURFACES!!
UNTIL THAT MOMENT, WE WILL LIE SILENTLY IN WAIT!!! MUA HA HA HA!
キーンコーン…
OKAY... MAYBE SHE WAITED A BIT TOO LONG.
....
SCHOOL'S OUT

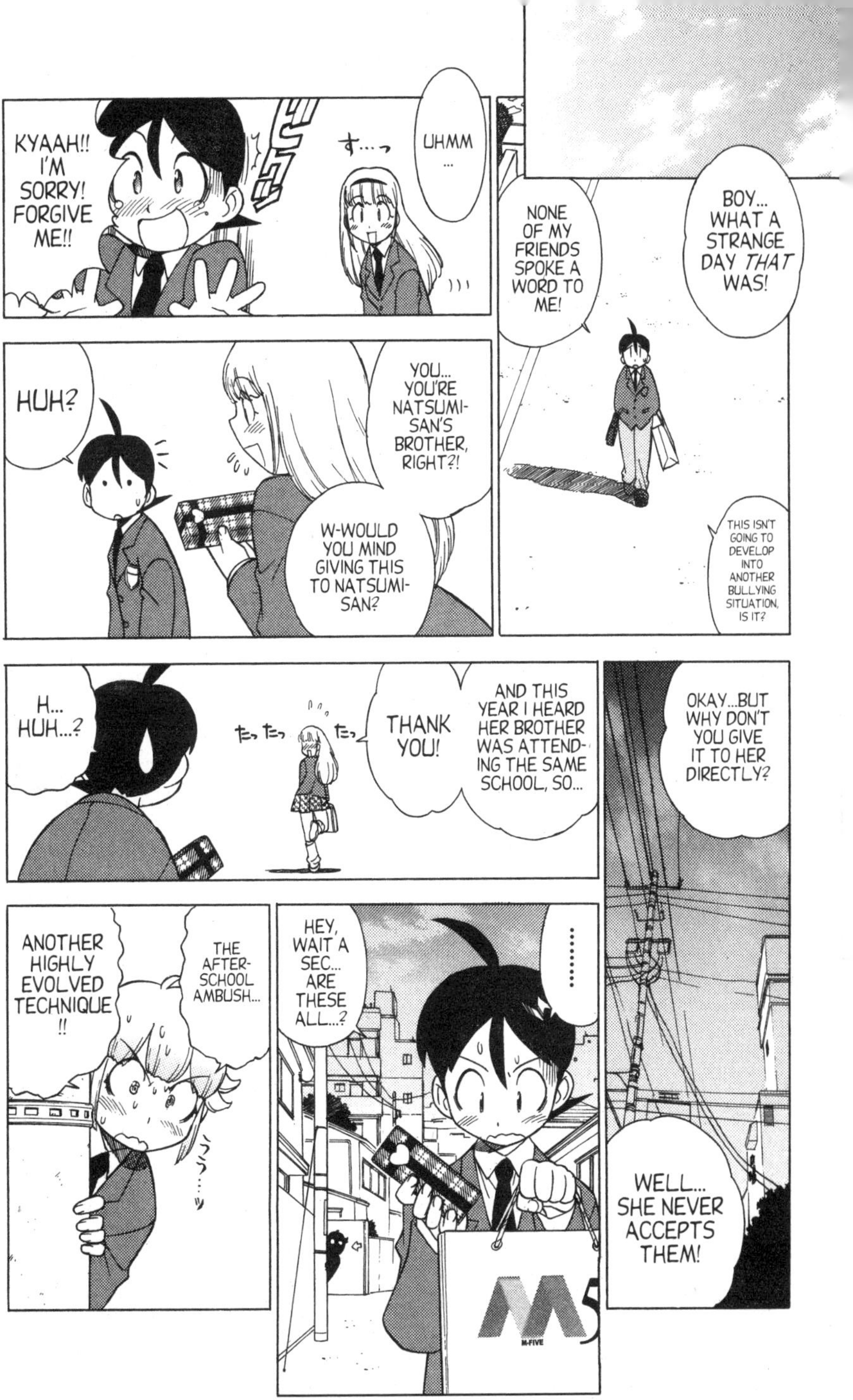

BOY... WHAT A STRANGE DAY *THAT* WAS!
NONE OF MY FRIENDS SPOKE A WORD TO ME!
THIS ISN'T GOING TO DEVELOP INTO ANOTHER BULLYING SITUATION, IS IT?
UHMM ...
す…っ
KYAAH!! I'M SORRY! FORGIVE ME!!
YOU... YOU'RE NATSUMI-SAN'S BROTHER, RIGHT?!
W-WOULD YOU MIND GIVING THIS TO NATSUMI-SAN?
HUH?
OKAY...BUT WHY DON'T YOU GIVE IT TO HER DIRECTLY?
WELL... SHE NEVER ACCEPTS THEM!
AND THIS YEAR I HEARD HER BROTHER WAS ATTENDING THE SAME SCHOOL, SO...
THANK YOU!
たっ たっ たっ
H... HUH...?
....
HEY, WAIT A SEC... ARE THESE ALL...?
M-FIVE
THE AFTER-SCHOOL AMBUSH...
ANOTHER HIGHLY EVOLVED TECHNIQUE !!
フフ…ッ

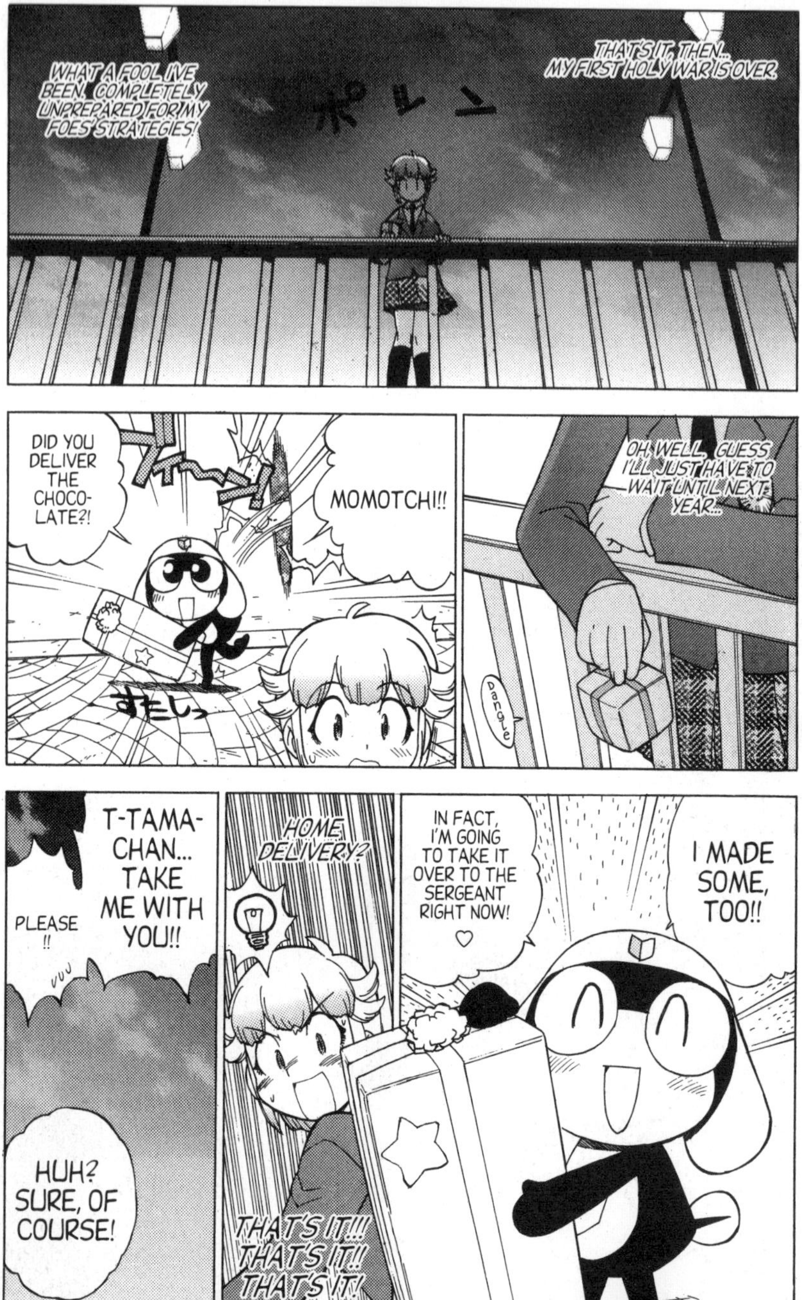
THAT'S IT, THEN... MY FIRST HOLY WAR IS OVER.
WHAT A FOOL I'VE BEEN, COMPLETELY UNPREPARED FOR MY FOES' STRATEGIES!
ポレン
OH WELL. GUESS I'LL JUST HAVE TO WAIT UNTIL NEXT YEAR...
Dangle
MOMOTCHI!!
DID YOU DELIVER THE CHOCO-LATE?!
I MADE SOME, TOO!!
IN FACT, I'M GOING TO TAKE IT OVER TO THE SERGEANT RIGHT NOW! ♡
HOME DELIVERY?
THAT'S IT!!! THAT'S IT!! THAT'S IT!
T-TAMA-CHAN... TAKE ME WITH YOU!!
PLEASE !!
HUH? SURE, OF COURSE!

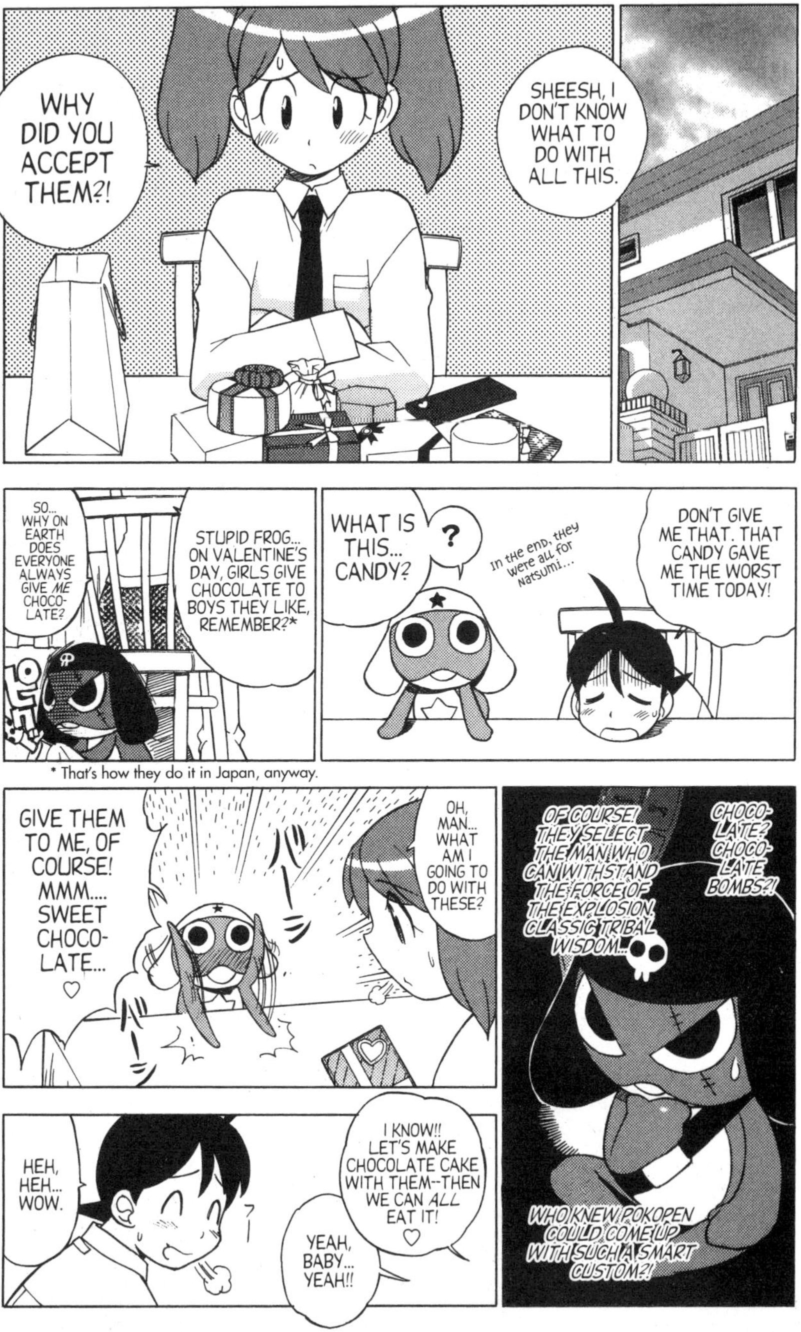
SHEESH, I DON'T KNOW WHAT TO DO WITH ALL THIS.
WHY DID YOU ACCEPT THEM?!
DON'T GIVE ME THAT. THAT CANDY GAVE ME THE WORST TIME TODAY!
In the end, they were all for Natsumi...
?
WHAT IS THIS... CANDY?
STUPID FROG... ON VALENTINE'S DAY, GIRLS GIVE CHOCOLATE TO BOYS THEY LIKE, REMEMBER?*
SO... WHY ON EARTH DOES EVERYONE ALWAYS GIVE *ME* CHOCOLATE?
CHOCOLATE? CHOCOLATE BOMBS?!
OF COURSE! THEY SELECT THE MAN WHO CAN WITHSTAND THE FORCE OF THE EXPLOSION. CLASSIC TRIBAL WISDOM...
WHO KNEW POKOPEN COULD COME UP WITH SUCH A SMART CUSTOM?!
OH, MAN... WHAT AM I GOING TO DO WITH THESE?
GIVE THEM TO ME, OF COURSE! MMM.... SWEET CHOCOLATE... ♡
I KNOW!! LET'S MAKE CHOCOLATE CAKE WITH THEM--THEN WE CAN *ALL* EAT IT! ♡
YEAH, BABY... YEAH!!
HEH, HEH... WOW.

* That's how they do it in Japan, anyway.

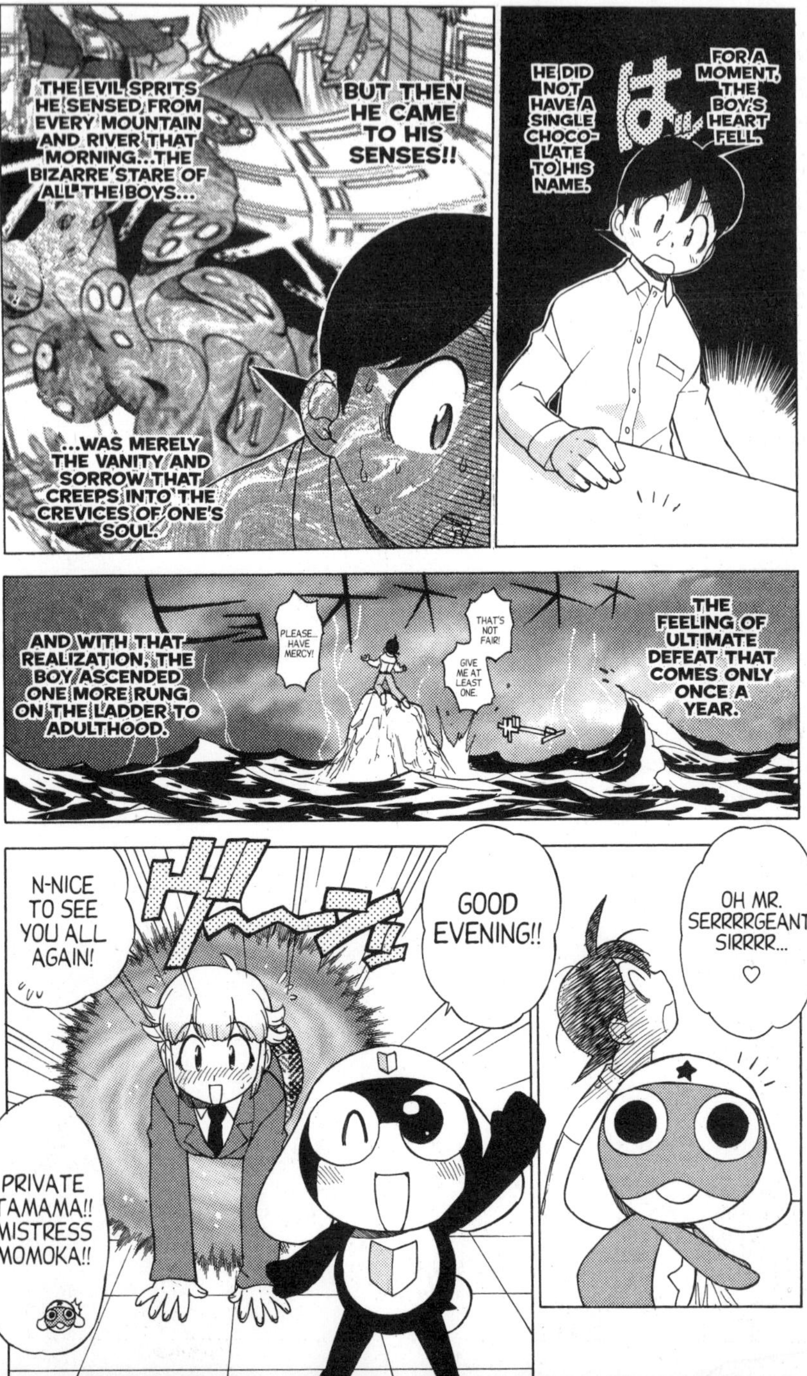

FOR A MOMENT, THE BOY'S HEART FELL.
はッ
HE DID NOT HAVE A SINGLE CHOCO-LATE TO HIS NAME.
BUT THEN HE CAME TO HIS SENSES!!
THE EVIL SPRITS HE SENSED FROM EVERY MOUNTAIN AND RIVER THAT MORNING...THE BIZARRE STARE OF ALL THE BOYS...
...WAS MERELY THE VANITY AND SORROW THAT CREEPS INTO THE CREVICES OF ONE'S SOUL.
THE FEELING OF ULTIMATE DEFEAT THAT COMES ONLY ONCE A YEAR.
THAT'S NOT FAIR!
GIVE ME AT LEAST ONE.
PLEASE... HAVE MERCY!
AND WITH THAT REALIZATION, THE BOY ASCENDED ONE MORE RUNG ON THE LADDER TO ADULTHOOD.
OH MR. SERRRRGEANT, SIRRRR... ♡
GOOD EVENING!!
N-NICE TO SEE YOU ALL AGAIN!
PRIVATE TAMAMA!! MISTRESS MOMOKA!!

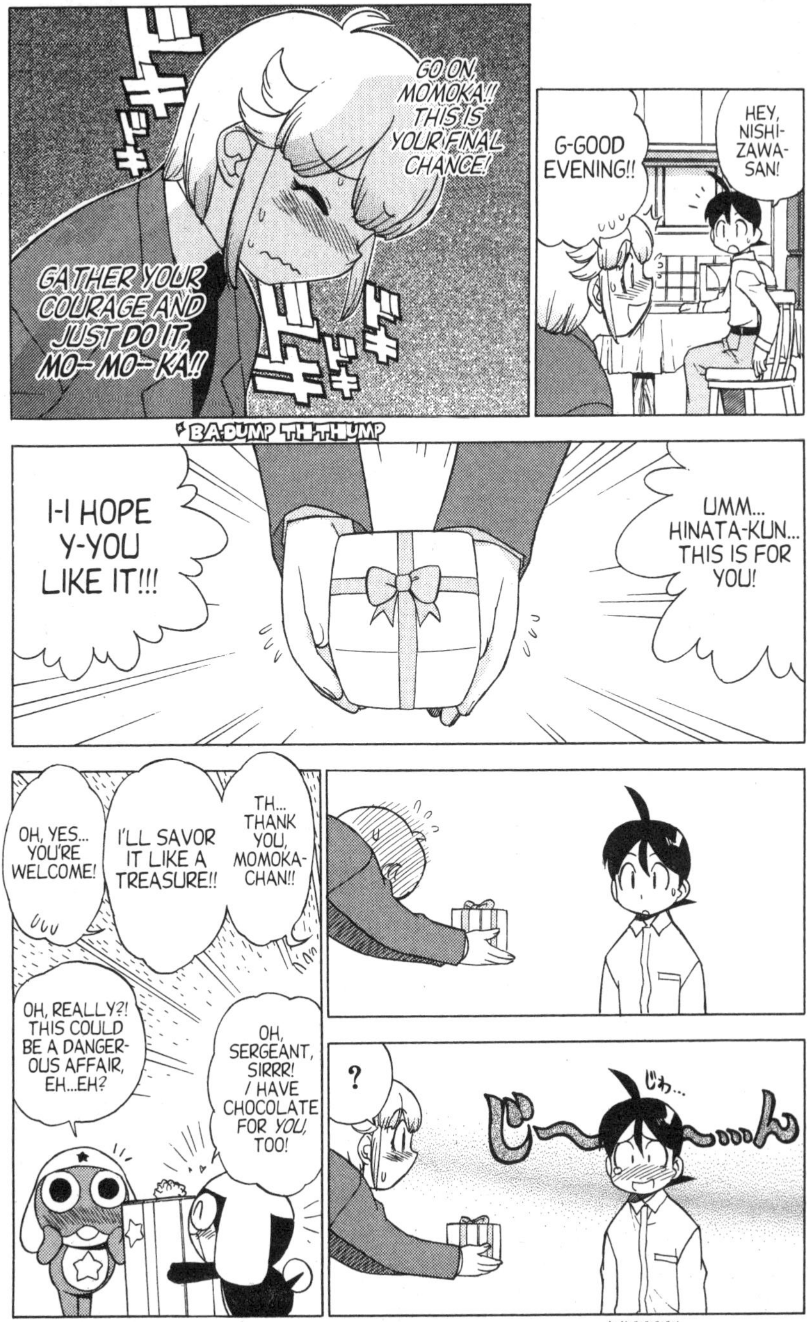
HEY, NISHI-ZAWA-SAN!
G-GOOD EVENING!!
ドキドキ
GO ON, MOMOKA!! THIS IS YOUR FINAL CHANCE!
GATHER YOUR COURAGE AND JUST DO IT, MO-- MO-- KA!!
ドキドキドキ
UMM... HINATA-KUN... THIS IS FOR YOU!
I-I HOPE Y-YOU LIKE IT!!!
?
じわ…
じ〜〜…ん
TH... THANK YOU, MOMOKA-CHAN!!
I'LL SAVOR IT LIKE A TREASURE!!
OH, YES... YOU'RE WELCOME!
OH, SERGEANT, SIRRR! I HAVE CHOCOLATE FOR YOU, TOO!
OH, REALLY?! THIS COULD BE A DANGER-OUS AFFAIR, EH...EH?

* BA-DUMP TH-THUMP

* AWWWWW...

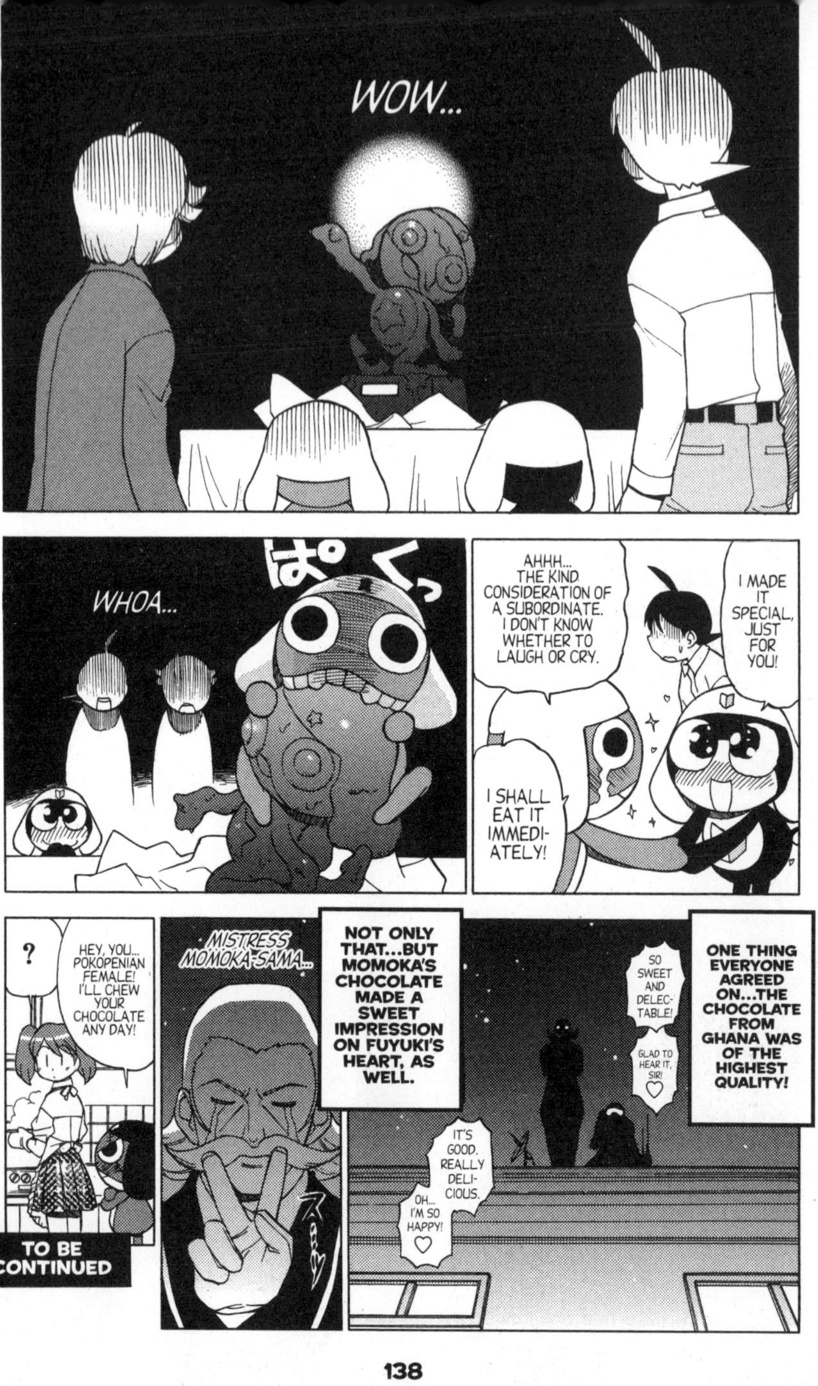
WOW...
I MADE IT SPECIAL, JUST FOR YOU!
AHHH... THE KIND CONSIDERATION OF A SUBORDINATE. I DON'T KNOW WHETHER TO LAUGH OR CRY.
I SHALL EAT IT IMMEDI-ATELY!
ぱくっ
WHOA...
ONE THING EVERYONE AGREED ON...THE CHOCOLATE FROM GHANA WAS OF THE HIGHEST QUALITY!
SO SWEET AND DELEC-TABLE!
GLAD TO HEAR IT, SIR! ♡
IT'S GOOD. REALLY DELI-CIOUS.
OH... I'M SO HAPPY! ♡
NOT ONLY THAT...BUT MOMOKA'S CHOCOLATE MADE A SWEET IMPRESSION ON FUYUKI'S HEART, AS WELL.
MISTRESS MOMOKA-SAMA...
HEY, YOU... POKOPENIAN FEMALE! I'LL CHEW YOUR CHOCOLATE ANY DAY!
?
TO BE CONTINUED

ENCOUNTER XIX-
THE 623 INCIDENT!!

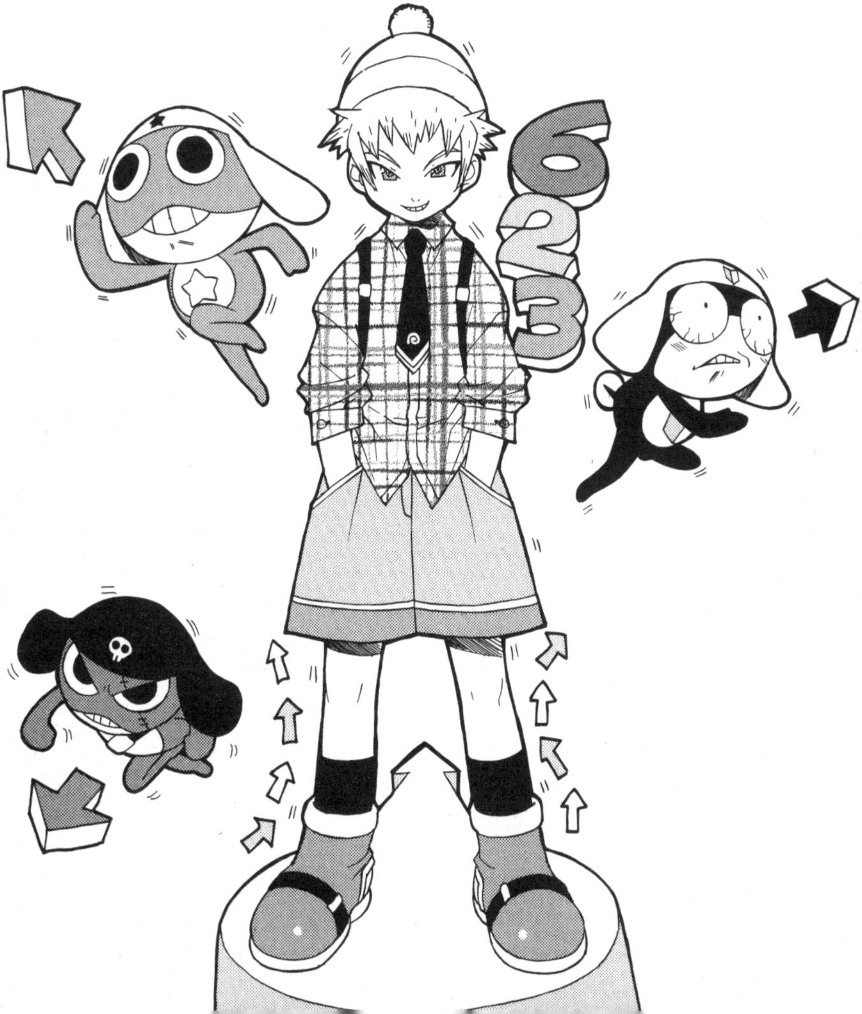
623

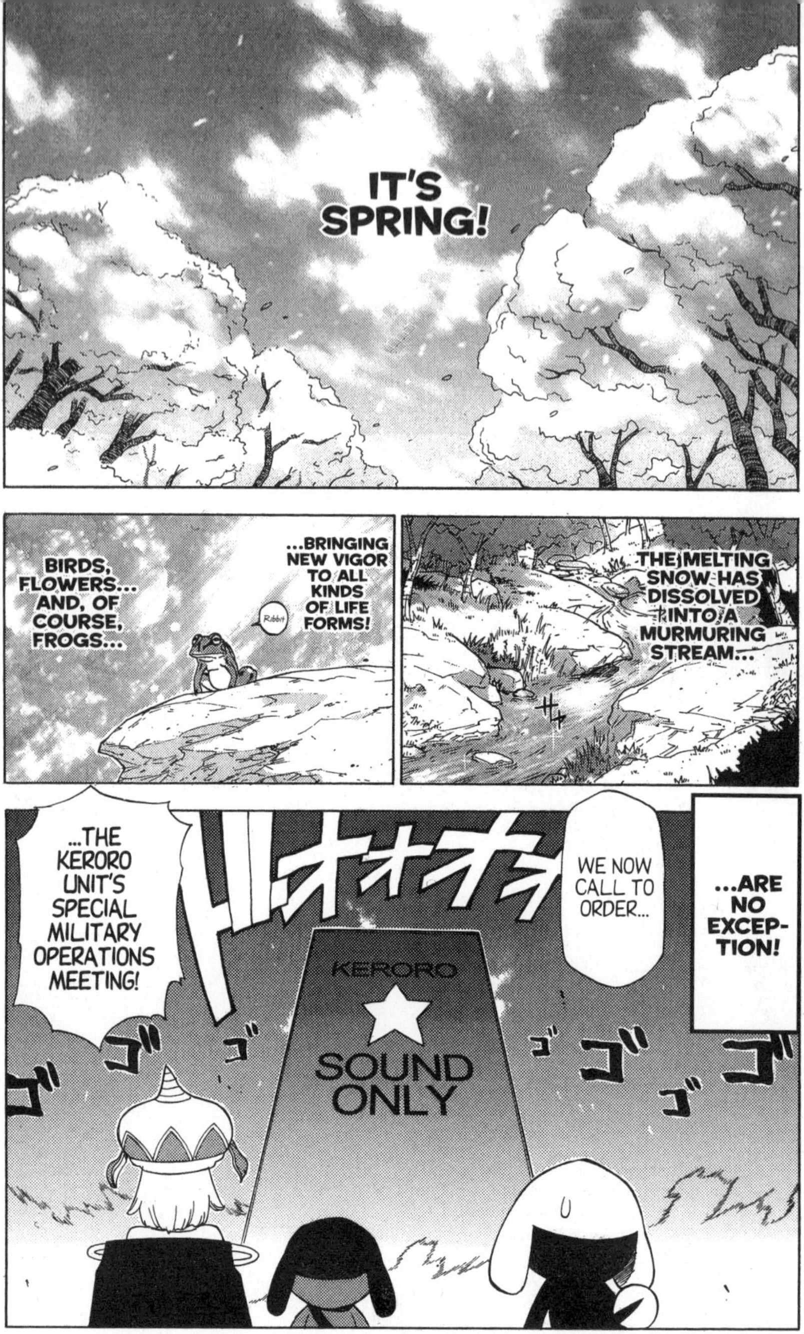
IT'S SPRING!
THE MELTING SNOW HAS DISSOLVED INTO A MURMURING STREAM...
...BRINGING NEW VIGOR TO ALL KINDS OF LIFE FORMS!
Ribbit
BIRDS, FLOWERS... AND, OF COURSE, FROGS...
...ARE NO EXCEPTION!
WE NOW CALL TO ORDER...
...THE KERORO UNIT'S SPECIAL MILITARY OPERATIONS MEETING!
KERORO
SOUND ONLY

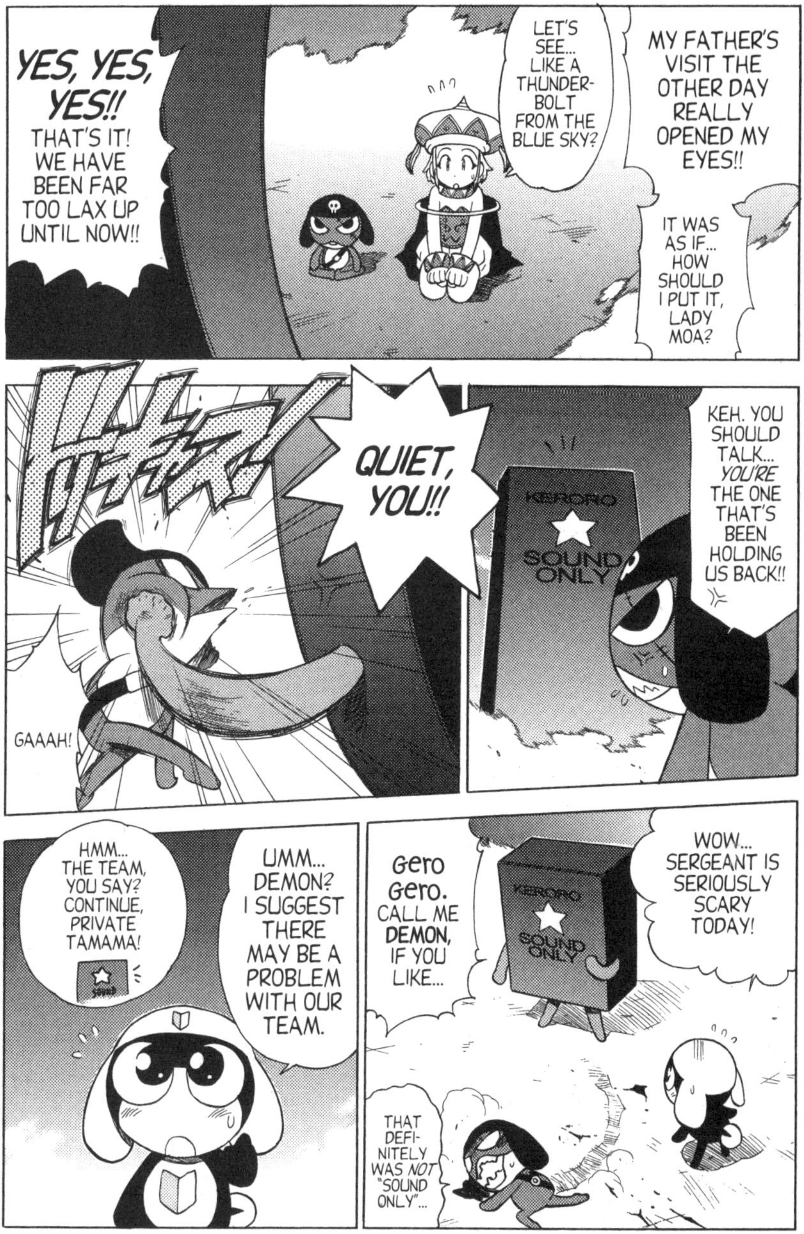
MY FATHER'S VISIT THE OTHER DAY REALLY OPENED MY EYES!!
IT WAS AS IF... HOW SHOULD I PUT IT, LADY MOA?
LET'S SEE... LIKE A THUNDER-BOLT FROM THE BLUE SKY?
YES, YES, YES!! THAT'S IT! WE HAVE BEEN FAR TOO LAX UP UNTIL NOW!!
KEROR0 SOUND ONLY
KEH. YOU SHOULD TALK... *YOU'RE* THE ONE THAT'S BEEN HOLDING US BACK!!
QUIET, YOU!!
GAAAH!
WOW... SERGEANT IS SERIOUSLY SCARY TODAY!
KERORO SOUND ONLY
Gero Gero. CALL ME **DEMON,** IF YOU LIKE...
THAT DEFI-NITELY WAS *NOT* "SOUND ONLY"...
UMM... DEMON? I SUGGEST THERE MAY BE A PROBLEM WITH OUR TEAM.
HMM... THE TEAM, YOU SAY? CONTINUE, PRIVATE TAMAMA!

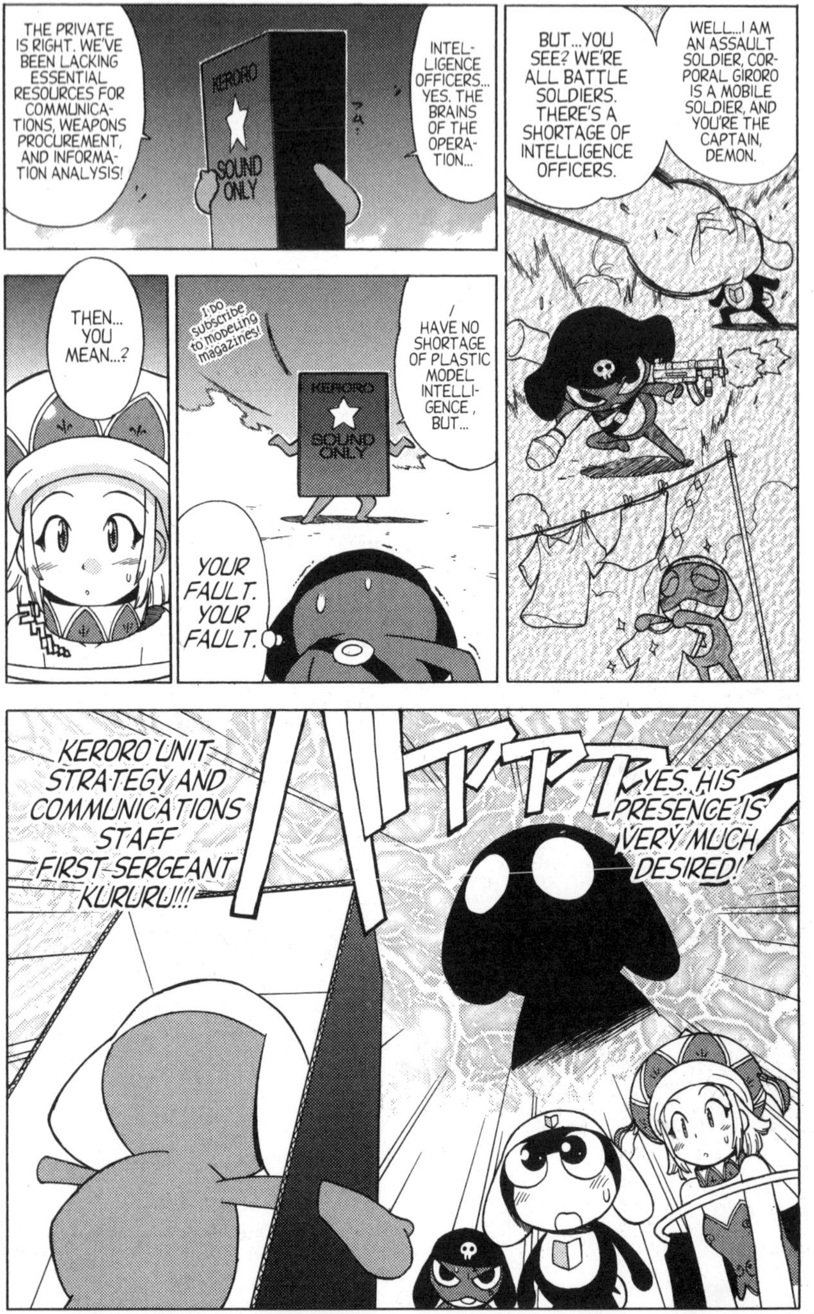
WELL...I AM AN ASSAULT SOLDIER, CORPORAL GIRORO IS A MOBILE SOLDIER, AND YOU'RE THE CAPTAIN, DEMON.
BUT...YOU SEE? WE'RE ALL BATTLE SOLDIERS. THERE'S A SHORTAGE OF INTELLIGENCE OFFICERS.
INTELLIGENCE OFFICERS... YES. THE BRAINS OF THE OPERATION...
THE PRIVATE IS RIGHT. WE'VE BEEN LACKING ESSENTIAL RESOURCES FOR COMMUNICATIONS, WEAPONS PROCUREMENT, AND INFORMATION ANALYSIS!
KERORO
SOUND ONLY
I HAVE NO SHORTAGE OF PLASTIC MODEL INTELLIGENCE, BUT...
I DO subscribe to modeling magazines!
KERORO
SOUND ONLY
YOUR FAULT. YOUR FAULT.
THEN... YOU MEAN...?
YES. HIS PRESENCE IS VERY MUCH DESIRED!
KERORO UNIT STRATEGY AND COMMUNICATIONS STAFF FIRST SERGEANT KURURU!!!

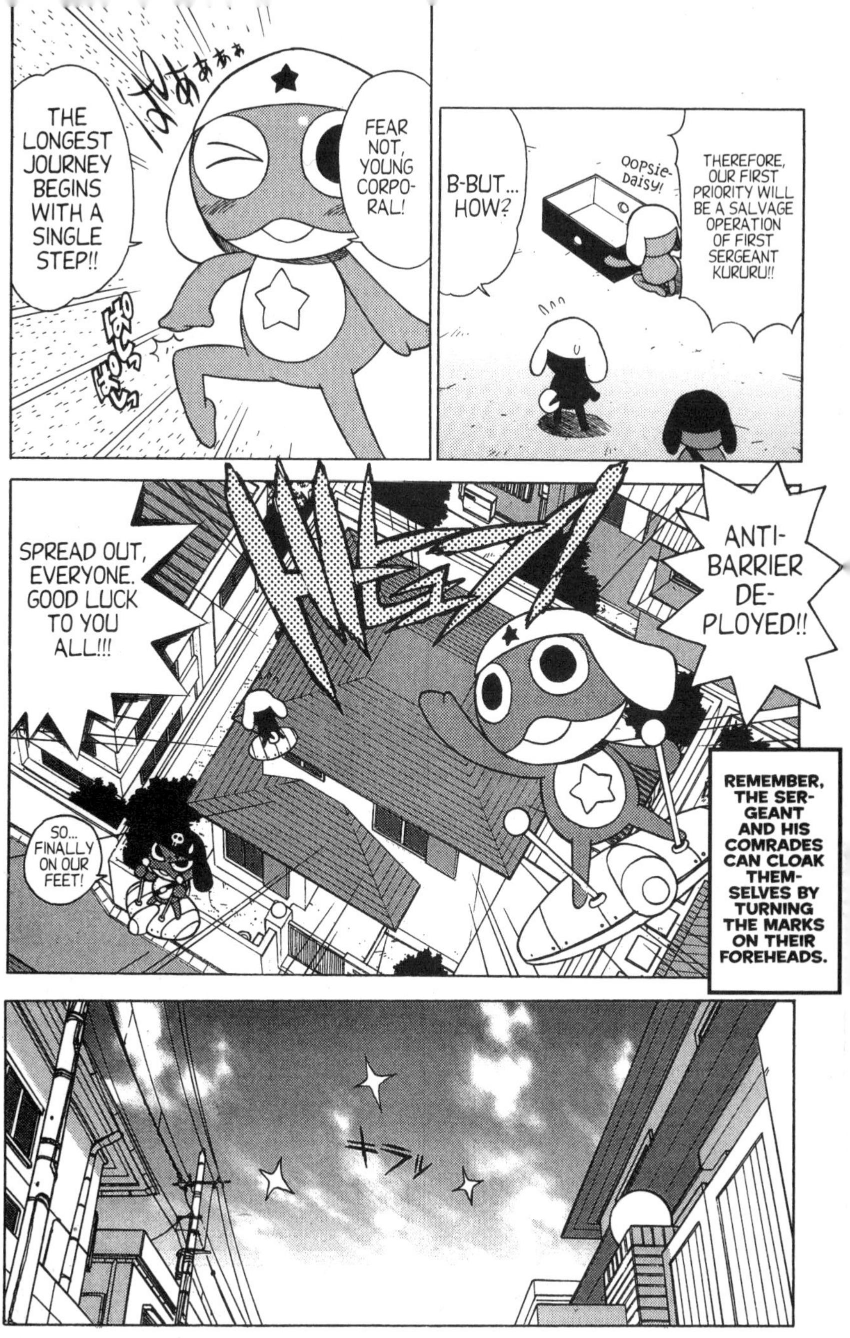
THEREFORE, OUR FIRST PRIORITY WILL BE A SALVAGE OPERATION OF FIRST SERGEANT KURURU!!
Oopsie-Daisy!
B-BUT... HOW?
FEAR NOT, YOUNG CORPORAL!
THE LONGEST JOURNEY BEGINS WITH A SINGLE STEP!!
ANTI-BARRIER DE-PLOYED!!
REMEMBER, THE SERGEANT AND HIS COMRADES CAN CLOAK THEMSELVES BY TURNING THE MARKS ON THEIR FOREHEADS.
SPREAD OUT, EVERYONE. GOOD LUCK TO YOU ALL!!!
SO... FINALLY ON OUR FEET!

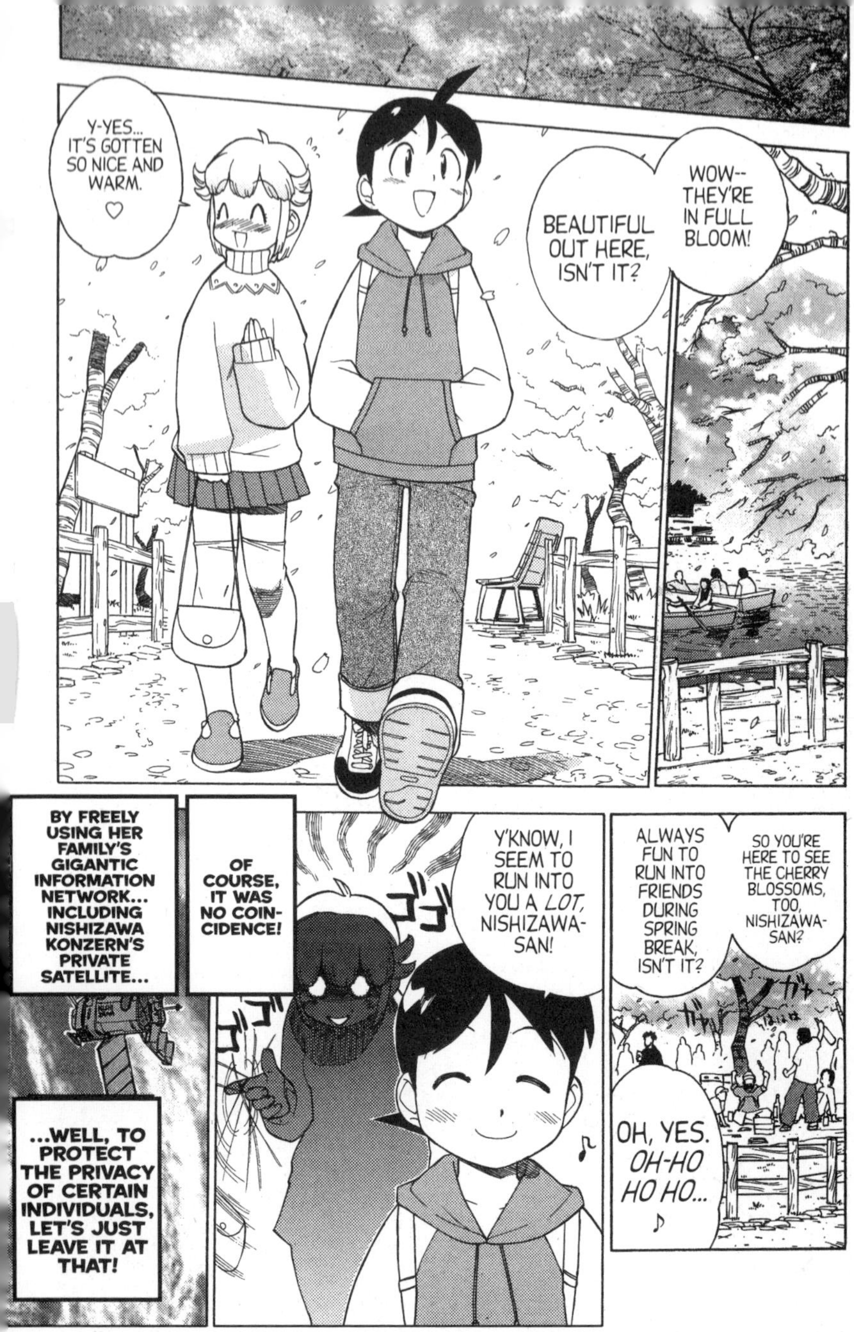
WOW-- THEY'RE IN FULL BLOOM!
BEAUTIFUL OUT HERE, ISN'T IT?
Y-YES... IT'S GOTTEN SO NICE AND WARM. ♡
SO YOU'RE HERE TO SEE THE CHERRY BLOSSOMS, TOO, NISHIZAWA-SAN?
ALWAYS FUN TO RUN INTO FRIENDS DURING SPRING BREAK, ISN'T IT?
ガヤ
ガヤ
OH, YES. OH-HO HO HO... ♪
Y'KNOW, I SEEM TO RUN INTO YOU A LOT, NISHIZAWA-SAN!
ゴゴ
ゴゴ
OF COURSE, IT WAS NO COINCIDENCE!
BY FREELY USING HER FAMILY'S GIGANTIC INFORMATION NETWORK... INCLUDING NISHIZAWA KONZERN'S PRIVATE SATELLITE...
...WELL, TO PROTECT THE PRIVACY OF CERTAIN INDIVIDUALS, LET'S JUST LEAVE IT AT THAT!

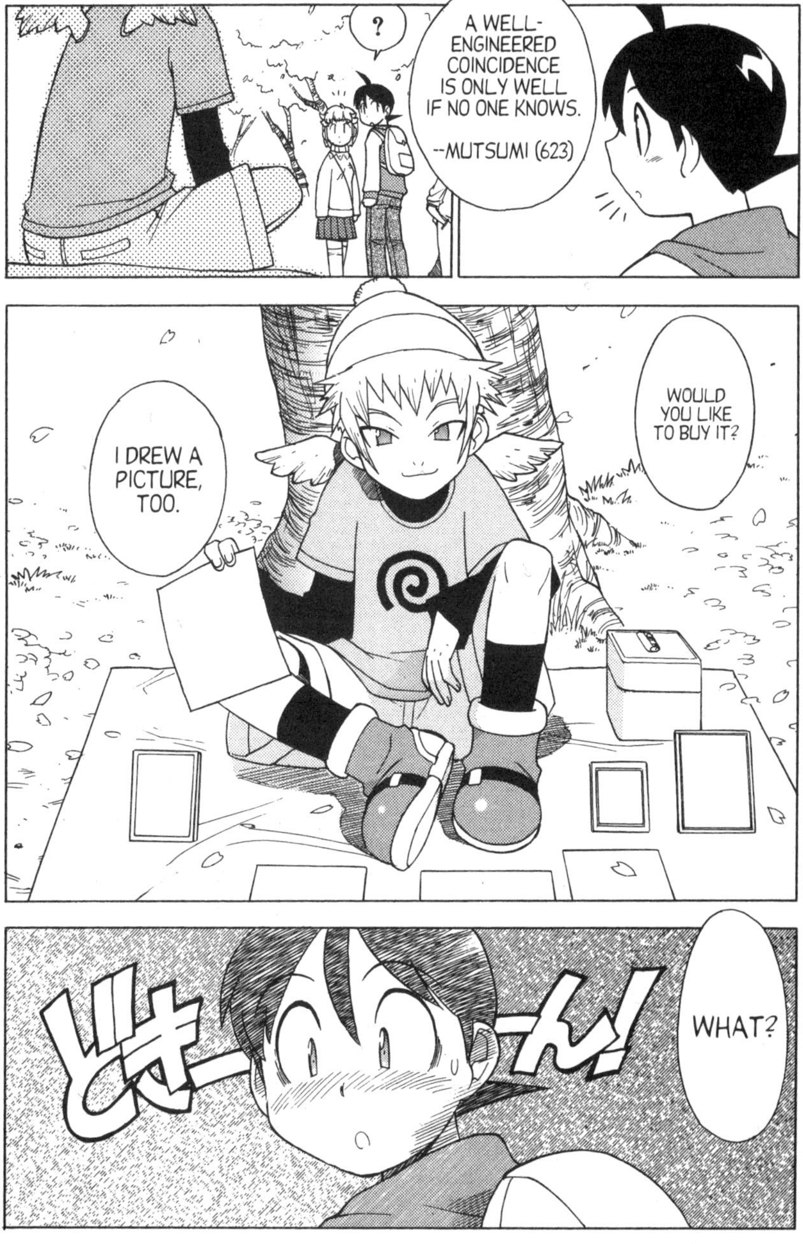
A WELL-ENGINEERED COINCIDENCE IS ONLY WELL IF NO ONE KNOWS.
--MUTSUMI (623)
?
WOULD YOU LIKE TO BUY IT?
I DREW A PICTURE, TOO.
WHAT?
どきーん!

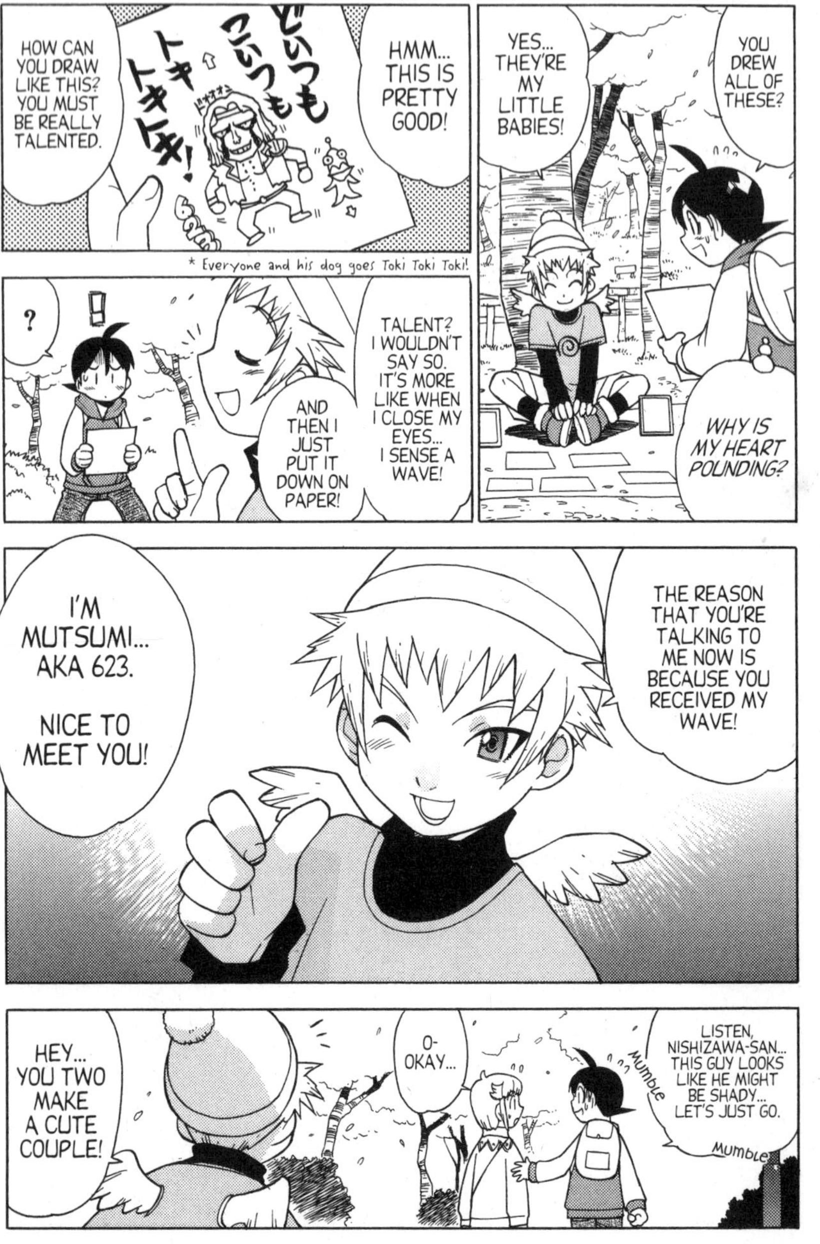
YOU DREW ALL OF THESE?
YES... THEY'RE MY LITTLE BABIES!
WHY IS MY HEART POUNDING?
HMM... THIS IS PRETTY GOOD!
どいつもこいつもトキトキトキ!
HOW CAN YOU DRAW LIKE THIS? YOU MUST BE REALLY TALENTED.
* Everyone and his dog goes Toki Toki Toki!
TALENT? I WOULDN'T SAY SO. IT'S MORE LIKE WHEN I CLOSE MY EYES... I SENSE A WAVE!
AND THEN I JUST PUT IT DOWN ON PAPER!
!
?
THE REASON THAT YOU'RE TALKING TO ME NOW IS BECAUSE YOU RECEIVED MY WAVE!
I'M MUTSUMI... AKA 623.
NICE TO MEET YOU!
LISTEN, NISHIZAWA-SAN... THIS GUY LOOKS LIKE HE MIGHT BE SHADY... LET'S JUST GO.
Mumble
Mumble
O-OKAY...
HEY... YOU TWO MAKE A CUTE COUPLE!

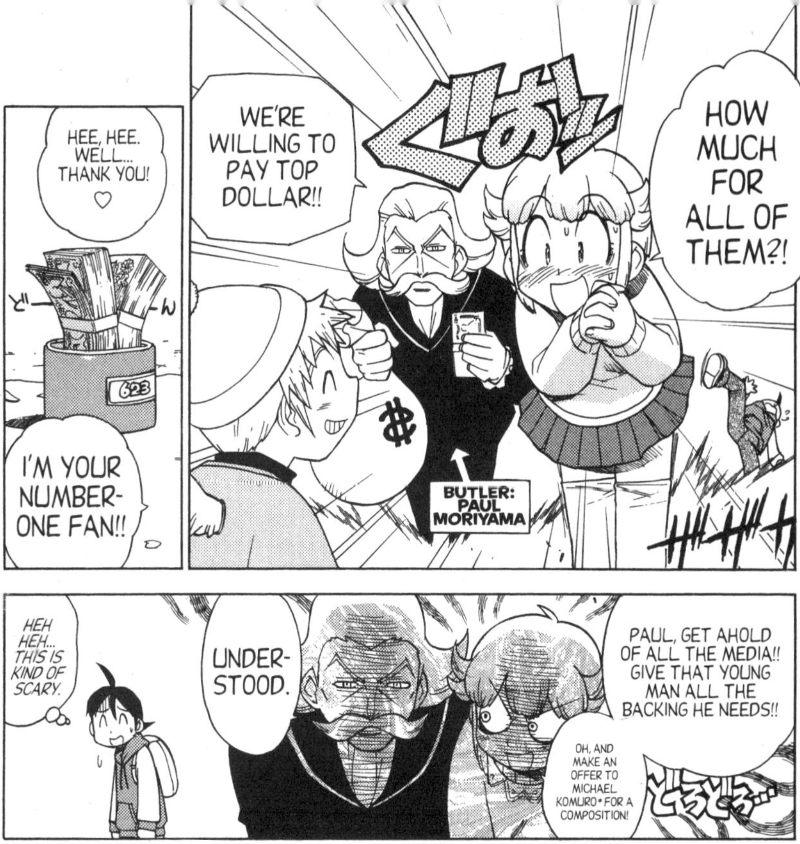
HOW MUCH FOR ALL OF THEM?!
WE'RE WILLING TO PAY TOP DOLLAR!!
BUTLER: PAUL MORIYAMA
HEE, HEE. WELL... THANK YOU! ♡
623
I'M YOUR NUMBER-ONE FAN!!
PAUL, GET AHOLD OF ALL THE MEDIA!! GIVE THAT YOUNG MAN ALL THE BACKING HE NEEDS!!
OH, AND MAKE AN OFFER TO MICHAEL KOMURO* FOR A COMPOSITION!
UNDERSTOOD.
HEH HEH... THIS IS KIND OF SCARY.

* Probably a combination of Michael Jackson and Tetsuya Komuro.

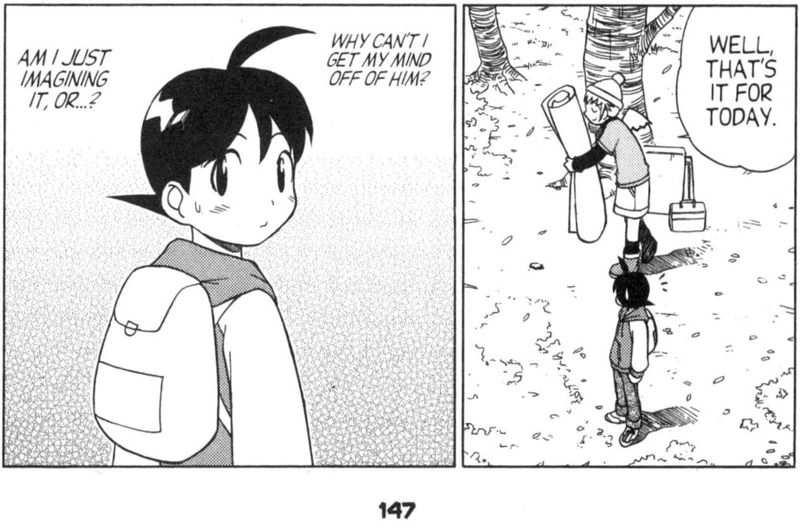
WELL, THAT'S IT FOR TODAY.
WHY CAN'T I GET MY MIND OFF OF HIM?
AM I JUST IMAGINING IT, OR...?

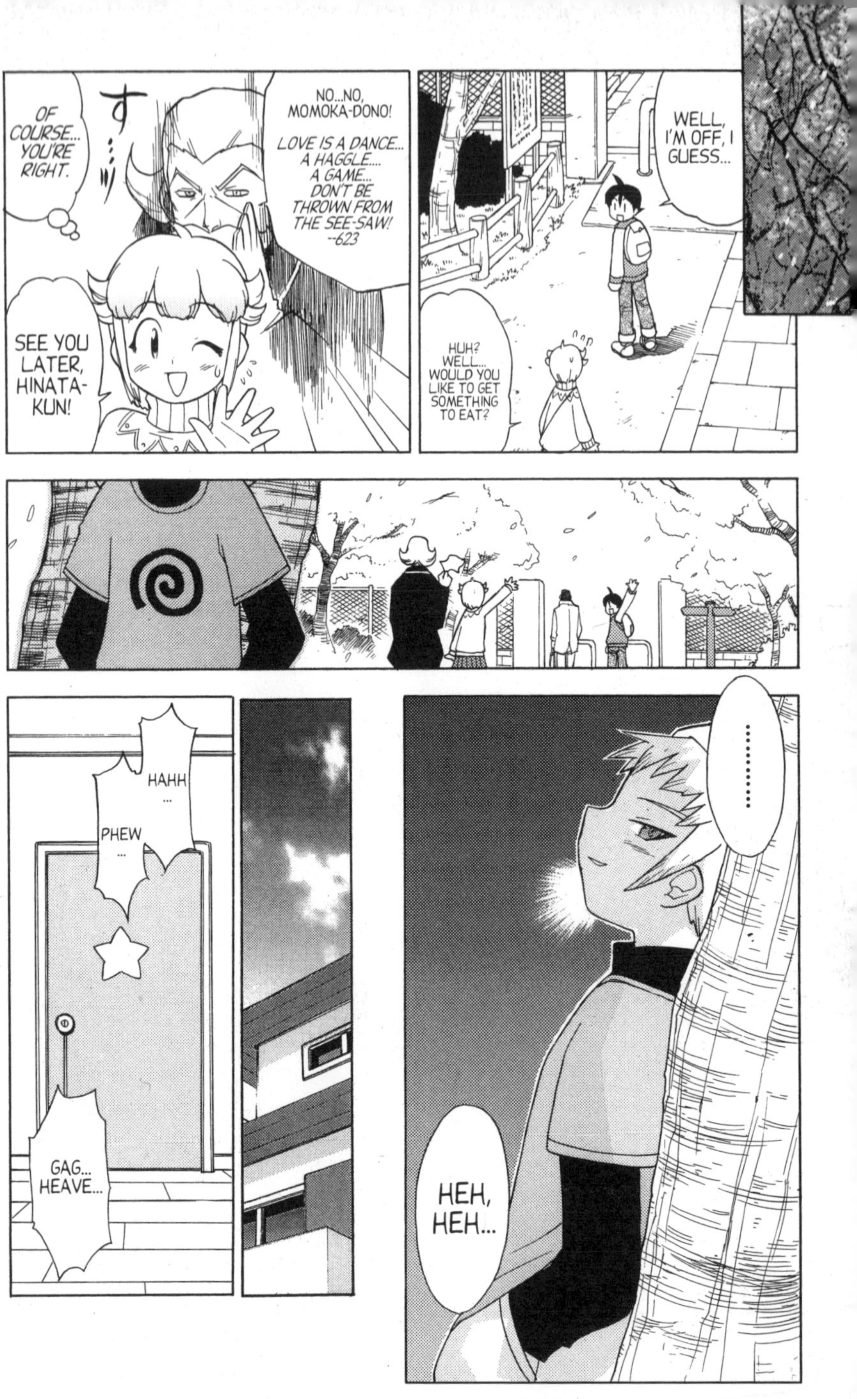
WELL, I'M OFF, I GUESS...
HUH? WELL... WOULD YOU LIKE TO GET SOMETHING TO EAT?
NO...NO, MOMOKA-DONO!
LOVE IS A DANCE... A HAGGLE.... A GAME... DON'T BE THROWN FROM THE SEE-SAW! --623
OF COURSE... YOU'RE RIGHT.
す
SEE YOU LATER, HINATA-KUN!
....
HEH, HEH...
HAHH ...
PHEW ...
GAG... HEAVE...

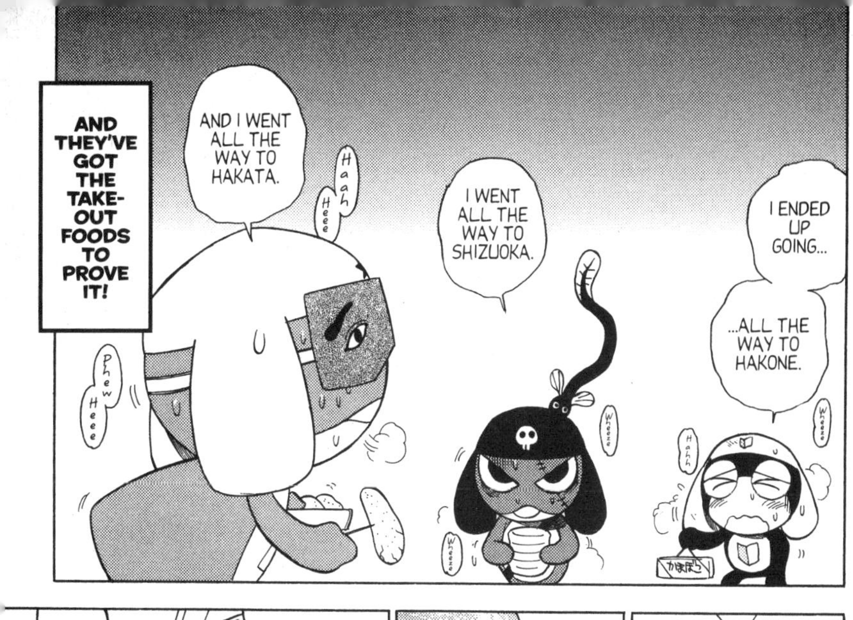
I ENDED UP GOING...
...ALL THE WAY TO HAKONE.
Wheeze
Hahh
I WENT ALL THE WAY TO SHIZUOKA.
Wheeze
AND I WENT ALL THE WAY TO HAKATA.
Haah Heee
Phew Heee
AND THEY'VE GOT THE TAKE-OUT FOODS TO PROVE IT!
WE CAN'T GO ON SEARCHING WITHOUT ANY CLUES!
HMM, YES... IT'S LIKE LOOKING FOR A CONTACT LENS IN A DESERT. THOSE ANCIENT POKOPENIAN PHILOSOPHERS REALLY KNEW HOW TO PUT THINGS!
Hmm...
Sigh...
WONDERFUL! ANOTHER WASTED EFFORT, LED BY SERGEANT STUPIDO!!
YOUR PLANS ARE ALWAYS SO--
I'VE HAD ENOUGH OF YOUR NEGATIVE ATTITUDE!! EAT *THIS!!*
UNNH?!

* The Sergeant just fed Giroro a local specialty from Hakata: salted cod roe with chilies.

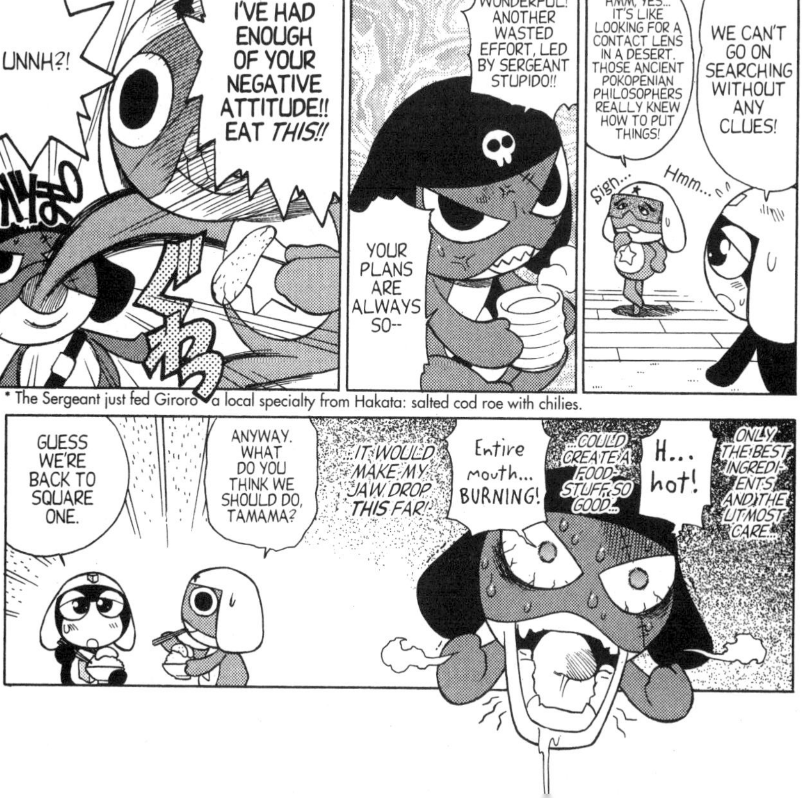
ONLY THE BEST INGREDIENTS AND THE UTMOST CARE...
H... hot!
...COULD CREATE A FOODSTUFF SO GOOD...
Entire mouth... BURNING!
...IT WOULD MAKE MY JAW DROP THIS FAR!
ANYWAY. WHAT DO YOU THINK WE SHOULD DO, TAMAMA?
GUESS WE'RE BACK TO SQUARE ONE.

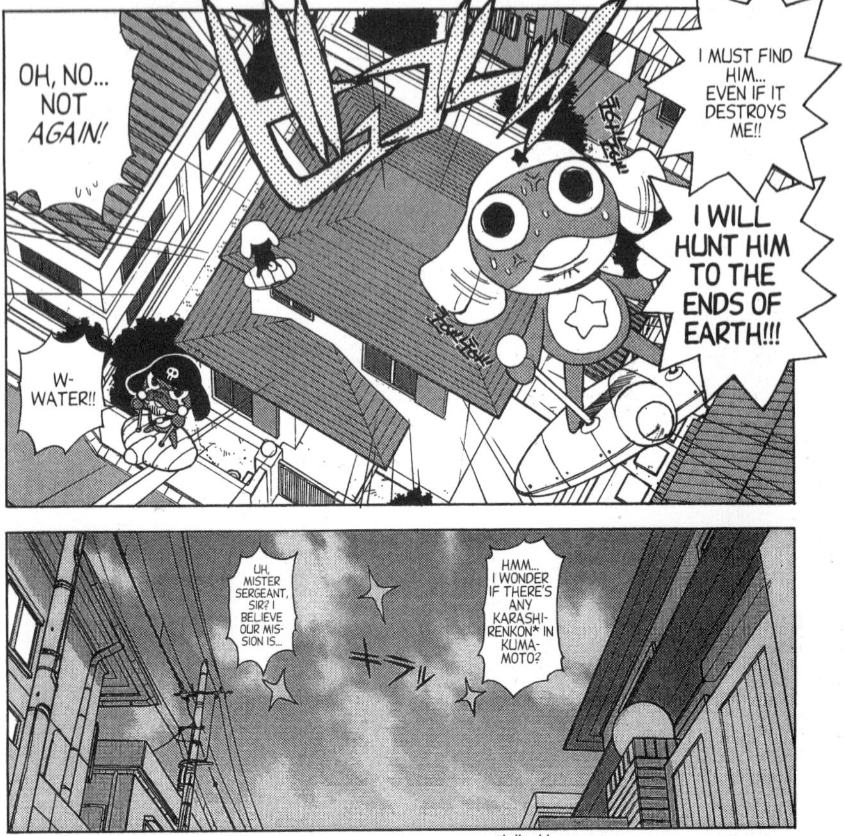
I MUST FIND HIM... EVEN IF IT DESTROYS ME!!
I WILL HUNT HIM TO THE ENDS OF EARTH!!!
OH, NO... NOT AGAIN!
W-WATER!!
HMM... I WONDER IF THERE'S ANY KARASHI-RENKON* IN KUMAMOTO?
UH, MISTER SERGEANT, SIR? I BELIEVE OUR MISSION IS...

* Chillied lotus root.

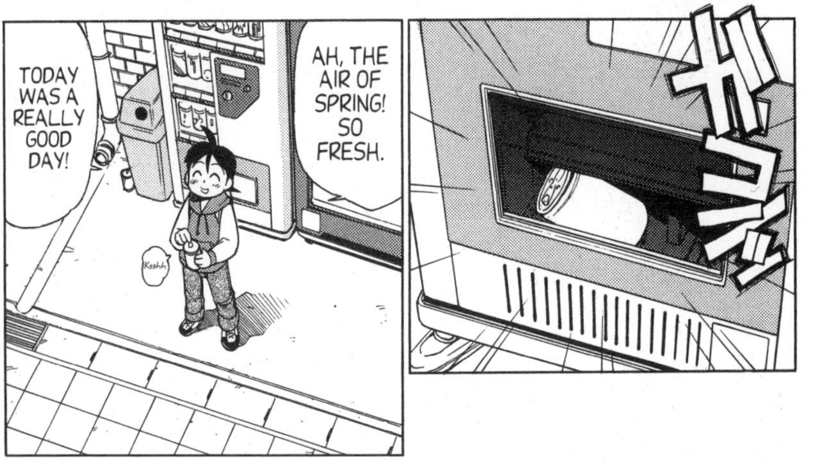
AH, THE AIR OF SPRING! SO FRESH.
TODAY WAS A REALLY GOOD DAY!
Ksshh

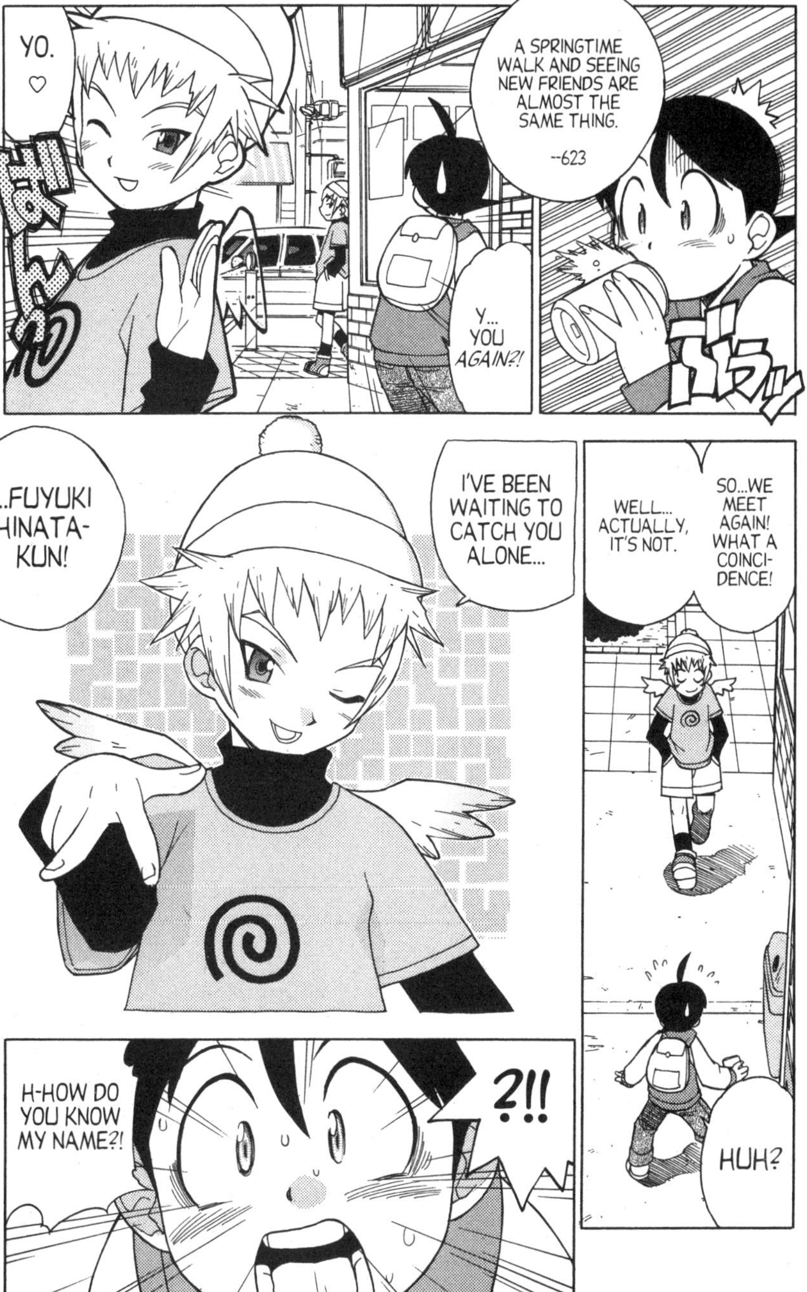
A SPRINGTIME WALK AND SEEING NEW FRIENDS ARE ALMOST THE SAME THING.
--623
Y... YOU *AGAIN?!*
YO. ♡
SO...WE MEET AGAIN! WHAT A COINCI-DENCE!
WELL... ACTUALLY, IT'S NOT.
HUH?
I'VE BEEN WAITING TO CATCH YOU ALONE...
...FUYUKI HINATA-KUN!
?!!
H-HOW DO YOU KNOW MY NAME?!

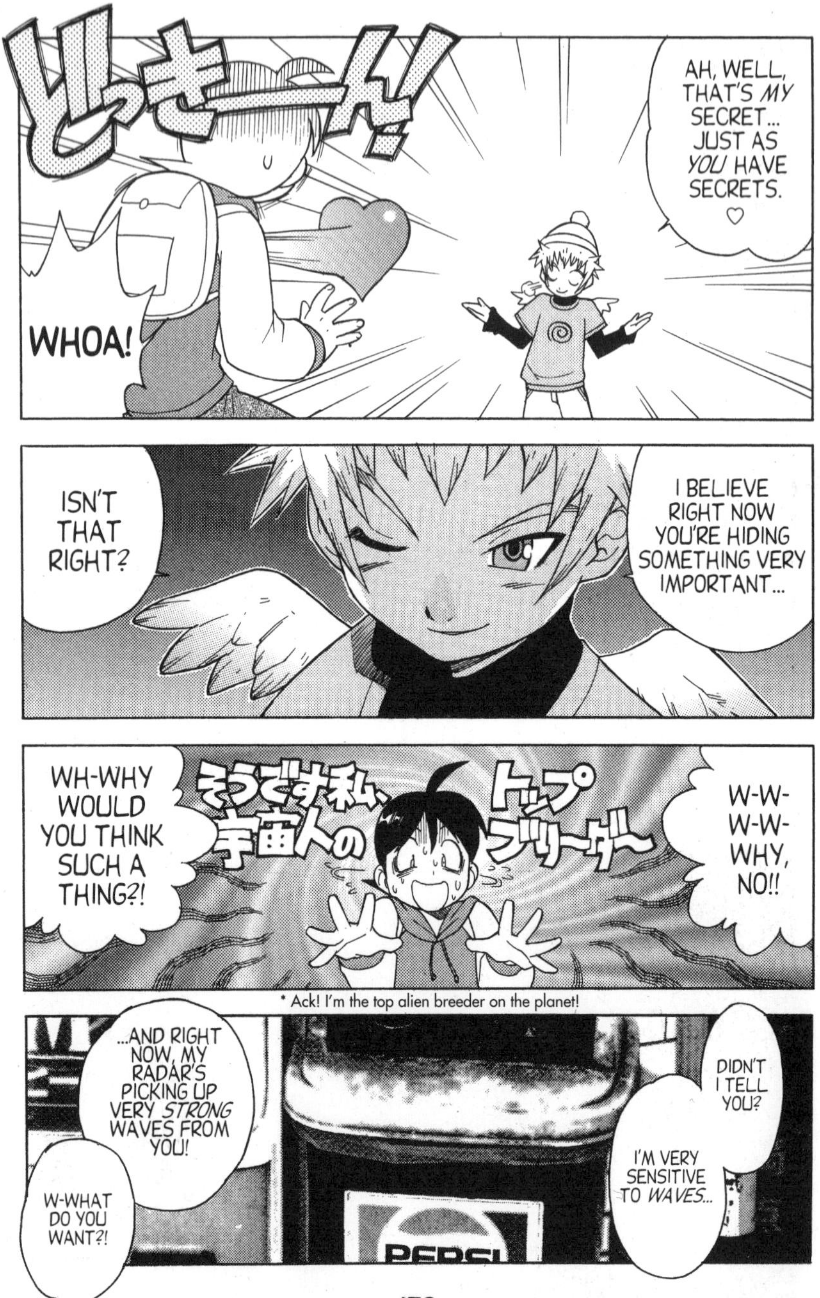
AH, WELL, THAT'S *MY* SECRET... JUST AS *YOU* HAVE SECRETS. ♡
どっきーん!
WHOA!
I BELIEVE RIGHT NOW YOU'RE HIDING SOMETHING VERY IMPORTANT...
ISN'T THAT RIGHT?
W-W-W-W-WHY, NO!!
そうです私、宇宙人の
トップブリーダ〜
WH-WHY WOULD YOU THINK SUCH A THING?!
* Ack! I'm the top alien breeder on the planet!
DIDN'T I TELL YOU?
I'M VERY SENSITIVE TO *WAVES*...
...AND RIGHT NOW, MY RADAR'S PICKING UP VERY *STRONG* WAVES FROM YOU!
W-WHAT DO YOU WANT?!
PEPSI

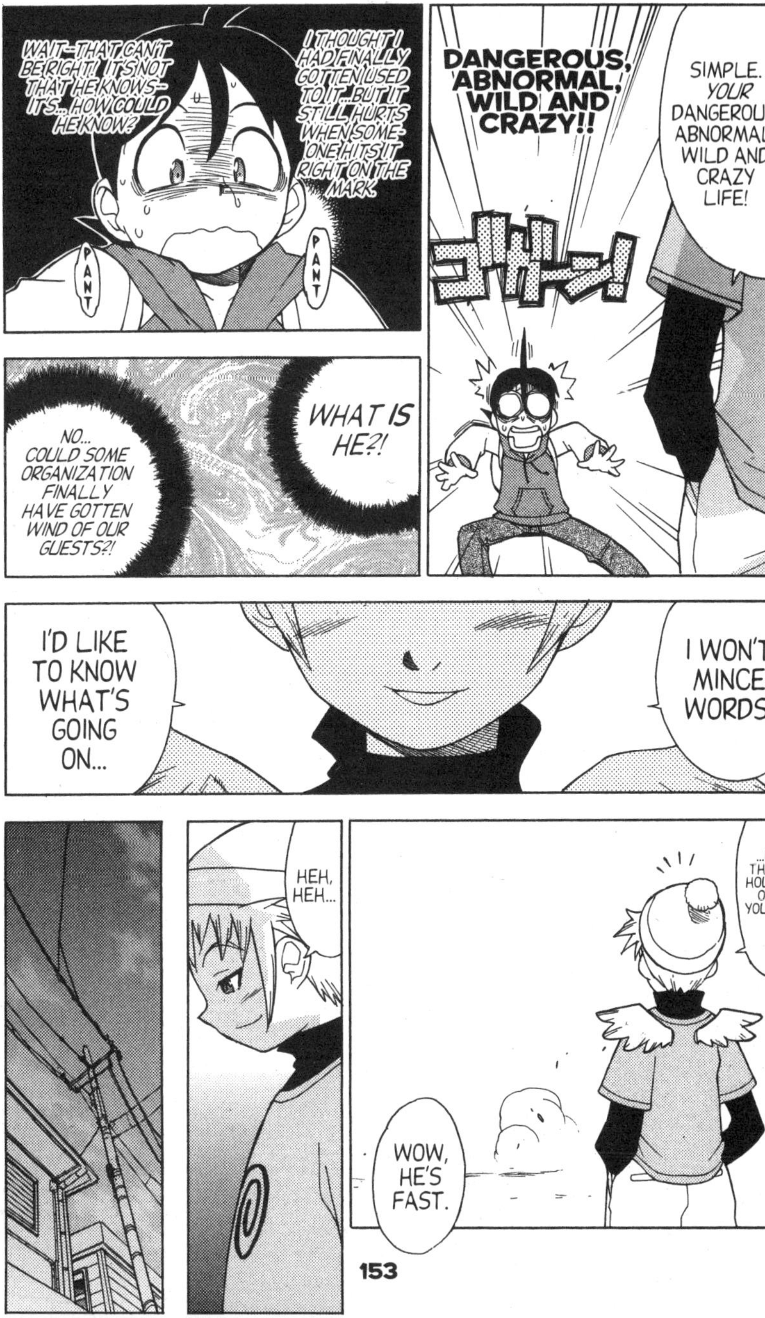
SIMPLE. YOUR DANGEROUS, ABNORMAL, WILD AND CRAZY LIFE!
DANGEROUS, ABNORMAL, WILD AND CRAZY!!
ゴガーン!
I THOUGHT I HAD FINALLY GOTTEN USED TO IT... BUT IT STILL HURTS WHEN SOME-ONE HITS IT RIGHT ON THE MARK.
WAIT—THAT CAN'T BE RIGHT! IT'S NOT THAT HE KNOWS— IT'S... HOW COULD HE KNOW?
PANT
PANT
WHAT IS HE?!
NO... COULD SOME ORGANIZATION FINALLY HAVE GOTTEN WIND OF OUR GUESTS?!
I WON'T MINCE WORDS.
I'D LIKE TO KNOW WHAT'S GOING ON...
...IN THAT HOUSE OF YOURS.
WOW, HE'S FAST.
HEH, HEH...

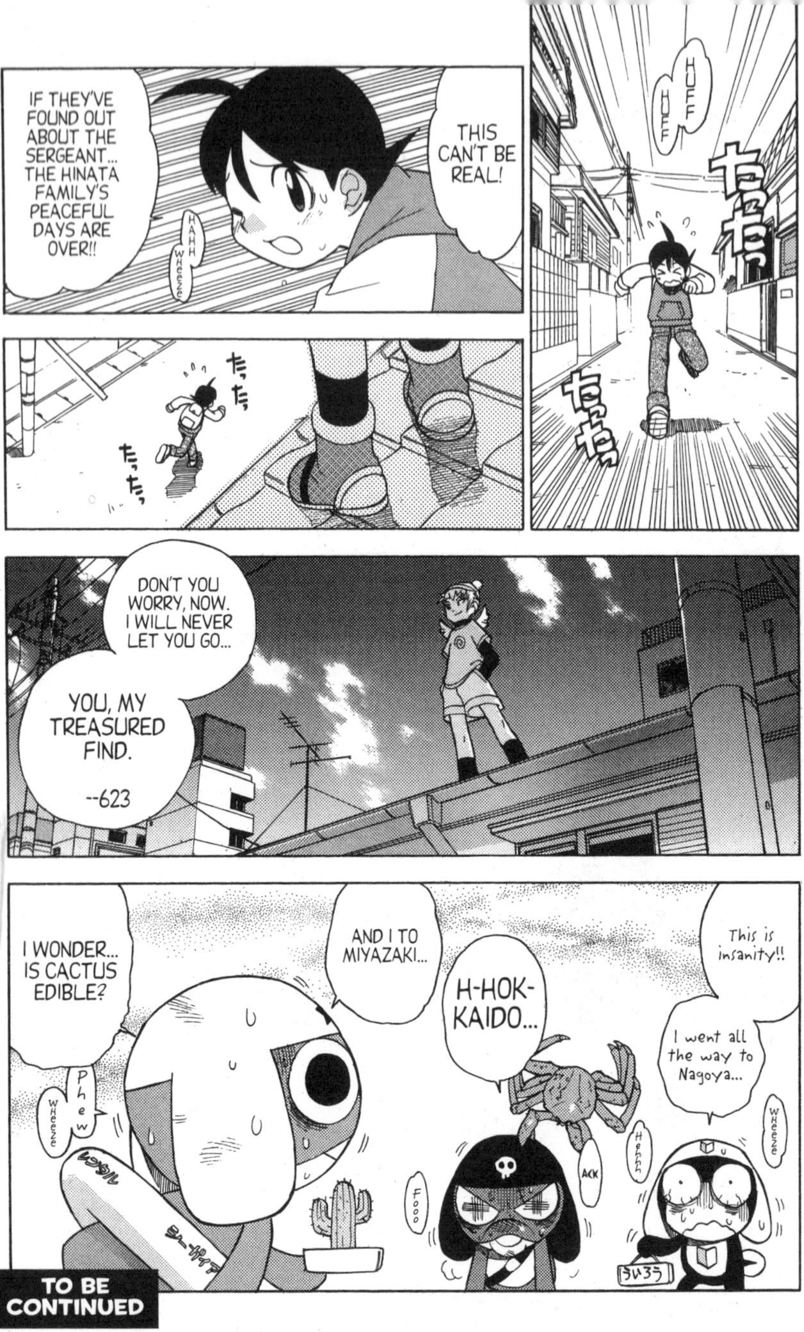
HUFF
HUFF
たったっ
たったっ
THIS CAN'T BE REAL!
IF THEY'VE FOUND OUT ABOUT THE SERGEANT... THE HINATA FAMILY'S PEACEFUL DAYS ARE OVER!!
HAHH
Wheeze
たったっ
たったっ
DON'T YOU WORRY, NOW. I WILL NEVER LET YOU GO...
YOU, MY TREASURED FIND.
--623
This is insanity!!
I went all the way to Nagoya...
Wheeze
Hehhh
ういろう
ACK
H-HOK-KAIDO...
Fooo
AND I TO MIYAZAKI...
I WONDER... IS CACTUS EDIBLE?
Phew
Wheeze
TO BE CONTINUED

ENCOUNTER XX
A FOURTH VISITOR

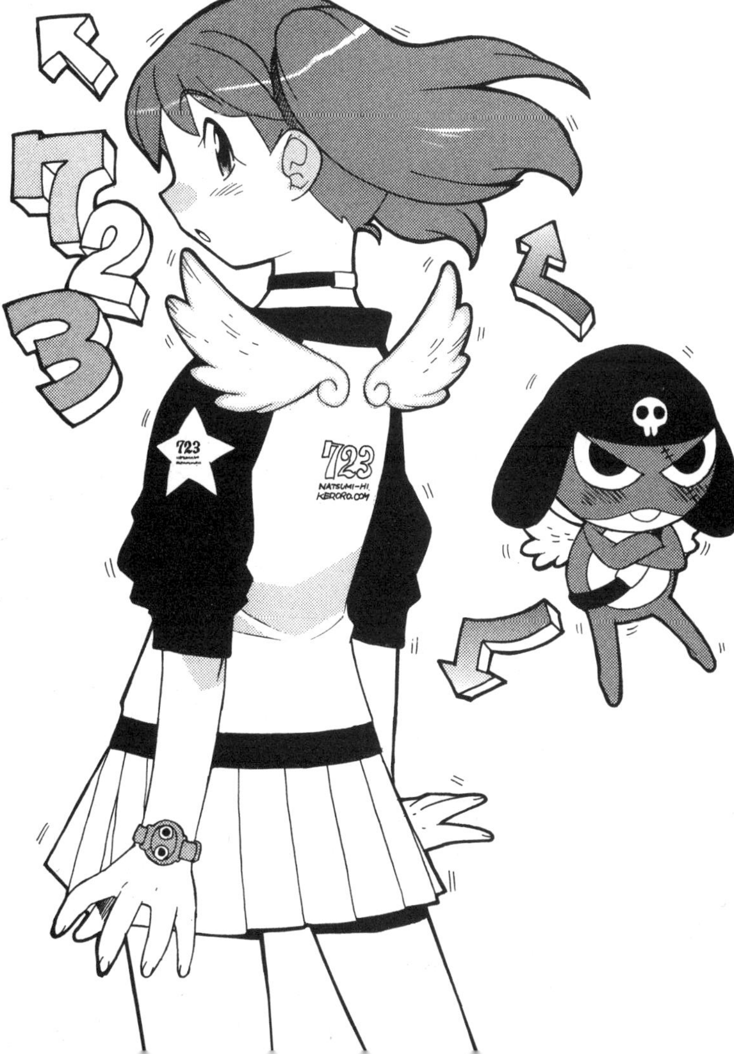
723
723
NATSUMI-HI
KERORO.COM

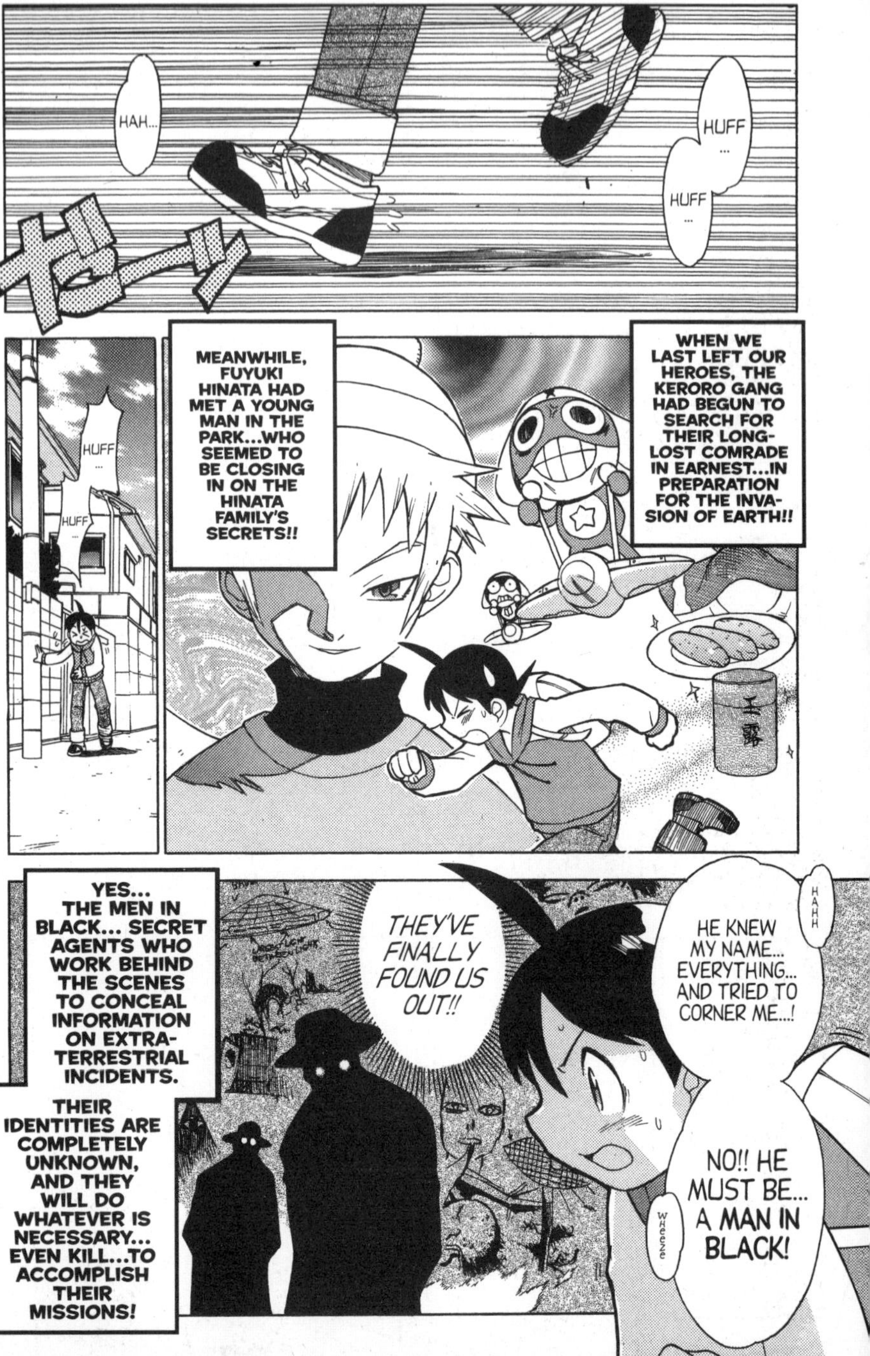
HUFF...
HUFF...
HAH...
WHEN WE LAST LEFT OUR HEROES, THE KERORO GANG HAD BEGUN TO SEARCH FOR THEIR LONG-LOST COMRADE IN EARNEST...IN PREPARATION FOR THE INVASION OF EARTH!!
MEANWHILE, FUYUKI HINATA HAD MET A YOUNG MAN IN THE PARK...WHO SEEMED TO BE CLOSING IN ON THE HINATA FAMILY'S SECRETS!!
HUFF...
HUFF...
HAHH
HE KNEW MY NAME... EVERYTHING... AND TRIED TO CORNER ME...!
THEY'VE FINALLY FOUND US OUT!!
YES... THE MEN IN BLACK... SECRET AGENTS WHO WORK BEHIND THE SCENES TO CONCEAL INFORMATION ON EXTRA-TERRESTRIAL INCIDENTS.
NO!! HE MUST BE... A MAN IN BLACK!
WHEEZE
THEIR IDENTITIES ARE COMPLETELY UNKNOWN, AND THEY WILL DO WHATEVER IS NECESSARY... EVEN KILL...TO ACCOMPLISH THEIR MISSIONS!

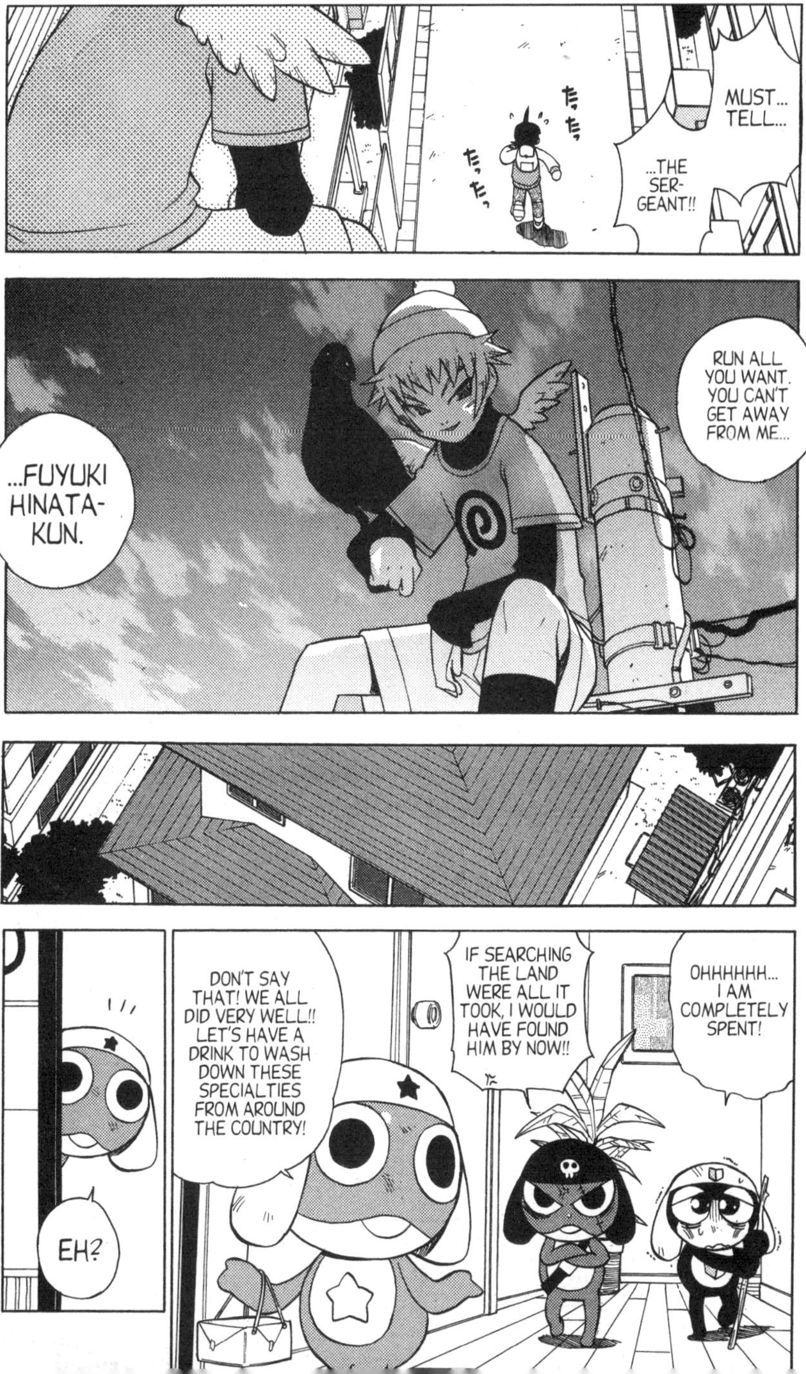
MUST... TELL...
...THE SER-GEANT!!
たっ たっ
たっ たっ
RUN ALL YOU WANT. YOU CAN'T GET AWAY FROM ME...
...FUYUKI HINATA-KUN.
OHHHHHH... I AM COMPLETELY SPENT!
IF SEARCHING THE LAND WERE ALL IT TOOK, I WOULD HAVE FOUND HIM BY NOW!!
DON'T SAY THAT! WE ALL DID VERY WELL!! LET'S HAVE A DRINK TO WASH DOWN THESE SPECIALTIES FROM AROUND THE COUNTRY!
EH?

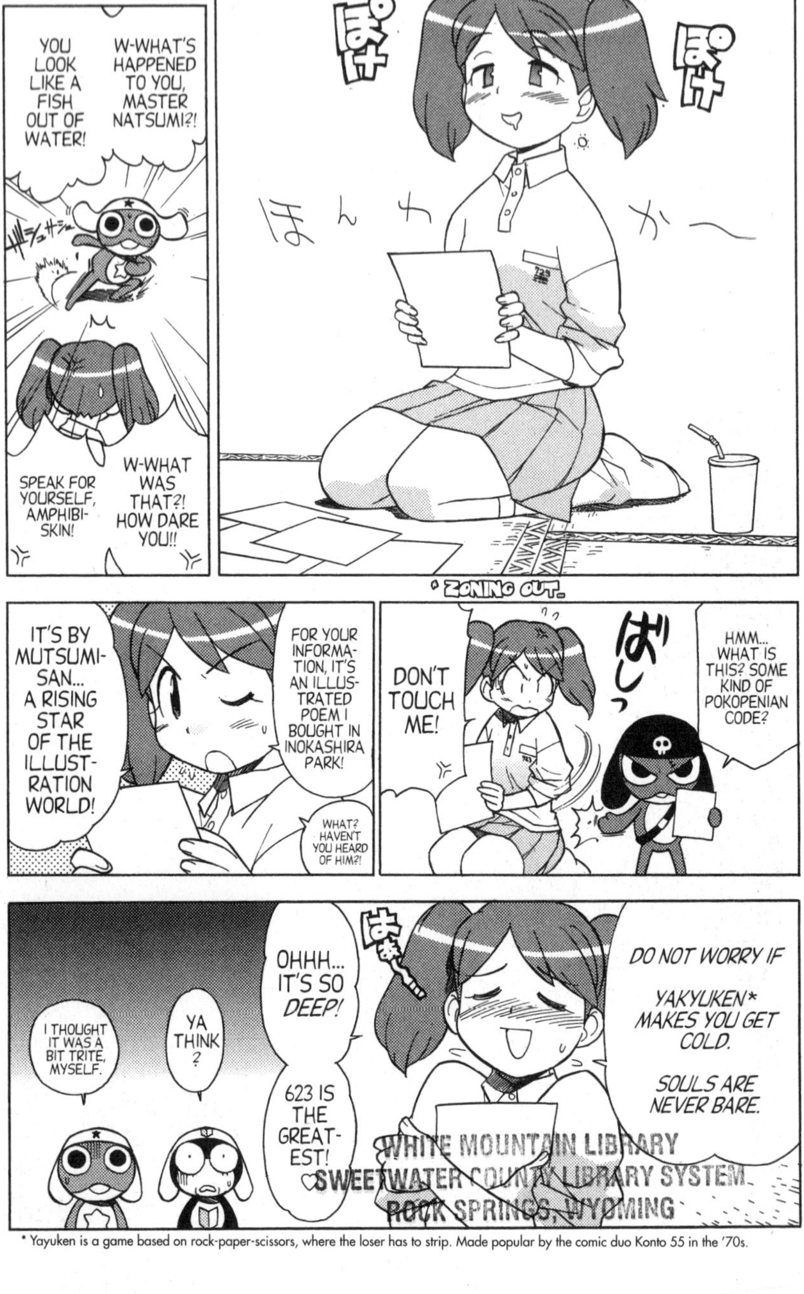
ぽけ
ぽけ
ほんわかー
* ZONING OUT.
W-WHAT'S HAPPENED TO YOU, MASTER NATSUMI?!
YOU LOOK LIKE A FISH OUT OF WATER!
W-WHAT WAS THAT?! HOW DARE YOU!!
SPEAK FOR YOURSELF, AMPHIBI-SKIN!
HMM... WHAT IS THIS? SOME KIND OF POKOPENIAN CODE?
ぱしっ
DON'T TOUCH ME!
FOR YOUR INFORMATION, IT'S AN ILLUSTRATED POEM I BOUGHT IN INOKASHIRA PARK!
IT'S BY MUTSUMI-SAN... A RISING STAR OF THE ILLUSTRATION WORLD!
WHAT?! HAVEN'T YOU HEARD OF HIM?!
DO NOT WORRY IF YAKYUKEN* MAKES YOU GET COLD.
SOULS ARE NEVER BARE.
はぁ〜
OHHH... IT'S SO *DEEP*!
623 IS THE GREAT-EST! ♡
YA THINK?
I THOUGHT IT WAS A BIT TRITE, MYSELF.

* Yayuken is a game based on rock-paper-scissors, where the loser has to strip. Made popular by the comic duo Konto 55 in the '70s.

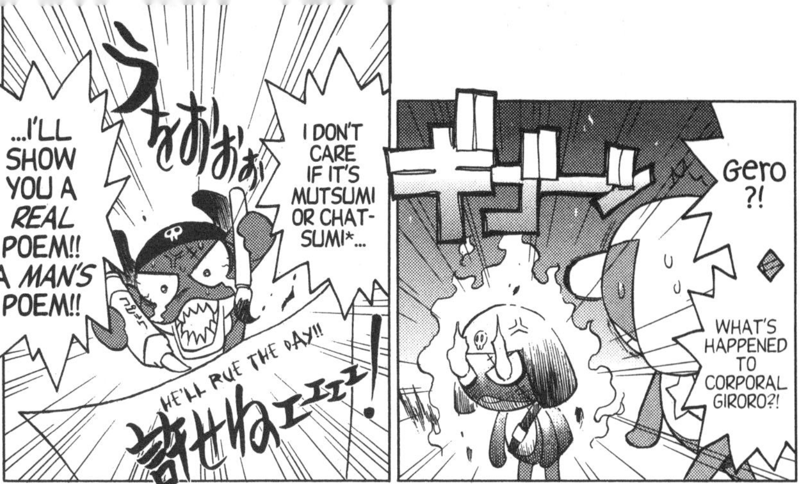
Gero ?!
WHAT'S HAPPENED TO CORPORAL GIRORO?!
I DON'T CARE IF IT'S MUTSUMI OR CHAT-SUMI*...
うをおおお
...I'LL SHOW YOU A *REAL* POEM!! A *MAN'S* POEM!!
HE'LL RUE THE DAY!!
許せねエエエ!

* A lowly tea leaf picker

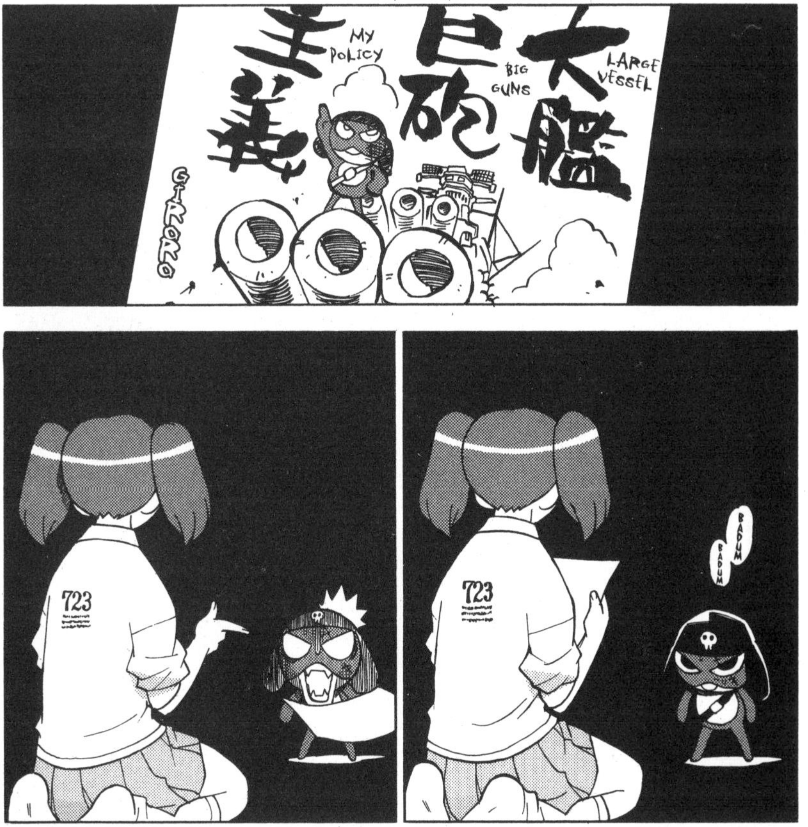
大艦
LARGE VESSEL
巨砲
BIG GUNS
主義
MY POLICY
GIRORO
BADUM BADUM

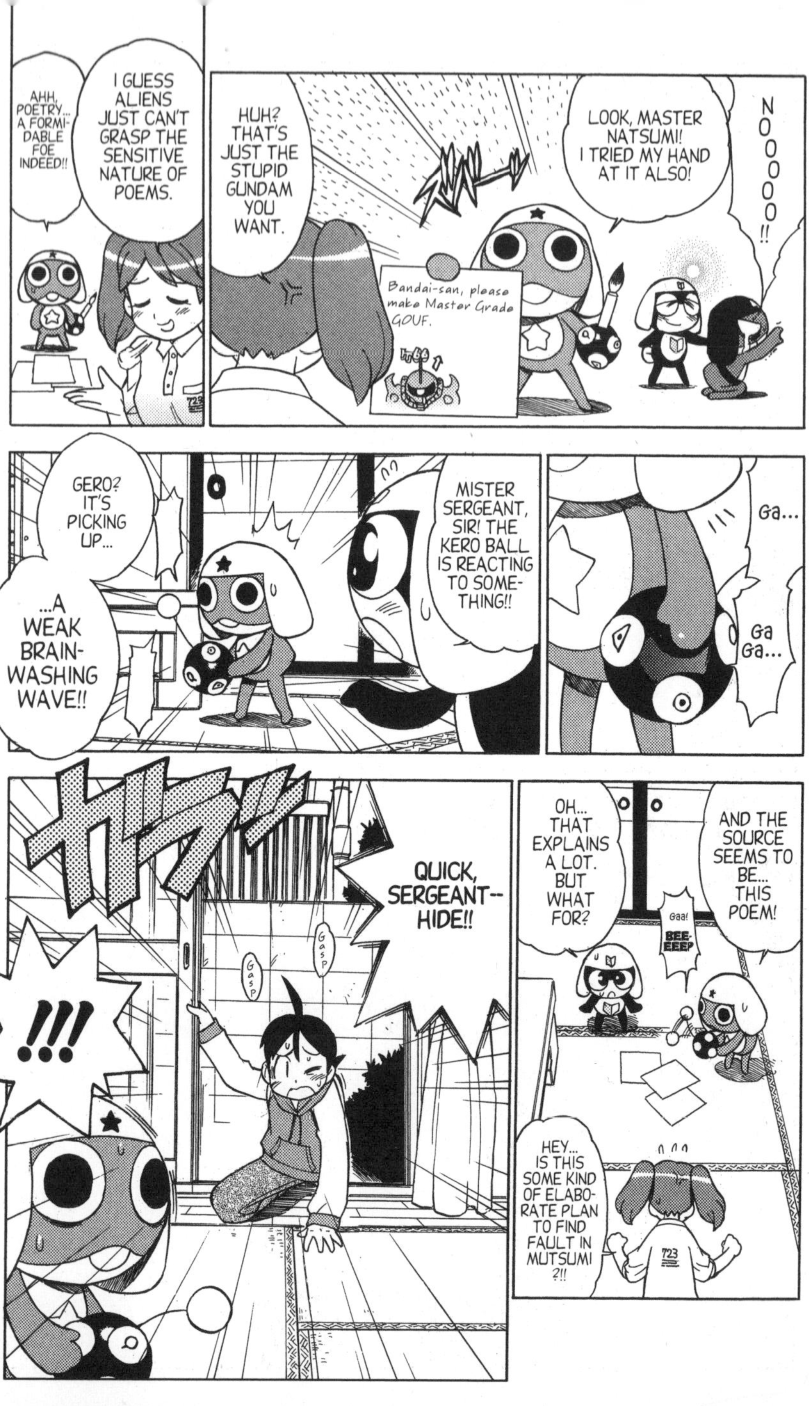

NOOOOO!!
LOOK, MASTER NATSUMI! I TRIED MY HAND AT IT ALSO!
Bandai-san, please make Master Grade GOUF.
HUH? THAT'S JUST THE STUPID GUNDAM YOU WANT.
I GUESS ALIENS JUST CAN'T GRASP THE SENSITIVE NATURE OF POEMS.
AHH, POETRY... A FORMIDABLE FOE INDEED!!
Ga...
Ga Ga...
MISTER SERGEANT, SIR! THE KERO BALL IS REACTING TO SOMETHING!!
GERO? IT'S PICKING UP...
...A WEAK BRAIN-WASHING WAVE!!
AND THE SOURCE SEEMS TO BE... THIS POEM!
Gaa!
BEE-EEEP
OH... THAT EXPLAINS A LOT. BUT WHAT FOR?
HEY... IS THIS SOME KIND OF ELABORATE PLAN TO FIND FAULT IN MUTSUMI?!!
QUICK, SERGEANT-- HIDE!!
Gasp
Gasp
!!!

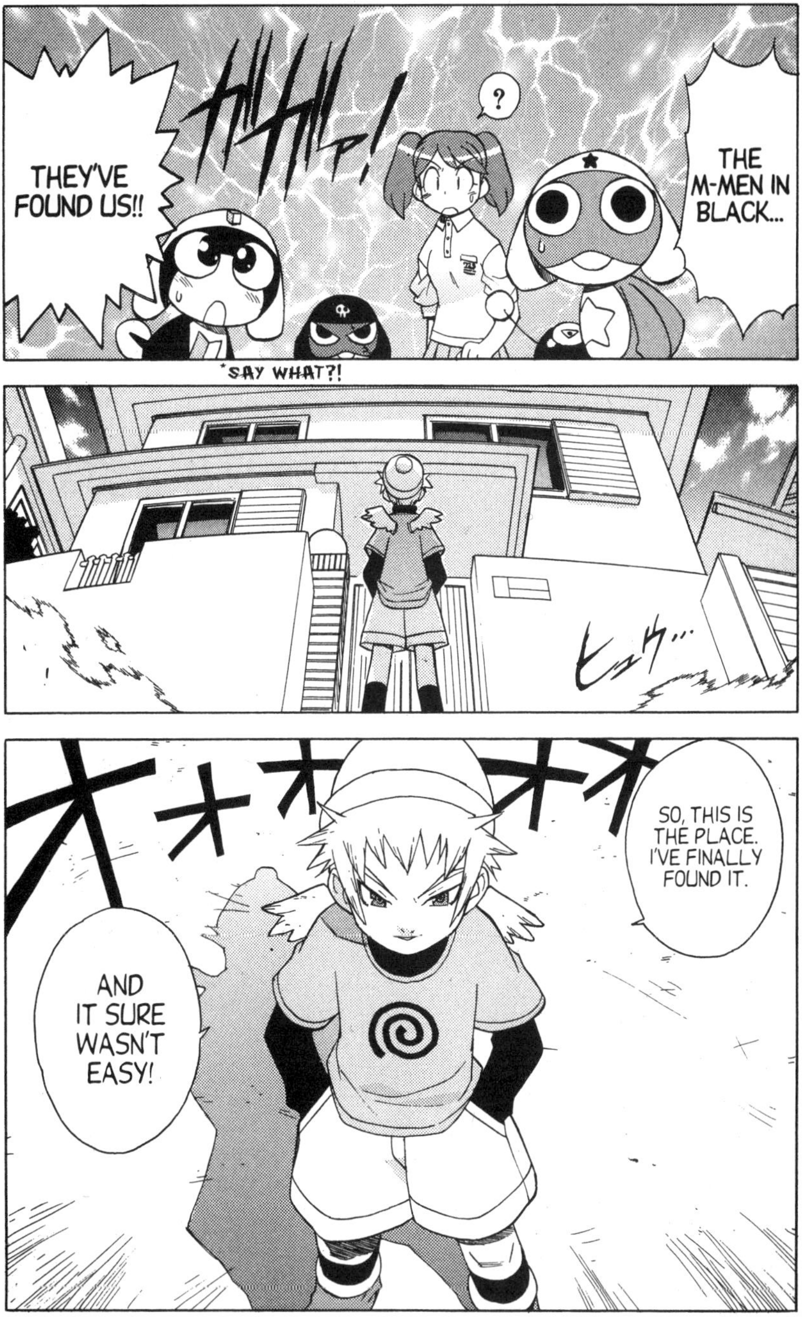
THE M-MEN IN BLACK...
?
THEY'VE FOUND US!!
*SAY WHAT?!
SO, THIS IS THE PLACE. I'VE FINALLY FOUND IT.
AND IT SURE WASN'T EASY!

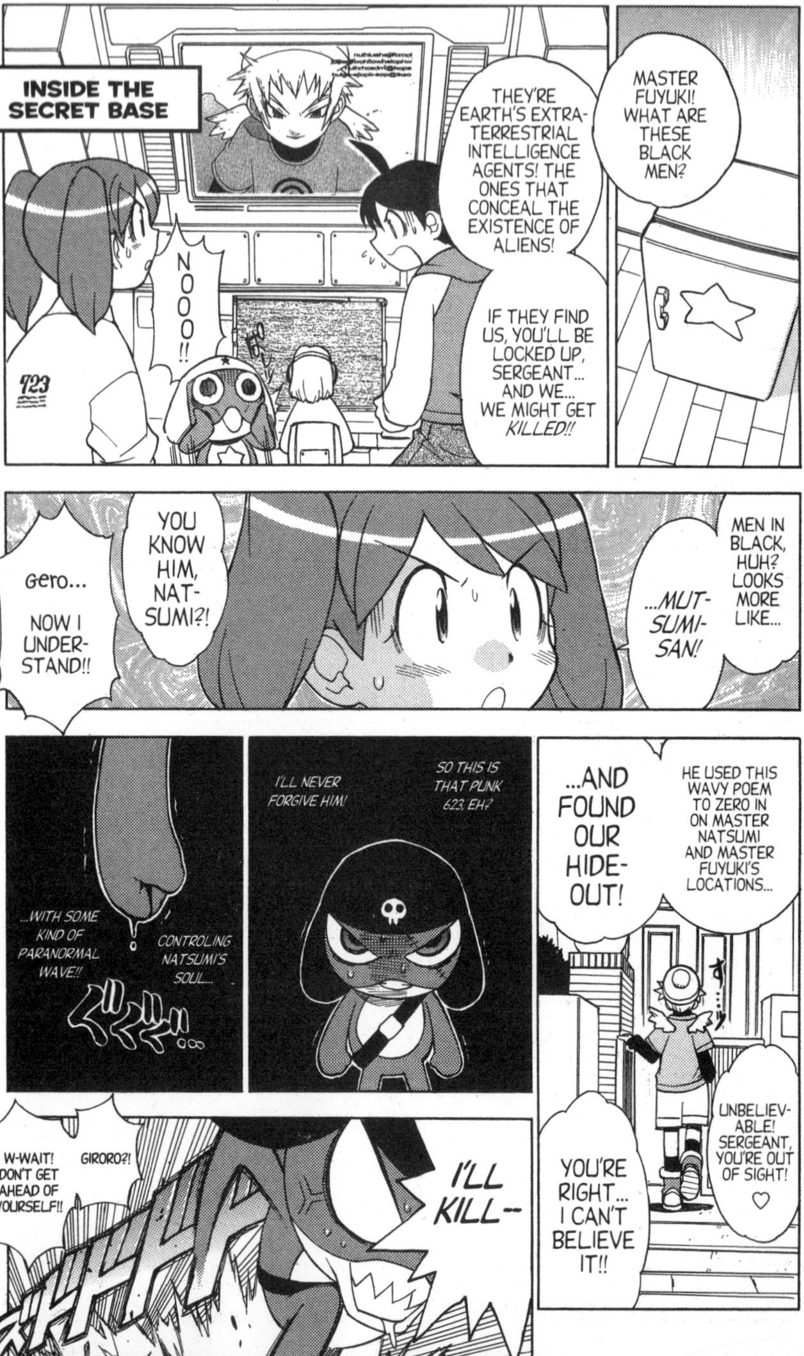
MASTER FUYUKI! WHAT ARE THESE BLACK MEN?
THEY'RE EARTH'S EXTRA-TERRESTRIAL INTELLIGENCE AGENTS! THE ONES THAT CONCEAL THE EXISTENCE OF ALIENS!
INSIDE THE SECRET BASE
IF THEY FIND US, YOU'LL BE LOCKED UP, SERGEANT... AND WE... WE MIGHT GET *KILLED!!*
NOOOO!!
723
MEN IN BLACK, HUH? LOOKS MORE LIKE...
...*MUT-SUMI-SAN!*
YOU KNOW HIM, NAT-SUMI?!
Gero...
NOW I UNDER-STAND!!
HE USED THIS WAVY POEM TO ZERO IN ON MASTER NATSUMI AND MASTER FUYUKI'S LOCATIONS...
...AND FOUND OUR HIDE-OUT!
UNBELIEV-ABLE! SERGEANT, YOU'RE OUT OF SIGHT! ♡
YOU'RE RIGHT... I CAN'T BELIEVE IT!!
SO THIS IS THAT PUNK 623, EH?
I'LL NEVER FORGIVE HIM!
CONTROLING NATSUMI'S SOUL...
...WITH SOME KIND OF PARANORMAL WAVE!!
I'LL KILL--
GIRORO?!
W-WAIT! DON'T GET AHEAD OF YOURSELF!!

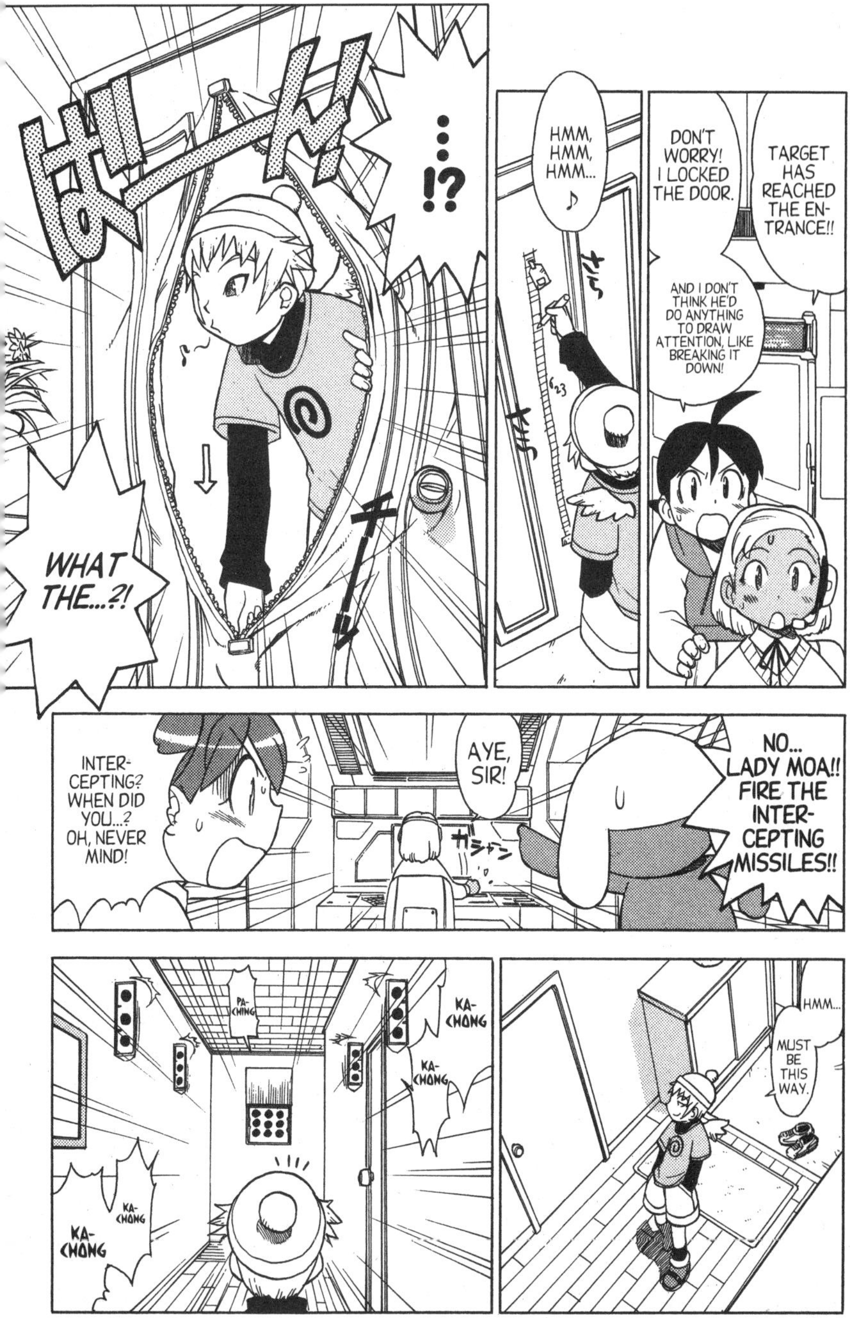
TARGET HAS REACHED THE ENTRANCE!!
DON'T WORRY! I LOCKED THE DOOR.
AND I DON'T THINK HE'D DO ANYTHING TO DRAW ATTENTION, LIKE BREAKING IT DOWN!
HMM, HMM, HMM... ♪
...!?
WHAT THE...?!
NO... LADY MOA!! FIRE THE INTERCEPTING MISSILES!!
AYE, SIR!
INTERCEPTING? WHEN DID YOU...? OH, NEVER MIND!
HMM...
MUST BE THIS WAY.
KA-CHONG
PA-CHING
KA-CHONG
KA-CHONG
KA-CHONG

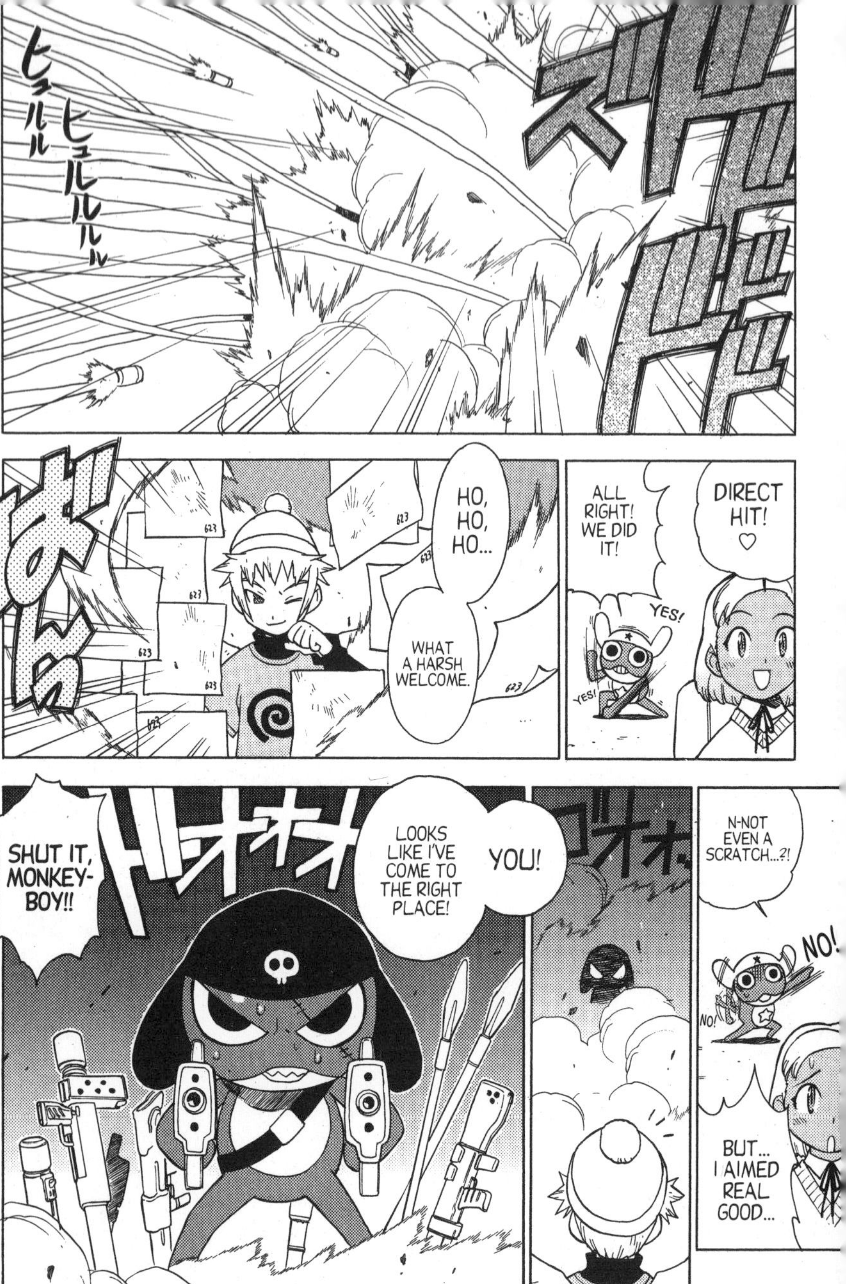
DIRECT HIT! ♡
ALL RIGHT! WE DID IT!
YES!
YES!
HO, HO, HO...
WHAT A HARSH WELCOME.
N-NOT EVEN A SCRATCH...?!
NO!
NO!
BUT... I AIMED REAL GOOD...
YOU!
LOOKS LIKE I'VE COME TO THE RIGHT PLACE!
SHUT IT, MONKEY-BOY!!

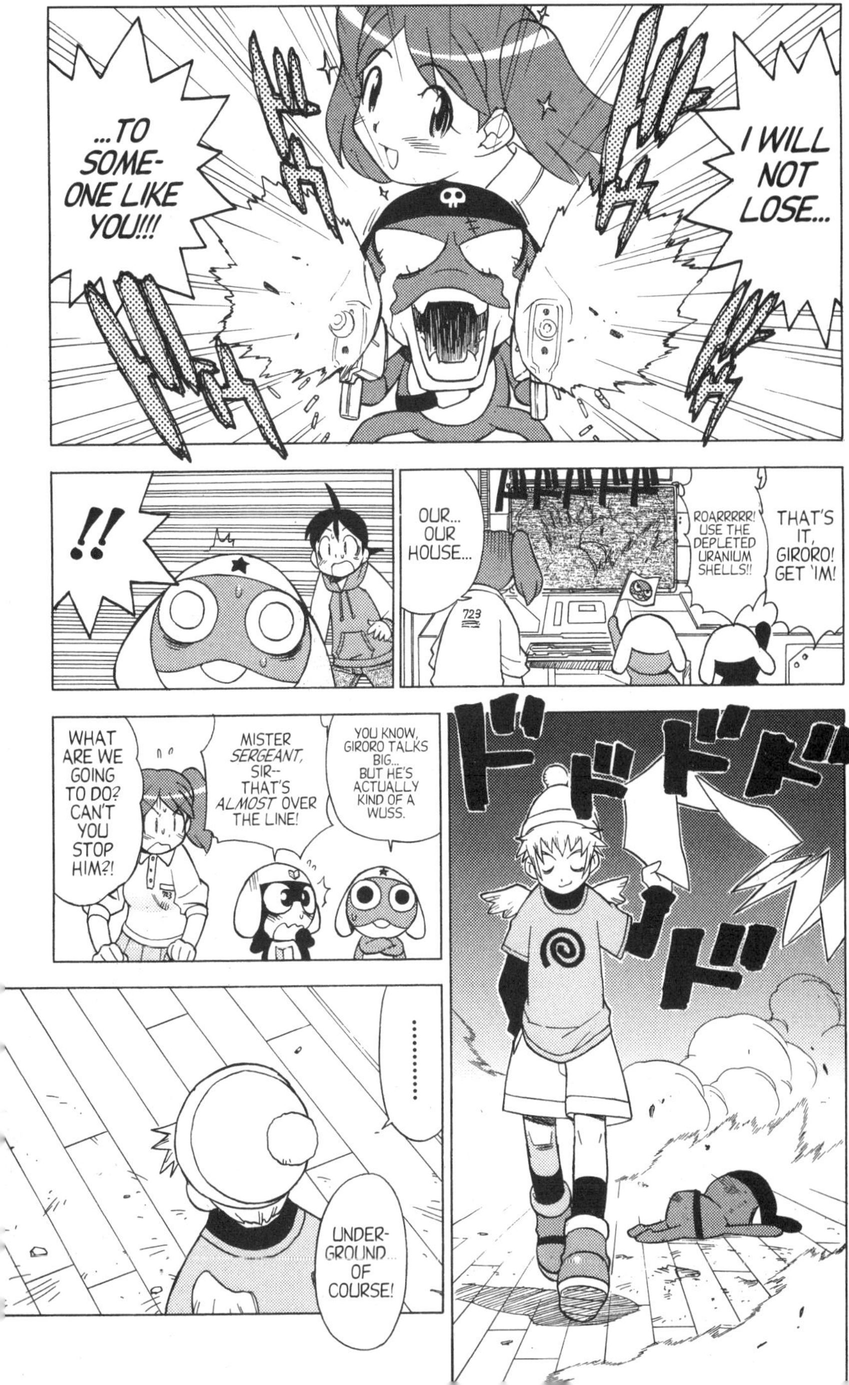
I WILL NOT LOSE...
...TO SOME-ONE LIKE YOU!!!
THAT'S IT, GIRORO! GET 'IM!
ROARRRRR! USE THE DEPLETED URANIUM SHELLS!!
OUR... OUR HOUSE...
!!
ドドドドド
YOU KNOW, GIRORO TALKS BIG... BUT HE'S ACTUALLY KIND OF A WUSS.
MISTER *SERGEANT*, SIR-- THAT'S *ALMOST* OVER THE LINE!
WHAT ARE WE GOING TO DO? CAN'T YOU STOP HIM?!
....
UNDER-GROUND... OF COURSE!

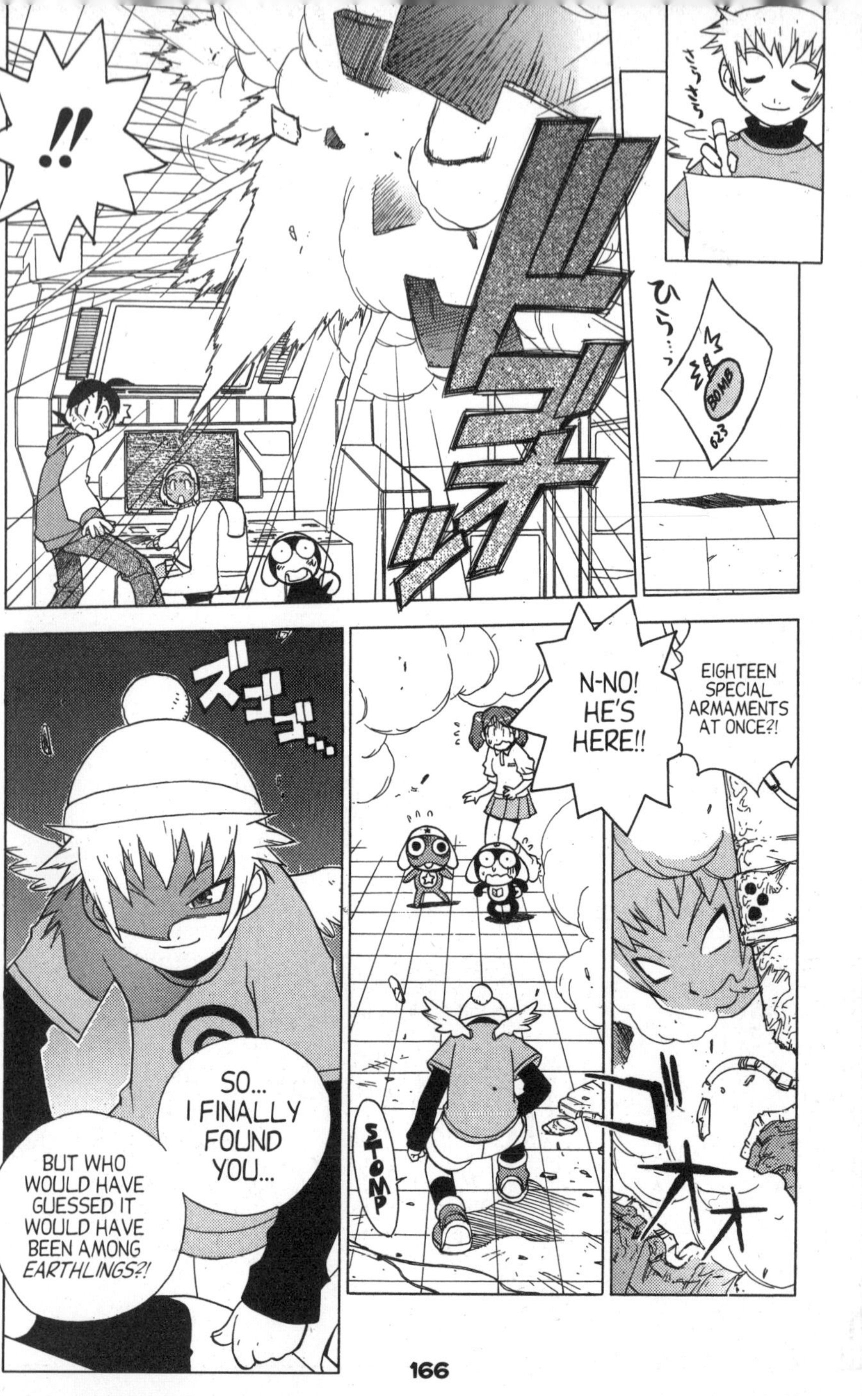

ひら…っ
BOMB
623
!!
ドゴオッ
EIGHTEEN SPECIAL ARMAMENTS AT ONCE?!
ゴオオ
N-NO! HE'S HERE!!
STOMP
ズゴゴ…
SO... I FINALLY FOUND YOU...
BUT WHO WOULD HAVE GUESSED IT WOULD HAVE BEEN AMONG *EARTHLINGS*?!

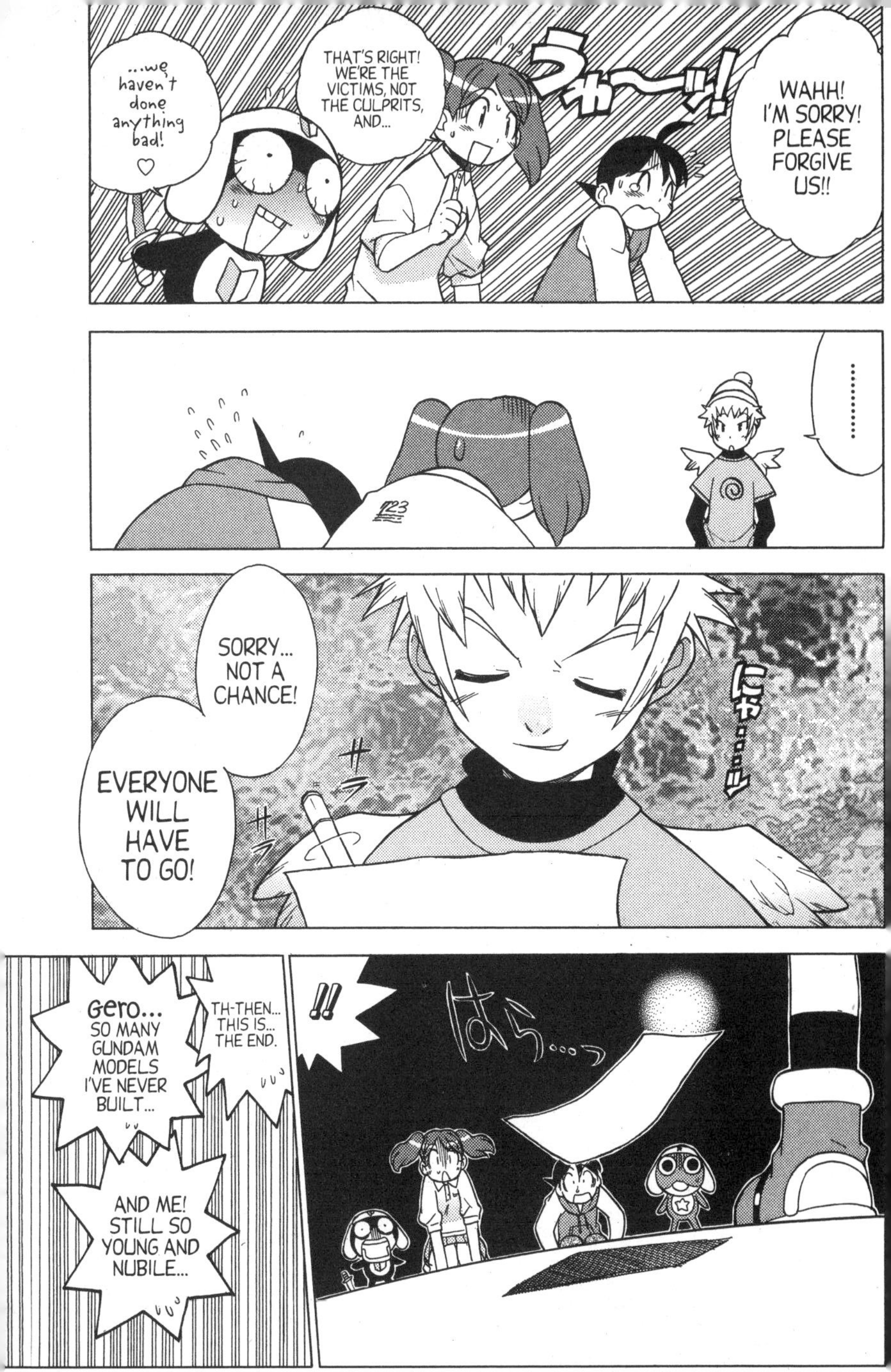
WAHH! I'M SORRY! PLEASE FORGIVE US!!
うわ〜〜ッ!
THAT'S RIGHT! WE'RE THE VICTIMS, NOT THE CULPRITS, AND...
...we haven't done anything bad! ♡
....
にゃ…ッ
SORRY... NOT A CHANCE!
EVERYONE WILL HAVE TO GO!
!!
はら…っ
TH-THEN... THIS IS... THE END.
Gero... SO MANY GUNDAM MODELS I'VE NEVER BUILT...
AND ME! STILL SO YOUNG AND NUBILE...

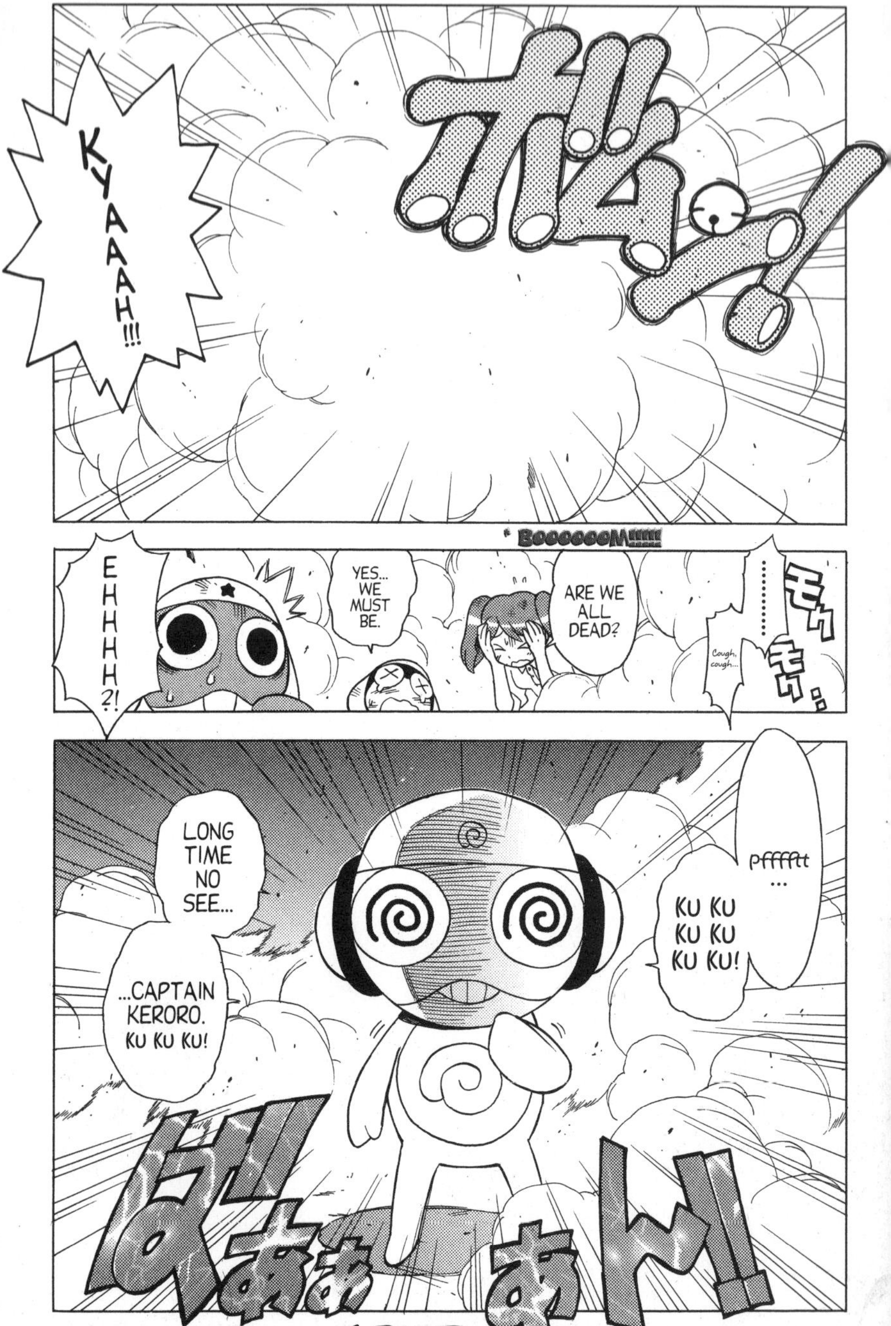
KYAAAAH!!!
BOOOOOOM!!!!!
Cough, cough...
......
ARE WE ALL DEAD?
YES... WE MUST BE.
EHHHHH?!
pffffft ...
KU KU KU KU KU KU!
LONG TIME NO SEE...
...CAPTAIN KERORO. KU KU KU!
POOF

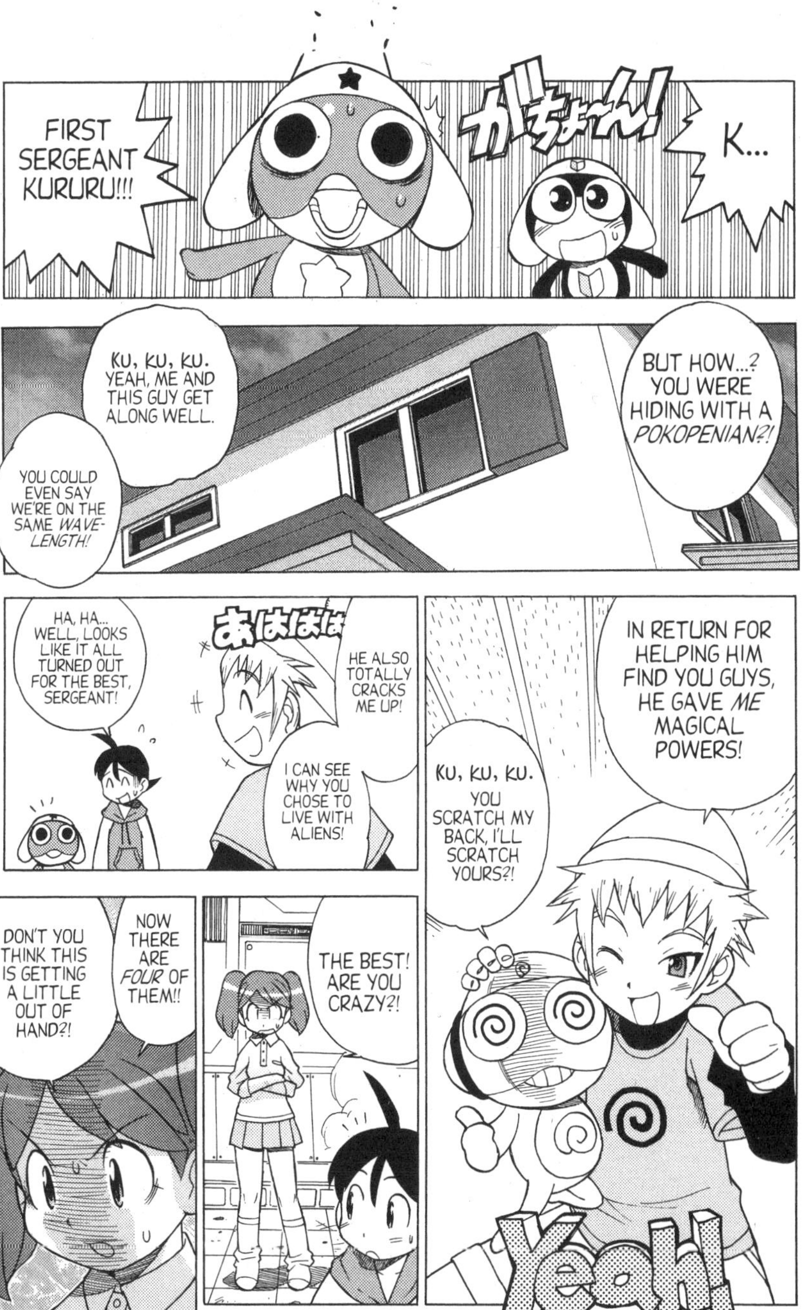
K...
がちゃ〜ん!
FIRST SERGEANT KURURU!!!
BUT HOW...? YOU WERE HIDING WITH A *POKOPENIAN*?!
KU, KU, KU. YEAH, ME AND THIS GUY GET ALONG WELL.
YOU COULD EVEN SAY WE'RE ON THE SAME *WAVE-LENGTH*!
IN RETURN FOR HELPING HIM FIND YOU GUYS, HE GAVE *ME* MAGICAL POWERS!
KU, KU, KU. YOU SCRATCH MY BACK, I'LL SCRATCH YOURS?!
Yeah!
HE ALSO TOTALLY CRACKS ME UP!
あははは
I CAN SEE WHY YOU CHOSE TO LIVE WITH ALIENS!
HA, HA... WELL, LOOKS LIKE IT ALL TURNED OUT FOR THE BEST, SERGEANT!
THE BEST! ARE YOU CRAZY?!
NOW THERE ARE *FOUR* OF THEM!!
DON'T YOU THINK THIS IS GETTING A LITTLE OUT OF HAND?!

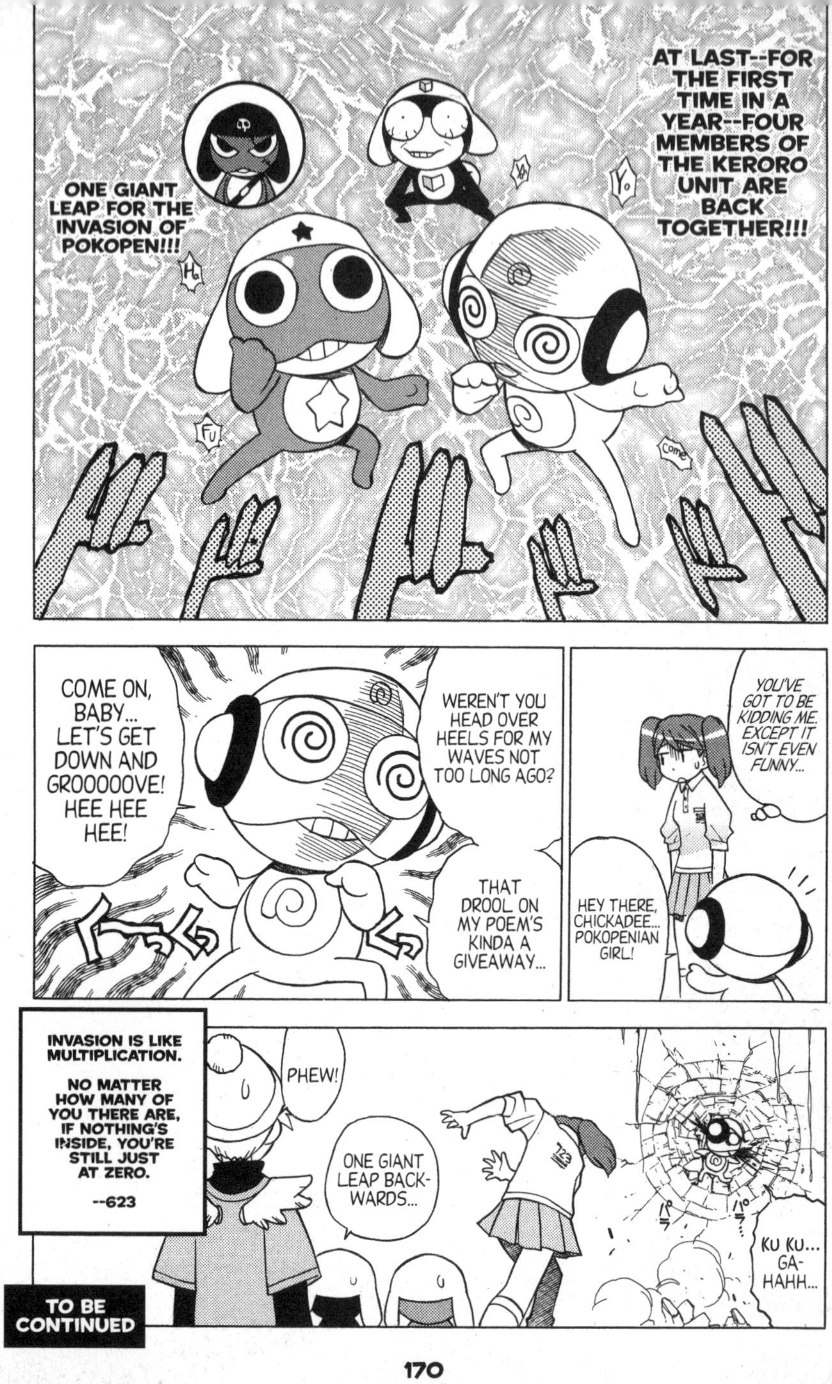
AT LAST--FOR THE FIRST TIME IN A YEAR--FOUR MEMBERS OF THE KERORO UNIT ARE BACK TOGETHER!!!
Yo
Ya
Come
ONE GIANT LEAP FOR THE INVASION OF POKOPEN!!!
Ha
Fu
YOU'VE GOT TO BE KIDDING ME. EXCEPT IT ISN'T EVEN FUNNY...
HEY THERE, CHICKADEE... POKOPENIAN GIRL!
WEREN'T YOU HEAD OVER HEELS FOR MY WAVES NOT TOO LONG AGO?
THAT DROOL ON MY POEM'S KINDA A GIVEAWAY...
COME ON, BABY... LET'S GET DOWN AND GROOOOOVE! HEE HEE HEE!
KU KU... GA-HAHH...
ONE GIANT LEAP BACK-WARDS...
PHEW!
INVASION IS LIKE MULTIPLICATION.
NO MATTER HOW MANY OF YOU THERE ARE, IF NOTHING'S INSIDE, YOU'RE STILL JUST AT ZERO.
--623
TO BE CONTINUED

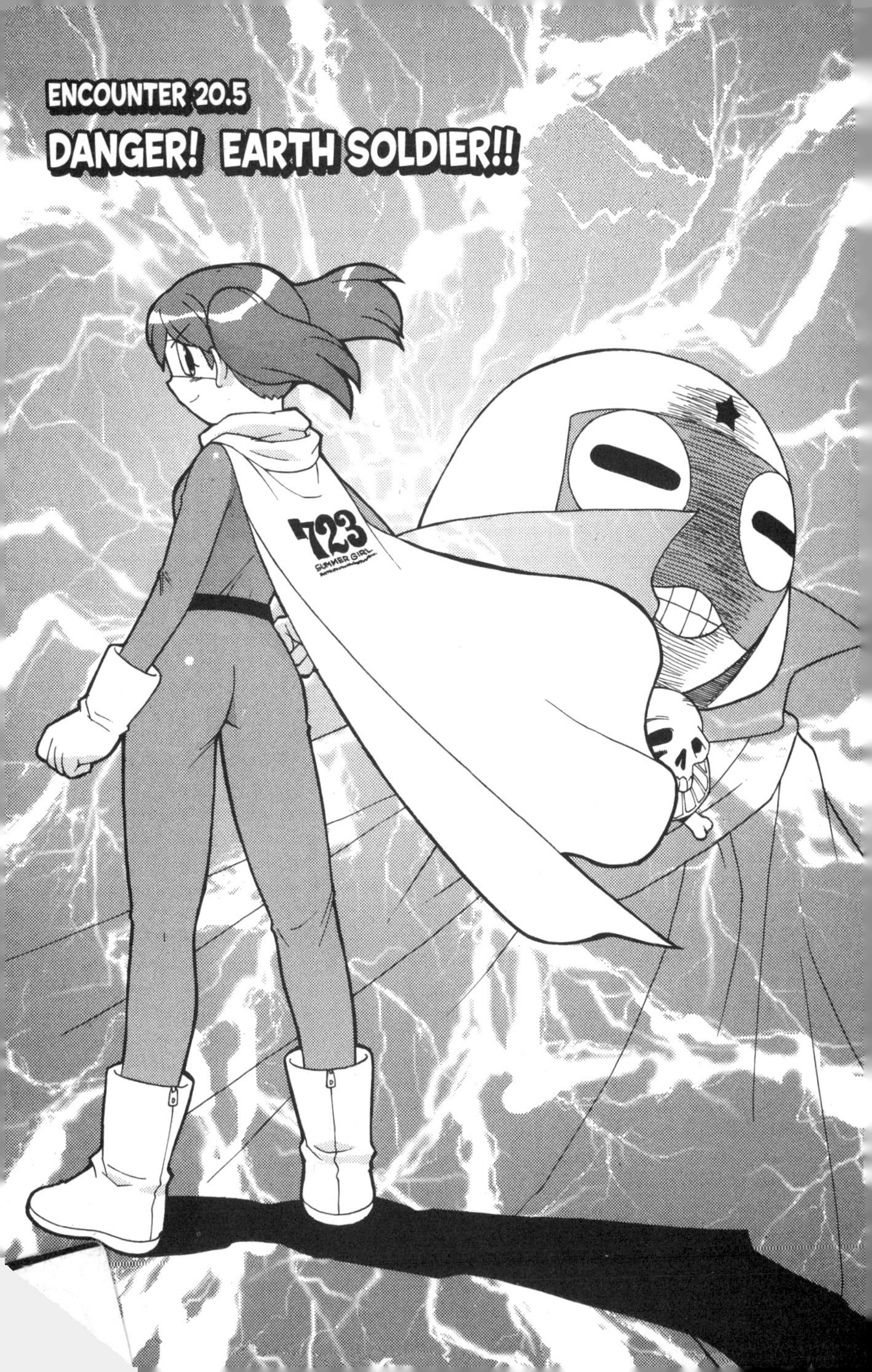
ENCOUNTER 20.5
DANGER! EARTH SOLDIER!!
723
SUMMER GIRL

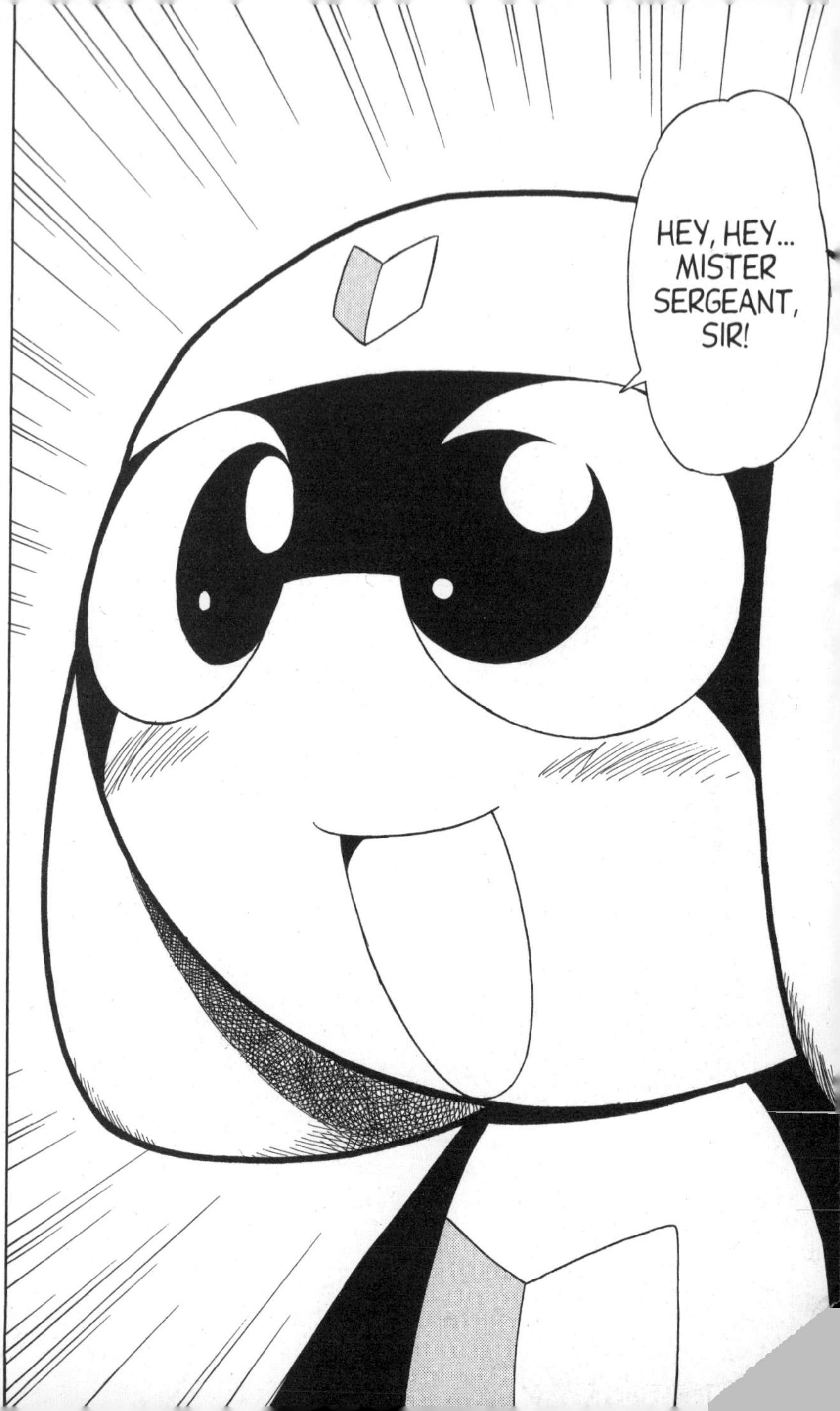
HEY, HEY... MISTER SERGEANT, SIR!

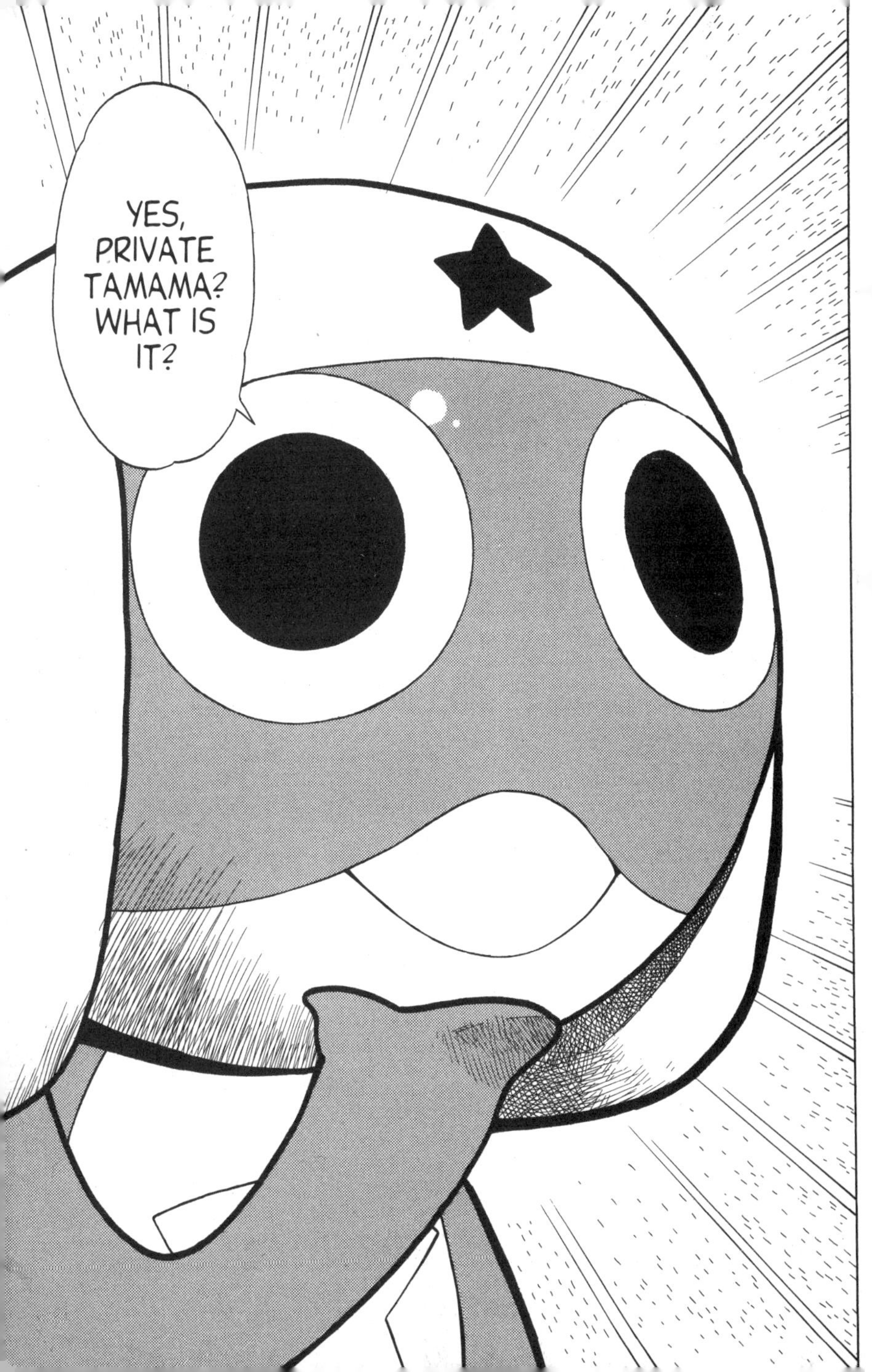
YES, PRIVATE TAMAMA? WHAT IS IT?

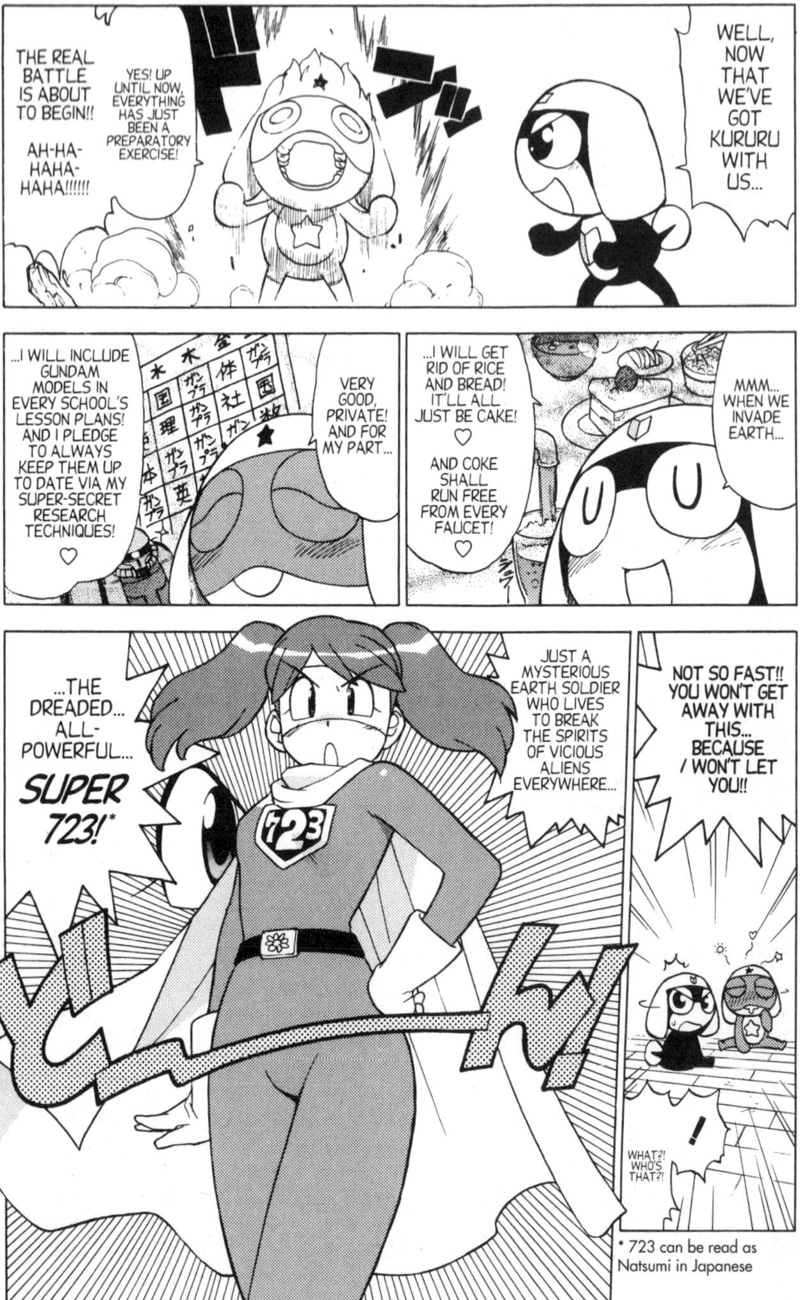
WELL, NOW THAT WE'VE GOT KURURU WITH US...
YES! UP UNTIL NOW, EVERYTHING HAS JUST BEEN A PREPARATORY EXERCISE!
THE REAL BATTLE IS ABOUT TO BEGIN!!
AH-HA-HAHA-HAHA!!!!!!
MMM... WHEN WE INVADE EARTH...
...I WILL GET RID OF RICE AND BREAD! IT'LL ALL JUST BE CAKE! ♡
AND COKE SHALL RUN FREE FROM EVERY FAUCET! ♡
VERY GOOD, PRIVATE! AND FOR MY PART...
...I WILL INCLUDE GUNDAM MODELS IN EVERY SCHOOL'S LESSON PLANS! AND I PLEDGE TO ALWAYS KEEP THEM UP TO DATE VIA MY SUPER-SECRET RESEARCH TECHNIQUES! ♡
NOT SO FAST!! YOU WON'T GET AWAY WITH THIS... BECAUSE *I* WON'T LET YOU!!
!
WHAT?! WHO'S THAT?!
JUST A MYSTERIOUS EARTH SOLDIER WHO LIVES TO BREAK THE SPIRITS OF VICIOUS ALIENS EVERYWHERE...
...THE DREADED... ALL-POWERFUL... SUPER 723!*

* 723 can be read as Natsumi in Japanese

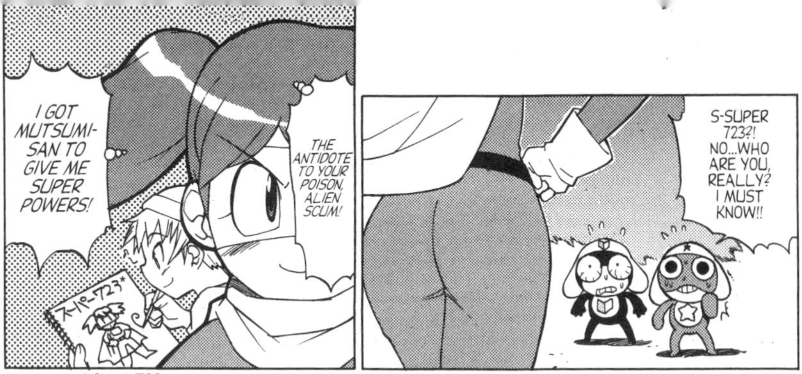
S-SUPER 723?! NO...WHO ARE YOU, REALLY? I MUST KNOW!!
THE ANTIDOTE TO YOUR POISON, ALIEN SCUM!
I GOT MUTSUMI-SAN TO GIVE ME SUPER POWERS!
スーパー723*

* Super 723

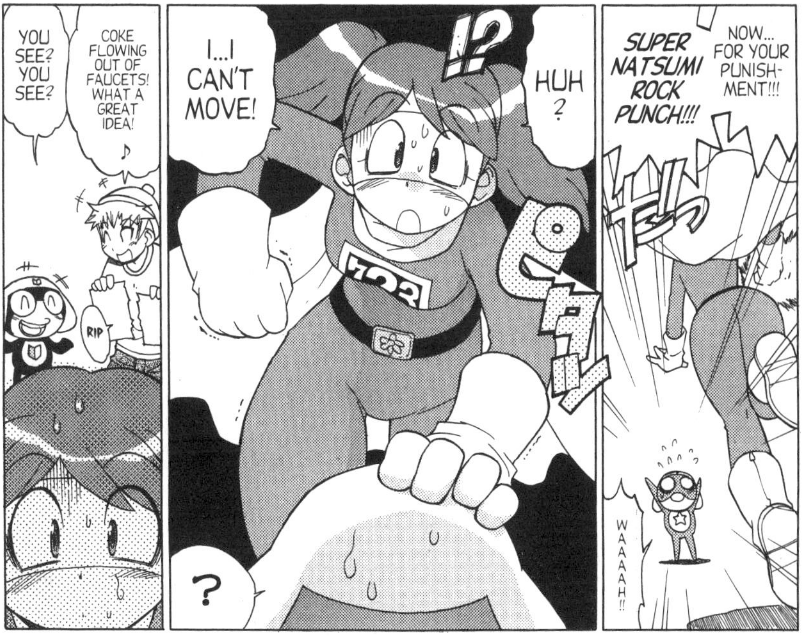
NOW... FOR YOUR PUNISH-MENT!!!
SUPER NATSUMI ROCK PUNCH!!!
WAAAAAH!!
!?
HUH?
I...I CAN'T MOVE!
?
COKE FLOWING OUT OF FAUCETS! WHAT A GREAT IDEA! ♪
YOU SEE? YOU SEE?
RIP

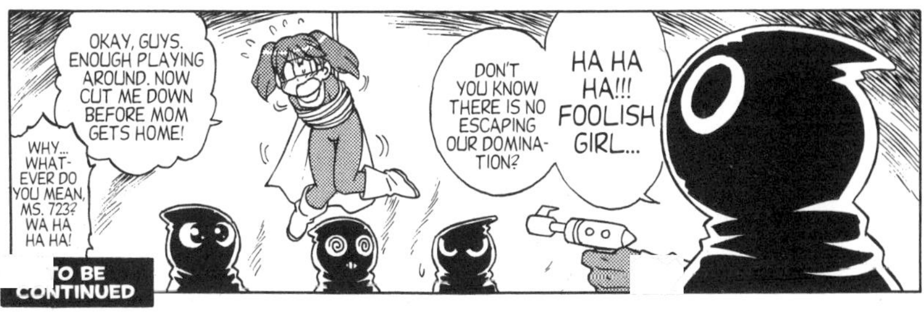
HA HA HA!!! FOOLISH GIRL...
DON'T YOU KNOW THERE IS NO ESCAPING OUR DOMINA-TION?
OKAY, GUYS. ENOUGH PLAYING AROUND. NOW CUT ME DOWN BEFORE MOM GETS HOME!
WHY... WHAT-EVER DO YOU MEAN, MS. 723? WA HA HA HA!
TO BE CONTINUED

JAPAN STAFF

MINE YOSHIZAKI
OYSTER
GOMOKU AKATSUKI
RYOICHI KOGA
MADARA

TO BE CONTINUED
IN VOLUME 3

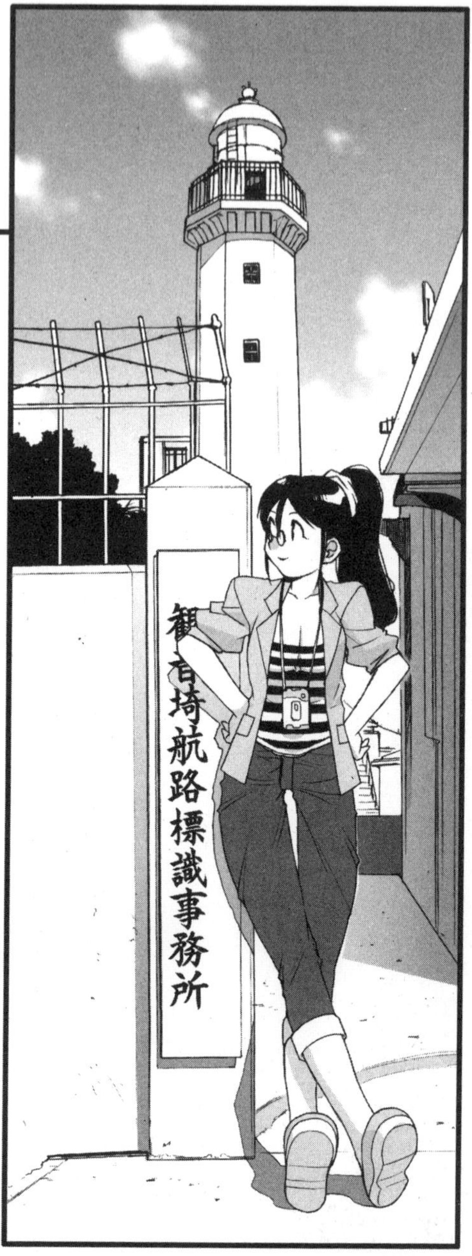
観音埼航路標識事務所

MOTHER AKI

Translator - Yuko Fukami
English Adaptation - Carol Fox
Copy Editor - Tim Beedle
Retouch and Lettering - Jose Macasocol, Jr.
Cover Layout - Raymond Makowski
Graphic Designer - James Lee

Editor - Paul Morrissey
Digital Imaging Manager - Chris Buford
Pre-Press Manager - Antonio DePietro
Production Managers - Jennifer Miller and Mutsumi Miyazaki
Art Director - Matt Alford
Managing Editor - Jill Freshney
VP of Production - Ron Klamert
President & C.O.O. - John Parker
Publisher & C.E.O. - Stuart Levy

Email: info@TOKYOPOP.com
Come visit us online at www.TOKYOPOP.com

A  Manga

TOKYOPOP Inc.
5900 Wilshire Blvd. Suite 2000
Los Angeles, CA 90036

SGT. Frog Vol. 2

ISBN: 1-59182-704-3

First TOKYOPOP printing: May 2004

10 9 8 7 6 5 4 3 2 1

Printed in the USA

PRINCESS AI
PSYCHIC ACADEMY
RAGNAROK
RAVE MASTER
REALITY CHECK
REBIRTH
REBOUND
REMOTE
RISING STARS OF MANGA
SABER MARIONETTE J
SAILOR MOON
SAINT TAIL
SAIYUKI
SAMURAI DEEPER KYO
SAMURAI GIRL REAL BOUT HIGH SCHOOL
SCRYED
SEIKAI TRILOGY, THE
SGT FROG
SHAOLIN SISTERS
SHIRAHIME-SYO: SNOW GODDESS TALES
SHUTTERBOX
SKULL MAN, THE
SMUGGLER
SNOW DROP
SORCERER HUNTERS
STONE
SUIKODEN III
SUKI
THREADS OF TIME
TOKYO BABYLON
TOKYO MEW MEW
TRAMPS LIKE US
TREASURE CHESS
UNDER THE GLASS MOON
VAMPIRE GAME
VISION OF ESCAFLOWNE, THE
WARRIORS OF TAO
WILD ACT
WISH
WORLD OF HARTZ
X-DAY
ZODIAC P.I.

NOVELS

CLAMP SCHOOL PARANORMAL INVESTIGATORS
KARMA CLUB
SAILOR MOON
SLAYERS

ART BOOKS

ART OF CARDCAPTOR SAKURA
ART OF MAGIC KNIGHT RAYEARTH, THE
PEACH: MIWA UEDA ILLUSTRATIONS

ANIME GUIDES

COWBOY BEBOP
GUNDAM TECHNICAL MANUALS
SAILOR MOON SCOUT GUIDES

TOKYOPOP KIDS

STRAY SHEEP

CINE-MANGA™

ALADDIN
ASTRO BOY
CARDCAPTORS
CONFESSIONS OF A TEENAGE DRAMA QUEEN
DUEL MASTERS
FAIRLY ODDPARENTS, THE
FAMILY GUY
FINDING NEMO
G.I. JOE SPY TROOPS
JACKIE CHAN ADVENTURES
JIMMY NEUTRON: BOY GENIUS, THE ADVENTURES OF
KIM POSSIBLE
LILO & STITCH
LIZZIE MCGUIRE
LIZZIE MCGUIRE MOVIE, THE
MALCOLM IN THE MIDDLE
POWER RANGERS: NINJA STORM
SHREK 2
SPONGEBOB SQUAREPANTS
SPY KIDS 2
SPY KIDS 3-D: GAME OVER
TEENAGE MUTANT NINJA TURTLES
THAT'S SO RAVEN
TRANSFORMERS: ARMADA
TRANSFORMERS: ENERGON

For more
information visit
www.TOKYOPOP.com

02.03.04T

MANGA

.HACK//LEGEND OF THE TWILIGHT
@LARGE
ABENOBASHI: MAGICAL SHOPPING ARCADE
A.I. LOVE YOU
AI YORI AOSHI
ANGELIC LAYER
ARM OF KANNON
BABY BIRTH
BATTLE ROYALE
BATTLE VIXENS
BRAIN POWERED
BRIGADOON
B'TX
CANDIDATE FOR GODDESS, THE
CARDCAPTOR SAKURA
CARDCAPTOR SAKURA - MASTER OF THE CLOW
CHOBITS
CHRONICLES OF THE CURSED SWORD
CLAMP SCHOOL DETECTIVES
CLOVER
COMIC PARTY
CONFIDENTIAL CONFESSIONS
CORRECTOR YUI
COWBOY BEBOP
COWBOY BEBOP: SHOOTING STAR
CRAZY LOVE STORY
CRESCENT MOON
CULDCEPT
CYBORG 009
D•N•ANGEL
DEMON DIARY
DEMON ORORON, THE
DEUS VITAE
DIGIMON
DIGIMON TAMERS
DIGIMON ZERO TWO
DOLL
DRAGON HUNTER
DRAGON KNIGHTS
DRAGON VOICE
DREAM SAGA
DUKLYON: CLAMP SCHOOL DEFENDERS
EERIE QUEERIE!
ERICA SAKURAZAWA: COLLECTED WORKS
ET CETERA
ETERNITY
EVIL'S RETURN
FAERIES' LANDING
FAKE
FLCL
FORBIDDEN DANCE
FRUITS BASKET
G GUNDAM
GATEKEEPERS
GETBACKERS

GIRL GOT GAME
GRAVITATION
GTO
GUNDAM BLUE DESTINY
GUNDAM SEED ASTRAY
GUNDAM WING
GUNDAM WING: BATTLEFIELD OF PACIFISTS
GUNDAM WING: ENDLESS WALTZ
GUNDAM WING: THE LAST OUTPOST (G-UNIT)
HANDS OFF!
HAPPY MANIA
HARLEM BEAT
I.N.V.U.
IMMORTAL RAIN
INITIAL D
INSTANT TEEN: JUST ADD NUTS
ISLAND
JING: KING OF BANDITS
JING: KING OF BANDITS - TWILIGHT TALES
JULINE
KARE KANO
KILL ME, KISS ME
KINDAICHI CASE FILES, THE
KING OF HELL
KODOCHA: SANA'S STAGE
LAMENT OF THE LAMB
LEGAL DRUG
LEGEND OF CHUN HYANG, THE
LES BIJOUX
LOVE HINA
LUPIN III
LUPIN III: WORLD'S MOST WANTED
MAGIC KNIGHT RAYEARTH I
MAGIC KNIGHT RAYEARTH II
MAHOROMATIC: AUTOMATIC MAIDEN
MAN OF MANY FACES
MARMALADE BOY
MARS
MARS: HORSE WITH NO NAME
METROID
MINK
MIRACLE GIRLS
MIYUKI-CHAN IN WONDERLAND
MODEL
ONE
ONE I LOVE, THE
PARADISE KISS
PARASYTE
PASSION FRUIT
PEACH GIRL
PEACH GIRL: CHANGE OF HEART
PET SHOP OF HORRORS
PITA-TEN
PLANET LADDER
PLANETES
PRIEST

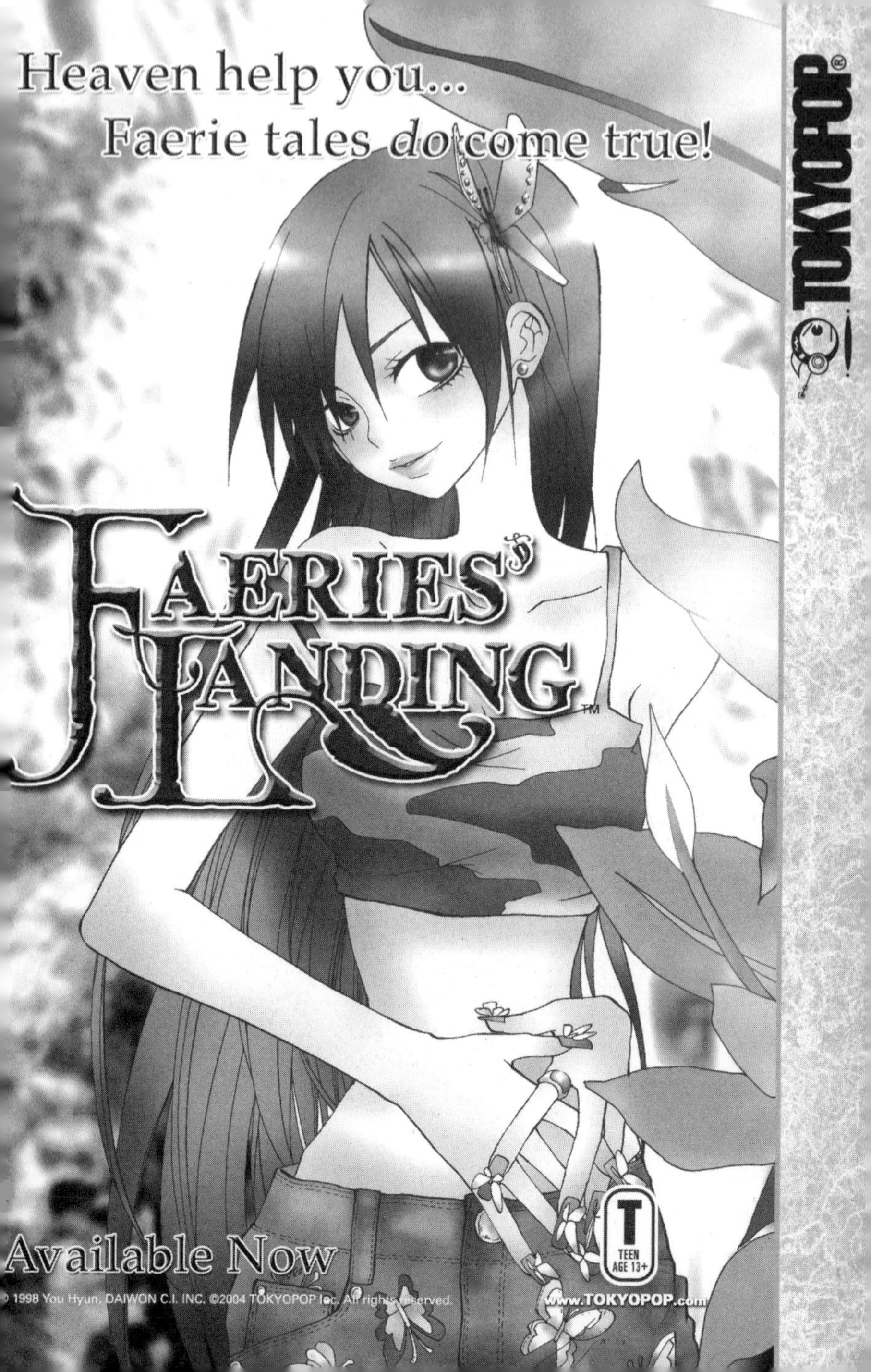

Heaven help you...
Faerie tales *do* come true!
FAERIES' LANDING™
Available Now
T
TEEN
AGE 13+
© 1998 You Hyun, DAIWON C.I. INC. ©2004 TOKYOPOP Inc. All rights reserved.
www.TOKYOPOP.com
TOKYOPOP®

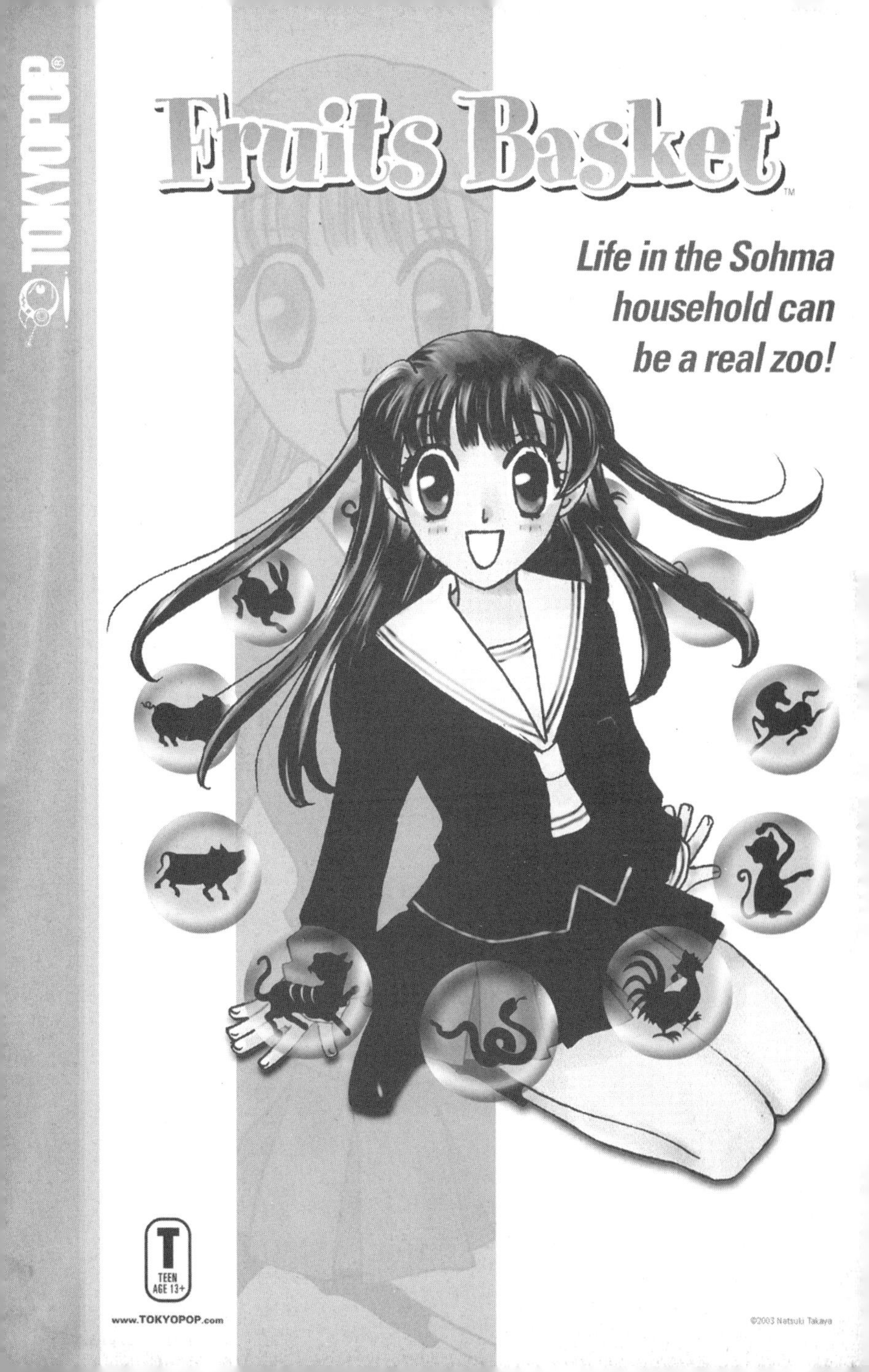
TOKYOPOP
Fruits Basket™
Life in the Sohma household can be a real zoo!
T TEEN AGE 13+
www.TOKYOPOP.com
©2003 Natsuki Takaya

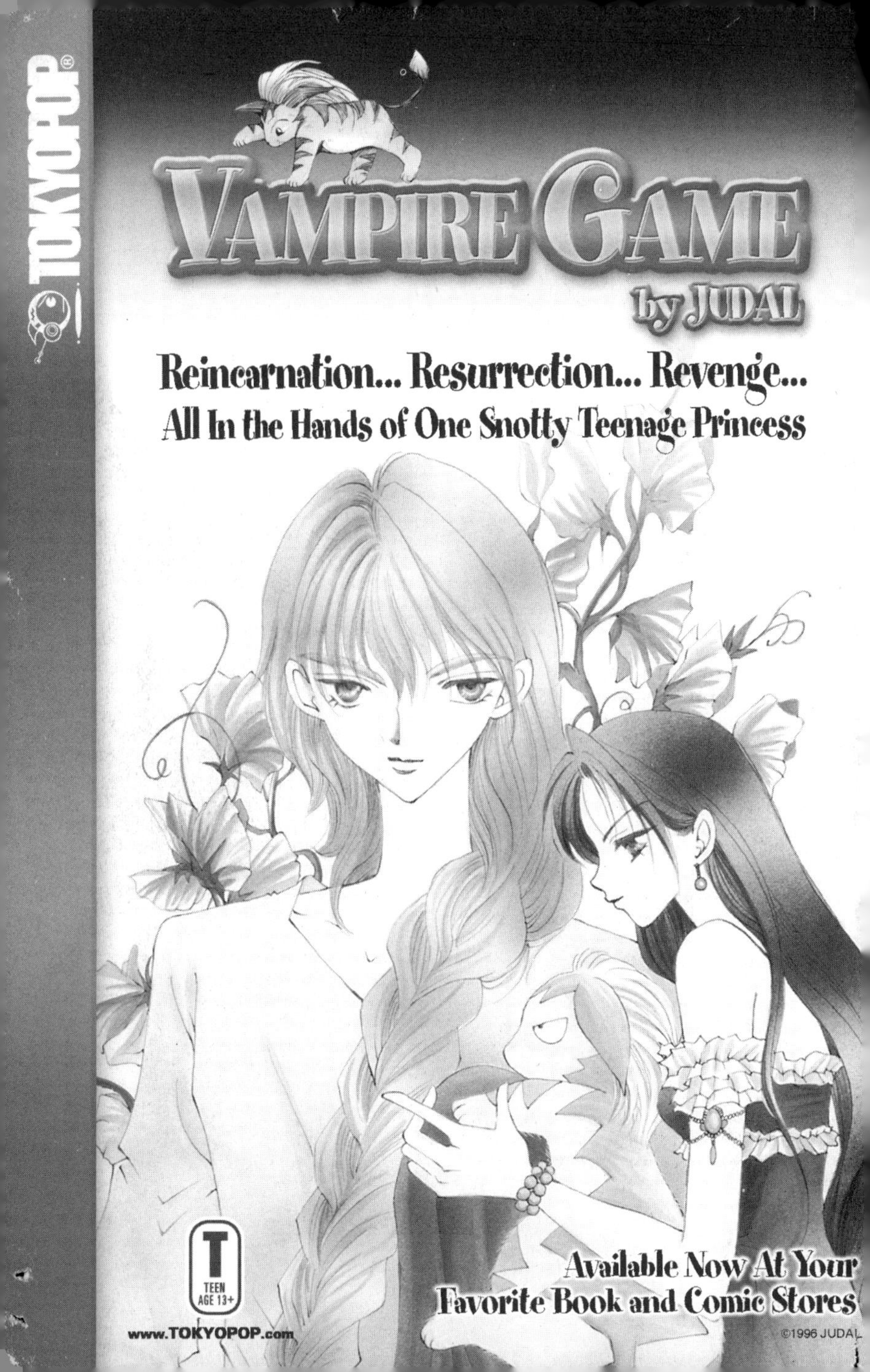
TOKYOPOP
VAMPIRE GAME
by JUDAL
Reincarnation... Resurrection... Revenge...
All In the Hands of One Snotty Teenage Princess
T
TEEN
AGE 13+
Available Now At Your
Favorite Book and Comic Stores
www.TOKYOPOP.com
©1996 JUDAL

STOP!

This is the back of the book.
You wouldn't want to spoil a great ending!

This book is printed "manga-style," in the authentic Japanese right-to-left format. Since none of the artwork has been flipped or altered, readers get to experience the story just as the creator intended. You've been asking for it, so TOKYOPOP® delivered: authentic, hot-off-the-press, and far more fun!

DIRECTIONS

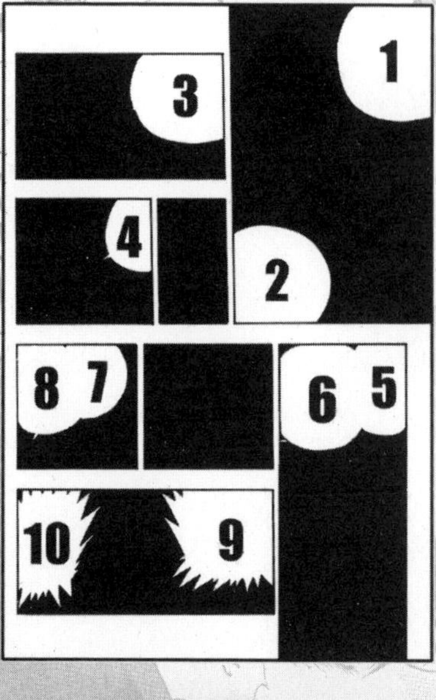
1
2
3
4
5
6
7
8
9
10

If this is your first time reading manga-style, here's a quick guide to help you understand how it works.

It's easy... just start in the top right panel and follow the numbers. Have fun, and look for more 100% authentic manga from TOKYOPOP®!

100% AUTHENTIC MANGA

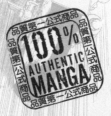